The East End of London about 1900 sh[ow]...
of Jewish Residents.

(Adapted from Russell and Lewis: *The Jew in London* and reproduced from V. D. Lipman: *Social History of the Jews in England 1850–1950* Watts & Co.)

THE JEWISH IMMIGRANT
IN ENGLAND, 1870-1914

THE JEWISH IMMIGRANT
IN ENGLAND, 1870-1914

BY

LLOYD P. GARTNER

Detroit – Wayne State University Press – 1960

FIRST PUBLISHED IN 1960

© *George Allen & Unwin Ltd., London, England*

All rights reserved

DS135
E5
G35
1960x

PRINTED IN GREAT BRITAIN
BOUND IN THE UNITED STATES OF AMERICA

To My Father
and My Mother

JAN 1 1 1962

FOREWORD

The commanding importance of migration in modern Jewish history has been generally recognized. But except for statistical investigations, the story of emigration, settlement, and adaptation has not received the attention it merits. The valuable work of sociologists and economists has been handicapped by the lack of historic perspective which they rightfully expect of the historian. This study attempts to tell the history of the immigrant who settled in England between 1870 and 1914, both as an individual and as a member of an immigrant community. If the treatment suggests a 'school' it is that of the American historian Marcus Lee Hansen who conceived the immigrant as a person who exchanged societies and had to synthesize two cultures in so doing. My debt to Hansen is deep although he has not supplied a single citation.

This is a work of Jewish history, with an English background. While I hope that English and other historians will find things in it which interest them, I have primarily seen these immigrants as Jews sharing in the historic experience of their people. I have written about migration to England because, unlike America, the number of immigrants is small enough to be manageable. Moreover, unlike the Dominions, English society was economically and culturally mature, thus making clear the contrast between the immigrants and their new land. Migration to England is unorganized—unlike Argentina—and there is no ideology at the root of it, so it also does not resemble the settlement in Palestine. We are dealing with a spontaneous movement of people which flowed unencouraged by outsiders.

Nobody has written a book about Jewish immigrants in England since Georg Halpern's short thesis of 1902, which still retains value. Halpern literally wrote in the midst of his subject. Now is a propitious time to write again, while many of the scenes and persons of the pre-1914 years are with us yet and some historic perspective is already attainable. In forty years, if not sooner, living memory of the period will have disappeared, and probably little will remain to be seen. The nice balance between perspective and observation is not easy to strike; others will judge to what extent I have succeeded.

As an American, I also know that whatever advantage comes from a 'long range' trans-Atlantic view is more than cancelled out by the absence of intimate knowledge of English and English-Jewish life. Kind hospitality and friendly guidance in England helped me not a little to compensate for this shortcoming.

I venture here to express the hope that the distinguished and historically conscious Jewry of England will not permit the records of the immigrant period from 1870 to 1914 to be lost or destroyed by neglect. However, this is in a fair way of happening. Very, very little can be located of the Yiddish press which once flourished, and many decadent and defunct institutions' records will vanish if measures are not taken by outsiders. The same applies to personal records, such as letters, diaries, and even steamship tickets. It is not for me to suggest how this can be accomplished, but it requires less money than persistence.

This work is somewhat a pioneer attempt, and contains many lacunae. It will have achieved its greatest success if others feel inclined to fill them in. We need studies of the operation of the Aliens Act; the mutual influences of American and British immigration policies; Provincial immigrant communities; emigration from England to America and the Empire; anti-alienism and anti-Semitism; and many more.

This study was written during several years with pauses and interruptions. Of all who have given me of their time and knowledge, I am most indebted to Professor Salo W. Baron, for his wise and patient guidance at every step. He sponsored this work when it was presented (in a somewhat different form) as a thesis at Columbia University. The late Professor John Bartlet Brebner placed me in his debt for his kindly yet searching and comprehensive review of this work. Dr Philip Friedman was similarly gracious and helpful.

Dr Cecil Roth read this work and encouraged me with kind opinion and learned suggestions. Professor and Mrs D. V.

Glass gave experienced advice. Dr V. D. Lipman has been most helpful in many important ways.

Many friends in England and America advised me and called material to my attention. In England, I am thankful to Mr Henry Shaw, Mr C. Abramsky, Mr I. Finestein, Mr A. R. Rollin, and Dr B. Homa. Among others, the Misses Paula, Nina, and May Hirschbein, the Rev J. K. Goldbloom, and the late Professor Selig Brodetsky favoured me with personal statements. Institutional representatives, especially Mr Mark Fineman of the Jewish Board of Guardians in London, Mr D. Guedalla of the Jews' Temporary Shelter, and Messrs A. G. Brotman and R. Levy of the Jewish Board of Deputies, courteously made available the material well preserved at their offices. The officials of the Jewish Boards of Guardians of Manchester and Liverpool, the United Synagogue, the Stepney and Brady Jewish Boys' Clubs, were likewise helpful. The Mocatta Library of the Jewish Historical Society made its fine collection available to me.

Even study in England could not substitute for the riches of the unequalled Jewish libraries in New York City. I should like to single out the Jewish Division of the New York Public Library and its ever-helpful Chief, Mr Abraham Berger, for courteous and unflagging service. The library of YIVO, and Miss Dina Abramowitz, were always cordial and helpful. I owe much to Mrs Eileen Reidy for secretarial services. Besides the Alexander Kohut Memorial Foundation's grant, I am obliged to the Littauer Foundation for aiding the final stages of my research.

With so much wisdom and kindness at my service, how much more am I alone to blame for the shortcomings of this study!

LLOYD P. GARTNER

The Jewish Theological Seminary of America
New York City
August, 1959

CONTENTS

CONTENTS

I

INTRODUCTION

HISTORIC BACKGROUNDS OF
JEWISH MIGRATION

The Jews of the late nineteenth and early twentieth centuries who set forth from their lands and homes to other countries and continents decisively changed the probable course of Jewish history. Each of them is the true subject in the history of migration, for behind the historic 'causes' or 'forces' or 'factors', was a family or a person who had to make an individual choice to move, and then carry it through to the ultimate destination. This study is a chapter in that saga of movement, and deals with a land where many thousands found safety and freedom, whose shores were kept freely open to immigrants from the days of Jewish Resettlement three centuries ago until the early years of the present century. Throughout this age of the open door in England, the lands of Eastern Europe were hostile to their Jews. The stimulus to Jews to move westward began three centuries ago, and reached its climax a few decades ago. We shall treat here the climactic years between 1870 and 1914, when borders were open, transportation relatively safe, fares cheap enough, and reasons to leave abundant.

Our study is a segment not only of modern Jewish history, but of the greatest age of voluntary migration. Jewish emigrants in their multitudes accompanied millions of hopeful people from every country in Europe, en route to practically every country in the Western Hemisphere and elsewhere, with the United States standing paramount among them. Our interest, however, is in a country which sent forth many emigrants for every immigrant it received. England, in the forefront of lands of emigration, was but a backwater of immigration.[1]

[1]W. Cunningham, *Alien Immigration to England*, London, 1897, is a brief historical survey; S. C. Johnson, *A History of Emigration from the United Kingdom*

Migration is a commanding theme only in modern history, while in Jewish history the subject is, as is well known, a constant one. The modern direction of Jewish migration appeared first in the mid-seventeenth century, when the earlier flight of Marranos from Spain and Portugal was no longer important. From that time, Jewish migrations, which had earlier tended to move east to Slavic lands, began the reverse trend. The Chielmienicki massacres of 1648-1649, and subsequent repetitions in 1656 and 1668, were a bloody symbol of the deterioration in the position of the Jews in Eastern Europe. The first omens of this westward migration appeared when thousands of Jews streamed westward from the scenes of the butchery in Poland and the Ukraine. In the west, two new outlets appeared in these decades which later assumed supreme significance: England and the American colonies. It is not the present purpose to describe how Dutch Jewry, from its centre in Amsterdam, helped to lay a base for Jewish settlement in English-speaking lands by the pleas of Manasseh ben Israel, the example of the prosperous outcome of religious toleration, and by the Dutch West India Company's instructions to an unwilling Peter Stuyvesant. Two centuries elapsed before full advantage was taken of the possibilities offered by the events of the 1650's and 1660's.[2]

England's and America's doors were open, but one difference between them stands out. England held forth attractions, but it never rivalled the lure of America, the fabled 'goldene medineh' (golden land) to the west. But America was distant and England was near, especially until the later nineteenth century.

England's position in Jewish migration is unique. As a land of immigration, she stands second only to the United States, although, to be sure, it is a very distant second. In 1914, no

to North America, 1783-1912, London, 1913, on the main stream; Mark Wischnitzer, To Dwell in Safety, Philadelphia, 1949, deals principally with organized Jewish migration; Walter F. Willcox, ed., International Migrations, 2 vols., N.Y., 1929, 1931, contains a serviceable chapter on the Jews by Liebman Hersch (II, pp. 471-521). M. L. Hansen, The Atlantic Migration 1607-1860, Cambridge, Mass., 1940, is stimulating for its approach.

[2]Lucien Wolf, Manasseh ben Israel's Mission to Oliver Cromwell, London, 1901; Herbert I. Bloom, The Economic Activities of the Jews of Amsterdam in the Seventeenth and Eighteenth Centuries, Williamsport, Pa., 1937, shows some underlying economic connections, as on pp. 109, 190-91.

city other than New York and Chicago contained more East European immigrants than London, in addition to its not inconsiderable number of native Jews. Cities like Manchester and Leeds were the domicile of tens of thousands of immigrant Jews, and in every larger and many smaller English cities an immigrant community could be found dwelling together. The prominence of England as a land of immigrant settlement would alone merit study. Yet England also played a second role in Jewish migration, that of a land of transmigration. At its simplest, this meant only disembarkation at an English port after crossing the Channel or North Sea, followed by a railroad ride, and embarkation upon a second ship to cross the Atlantic. Hundreds of thousands of Jewish migrants knew no more of England than this, but countless others dallied for periods from a week to a lifetime. Some stopped only to buy a ticket, or to earn enough in order to buy; their stay was not long. Others, the wives and children of men who had already gone ahead, followed in the trail of the head of the family. Then there were persons who had determined to migrate, yet were not certain what their destination would finally be. Coming to England first, they tried their luck, and perhaps stayed on. Naturally, there is no means of knowing how many migrants belong in any of these groups. This second role, that of a 'staging area' for masses of Jewish as well as non-Jewish transmigrants, fell to England during the 1840's and 1850's, when fast English steamships and low fares competed effectively with the previously dominant German shippers. Our study does not intentionally deal with transmigrants, but it does nevertheless because thousands of Jewish migrants came to America after spending years in England. We do not know who they were, but there is no doubt of their existence.

JEWISH COMMUNAL BACKGROUNDS

Not long after the initial recognition of the Jews' presence in England and the tolerance extended to them (which is all that the legal aspect of the Resettlement signifies) the first unwanted immigrants put in their appearance. Early in 1669 the irritated *Mahamad* (Council) of the Sefardi community (the Ashkenazim were not yet organized) peremptorily instructed all foreigners who were in this city and those who should come for the future in the expectation that Ceddacka [charity] would support them, should within five days depart from the country; and in case that they should not do so, that they should not come to the Synagogue; and for their passage the Ceddacka will aid them with what may be possible.[3]

By the close of the seventeenth century, the Ashkenazim were organized to take care of their own. Besides some affluent arrivals from the Sefardi community in Amsterdam and an eighteenth century Italian influx, much greater numbers of Ashkenazim from the areas around Amsterdam and Hamburg made their way to London. Well into the nineteenth century the Jews already in England were embarrassed by unceasing accessions to their numbers of poor Jews from the jobless, unskilled mass which was vegetating in Holland and northern Germany.

Early immigrants to England from Slavic lands did not come directly, but more often arrived after many stops en route. Sometimes the son of a Jew who moved to Germany lengthened his father's trail by going ahead to England. Rabbi David Tevele Schiff of the Great Synagogue, who died in 1792, remitted funds to Rabbi Akiva Eger of Posen for distribution to relatives of London Jews living in Poland—a symptom of the early migration from Polish lands to England.[4]

Many immigrants set up as tradesmen and country peddlers, while others were silversmiths and jewellers. However, a notorious segment were criminals: highwaymen, thieves, receivers of stolen goods, and coin-clippers. In that age of urban turbulence, the Jewish community was expected to look after its own needy, and one means was to prevent Jewish paupers from coming to England. Others, already resident, were sent back; Oglethorpe's Georgia venture of 1732 was the

[3]Lionel D. Barnett, ed., *El Libro de los Acuerdos Being the Records and Accompts of the Spanish and Portuguese Synagogue of London*, Oxford, 1931, p. 28; *cf.* pp. 19, 48-49, 78. The texts are given entirely in translation. Lucien Wolf, *Essays in Jewish History*, ed. Cecil Roth, London, 1934, p. 123.

[4]Charles Duschinsky, *The Rabbinate of the Great Synagogue*, 1756-1842, Oxford, 1921, p. 141. Schiff's letters to his brother in Frankfort give many glimpses into the Anglo-German Jewish milieu of the day. See *The Case of Henry Simons, a Polish Jew Merchant . . .* London, 1753, p.3.

occasion of an unsuccessful attempt to colonize poor London Jews in that American colony.[5]

Meanwhile, the first institutions of the re-established Jewish community were founded, centred in the synagogue. From the outset, Ashkenazim and Sefardim organized separately and long remained punctiliously apart, socially and communally. The organic growth of the Ashkenazim out of the Great Synagogue, their parent house of worship in England, is practically the constitutional history of the Jewish community. Thus the rabbi of the Great Synagogue was recognized in London and later in the Provinces as the principal religious authority, even by synagogues with rabbis of their own. Practically, this meant the issuance of rabbinic responsa, the settlement of religious disputes, granting of marriage and divorce documents, and the licensing of *shohetim* and butchers. From this *de facto* primacy arose the office of Chief Rabbi, first of England and later of the Empire; cognate religious needs gave birth to the Chief Rabbi's *Beth Din* (court). By 1845, when Nathan Marcus Adler was installed, the office and its functions were spelled out. When Jews settled in outlying parts of London and built synagogues in their new vicinities, they regarded themselves as 'branches' of the parent Great Synagogue. In 1870, this relation was written into law by the United Synagogue Act, which confirmed the financial and religious union of the main London orthodox synagogues.[6]

When emissaries had to be sent to the outside world or representations made to the Government, they went in the name of the synagogally organized community. After a few

[5]In general, see several works of Cecil Roth: *A History of the Jews in England*, 2nd ed., Oxford, 1949, pp. 190, 197-202, 225-27; *The Rise of Provincial Jewry*, London, 1950, pp. 15-26; 'The Lesser London Synagogues of the Eighteenth Century,' *Miscellanies of the Jewish Historical Society of England*, III (1937), pp. 1-8; 'The Portsmouth Community and its Historical Background,' *Transactions of the Jewish Historical Society of England*, XIII (1936), esp. pp. 166-67; also M. Dorothy George, *London Life in the XVIIIth Century*, 2nd ed., London, 1930, pp. 125-32, and the contemporary observations of Patrick Colquhoun, *A Treatise on the Police of the Metropolis*, 6th ed., London, 1800, pp. 119-21, 182-83, 190, 292, 319-21, 568, 637.

[6]Cecil Roth, *The Great Synagogue, 1690-1940*, London, 1950, *passim;* V. D. Lipman, *Social History of the Jews in England, 1850-1950*, London, 1954, treats with precision the main lines of communal development, esp. pp. 34-64. Charles Duschinsky, *op. cit.*, contains valuable source materials and refers to others in MS., although it is largely biographical and not well organized.

contretemps, the representatives of the earliest houses of worship united loosely about 1760 as the London Committee of Deputies of British Jews, later known as the Board of Deputies of British Jews. This famous body, the legal representative of the Jewish community, drew its members from synagogal constituencies.

It was assumed that every Jew was associated with a synagogue as a member or, failing that, as a beneficiary of its charities. Such functions of Jewish communities as charity, education, and burial were vested in the English synagogue community, much as had been the immemorial practice of Continental communities. But charity of this type, while commendable for its intentions and passable by the standards of the day, grew inadequate for the native Jewish poor and hopeless for the many unsynagogued immigrants. Indiscriminate handouts to 'the strange poor' by the main City synagogues often caused riotous scenes, and encouraged chronic beggary. A group of young Victorian Jews, imbued with the Benthamite ideas of their time and eager to apply the new techniques of 'charity organisation' to their own community, founded the Board of Guardians for the Relief of the Jewish Poor in 1859. At first their clientele was to be only 'the strange poor', those without an established claim on the charity of a particular synagogue. However, within a few years the Board distributed most of the charitable funds in London, earning the designation of 'the almoner of the Jewish community'. The United Synagogue recognized the Jewish Board of Guardians as its charitable arm, and granted it liberal support. In philanthropic circles the Board enjoyed a reputation as a model charity. Poor Law authorities customarily handled their Jewish cases through it. This pre-eminent English Jewish charity, and its counterparts in the Provinces originated in a synagogal framework and never abandoned that connection, regarding themselves in some ways as surrogates for the charitable obligations of individual houses of worship.[7]

[7]V. D. Lipman, *op. cit.*, pp. 54–58 is useful; Laurie Magnus, *The Jewish Board of Guardians and the Men Who Made It*, London, 1909, is not. See now V. D. Lipman's valuable *A Century of Social Service 1859-1959. The History of the Jewish Board of Guardians*, London, 1959, which treats its subject broadly. It appeared too late to be used here.

The solidity and stability which the Jewish community and its institutions attained by the middle of the nineteenth century reflected the position of its dominant group. A few families, interrelated by constant marriage into each other, comprised the ruling elite of the community. The oligarchy is nearly complete when the families and family connections of Louis Cohen's descendants, Montefiore, Samuel, Mocatta, Goldsmid, Franklin, Henriques, Lucas, and transcending all others, Rothschild (practically the Royal Family of the community) are added together. They were religiously observant, and contributed time and money to communal affairs. Socially and economically, they were quite homogeneous; banking, stock-brokerage, and wholesale and commission mercantile transactions were their occupations, in which less affluent fellow-Jews also aspired to succeed. Fewer Jews were to be found in the arts, sciences, and professions.

EAST EUROPEAN BACKGROUNDS

A careful inquiry into the causes of Jewish emigration from Russia and Poland in its climactic generation would be little less than a history of those communities. The causes may perhaps be divided into those internal and external, or inherent and imposed. The most fundamental fact in nineteenth century Jewry in the Russian Empire was its multiplication from about 1,000,000 souls in 1800 to over 5,189,000 in 1897, the latter figures excluding probably 1,000,000 emigrants and their progeny. The increase of Jews in other lands of Eastern Europe was probably as great. There were 811,000 Jews in Galicia (1900), 266,000 in Roumania (1899), and 96,000 in Bukovina (1900), whose way of life resembled that of Russian and Polish Jewry. The same may be said of a large proportion of the 851,000 Jews in Hungary in 1900. The economic structure of Jewish life failed to expand with the needs imposed by this unprecedented increase. On the contrary, the narrow basis of petty trades and crafts was increasingly attenuated by the newer economic developments, which did not grant the Jews a role sufficient for their needs. With a full measure of inner difficulties, matters were at their worst in Russia, where they were aggravated by the anti-Jewish policy of the Czarist autocracy. After more than a generation of earlier attempts at enforced western-ization, the Russian government settled down to a régime of calculated oppression. Of all its restrictions and petty tyrannies, those most harmful were the limitations on domicile. Under them, the great majority of Jews, lacking special professional or mercantile qualifications, had to reside in the Pale of Settle-ment of Poland and western Russia. Within those territories, they were kept off the land, excluded from the larger cities, and finally driven off a wide swath of border areas. Pogrom outrages, at first passively watched and later connived at by the government, made the Jews' cup of troubles overflow.[8]

This study proposes to accompany the migrant from his departure from Eastern Europe through the several stages of settlement in England. A Jew's exodus from Russia or Poland by no means meant his severance from the social and cultural heritage of that Jewish sphere, for every emigrant took some of it with him; it could never be all transplanted nor was it ever wholly discarded. The foreign heritage continued not only in personal and cultural life but in economic activity as well. The study of an immigrant community requires an understanding of the background which many immigrants consciously and each of them unconsciously was preserving. Writers who treat immigrants as a sort of *tabulae rasae*, passively absorbing what-ever the new country offered and complying with what it demanded, are no wiser than the over-eager Anglicizers who who expected exactly this.

The maintenance of their culture came easier to the Jews than to other migrant peoples, for they were long schooled in migration, and their intangible baggage was in some ways unique. Judaism was rooted in Jewish history, language, and religious belief and observance, and not in any specific place— although the memory of Palestine and the hope for restoration remained very much alive. Unlike Polish migrants from Eastern

---

[8]Arthur Ruppin, *Die Soziologie der Juden*, 2 vols., Berlin, 1930, I, pp. 67-78; *The Jews of Today*, London, 1913, pp. 33-44; Alfred Nossig, ed., *Juedische Statistik*, Berlin, 1903, pp. 259-316; on political and economic developments, Philipp Friedmann, 'Wirtschaftliche Umschichtungsprozesses und Industrialisierung in der polnischen Judenschaft 1800-1870,' *Jewish Studies in Memory of George Alexander Kohut*, N.Y., 1935, pp. 178-247; S. M. Dubnow, *History of the Jews in Russia and Poland*, 3 vols., Philadelphia, 1916-1918, II, pp. 154-206, 243 *et seq.*

Europe, whose emigration commenced in large numbers nearer the end of the nineteenth century, the Jews were not peasants but townsfolk, having the greater mobility of urban life. Hence both Judaism and the Jews could move and adapt themselves to new surroundings, and immigrant Jewish communities arose in every Western country, above all in the United States. In America the Jewish immigrants formed but one among many ethnic groups struggling to establish themselves in American life, and shared important features in common with Germans, Italians, Poles, and others. Immigrant Jews in England—a group closely resembling in background and social structure the far larger one across the Atlantic—stood alone, without substantial organized immigrant communities at its side. Most non-Jewish immigrants in England were temporary residents and sometimes political refugees like Mazzini, Kossuth, and Herzen, whose minds and acts were focussed upon their homelands. Permanent residents seldom aspired to do more than quickly become English. Hence there is a great contrast between the external settings of immigrant Jewry in England and America. The cardinal fact in common is the existence of a sturdy communal life and a distinctive social milieu. Our study will view the gradual adjustment to English life of the Jewish immigrant and his community.

II

THE FLOW OF IMMIGRATION

In the closing days of 1888, Nathan Adler, Chief Rabbi of England from 1845 until he retired in 1880, addressed a circular from his retreat in Brighton to his East European colleagues upon an urgent matter. At eighty-five years and with a little more than a year of life remaining, he brought to the notice of East European readers the plight of the immigrant 'unfortunates who have come here to seek rest. . . .' The outlook for them was dire:

. . . many of them are lost without livelihoods . . . it is difficult for them to support themselves and their households, and at times they contravene the will of their Maker on account of poverty and over-work, and violate the Sabbath and Festivals. Some have been ensnared in the net of the missionaries and renounced their religion, may the Merciful save. Woe to the eyes which see and to the ears which hear such things.

The charities of the rich English Jews could not suffice:

. . . it is impossible, for one city cannot support all the refugees of other countries, besides the poor who already reside in it. There are many who believe that all the cobblestones of London are precious stones, and that it is the place of gold. Woe and alas, it is not so. . . .

The aged rabbi, originally from Hanover, was well known in Eastern Europe for his scholarship and for the prestige of the position he occupied and had turned over to his son. Summoning his influence, he therefore entreated

. . . every rabbi of a community kindly to preach in the synagogue and house of study, to publicize the evil which is befalling our brethren who have come here, and to warn them not to come to the land of Britain for such ascent is a descent.[1]

This warning to stay away from England was one of many, though its source is unusual. Two years earlier, the Jewish

---

[1] *HaMeliz*, XXVIII, 287 (December 30, 1888-January 11, 1889). The identical warning was also printed in *HaMaggid*, XXXIII, 1 (January 3, 1889).

Board of Guardians which bore the brunt of responsibility for charity in the Metropolis, sent a warning in sternest terms to the European Jewish press. Reciting the tribulations of both the English working men and native English Jews who could find no work, the Guardian proceeded a *fortiori*: '. . . how much more bitter and evil is the lot of the foreigners who come.' Such persons, who lack the resources either to go forward to America or back to Russia, could not possibly subsist in England. The advice to them could hardly have been bleaker:

. . . In order to avoid trouble in the coming days we beseech every right-thinking person among our brethren in Germany, Russia, and Austria to place a barrier to the flow of foreigners, to persuade these voyagers not to venture to come to a land they do not know. It is better that they live a life of sorrows in their native place than bear the shame of famine and the disgrace of the missionaries and perish in destitution in a strange land.[2]

Yet if the reader turned the page, he came upon the remarks of an immigrant Jewish peddler writing from the Provinces:

These brethren of ours [who emigrate] will not be frightened by this announcement as they are not frightened by the many announcements heard from America and France.[3]

Disapproval of migration was not confined to Western Jews, the reluctant hosts to impoverished migrants. Many Jewish notables of Eastern Europe were likewise distressed to see immense numbers among their people so despair of

[2]*HaMeliz*, XXII, 155 (November 25–December 7, 1886). Other specimen 'warnings': *JC*, April 16, 1880; Board of Guardians, *Minutes*, November 10, 1884, January 9, 1888, and *Minute Letter Book, ad loc.*; November 3, 1893, and Letter, I. Spielmann to M. Stephany, October 13, 1893, *Minute Letter Book, ad loc.*; *HaMeliz*, XIV, 2 (July 24–August 5, 1878); XV, 35 (September 2–14, 1879); XVII, 49 (December 27, 1881–January 8, 1882); XXVI, 155 (November 25 December 7, 1886); XXXII, 116 (May 27–June 8, 1892); XXIV, 8 (January 10–22, 1894); *HaMaggid*, XXVI, 14 (April 13, 1882), 25 (June 28, 1882); XXXI, 21 (June 2, 1887).
[3]*HaMeliz*, XXVI, 155 (November 25–December 7, 1886). A complaint is registered that Jews pay no attention to warnings to stay at home: *Idem*, XXXI, 78 (March 3–15, 1891); report of R. B. Morier to Lord Salisbury, St. Petersburg, May 12, 1888, in House of Commons Select Committee on Emigration and Immigration (Foreigners), *First Report*, 1888, p. 205.

their future in Russia, Poland, Galicia, and Rumania that they left to seek new homes. Migration undermined the policy which these leaders were striving to establish, one aiming at the political and economic reconstruction of East European Jewry. Rather than emigrate, the most prominent spokesmen of Western as well as Eastern Jewry wished the masses to remain at home and improve themselves. Vocational training and diversification would win for them a firm place in their respective national economies, dress and language reform and educational improvement would gain for them social acceptance in their countries. These measures would cause anti-Semitism to decrease; unfair discriminations would presently be removed; their material condition would gain. These westernizing reforms were fostered not only by Jewish well-wishers abroad, but by a growing and influential section of the intellectual classes and the new wealth at home. But East European Jewish history did not follow the course it had in the West. By the irony of history, those who disregarded the counsel of the learned and affluent and migrated, secured all of these goals. Those who remained endured decades of disappointment and frustration before they apparently attained emancipation.

THE IMMIGRANT'S IMAGE OF ENGLAND

Let us review the emigrant's course from the time he decided to leave town and family until his arrival and initial settlement in England.

Naturally, the emigrant sought to learn what he could about the new land. The great questions in his mind were: could he make a living? could he live in relative freedom? and, at least to many, could he preserve his Jewishness? He had to find his answers in a wide variety of sources dependable and dubious, from public information and from private communication. Hebrew and Yiddish periodicals printed frequent reports from England, as they did from America, by which emigrants could augment the knowledge which they garnered from word of mouth or letters from friends and relatives who had already emigrated. The emigrant did not absorb all that the press had to tell him, for only a minority read Hebrew, and the Yiddish press was slow in developing.[4] Letters from England conveying impressions and counsel became common property in small towns where emigration was seldom far from anyone's thoughts. As one emigrant expressed it,

. . . when a letter comes from abroad, especially with money, in the evening everyone all over the place knows who sent the money, who received the money, and everything; and that makes people come over here very often.[5]

Unfortunately, hardly any specimen letters can be found. There is also a strange but complete absence of emigrant guide books before 1905,[6] so that unlike emigrants from England and Ireland, Germany and Scandinavia, the Jew who left Russia or Poland had nothing fuller to advise him than meagre letters, ambiguous word of mouth, and the often inaccurate press. For some emigrants, the only tangible information was an address in England.[7]

The composite picture which was formed by this knowledge regarded England as a free country where an immigrant would have to work extremely hard to earn very little, and a fortunate few might become prosperous. In this mental image, an immigrant might expect to live in freedom but almost sealed off from the rest of the population, and endure public dislike. All in all, the picture was essentially true. It was well known abroad that the Jews enjoyed civil and political rights in England, and the lordly station of such families as Rothschild showed what peaks might be attained by Jews in Queen

[4]Hardly any immigrant who tells his own story speaks of press reports as a factor in inducing him to come; the unvarying emphasis is upon personal reports which they received. For example, Solomon Wildman, boot finisher, came to England at the advice of 'some friends.' (House of Lords, Commission on the Sweating System, *Report*, I, 1888, Min. 576 ff.) *Cf.* House of Commons Select Committee . . . *First Report* . . . 1888, Min. 1431-32, 1477, 1531-39, 1606, 1680, 1721-22.

[5]Royal Commission on Alien Immigration, *Minutes of Evidence,* Cd. 1742, 1903, (Abbr. Cd. 1742) Min. 3363.

[6]The sole guides intended for East European emigrants are Aaron J. L. Horowitz' somewhat fugitive Hebrew work, *Rumaniah veAmerika* (Rumania and America), Berlin, 1874; and, beginning in 1907, *Der Yudisher Emigrant* of the Jewish Colonization Association, which also published *Algemeine Yediyes far Die Vus Villen Foren in Fremde Lender* (General Information for Those Who Wish to Travel in Foreign Countries), 1905.

[7]Ellis Franklin claimed that 'the address of the [Poor Jews' Temporary] Shelter was bought and sold' in Eastern Europe. House of Commons Select Committee . . . *First Report* . . . 1888, Min. 1683-86; Cd. 1742, Min. 3410.

Victoria's realm. The shining vista of England as the haven and protector of freedom, which was created among Jews to some extent by the philanthropic efforts of Sir Moses Montefiore, was not noticeably tarnished, at least until the era of the Aliens Act of 1905. However, the distaste and at times hostility which the English working classes showed to Jewish immigrants when they lived near them was also reported back to the Pale of Settlement. Stirrings of anti-alienism or anti-Semitism were seldom underestimated:

. . . the spirit of the native workers and farmers is very bitter against the aliens (especially our coreligionists from Russia) in a very terrible and alarming way.[8]

Yet all of this, even when exaggerated for foreign consumption in attempts to frighten away prospective immigrants, seems to have had little measurable effect. Oppression and poverty made Russia infinitely worse than England, and this fact was simply too well known to be obscured by any amount of drumming on the Jews' fears.

With this minimum of freedom and personal safety assured, the prospective emigrant wanted to learn of his opportunities to make a living. Here, too, extensive efforts were made to depict a grim state of affairs in both lean and plentiful years. The themes of unavoidable unemployment and probable pauperism remained dominant, varying but slightly from Nafthali Levy's prototype warning in 1878:

Most of these immigrant brethren of ours are artisans of different kinds, always working hard and supporting their families scantily. Terrible is the lot of a fellow countryman when he first arrives here. . . .[9]

The trusting reader should have expected little less than destitution upon the streets of London or Manchester if he were so foolhardy as to ignore assurances that he could never make a living:

. . . bitter and evil is their fate here in England and in America, where they must stand upon their feet to perform labour which

[8]*HaMeliz*, XXXIII, 1 (January 2–14, 1892); see also *idem*, XXVI, 178 (December 10–22, 1886); XXXI, 173 (August 4–16, 1891).
[9]*Idem*, XIV, 2 (July 24–August 5, 1878).

exhausts them and breaks the body; all this for meagre bread and water of affliction. Their life is no life, for by the hard labour which they perform old age overtakes them in the springtime of their years.[10]

Diplomatic officials joined in warning the emigrants who applied at a British Consulate for the formality of a British visa. The Consul-General at Odessa 'always warned those who are proceeding to England to settle there that England is over crowded with unemployed workmen and that it is most undesirable that people should proceed there . . . but they invariably insist on going as their friends send them glowing accounts and also money to pay their passage.'[10a] These warnings were most frequent in such troubled years as 1882, 1886, and 1892. However, personal letters from England were more influential, and the sight of cash remittances must have been irresistible to many ambitious young men:

. . . people began to leave our town, which is a small town, and began sending over money very often, and that made up my mind that I should go over there as well, and so I came here. Especially a man left our place—an old man who had no trade at all. He was here only a few months, and he sent over £30. I made up my mind. 'I am a mechanic. I believe when I go over there I shall be able to make more money than he can.'[11]

Ten years later, in 1899, the now settled immigrant received a letter from his brother 'absolutely begging for me to send for him. . . .' But now the shoe was on the other foot and the importunate brother received fraternal admonition:

If you have got a potato and a cup of tea to it, stop where you are, because people coming over here, if they are foreigners, cannot make no fortune (sic).[12]

Some immigrants were interested in the religious prospect before them. There were religious leaders in Eastern Europe who warned faithful Jews not to endanger their Judaism by emigrating 'to lands where they are religiously dissolute and

[10]*Idem*, XXXII, 116 (May 27–June 8, 1892).
[10a]C. E. Stewart, Consul-General at Odessa, to Secretary of State, February 12, 1894. F. O. 65–1479.
[11]Cd. 1742, Min. 3361.
[12]Cd. 1742, Min. 3458.

transgress the commands of the Torah, such as shaving the beard and so forth. . . .' Such lands were especially undesirable for children. 'Whoever cannot return home for some reason and must bring his wife and infants to join him should in no case advise his older sons, who do not depend upon him, to come also . . . it is proper for them to remain in their native land and walk in the ways of the Lord.'[12a] The immigrant should 'place his entire hope that God may aid him to flee' back to Eastern Europe. The above was the advice of Rabbi Israel Meir Kahan (1839-1933, the 'Hafez Hayyim'), a widely revered leader of extreme orthodoxy. Such hostility to emigration probably discouraged many pious Jews from emigrating. However, other religious leaders took a more moderate view of emigration. The native Jews of England had long been praised for their faithful observance of traditional Judaism, and their well-organized community was elevated as a model. Despite occasional laments over unlearned or superficial English Judaism, there can have been little doubt of the religious acceptability of England as a land for Jewish settlement in comparison with the much laxer situation in America as it was reported back to Eastern Europe. When pious immigrants seceded to form a separate communal establishment, the press on the Continent published attacks on the schismatics' temerity for disputing the authentic orthodoxy of the native Jews.[13] Incredulity must have greeted the occasional alarms that Christian missionaries would surely ensnare destitute immigrants, and that apostasy was an all too likely outcome for poor immigrants.

THE WAY TO ENGLAND

Yet whatever the risks, Jews migrated by the million, and over 120,000 came to England in our period. There are three stages in the immigrant's odyssey: from home to the port city, the

[12a]Kahan, Israel Meir, *Nidhey Yisrael* (The Dispersed of Israel) (Hebrew and Yiddish), Warsaw, 1894, reprinted with English translation, New York, 1951.
[13]Especially in despatches from London to *HaMeliz*, XXXI, 257, 262, 292 (November 19–December 1, 1891, November 29–December 11, 1891, December 31, 1891–January 12, 1892); XXXII, 5, 14, 53 (January 7–19, 1892, January 17–29, 1892, March 14–26, 1892).

sea voyage, and the reception when he debarked. Natural and man-made pitfalls lay astride this path throughout, and the latter were harder to overcome. The first step was to leave Russia without a passport, which took trouble and money to secure and was not granted to prospective conscripts. Smuggling out emigrants was a further undertaking of the ubiquitous shipping agents. A British diplomat learned unofficially; 'I am given to understand that the emigration agents take care that a certain number of emigrants are duly provided with passports to blind the officials, but that a certain portion of the hold of the vessel is partitioned off with matting, etc., in which a number of those who are not provided with passports are placed until such time as the official revision of the ship has been made, when these stowaways emerge from their hiding place . . . the returns [of emigration] given to me by Spiro & Co. and Karlsberg & Co. are intentionally incorrect.'[13a] Obviously, the emigration agents had allies among the Russian officials. A further instance, probably typical of many others, may be quoted here. A ship sailing from Riga 'took with her 160 passengers who were provided with passports . . . more likely about 200 will land in London. The emigrants are supposed to be bound for, either the United States of America, or South Africa, and might produce vouchers for this effect, but for a great part these vouchers are blinds and are given gratis by the emigration agents here.'[13b] More emigrants smuggled across the frontier and reached Memel in Germany, whence they moved ahead on their own resources or with assistance to Hamburg.[13c] This steady flow could not have occurred unless the Russian government turned a blind eye. We hardly ever hear of emigrants caught or turned back as they left Russia.

The main ports of embarkation for England in the later nineteenth century were Bremen, Hamburg, and Rotterdam. Libau rose to importance after 1900 when its earlier emphasis

[13a]A. Wagstaff, Consul at Riga, to Secretary of State, March 9, 1896. F.O. 65–1522.
[13b]A. Woodhouse, Vice-Consul at Riga, to Secretary of State, November 9, 1896. F.O. 65–1522.
[13c]W. G. Wagstaff, Consul at Riga, to Secretary of State, June 13, 1891. F.O. 65–1406.

on cargo shipping came to share importance with the emigration traffic. It had the particular advantage of avoiding a long railroad trip and a border crossing. Most of its emigrants were Jews.[14] The ports of debarkation were Glasgow, Grimsby, Harwich, and London. Other British ports, such as Southampton, Newcastle, or Bristol, were either smaller or did not bestride the main emigration routes. Liverpool, England's greatest port, received mainly Irish, while to Glasgow came transmigrants from Scandinavia, among whom there were no Jews. Grimsby in the Midlands, and Tilbury, on the Thames close to central London, berthed the vessels which bore East European Jews to England or points west. Under the shipping arrangements of the times, Grimsby was the port for transmigrants, who then crossed England to board an America-bound boat in Liverpool. London, however, was a terminal, so that the immigrant who landed at Tilbury was obliged to fend for himself if he intended to continue his voyage.[15] The travel situation at the turn of the present century, with its imperfections and abuses, which we shall see, was still immeasurably removed from the uncertainties of international migration when German and East European Jews first began to come to England in a steady stream in the mid-eighteenth century.

Until some two hundred years ago, European Jewish migrations took place upon the Continent, and consisted mostly of movements back and forth between Slavic and Germanic lands. Jews also colonized Little Russia, the Ukraine, and Roumania

[14] *Der Yudisher Emigrant*, II, 10 (June 4, 1908), pp. 1–13.

[15] On immigration from origin to destination, see Board of Trade (Alien Immigration), *Reports on the Volume and Effects of Recent Immigration from Eastern Europe to the United Kingdom*, C. 7406, 1894, pp. 3–24 (cited hereafter as C. 7406); as a member of the Royal Commission on Alien Immigration in 1902–1903, William Evans-Gordon toured the ports on the Continent and published his observations in the Commission's *Report*, Cd. 1742, 1903, as Min. 13349; see esp. pp. 462–66. F. E. Eddis, the Commission's Secretary, visited Rotterdam, and published his findings in *Ibid.*, Min. 21713. See also *Memorandum by Dr Theodore Thomson concerning arrival of Immigrants and Transmigrants*, in Sessional Papers for 1896, v. 67, p. 729 ff. For the dockside situation the Annual Reports of the Poor Jews' Temporary Shelter are especially helpful. For a specimen description of an arriving vessel, see Charles Booth, ed., *Life and Labour of the People*, I: *East London*, London, 1889, pp. 580–83. On the predominance of Hamburg, see House of Commons Select Committee . . . *First Report* . . . 1888, pp. 304–05.

from Poland and Lithuania. By the French Revolutionary era westward movement predominated, and such west European Jewish communities of the nineteenth century as Vienna, Berlin, and Paris were built not only by Jews who migrated thither from their immediate hinterlands, but by Eastern Jews moving west. The westward impulse touched England in the middle of the eighteenth century, when Ashkenazi Jews began to arrive in force. For about a century the Ashkenazi immigrants came mainly from Holland and north German principalities, and helped to give a pronounced Dutch cast to a large part of English Jewry. Germany continued to supply a small but distinguished emigration of Jews to England throughout the nineteenth century. These were emancipated Jews with Western education, which practically removed them from the customary category of immigrant. Such men as Behrens and Moser in Bradford, where there arose a textile centre, and Ludwig Mond, father of Imperial Chemical Industries, arrived in England with valuable technical knowledge and business connections. Others like Edgar Speyer and Ernest Cassel became powerful bankers, moving in the upper reaches of English society. Behind these economic giants was a small class of prosperous businessmen, mainly engaged in textiles, banking, and foreign trade. The German Jewish immigrants did not form a sub-community or occupy an immigrant quarter. Many were estranged from the Jewish community.[15a] From the early nineteenth century, more distant reservoirs were tapped as emigrants left for England not only from German lands but also from Poland and Lithuania. The emigration frontier crept eastward from Posen, the area of contact between German and Polish culture, to the Vilna-Suvalk region in north-eastern Poland, which long remained the principal source for East European migration. A rather special instance among the

[15a]J. M. Cohen, *The Life of Ludwig Mond*, London, 1956; Brian Connell, *Manifest Destiny*, London, 1953 (on Cassel); Ernest Jones, *The Life and Work of Sigmund Freud*, I, New York, 1953 (on Freud's brothers in England); C. C. Aronsfeld, 'Jewish Enemy Aliens in England during the First World War,' *Jewish Social Studies*, XVIII, 4 (October, 1956), pp. 275–283; A. R. Rollin, 'The Jewish Contribution to the British Textile Industry,' *Transactions of the Jewish Historical Society of England*, XVII (1951–52), pp. 45–51; Elie Halévy, *A History of the English People in the Nineteenth Century*, 2nd ed., repr. London, 1952, pp. 409–10.

C

towns in this vicinity concerns Krottingen, whose Jewish emigrants tended to follow their pioneer emigrants and settle in Sunderland. After a fire in 1889 laid Krottingen waste, perhaps a majority of the local Jews moved to Sunderland.[16] This is an extreme yet illuminating example of the tendency of Jews from townlets and villages in the Pale of Settlement to cluster together in England in the spot which pioneer emigrants from home had happened to select. On the other hand, emigration to England from Galicia and the Ukraine to the south appears to have been small, if we may judge from the paucity of 'Austrians' mentioned by contemporaries and the few immigrant societies which bore place names from those regions. One reason for the preponderance of Vilna and Suvalk emigrants is that territory's proximity to the west, and its relative nearness to the port cities on the North Sea and the Baltic, which could be reached by rail at an early date. As railroads cut deeper into Russia, emigration flowed from further and further inland. The locomotive may be as important in the history of Jewish migration as the steamship.

A whole array of vocations existed to fleece the emigrant when he came to the port city—keepers of immigrant hostels, railroad employees, ships' officers and crews, and pre-eminently, ticket agents. Many of these dealers were Jews who spoke Yiddish, and exploited their victims' trust in them. Stolen baggage, exorbitant lodging rates, misrepresentation of ships' facilities, and capricious shifts of sailing schedules occurred daily. One also hears of tickets sold to the wrong destination by unscrupulous agents. Testimony upon all of this is borne not only by emigrants, who might understandably attribute the errors they committed in their bewilderment to someone's malevolence, but by resident observers and representatives of philanthropic organizations.[17] In Hamburg, however, rudimentary protection was devised. The shippers

---

[16]Arnold Levy, *History of the Sunderland Jewish Community*, London, 1956, pp. 93-99.

[17]Jacob Finkelstein, 'Zikhroines fun a "fusgayer" fun Rumenieh kayn America' (Memoirs of a 'Fusgayer' from Rumania to America), *YIVO Bleter*, XXVI (1945), pp. 112-20; Hermann Landau on Hamburg in *JC*, December 13, 1889. The opening chapters on emigration in Samuel Chotzinoff, *A Lost Paradise*, N.Y., 1955, are an excellent autobiographical account; Cd. 1742, Min. 3394-3409; 'Emigrant Hostels in Hamburg,' *JC*, July 25, 1902.

maintained emigrant hostels to control contagious disease and
prevent the cheating of the travellers, and the results may be
deemed satisfactory. Many emigrants partially circumvented
such dishonesty by having tickets already in their possession.
However, in periods of emergency many simply arrived in
Bremen or Hamburg to cast about helplessly for passage.
Not only were tickets sold in the towns and cities of the Pale,
where the same cheating could be perpetrated, but they were
sent by relatives who had already emigrated. Such remittance
was perhaps the safest means, because the remitter was shielded
by personal experience. Ticket agencies transacted their
business not only in Eastern Europe and port cities, but also
in railroad termini like Berlin, Vienna, and Breslau, in London
and the major English cities, and in America. They often
combined their business with money-changing, an important
service but also a lucrative source of plunder on the Continent.
On the other hand, the prudent purchaser could save substantial amounts, depending upon the route he selected, the
season of the year, and competitive conditions between the
various companies.[18] One cause of England's popularity as a
transit point was the well known fact that a trans-Atlantic
journey was cheaper when it took ship from Liverpool instead
of directly from Hamburg. At one time it was cheaper to go
from Hamburg to London to Antwerp to New York than
directly![19] Furthermore, spring and summer were the emigration seasons, so that attractive rates were dangled before
prospective emigrants who would brave a winter's trip over-
land and overseas. However, few saved their money in this
hazardous way.

The calculating emigrant who scanned the voluminous
advertising of the steamship lines had a safer way to conserve

[18]The Hebrew and Yiddish press in Eastern Europe, England, and America
are filled with the advertising of steamship companies and agents. However,
prospectus and practice are separate matters, and the latter is hardly to be found
in the advertising. It was estimated that 1,000,000 rubles were remitted from
England to the Continent through the International Bank in the East End, besides
steamship tickets. G. R. Sims, *Living London*, 3 vols., London, 1903, I, p. 23.
See advt. by this bank in I. Suwalsky, *Betelin uMebutallin*, (Null and Void),
London, 1900, end papers. *JC*, January 1, 1904.

[19]C. 7406, pp. 12–15; Georg Halpern, *Der jüdischen Arbeiter in London*, Berlin,
1903, p. 15; *JC*, May 26, 1892. Cd. 1742, Min. 16285–86; *cf.* Ernest Pépin, *La
question des etrangers en Angle-terre*, Paris, 1914, pp. 157–58.

his limited resources. The main trans-Atlantic companies alternated between price-fixing among themselves and cut-throat competition. For example, after years of an 'Atlantic Shipping Ring' which aimed to eliminate the emigrants' saving in buying tickets in England, the 'Atlantic Rate War' erupted from 1902 to 1904. During inter-company hostilities, the fare from England to America was slashed from its custo-mary £6 10s to £2, while the fare of 120 marks from Germany remained stationary. A torrent of emigrants rushed to England to seize the opportunity; Jewish charitable organizations in England and on the continent quickly cleared their backlogs of emigration cases by despatching them during the bargain years.[20]

After three days' voyage across the North Sea in steerage, the people who debarked at Tilbury or Grimsby were thoroughly dishevelled and their clothes in tatters. Many of them had not changed garments since they commenced the long journey from home. Observers complained frequently of the immigrants' 'unsanitary' condition, but the unsightliness was the end result of an arduous journey.[21]

Few immigrants realized that a dangerous part of their voyage lay at its very end, at dockside. All was well for the immigrant whose friend or relative picked him out of the crowd, provided that mutual recognition did not take too much time. A motley mass of waterfront sharks and thieves lay in wait to despoil the others of money and baggage, under the guise of 'guides', 'porters', and runners for lodging houses. More contemptible were the Jews who used their knowledge of Yiddish to win immigrants' confidence only to defraud them. A more sinister person also lurked at the waterfront, the white slaver or his agent seeking out unaccompanied girls. The most consistent offenders were some lodging-house

[20]Poor Jews' Temporary Shelter, *Annual Report 1903–1904*, p. 4. The number of emigrants who sailed from England leaped from 4,725 from July 1 to September 30, 1903 to 13,685 for the same period in the following year. B. Huldermann, *Albert Ballin*, N.Y., 1922, contains revealing views into the business practices of the German and English shippers; Ballin's earliest business was the sale of emigrant tickets. London *Daily Chronicle*, May 26, 1904, quoted in *JC*, May 27, 1904.

[21]T. B. Eyges, *Zikhroines* . . . MS. in YIVO, New York; *Memorandum of Dr Theodore Thomson, loc. cit.*

keepers who guided the immigrant to flop-house accommo-
dations and charged him an exorbitant 2s 6d a day and another
5s for a 'guide' who simply tramped him aimlessly about the
city. After the victim was fleeced, if he was a transmigrant
en route to another British port he was put on a train supposedly to bring him to his destination. Actually he rode as
far as some nearby town, where he was dumped, destitute and
alone. The *Jewish Chronicle* concluded that 'the process of
robbery and chicanery . . . is quite as active in London as it is
on the Russian frontier.'[22] Credit for the prevention and
remedy of these abuses is due less to the London dock police,
who gave little active assistance, than to the prolonged efforts
of the Poor Jews' Temporary Shelter. It was the Shelter,
whose subvention came from a small proportion of the Jewish
community, which steadily pressed the fight and forced the
public authorities to take action. Its representatives who came
to meet a ship had to elbow their way through the collection
of scamps whose wiles they detected and stamped out. By the
turn of the century the Shelter could report with satisfaction
that

. . . at all events in this country, the sharks and crimps which formerly
infested the riverside and preyed on the ignorance and helplessness
of the newcomers, robbing them even of the little which had escaped
the rapacity of continental agents and others, have now very nearly
found their occupation gone. . . .[23]

As a measure of safety and public control was established
over the London docks, port authorities and police assumed
some of the functions which the Poor Jews' Temporary Shelter
undertook. However, nothing could be done in England to
protect the immigrant from yet greater abuses on the Continent.

[22] *JC*, August 21, 1891; *HaYehudi*, I, 1 (October 13, 1897); see some graphic
details supplied by Hermann Landau in House of Commons Select Committee . . .
First Report . . . 1888, Min. 2163–90.
[23] Poor Jews' Temporary Shelter, *Annual Report 1901–1902*, n.p. The Shelter
employed a carman, an interpreter, and a retired policeman as a guard. It also
assisted in the purchase of steamship tickets and in currency exchange. Its representatives met trains from Grimsby at Kings Cross Station. *Idem*, Executive
Minutes, 1887–1898, *passim;* Cd. 1742, Min. 16271. For a day at the docks see
JC, February 12, 1904.

THE TIDES OF IMMIGRATION[24]

The transition from predominantly Dutch and German immigration to immigration from Eastern Europe occurred between 1865 and 1875. It was still true in 1861 that 'Holland continues to supply the largest number of foreign paupers,'[25] yet the actual number of Dutch immigrants to England in the early 1860's was smaller than that of emigrants from England to America.[26] To be sure, immigrants from Eastern Europe had already been coming to England for some time. A high proportion of them was made up of roaming unattached individuals without family ties, or young men who left home and family. For example, young Joseph Lissack left his native Posen in 1836 in quest of a supposed inheritance in London. When he found this was chimerical, he began a successful career as a country peddler.[27] Joseph Harris of Neustadt near Suvalk, aged seventeen, came to England in 1852. Expecting no inheritance, he lost no time in betaking himself to rural Yorkshire with a peddler's pack and also enjoyed material success in due course.[28] Matthias Bentwich, ancestor of a notable Jewish family line, arrived in England from Peiser in Posen sometime around 1840. Two of his brothers went to Australia, just as a brother of Lissack had gone ahead to New York.[29] William Aronsberg of Courland settled in England in 1850 at the age of eighteen, and became a wealthy spectacle maker and manufacturer of precision tools in Manchester, a J.P., and the patron of Jewish immigrant institutions.[30] Rabbi Abraham Sussmann

[24]The statistical aspects of Jewish immigration have been summarized in the author's 'Notes on the Statistics of Jewish Immigration to England, 1870–1914,' *Jewish Social Studies*, XXI. See also Appendix.

[25]Jewish Board of Guardians, *Annual Report*, 1861, p. 10. An 1866 specimen of Dutch Jewish immigration is S. N. Behrman, *Duveen*, N.Y., 1952, pp. 51–54, 59–60; see Emanuel Shinwell, *Conflict Without Malice*, London, 1955, ch. 1.

[26]Jewish Board of Guardians, *Annual Report*, 1863, pp. 8–9, 21, 43; J. H. Stallard, *London Pauperism amongst Jews and Christians*, London, 1867, pp. 5–9.

[27]J. M. Lissack, *Jewish Perseverance*, 2nd ed. (sic), Bedford, 1851, pp. 68–71.

[28]Joseph Harris, *Random Notes and Reflections*, Liverpool, 1912, pp. 13, 15 ff.

[29]Norman and Margery Bentwich, *Herbert Bentwich the Pilgrim Father*, Jerusalem, 1940, pp. 9–10; J. M. Lissack, *op. cit.*, pp. 89–91.

[30]*HaMaggid Mishneh*, XXIII, 24 (June 18, 1879). J. L. Gordon (1831–1892), the poet of the Russian Hebrew Enlightenment, narrates an immigrant family story in his satire *Kozo shel Yad*, in which the father goes to Liverpool to mend his fortunes. Ll. 499 ff.

arrived from Poland around 1840, and served as chief *shohet*
in London for many years.[31] A notable case is that of Hermann
Landau, who came from Poland in 1864 and became a wealthy
banker and supporter of immigrant life in London.[32] These
successful life histories are naturally more prominent than those
typified by Yekuthiel Sussmann Schlosser (1796-1876), who
arrived in 1852 as an itinerant solicitor for a projected yeshibah
in Kalish. The money was not raised,

. . . and this man began bit by bit to worry about himself and ceased
concerning himself about the yeshibah. Since he too was also from
Russia-Poland he did not undertake any trade or skill, and poverty
compelled him to be a beggar here. At first he was an honourable
beggar, until he afterward became a common beggar like one of the
common beggars who, to our distress, are not few among the natives
of Russia and Poland [in England].[33]

The man died a pauper, 51 years after first leaving his family
in Plungyan.

The majority of early immigrants stood between these extremes of wealth and beggary and are typified by the laconic
recollections of two immigrant workmen. One came in 1870:

I was left an orphan, and I had a brother here, and he sent for me to
come here . . . my relations helped me with the fare to come to
London.[34]

A youthful immigrant of 1879:

I was 15 years old when I started away from Poland . . . I had
relatives living in this country, and my father gave me 20 roubles
to come over here to this country. He thought perhaps I should
be able to learn a trade over here to get on.[35]

By the onset of the era of mass migration, many such early
arrivals had become well-established English Jews. With
the end of the American Civil War, East European emigration

[31]See his commentary on laws of *shehitah*, *Bet Abraham*, Königsberg, 1853,
Part 2, p. 12; *HaMaggid*, XXIII, 15 (April 17, 1879). His son, Barnett Abrahams
was Dayan of the Sefardi (sic!) community in London, and his grandson was
Israel Abrahams, the distinguished Anglo-Jewish scholar.
[32]Cd. 1742, Min. 16266.
[33]Z. H. Dainow in *HaMaggid*, XX, 3 (January 19, 1876).
[34]Cd. 1742, Min. 3760-61.
[35]Cd. 1842, Min. 3569-70.

again flowed to North America, and some remained in England, contrary to their original intention of crossing the ocean.[36]

Perhaps the turning point from Dutch and German to East European immigration occurred in 1869-70, a year of famine in north-eastern Russia during which Jews were expelled from the border regions. At the same time, Rumania began systematically to persecute its Jews, forcing them out of their livelihoods and contriving to keep thousands in a state of permanent personal insecurity. The stream of young men from Eastern Europe was sharply augmented in 1875 and 1876, when many fled to avoid service in the armies of the Czar during the Russo-Turkish War. Such fleeing reservists may have set a pattern for later immigrants' occupations. They stayed away from peddling and took to such employment as clothes-pressing in London and waterproof-making in Manchester.[37] Later in the 1870's some intellectuals arrived, so that the immigrant quarter began to assume a cultural distinctiveness of its own. England received such varied personages as Jacob Reinowitz, Zvi Hirsch Dainow, Nahum Lipman, Morris Winchevsky, Aaron Liebermann, and E. W. Rabbinowitz at this time. However, a contemporary observer could not yet have foretold that the greatest demographic shift in Jewish history was getting under way. True, the Jewish Board of Guardians in London was concerned as early as 1872 with reports that Continental charitable bodies were clearing their dockets by despatching 'vagrant' Jews to England, and appointed a committee 'to enquire into the cause of the large influx of Jews from Poland with the view of suggesting a remedy to the Board.'[38] The usual warnings to stay away from England and reminders that no relief could be expected in the first six months of residence were placed in the European press.[39] An articulate young immigrant like Elijah Rabbinowitz appeared before the London Beth Din to plead for the establishment of an immigrant shelter in 1880. His principal argument

[36] J. H. Stallard, *op. cit.*, p. 7.
[37] J. G. Eccarius, *Der Kampf des Grossen und des Kleinen Kapitals oder Die Schneiderei in London*, Leipzig, 1876, p. 25; *HaMeliz*, XIV, 3, 4 (July 31–August 12, August 7–19, 1878).
[38] Jewish Board of Guardians, *Minutes*, November 27, 1872, March 25, 1873.
[39] *JC*, April 16, 1880.

was the danger of missionary allurements to the semi-destitute and not the quantity of helpless immigrants needing help and guidance.[40]

The dramatic need for fresh appraisal occurred in 1881–1882. In that year of widespread pogroms in southern Russia the malevolence of the Russian régime to the Jews was first fully realized. The Jewish intelligentsia in Eastern Europe was being led to re-examine painfully some of the articles of its faith in salvation by Jewish enlightenment and emancipation, and the millions of Jews pent up in the towns and villages of the Pale of Settlement contracted emigration fever. To the emancipated Jewries in Western countries, the events of 1881–1882 presaged the direction of their political effort and philanthropic activity for two generations to come. On the other hand, emigration did not begin on account of pogroms and would certainly have attained its massive dimensions even without the official anti-Semitism of the Russian Government. Witness Jewish emigration from the Habsburg territory of Galicia, where the Jews were emancipated in 1867 yet emigrated in proportions as great as those in Russia and Poland. The year 1881–1882 really signifies that a sense of urgency was given to emigration; that Jewish social thought in Eastern Europe noticeably shifted its bearings; that Jews throughout the Western world were put on notice to expect migration *en masse* to their more favoured lands. How directly the iniquitous treatment of the Jews in Russia affected England and the English Jews is expressed in the words of the *Jewish Chronicle*, that

. . . we have a considerable interest in the removal of the disabilities under which they labour . . . over ninety per cent. of our applicants to our Board of Guardians have been subjects of the Czar, and the larger proportion of our poor are invariably immigrants from Russia or Poland.[41]

It estimated that 'of the Jewish poor in the Metropolis it is probable that 90 per cent. are Russians.'[42] Not counted among them were the German Jewish immigrants, who formed a

[40]*Die Tsukunft*, II, 41 (April 16, 1886); memoirs in *'Iyyim*, I (1927), Part 4, pp. 66–67.
[41]*JC*, August 20, 1880.   [42]*JC*, October 1, 1880.

more prosperous group of tradesmen and skilled workmen. They came in small but steady numbers largely from German Poland, and their migration was comparatively unaffected by the crises in Russia.[43]

English Jewry did not expect so great a movement, and undertook to succour arriving refugees in 1881–82 while sending as many as possible to America, some to the Colonies, and returning to Russia those who looked unpromising. They wanted no new settlers in England, and aimed considerable efforts at preventing this.[44] The Jewish Board of Guardians relaxed its six months' rule during the emergency, but never abated its labours to avert the 'great danger of the emigrants coming over to England in still larger numbers.'[45] President Lionel L. Cohen alerted them to the 'obvious' fact that 'a movement is in progress which may assume vast proportions, and of which this country may not improbably become the centre. . . .'[46] A representative reported his 'considerable difficulties' with some immigrants who would not accept the Board's proffered alternatives of emigration overseas or

[43]Charles Booth, 'The Inhabitants of Tower Hamlets (School Board Division), their Condition and Occupations,' *Journal of the Royal Statistical Society*, L, 2 (June, 1887), pp. 366–67.

[44]See Zosa Szajkowski 'The European Attitude to East European Jewish Immigration (1881–93)," *Publications of the American Jewish Historical Society*, XLI, 2 (December, 1951), pp. 126–35, 138, 144, for examples of English Jewish unwillingness to receive immigrants for settlement. The same author's 'The Attitude of American Jews to East European Jewish Immigration (1881–93),' *Idem*, XL, 3 (March, 1951), pp. 226, 230, 232–33, 236, 239–40, quotes on the other hand, specimens of American Jewish protests at the unwanted 'passing-on' or 'dumping' of immigrants. The valuable unpublished material suffers from lack of comparison with published sources. The same author's 'How the Mass Migration to America Began,' *Jewish Social Studies*, IV, 4 (October, 1942), pp. 291–310, deals with 1870–90 upon the basis of Alliance Israélite Universelle archives. Jacob Lifschitz, *Zikhron Ya'akob* (Memoirs of Jacob), III, Kovno, 1930, pp. 93–95, mentions Asher's and Montagu's visit to Poland in the spring of 1882 for the 'sole' purpose of averting migration to England. They had other purposes. Lifschitz' interesting, but partisan and verbose, memoirs contain important original material concerning Jewish diplomatic efforts in the 1880's. The Russian and Hebrew letter given there (pp. 70–78) from 15 Russian Jews residing in London to Pobiedonostiev, dated January 19–31, 1882, evidently is connected with other activities then under way to relieve the position of the Russian Jews.

[45]*JC*, March 3, 1882; *cf. JC*, February 17, 1882. At the onset of the peak rush, it was observed that the emigrants arriving en route to America were '. . . a far superior class to the usual poor Jews that reach London from Poland.' *JC*, February 24, 1882.

[46]Jewish Board of Guardians, *Minutes*, February 27, 1882.

repatriation, but desired to remain in England.[47] The peak
of this first immigration rush was reached in the spring and
summer of 1882. By about July 20 of that crisis year, Mansion
House Fund relief had been granted to 2,220 persons, of whom
511 were 'assisted to remain in London.'[48] After twenty-six
weeks of frantic work, the Conjoint Committee of the Fund
and the Board of Guardians reported that 1,351 men, 386
women, and 541 children had received its aid, of whom 261 men,
78 women, and 87 children remained in England besides, no
doubt, many of the additional 232 men, 77 women, and 110
children who were denied aid because they 'refused to accept
the particular relief prescribed by the Committee.'[49] Thus,
as many as 845 of the total of 2,278 persons who applied for
charitable aid may have stayed in England for some period
of time, and some permanently.[50] Far more extensive was
emigration activity through English ports, chiefly Liverpool.
In the zenith between April 27 and July 12, 1882, the Mansion
House Commissioners in Liverpool used 31 steamships for the
despatch of 4,422 adults, 1,325 children, and 527 infants to
Canada and the United States.[51] These people were simply
passed on to America just as Continental relief committees
had shunted them on to England. The impact of this tide
upon the composition of London Jewry may be surmised from
the assertion in 1883 that of an estimated population of 44,000,
'nearly half . . . have only been in London, or indeed in England,
for an average of ten years or so.'[52] The increase in Leeds and
Manchester was in an even higher proportion.

Throughout the 1880's, migration proceeded at a heightened
pace, but without the Jewish communal assistance which had

[47]*JC*, March 3, 1882.   [48]*JC*, July 21, 1882.
[49]Letter, Lionel L. Cohen to Lionel L. Alexander, August 24, 1882, and 'Report
of Conjoint Committee for 26 weeks,' both in Board of Guardians, *Minute Letter
Book, ad loc.*
[50]The Mansion House Fund reported that the £108,759 which it collected
in 1882 was used for the relief of 10,310 persons in England and on the Continent,
of whom 8,596 went to America. *JC*, October 27, 1882. Of the 2,749 persons
aided in England, 1,207 emigrated and 624 were repatriated, leaving 918 un-
accounted for and presumably remaining in England. Jewish Board of Guardians.
Annual Report, 1905, p. 94 (gives cumulative figures of the Conjoint Committee
from 1882).
[51]Mansion House Fund. Liverpool Commission. *Memoir of Proceedings*, Liverpool, 1882, n.p.
[52]*JC*, October 12, 1883.

been forthcoming during the emergency period. A lower peak was touched in 1886 on account of Bismarck's expulsion of alien Poles from Prussia.[53] A youthful immigrant characterized immigrants who arrived at this time:

In England, chiefly in London, the emigrants were composed of those who had to leave their countries because of social conditions and had not enough fare [for America] and had to leave their homes suddenly, in haste, like refugees from mobilization, political refugees, and so on. About ninety per cent. of the immigrants in London had in mind to go on to America by saving up enough fare. The remaining ten per cent. remained in London, because their parents or children, family or fellow-townsmen made them comfortable, and they settled with the intention of remaining there permanently.[54]

The burden of the dormant Mansion House Fund's responsibilities, after it suspended activities at the close of 1882, fell upon the London and Provincial Jewish Boards of Guardians. These bodies received many new cases which were not the outcome solely of the hard times and social unrest in England at the close of the 1880's.[55]

Another hard blow struck East European Jewry in 1890 with the expulsion of the Jews from Russian cities like Moscow and Kiev and the rigorous enforcement of earlier decrees. All efforts by European Jewry to avert the enactments came to naught, and another surge of emigration brought another human wave to English and American shores.[56] Now, after ten years of intensive immigration, it was indeed realized that the movement in progress was of vast proportions, as uneasily

[53]To the irritation of English Jews, German Jews sent many expelled aliens on to England. The *JC* admitted: '. . . we are in a position to sympathize with our American cousins when we adopted the "passing-on" policy in 1882.' *JC*, November 12, 1886. Furthermore, it was impossible to return them to Hamburg because they were not allowed to land without means to continue their journey back to Russia. *JC*, November 5, 1886. Manchester Jewish Board of Guardians, *Minutes*, November 3, 1886. L. L. Alexander went to Hamburg to try to mitigate the ruling, and the community returned its cases via Rotterdam. Jewish Board of Guardians, *Minutes*, November 15, 1886. *Die Tsukunft*, III, 20 (November 19, 1886).

[54]T. Eyges, *Zikhroines* . . ., MS. in YIVO, New York.

[55]C. 7406, p. 12. The Appendix A of the Board of Guardians' Annual Reports presents figures on cases relieved by the Board. Reports of the Provincial Jewish Guardians, where available, show a similar rise.

[56](Russo-Jewish Committee), *The Persecution of the Jews in Russia*, London, 1891. The Czar refused to receive the memorial addressed to him by a distinguished English group on behalf of the Jews in Russia.

foretold by the deceased Lionel L. Cohen. No communal institution could stem immigration, nor could the establishment of 'border committees' turn back emigrants. On the other hand, an international Jewish Conference on migration in 1891 hardly advanced matters when representatives from each western Jewish community made clear their unwillingness to receive immigrants in more than insignificant numbers.[57] The Russo-Jewish Committee granted £25,000 to the counter-part committee in Berlin to assist in despatching an expected 18,000 refugees to America; 'on their side, the Berlin Committee undertook not to forward any Refugees on to England without previous consent asked and received.' The German group fulfilled this *quid pro quo* with 'unswerving loyalty,' so that only 'a few' reached English shores with Jewish communal funds. Many, however, came unaided.[58]

In the early 1890's the Board of Trade estimated the number of immigrants who actually settled in England as over 7,000 in 1891, about 3,000 in 1892, and less than 3,000 in 1893.[59] When we allow the same proportion of transmigrants to immigrants as that worked out by the statistical report, we may suppose that immigration remained relatively stationary at about 2,500 until the close of the 1890's. During these years, no political disaster or economic crisis befell East European Jewry, but the steady political and social pressures did not lessen. In contrast to the shocks and crises which spurred Jewish immigration from 1881 to 1891, the final decade of the nineteenth century witnessed the development of immigration into an unfailing substantial stream. These families depended little upon outside assistance but relied upon their own will and resourcefulness. They made an impression as people 'of a more capable and self-reliant nature than those who seek refuge here in times of acute persecution.'[60] The stories of

[57]M. Wischnitzer, *To Dwell in Safety*, Philadelphia, 1949, pp. 70–72, 320.
[58]Russo-Jewish Committee, *Annual Report*, 1891-92, p. 26. 'I am further told the Committee (in Königsberg) refuse any pecuniary assistance to Jews bound to the United Kingdom, and that the money they dispose of is largely received from Jewish sources in England and is sent on the express condition that no Jew be assisted to settle in the United Kingdom.' W. G. Wagstaff, Consul at Riga, to Secretary of State, May 14, 1892. F.O. 65–1426.
[59]C. 7406, pp. 3–15, 22–3.
[60]Jewish Board of Guardians, *Annual Report*, 1897, p. 16.

Samuel Chotzinoff (1889–   )[61] and Selig Brodetsky (1888–1954),[62] English mathematician and Zionist, mirror much of immigration during this relatively calmer period. Their families' decisions to emigrate were choices deliberately taken; routes of travel were carefully examined and advice was judiciously sought. Akiva Brodetsky, the father, preceded his family to England, and sent for his wife and young children when he had secured a slender footing in the new land. Later the father's parents followed. In spite of all of the Chotzinoffs' planning, they were nevertheless duped by a ticket dealer. In the fairly average year's span from November 1, 1893, through October 31, 1894, 3,954 persons came upon the rolls of the Poor Jews' Temporary Shelter, including such families as the Chotzinoffs. The largest group, 843 adults and 848 children, had come 'to join husbands or other relatives,' and a group of 1,148 were in England because of expulsion, 'threatened persecution,' or as 'indirect sufferers from restrictive laws.' Interestingly enough, 269 were en route back to Eastern Europe from America, in contrast to the 509 who were America-bound transmigrants.[63] This motley assortment of persons and reasons illumines the basic forces underlying migration very little, but does serve as a cross-section of an average migration year during relatively calm times.

The turn of the century brought a decade of turmoil. In almost consecutive order, East European Jewry underwent the Rumanian 'exodus' of 1900, the Kishinev outrage of 1903, the outbreak of the Russo-Japanese War in 1904, the Revolution of 1905, and its trail of pogroms lasting into 1906. Under these hammer blows, the semblance of orderly movement which had been preserved for some ten years vanished. Waves of Rumanian wanderers, fleeing conscripts, pogrom victims, and above all, Jews who simply despaired of improvement in Russia streamed into the British Isles in proportions which bewildered those who tried to organize the flow. An added magnet was the dissolution of the 'Atlantic Shipping Ring' and that price war

[61]Samuel Chotzinoff, *op. cit.*, pp. 38–45; a charming and useful book.
[62]W. P. Milne, 'Selig Brodetsky,' *Journal of the London Mathematical Society*, XXX, 1 (January, 1956), pp. 121–25; oral statements by Dr Brodetsky to the writer.
[63]Russo-Jewish Committee, *Report*, 1894, p. 27.

upon the high seas, the Atlantic Rate War from 1902 to 1904. Previously, English shippers had agreed with Continental firms that they would not sell their cheaper trans-Atlantic tickets to transmigrants. The connivances used by immigrants to outwit the shippers were abandoned and the fare dropped precipitously.[64] Furthermore, a recognizable number of Jews from South Africa sought refuge at the commencement of the Boer War. By 1907, the great waves had spent themselves, and the Aliens Act erected a barrier to uncontrolled torrents.

The Rumanian 'exodus' of 1899–1900,[65] a formless protest march across Europe which was joined in by several thousand young Jews, reached England and sought to continue still further. The apparent futility of the gesture incensed the leaders of the Jewish community:

> It is an outrage against the dictates of common sense and humanity, that such a senseless and hopeless movement should ever have been directed at these shores. . . .[66]

They exercised vigilance in keeping any of the *fusgayer* from remaining if it could be prevented, and pointed an accusing finger at the Jewish communities in port cities like Rotterdam, who had aided the procession to 'march' by ship to England: 'The responsibility is heavy of those who encouraged and assisted it.'[67] But settlement in England was not so easily averted. Of the 2,903 Rumanian Jews who arrived in the *fusgayer* movement, the Jewish Guardians in London returned 1,399 'mainly at their own request, and, naturally, never without their own consent.'[68] Another 375 went abroad, leaving 1,129 added to the books of the Guardians, to that body's displeasure. This undue proportion remaining in England is probably because the marchers arrived unaccom-

---

[64] Cd. 1742, Min. 1451–56; see above, Notes 14, 15.

[65] Zosa Szajkowski, 'Jewish Emigration Policy in the Period of the Rumanian "Exodus",' *Jewish Social Studies*, XIII, 1 (January, 1951), pp. 47–70; Joseph Kissman, *Studies in the History of Rumanian Jewry in the 19th and the Beginning of the 20th Centuries* (Yiddish), N.Y., 1944, ch. 1; Jacob Finkelstein, *op. cit.*, *YIVO Bleter*, XXVI (1945), pp. 105–128; Cd. 1742, Min. 15288–97.

[66] Jewish Board of Guardians, *Annual Report*, 1900, p. 16.

[67] *Ibid.*, p. 18; Jacob Finkelstein, *op. cit.*, pp. 121–25; Poor Jews' Temporary Shelter, *Annual Report*, 1899–1900, n.p.

[68] Jewish Board of Guardians, *Annual Report*, 1900, pp. 17–18; see also the testimony of the Board's President Leonard L. Cohen, in Cd. 1742, Min. 15278–97.

panied. Charitable bodies, however, refused to despatch married men overseas without their families.

Yet all this was of small consequence in comparison with the great tide set loose by the interlocked calamities of war, revolution and pogroms in Russia, and perhaps also by the approach of restrictive legislation in England. The years of 1905 and 1906 were the busiest in the history of Jewish immigration to England. In contrast to its annual average of 937 persons assisted to emigrate during the preceding ten years, the Conjoint Committee of the Russo–Jewish Committee and the Jewish Board of Guardians aided 3,847 and 2,796 persons in these two years, of whom, 2,746 in 1905 and 1,416 in 1906 neither returned to Russia nor went on to America at Jewish communal expense. Hence, at least 4,162 people were added to the immigrant population, at any rate for some period of time.[69] Probably thrice that many settled during those years without appearing in communal charitable records. Thus, of 4,000 to 5,000 reservists who landed in England to escape military service in Siberia during the Russo-Japanese War, some 1,500 are reported to have remained in England.[70]

The causes of emigration lay yet deeper:

No work, no commerce, the harvest is unpredictable, nothing for the workman to do, no one to whom to sell merchandise. And if one takes a general 'sideways view' of emigration, one would suppose it now plays the part of a thermometer to a sick person. If the sick person's temperature goes up, the mercury column rises a bit. It is exactly the same with emigration among the Jews. Now one does not need as many reasons to emigrate.[71]

Even in the Ukraine, an area previously troubled by pogroms yet not a major source of emigrants, 'there is not a single household among us where there is no one aspiring to go to America.'[72] A summary of reports from 100 towns and cities concluded that

. . . the main cause of emigration is simply that they can't earn a piece of bread. They write from thirty-four cities that one does not hear of

[69]*Idem*, 1907, Appendix A.
[70]Russo-Jewish Committee, *Report* for 1904, *q.v.* in *JC*, July 7, 1905.
[71]*Der Yudisher Emigrant*, I, 2 (November 5, 1907), p. 19.
[72]Reported from Lukashevka, *Idem*, I, 1 (October 15, 1907), p. 18.

emigration after the pogroms. In eighty-four cities the larger proportion of the emigrants is workmen and from forty-six cities a mass of traders and shopkeepers emigrates.[73]

In the words of a Warsaw observer, 'emigration has already become obviously a natural and steady fact in our life'.[74] Most of this emigration, however, stayed away from England. The United States and other countries of the New World seemed to offer greater opportunity, and an Aliens Act was now in the English statute books and presented a barrier which was more psychological than actual. To be sure, the Jewish immigrant population did increase. In 1911, 106,082 'Russians and Poles' were enumerated in England and Wales,[75] and it is reasonable to raise this figure to 120,000 by adding immigrant Jewry in Scotland and by including East European Jews from Germany, Austria, and Rumania.

NATIVE JEWRY AND IMMIGRATION

The Jews of England, like those of Western Europe and America, showed no pleasure at the arrival of immigrants, and did all in their power to persuade them not to come. However, no single policy or attitude consistently governed the attitude of the entire native Jewish community to immigration. England's geographic position permitted the Jewish community to send immigrants either forward to America or back to their native places. From the eighteenth century, the community encouraged emigration to America and the Colonies to reduce the number of its poor and the burden which they laid upon more affluent Jews. As early as Oglethorpe's settlement of Georgia in 1732, wealthy Jews participated as investors and sent along some of their own unwanted poor.[76] Such nineteenth century groups as the Jews' Emigration Society, the Emigration Committee of the Jewish Board of Guardians, and the

[73]Ben-Elijah pseud., *Ibid.*, p. 15.   [74]*Ibid.*, p. 19.
[75]*Census of England and Wales*, 1911, Cd. 7017, pp. 114 ff.
[76]Cecil Roth, *A History of the Jews in England*, 2nd ed., Oxford, 1949, pp. 198–202, 232–34; M. Dorothy George, *London Life in the XVIIIth Century*, 2nd ed., London, 1930, pp. 110–11, 125–30. The Elders of the Great Synagogue took steps in the second half of the eighteenth century to prevent immigration by encouraging government restrictions upon the embarkation of paupers from the Continent aboard British ships. *Ibid.*, p. 130.

D

Bevis Marks synagogue granted travel aid to poor but promising men with or without families.

Although immigration is a pervasive feature in every generation of Anglo-Jewish history, there was no comparable communal effort to deal with immigrants. Before the first crisis year of 1881–1882, the native community paid no consistent attention to immigrants and did not attempt to aid or advise them. In the decade of the 1870's, when Jews coming from Eastern Europe began to predominate among the yearly arrivals over Dutch and German Jews, the Jews in England were still unconcerned except as it seemed to augment the numbers of 'deserving poor'. Prosperity and depression each created worries of its own. The Jewish Guardians of Manchester explained to their subscribers that even 'a high rate of wages and a great demand for labour are likely to increase the calls on the Board' by attracting immigrant Jews who would eventually apply for its aid at some juncture.[77]

For fear of appearing too hospitable, the major charitable bodies resolutely left immigrants to their own devices, not extending them the least intimation that England desired them. One provision throughout the country required six months' residence in England in order to qualify an applicant for relief. Obviously, the rule intended to prevent arriving immigrants from depending upon charitable aid, and to accustom them to the well-advertised virtues of self-help. In later years, it was used to reassure both English Jews and Gentiles that no prospect of aid was tempting immigrants to come to England. Thus, difficult stages had to be passed without organized help from the Jewish community, although mutual aid among immigrants filled the vacuum. Critics justly observed that judicious aid at the dock-side and in the first stages of settlement could do much to spare both immigrants and natives later need for charity.[78]

The dominant view was that taken by leading families like Rothschild, Montefiore, and Mocatta, which impressed itself upon central institutions like the Jewish Boards of Guardians,

---

[77]Manchester Jewish Board of Guardians, *Annual Report*, 1872, n.p.
[78]For example, Leopold J. Greenberg in the *Jewish Year Book*, V, 1900–1901, pp. 382–383. (But compare his earlier views in *Idem*, I, 1896–1897, pp. 218–219.)

the United Synagogue, and the *Jewish Chronicle*. They would
have kept the gates of England always open to all, but would
give no encouragement and as little aid as possible to immigrants. Immigrants could be best dealt with by being sent
forward to America if they seemed like promising candidates
and if American Jews did not object too vehemently,[79] or back
to Eastern Europe if they could be persuaded to return. Until
the end of the century, this outlook held that 'the amelioration
of the condition of Russian Jews can only be effected in one
way—by their complete emancipation from political disabilities,' and that Russian Jews ought to put their faith in
this goal and remain in Russia.[80] The upholders of these views
were influential and socially prominent, and generous with
both time and money in Jewish and general communal endeavour.

This chilly, aloof policy toward new arrivals did not sit well
with a group which was closer in spirit and descent to the
immigrants. Such persons were Hermann Landau, a Polish
immigrant of 1864 and a successful stockbroker; Bernard
Birnbaum, a German immigrant and waterproof manufacturer;
and a pious and patriarchal native, Ellis A. Franklin. The
principal figure was the redoubtable Sir Samuel Montagu
(1832–1911). His family was in England several generations
but he stood close to the immigrant community as organizer
and patron of its institutions and M.P. for Whitechapel. Such
younger challengers of the oligarchic dominance of the community as Herbert Bentwich and Leopold J. Greenberg, who
took over the *Jewish Chronicle* in 1907, defended the cause of
alien immigration with greater ardour than had ever been
seen. These men's outlook did not advocate cordiality to
immigrants, but besides the open door it demanded a greater
measure of aid and comfort. This group furnished the most
articulate spokesmen for the immigrants' cause before the
Royal Commission in 1902–1903.

[79]However, American Jews did object, particularly in 1884 and 1900, for
precisely the reasons English Jews objected to receiving Jews from the Continent.
The archives of the Jewish Board of Guardians contain the sometimes agitated
correspondence between it and the United Hebrew Charities in New York concerning the shipment of emigrants by communal bodies.

[80]*JC*, May 20, 1881. This basic theme is well treated in Zosa Szajkowski,
'Emigration to America or Reconstruction in Europe,' *Publications of the American
Jewish Historical Society*, XLII, 2 (December, 1952), pp. 157–88.

The two views first clashed when the Poor Jews' Temporary Shelter opened in 1885.[81] Early in that year it came to light that Simon Cohen, a pious immigrant baker known to his contemporaries and to later recollection as 'Simha Becker', was personally maintaining a sort of shelter in Church Lane, a stone's throw from the principal intersection of the East End. The rooms which it occupied were a crude refuge for the homeless or jobless, where they could pray, study sacred literature, sleep somehow, and after a fashion, be fed and even clothed. Immigrants fresh off the boat were also accommodated by this austere but sincere hospitality. This transplantation of an East European charitable practice existed upon the largesse of other poor immigrants and mostly by the indefatigable efforts of 'Simha Becker'. When native Jewry learned of the immigrants' shelter in April, 1885, Frederic D. Mocatta and Lionel L. Alexander visited the place and pronounced the 'premises . . . unhealthy'. They also considered that 'such a harbour of refuge must tend to invite helpless Foreigners to this country, and therefore was not a desirable institution to exist'.[82] The Jewish Board of Guardians thereupon succeeded in having the refuge close its doors for more than sufficient sanitary reasons. However, this high-handed action roused a protest in the East End,[83] and more important, the pious baker's little 'harbour of refuge' found wealthy and important friends in Montagu, Franklin, and Landau. The latter advocated the founding of

an institution in which newcomers, having a little money, might obtain accommodation and the necessaries they required at cost price, and where they would receive useful advice.[84]

---

[81]The foundation of the Shelter is described in *JC*, March 27, April 3, May 15 and 29, June 5, 19, and 26, July 3, September 11, October 9, 16, 23, and 30. and November 13, 1885; April 16, 1886. Jewish Board of Guardians, *Minute Letter Book*, p. 192, January 9, 1888; House of Commons Select Committee . . . *First Report* . . . 1888, pp. 106–23 (esp. Min. 2157), 146–47, 312–13; *Idem, Second Report*, 1889, pp. 80–81, 92; C. 7406, pp. 29–35; Cd. 1742, Min. 16271; V. D. Lipman, *op. cit.*, pp. 92–93 is inaccurate.

[82]Jewish Board of Guardians, *Minutes*, April 13, 1885.

[83]A protest meeting was held in the Jewish Working Men's Club, and Mocatta appeared to defend the action of the Jewish Guardians. *Die Tsukunft*, I, 41 (May 1, 1885).

[84]*JC*, May 15, 1885.

He also warned of the risk that a separate Jewish community of immigrants might arise because the official community lacked sympathetic understanding.[85] The contrary view was voiced by the *Jewish Chronicle*:

> Able-bodied foreign Jews who have no prospect of finding or doing useful work must not be supported at a Jewish Refuge, but for the sake of themselves and their relatives abroad, as well as for their own, they must either earn their own living without charity or return to the land whence they came.[86]

The *Tsukunft* intimates the feelings of the immigrants toward native Jewry's policy when it ironically inquires— why is there no Jewish hospital in London? All the Jews will come to London to take sick. And why no Jewish hostel for the temporarily homeless? They will all gather in London to sleep. A Jewish soup kitchen for the hungry? They will all descend upon London to eat.[87]

The wealthy sponsors took over the refuge, gave it a building, and reopened it in October, 1885 as the Poor Jews' Temporary Shelter. It confined itself to immigrant aid alone, served two skimpy meals a day (a third, of bread and tea, was added in 1897),[88] and permitted no one to remain beyond fourteen days. For a while it also imposed a labour test upon every able-bodied person.[89] Not only did the Shelter give no dole, but in accord with enlightened philanthropic ideas of the time it declared that payment would be required of those who could afford it. Having sought to allay anxiety that the Shelter would make England appear over-hospitable to prospective immigrants, and having organized it along necessarily stern lines, the sponsors wanted a mutual accommodation with the Jewish Board of Guardians. Faced with a functioning *fait accompli*, the latter body had no choice but to negotiate with the unwanted Shelter. After prolonged bargaining, Lionel L. Cohen presented a proposed 'treaty' to his Board only to see it rejected because the majority would not make peace

[85] Jewish Board of Guardians, *Minutes*, May 11, 1885.
[86] *JC*, May 15, 1885.
[87] *Die Tsukunft*, I, 28 (January 23, 1885).
[88] Poor Jews' Temporary Shelter, *Minutes*, September 13, 1897.
[89] This requirement and the alleged insufficiency of the diet were bitterly protested by a writer in *Ha Maggid*, XXXI, 2 (January 13, 1887).

with the idea of a Shelter.[90] Matters proceeded for years in a state of mutual non-recognition until about 1900, when the Rumanian 'exodus' forced a measure of co-operation which was subsequently continued. Going its own way, the Poor Jews' Temporary Shelter accommodated from 1,000 to 4,000 immigrants and transmigrants per annum, aiding them from dockside until they boarded another ship or found a job or a place to live.[91] Thus, the Shelter and the Guardians originally embodied opposing outlooks on immigration policy, but the passage of time and the multiplication of immigrants blunted the arguments and immersed both sides in work to a point where *de facto* co-operation was essential. Perhaps they gradually realized that no policy of theirs could really halt or slow immigration.

There were also immigration restrictionists within the Jewish community. The terms of appeals for charitable funds make it clear that there were Jews who disapproved of charitable assistance, even after six months of residence, as an invitation to Jewish 'pauper classes' to descend upon England. Perhaps the most characteristically anti-immigration group in the Jewish community was the older generation of Dutch and sometimes Russian and Polish artisans resident in the immigrant quarter. Theirs were the same trades as the immigrants', and they felt their painfully gained social and economic status menaced by foreign Jews.[92]

As the community slowly came to grips with the social

[90]The proposed articles of the agreement included: 1. no cash relief to be provided; 2. no workshop to be opened by the Shelter in order to make work; 3. only single males to be admitted; 4. fourteen day limit with no re-entry permitted; 5. persons not finding employment upon leaving the Shelter would be referred to the Board for repatriation; 6. the Shelter could conduct its own solicitations, since it reached classes not reached by the Board; 7. the Guardians to approve changes in the Shelter's rules; 8. three representatives to sit on each other's boards. *JC,* October 9, 1885.

[91]There were immigrant shelters in Provincial cities. However, they did not receive immigrants from the docks, and their scope and operations were accordingly smaller. The Jewish Ladies' Association, later the Jewish Association for the Protection of Girls and Women, performed services of shelter and protection for unaccompanied girls and women.

[92]Such testimony to the Royal Commission on Alien Immigration (Cd. 1742) as that of William Silverstone, Zachariah Solomons, S. V. Amstell, Isaac Lyons; also letter of I. Pou in *JC,* September 28, 1894; Henry De Jonge to House of Commons Select Committee . . . *First Report* . . . 1888, Min. 962 ff.; C. Russell and H. S. Lewis, *The Jew in London,* London, 1900, pp. 24–25, 167–68.

questions raised by immigration, suggestions were heard as early as 1886 to approach the Government in order to limit immigration. The weight of the *Jewish Chronicle*, representing the Rothschild view, swung heavily against any such move, as N. S. Joseph had suggested at the Jewish Board of Guardians:

> It is a new and astounding thing for the Board of Guardians to hint that the multiplication of the foreign poor may one day become a public evil of which the intervention of the State may be demanded. It must not be demanded by Jews at least. . . . Such a proposal is full of danger. The letters which spell exclusion are not very different from those which compose expulsion.[93]

As the conservative M.P. for Islington, Benjamin L. Cohen informed the anti-alien lobby in Parliament that he and certain other Jewish M.P.'s were 'disposed to assist in the establishment of such regulations as would discourage the immigration of undesirable persons, provided that precautions were taken to preserve inviolate the right of asylum. . . .'[94] He admonished the native Jewish community as President of the Jewish Board of Guardians that proposed anti-alien measures were not anti-Jewish in intent nor would they deny the right of asylum. The Jews should 'make it clear not to endeavour to oppose any action which the responsible advisors of the Crown may deem necessary for the national interests which we are as desirous to protect as our fellow-citizens. . . .'[95] Cohen voted for the Aliens Act in 1905, and received a baronetcy soon after.

The regnant policy of discouragement to immigration and aloofness to the newcomers' plight was again sharply challenged in 1892 and 1893. N. S. Joseph (1834–1909), a tireless pillar of communal labour, amateur theologian, and brother-in-law of the Chief Rabbi, coupled his espousal of restriction with a realization that it was urgent to assist 'green' immigrants. As a first step, the Russo-Jewish Committee established a Visiting Committee and an Information and Location Bureau

[93]*JC*, February 26, 1886.
[94]*The Times*, March 21, 1894, quoted in *JC*, March 23, 1894.
[95]To the Annual Meeting of the Jewish Board of Guardians. N. S. Joseph declared there that he favoured 'any Government that would promote a reasonable measure of restriction, not only as Englishmen and Jews . . . but also as humanitarians.' *JC*, April 6, 1894. See letter of F. D. Mocatta to the Rev. J. F. Stern attacking Jewish opponents of immigration, dated May 13, 1894, in *JC*, January 20, 1906.

for Immigrants in 1893. Lionel L. Alexander, Honorary
Secretary of the Board of Guardians, bitterly assailed the
'new departure,' and interpreted the modest effort as a repre-
hensible 'seeking out of immigrants on arrival for the purpose
of taking them under the wing and care of a charitable organisation.'[96] Under the great influence of Sir Julian Goldsmid,
President of the Russo-Jewish Committee and Deputy Speaker
of the House of Commons, a harmonious arrangement was
reached.[97] However, Alexander resigned in adamant opposition, unable to swerve from the older view that the Jewish
community could best protect itself from the charge of fostering immigration by ignoring the immigrant.

The shifts and cross-currents of communal policy on immigrants are of some significance. The Jewish community of
England was the most highly organized and cohesive Jewish
community in the western world, and stood in a position to do
much for the immigrant. Its attitude was not that of German
Jewry, which was totally hostile, nor can it be compared with
the passivity of the Jews in France. As to the very fluid Jewish
communal organization in America, it was completely over-
whelmed by the magnitude of the influx. English Jewry steered
a sometimes unclear middle course, neither welcoming nor
repelling immigrants. It performed modest offices of aid and
comfort at the dock-side, and, as we shall see, rendered major
services to East European Jews who made homes in England.

[96]Letter to 'Dear Benny' (Benjamin L. Cohen), December 22, 1892, in Jewish
Board of Guardians, *Minutes*, January 5, 1893.
[97]Negotiations were prolonged from November 1892, to June, 1893, of which
a large and instructive file is preserved in the archives of the Board.

III

OLD TRADES IN A NEW SETTING

The immigrant began to support himself practically from the day he came to England. Often before he exhausted his two weeks' eligibility at the Poor Jews' Temporary Shelter, or within days of his arrival at friends' or relatives' lodgings, he had found a job and was making his way in the new country. However, he had to accustom himself not only to his allotted task in a workshop but also to a completely different economic environment from the one he had left behind. For in England, still the world's leading industrial nation, no great new industry or undeveloped region beckoned with opportunities for employment. Moreover, there was already an adequate supply of native and Irish labour for the hard, unskilled jobs. Above all, England was a factory country, and very few immigrants had ever worked in a factory. They had worked in little workshops back in Russia and Poland, and that is where they continued to work in England. Not many possessed more than superficial vocational skill, and much of their training and experience was quite useless under English conditions, since English trades which were controlled by guild-like trade union rules were not open to Jewish immigrants, and others, such as printing or high quality tailoring, required a level of skill which the immigrant worker did not reach. It is a piquant commentary upon the conditions of immigrant life that in a new and liberal land the Jewish immigrant worker earned his livelihood in a narrower range of trades than he had under the conditions of the Russian Pale of Settlement.

We may learn something about the immigrants' vocations from their responses to the Poor Jews' Temporary Shelter's inquiry as to the 'callings' of their lodgers.[1] With some necessary

[1]The sample is the sum of 9,047 answers in the years 1895–1896, 1899–1900, 1901–1902, 1903–1904, and 1907–1908, found in the Poor Jews' Temporary Shelter, *Annual Report* for the respective years. 'Dealer,' 'Merchant,' 'Traveller,' are here regarded as one, and the various branches of tailoring are assimilated under one heading. Despite some vague classifications, it probably has a rough validity.

simplification, we find that of the 9,047 respondents, 2,599
(29 per cent.) had made garments of some sort before coming
to England, and 2,054 (23 per cent.) were in trade and commerce, 977 persons (9 per cent.) made boots and shoes, 719
(7 per cent.) described themselves as carpenters, and 205
(2 per cent.) were in agriculture. The remaining 2,493 immigrants were spread thinly among a large variety of trades,
including butchers, bakers, printers, coopers, barbers, furriers,
jewellers, coachmen, locksmiths, bricklayers, cigar-makers,
painters, and descending numerically to one acrobat. Their
proficiency and earnings at these trades are unknown, nor do
we learn how many others were economic drifters—the 'luft-
menschen' of East European Jewry. Despite the seeming
diversity of this list, under the conditions of immigrant economic
life it was actually quite narrow. Yet with all their limitations
these East European Jewish occupations laid the foundation
of the immigrant community's economy. However, much painful
adaptation was needed to find their place in the English scene,
and to merge their special qualities into the surrounding
economy.

PEDDLING AND RETAIL TRADE

The immigrant tradesman or peddler might have been a
peddler in the old country, the keeper of a miniscule store,
or merely a hanger-on at the local market. Until the middle
of the nineteenth century, the Jews of England, especially
in the Provinces, were considerably occupied in hawking and
peddling. Countryside peddling was perhaps the most lucrative form. Joseph Harris, a youthful Polish immigrant of 1853,
describes his early experiences tramping the moors of
Yorkshire:

When I commenced business I did not know a word of English.
I was taught to say, 'Will you buy?' I did not know what the words
meant; I could not understand a word that was spoken to me. . . .
On an average my weekly expenses for some time were about five
shillings. . . . My lodgings were from threepence to sixpence per
night, and I managed to get a clean change of bed-linen wherever
I stayed. . . .
As for food, I used to buy 1½ lb. of bread, 1 oz. of tea, 2 oz. of butter,

and $\frac{1}{2}$ lb. of sugar. The bread and butter served me for supper and breakfast, and what was left I carried in my pocket for dinner. The tea lasted me for two days and the sugar for three. . . .[2]

The pious and frugal immigrant prospered, and he met compatriots whose peddling routes crossed his.[3] But countryside peddling as a road to riches became less certain, and in time was sooner identified with impoverishment:

. . . a very large proportion of the Jewish poor are but little removed from the pauper classes. Many of them are petty traders or pedlars. . . .[4]

Joseph Harris ultimately manufactured the watches which he had sold to rural buyers;[5] but the Manchester jewellery travellers of the 1880's found the very selling a difficult task. They were evidently salesmen employed on commission.

These travellers go about from door to door knocking and asking, 'Will you buy a watch?' They must knock enough doors until they find a buyer. The businessmen who employ the travellers do good business, but the travellers live a miserable life. As soon as they show their nose with the box they are told, 'Not today!', or others slam the door on sight and leave him standing in the street like a dummy. . . . In general the jewellery traveller is regarded by Englishmen as a bit of a swindler. In the country children pursue them in the streets and shout: 'Buy a watch! Buy a watch!' And the traveller must see, hear, and hold his tongue.[6]

Peddling declined in London and later in the Provinces because the retail trade network gradually covered the land. From an historic way to wealth it was reduced to a fruitless, exhausting occupation which led nowhere. So it seemed to Joel Elijah Rabbinowitz, Hebrew writer by choice and peddler by necessity:

. . . The peddler also trudges about from town to town and from city to city staggering under his burden. He is parched in the summer and frozen in the winter, and his eyes wither in their sockets before he gets sight of a coin. The farmers have wearied of these peddlers

[2]Joseph Harris, *Random Notes and Reflections*, Liverpool, 1912, pp. 23, 27.
[3]*Ibid.*, p. 34. For a similar account, *cf.* J. M. Lissack, *Jewish Perseverence*, 2nd ed. (sic.), London, 1851.
[4]*JC*, January 28, 1881.   [5]Joseph Harris, *op. cit.*, p. 47.
[6]Nathan Berlin in *Die Tsukunft*, IV, No. 197 (June 1, 1888). See also Royal Commission on Alien Immigration, *Minutes of Evidence*, Cd. 1742, 1903, Min. 21288–89 (cited hereafter as Cd. 1742).

who stand before their doors daily. Still worse is the lot of the peddler who is faithful to his religion and refuses to defile himself with forbidden foods; he is bound to sink under his load.[7]

Country peddling declined more slowly among immigrants in smaller and more outlying Jewish communities. In Liverpool and Glasgow it remained in the 1880's; in the Scottish city as many as 600 of its 6,000 Jews were hawking and travelling in 1906. The proportion in the smaller Edinburgh community was even higher.[8] The Scots-Jewish peddlers' vocabulary, a combination of Yiddish and English with a Scottish burr, produced an interesting but transitory linguistic hybrid. (Such as, 'Aye mon, ich hob' getrebblt mit de five o'clock train.')[9]

There were other outdoor trades to occupy the immigrant. Window mending and glaziery was a common form of urban peddling in the 1860's and 1870's, and in Hull and probably elsewhere it lingered on longer.[10] The glazier-window mender carried about plates of glass and other saleable articles which he sold as he called on houses. His lot was no better than the peddler's:

> The glazier . . . never has any free time. From morning to night he makes his rounds in streets and market places with a boxful of glass on his back and with his eyes raised to the lofty walls, seeking out a broken window. Wherever he turns he encounters ten compatriots looking for what he cannot find.[11]

While fewer immigrants were peddlers and glaziers, others sold their wares from stalls in the streets. Securing a foothold was not easy, for the English street-selling trades had long

---

[7]*HaMeliz*, XXVI, 178 (December 10–22, 1886). The prevalence of peddling and glaziery is noted in the Report of the Chief Inspector of Factories and Workshops for 1891, C. 6720, p. 14.

[8]*The Polish Yidel*, I, 10, September 26, 1884; *Arbeiter Freind*, IV, 6, February 8, 1889.

[9]Interestingly described in David Daiches, 'Trebblers, Bleggages, Persians,' *The New Yorker*, XXX, 18, June 19, 1954, pp. 78 ff. On Glasgow, see *JW*, June 22, 1906; on Liverpool, Cd. 1742, Min. 21448; on Leeds, *The Polish Yidel*, I, 15, October 31, 1884.

[10]*JC*, March 14, 1884. J. H. Stallard, *London Pauperism amongst Jews and Christians*, London, 1867, p. 9; *The Home and Synagogue of the Modern Jew*, London, c. 1870, p. 132. He was also called a 'window salesman'. House of Commons Select Committee on Emigration and Immigration (Foreigners), *First Report*, 1888, Min. 1492; Cd. 1742, Min. 2628, 9582–83; *Die Tsukunft*, I, 22 (December 19, 1884). He is still heard of in 1902, although he had 'almost disappeared' in Manchester. Cd. 1742, Min. 8967; Manchester *Evening News*, January 28, 1903.

[11]Joel Elijah Rabbinowitz in *HaMeliz*, *loc. cit.*

traditions and recognized *mores*. The Jew had to wedge his
barrow into a pitch (place in the street) where an English
costermonger might have stood for many years. Bitter were the
'costers' complaints that their Jewish competitors grabbed
the pitches which they had occupied for many years, did business
for unfairly long hours, undersold, and generally disrupted
the accepted usages of the trade.[12] The Jews and their de-
fenders replied that the English 'costers' merely hated Jews
and had always excluded them from their union. To the charge
that foreign Jews would not buy from the native English,
answer was made that Jews would not necessarily buy from
their own people, once they learned the rudiments of price
and quality.[13] These complaints resounded loudest in Petticoat
Lane when that historic London street market situated in the
Jewish quarter was taken over by Jewish traders in the 1880's
and 1890's. The Jews also entered the costermongers' union
in such numbers that the Whitechapel branch was one-third
Jewish, although on the other hand, the Fulham union, a non-
Jewish area of London, would admit no Jew to membership.[14]
Undeniably, food sellers in Petticoat Lane and their Provincial
counterparts lost considerably because the neighbouring Jews
did prefer to buy from Jewish dealers. Only 198 'Russians and
Poles' in East London and Hackney were 'describing themselves as travellers, hawkers, costers, etc.' in 1891, with 242
in Manchester and an additional 89 in Leeds, but these figures
rose considerably in the following score of years.[15]

A rung above the out-door traders stood the shopkeepers.
Despite the historic prominence of Jews in trade, few East
European Jews attained the level of keeping shops of their own.
As of 1891, 510 'Russian and Polish' retail tradesmen and shop
assistants lived in East London and Hackney, plus 128 in Man-
chester and 76 in Leeds, including kosher butchers licensed by

[12]See the typical testimony of H. W. Blake, Cd. 1742, Min. 7686 ff., esp. Min.
7896.
[13]In defence, see the testimonies of John B. Lyons (Cd. 1742, Min. 19855 ff.),
Benjamin Davis (*Ibid.*, Min. 19933 ff., esp. Min. 19934), and Moss Phillips
(*Ibid.*, 19980 ff.).
[14]*Ibid.*, Min. 7696, 7850–51, 8129.
[15]Board of Trade (Alien Immigration), *Reports on the Volume and Effects of
Recent Immigration from Eastern Europe into the United Kingdom*, C. 7406, 1894,
pp. 154–56. (Hereafter cited as C. 7406.)

the Jewish communal authorities.[16] Many of these Jewish shopkeepers were the heirs of displaced English shopkeepers in the Judaized streets of the East End, Strangeways and Red Bank, and the Leylands. Here, too, English tradesmen complained vehemently as their native customers moved away before the tide of foreign Jews, from whom they could expect much less patronage.[17] Among no group was anti-alienism and its more virulent development, anti-Semitism, more fierce. Displaced or embattled English shopkeepers were Major Evans Gordon's most zealous constituents in his anti-alien battles at the turn of the century. These opponents charged that the immigrant Jews' shops were cheap and dirty, lacking in the amenities of retail trade, and kept open all day and most of the night. The greatest friction was caused by the problem of Sabbath observance for, subject to certain limitations upon Sunday hours, the Jews were legally authorized to observe the Jewish instead of the English Sabbath. It was claimed, however, that some Jewish stores and street stalls observed neither day. With the undoubted existence of some such cases as their proof, the beleaguered English tradesmen were convinced that their Jewish rivals were too grasping to keep any day of rest, and thrice-told tales of the Jew supported their views. In the Borough Councils within London, where their influence was strong, the native shopkeepers did all they could to press for stringent Sunday trading ordinances, which would have harmed Jewish tradesmen by denying them enough hours on Sunday to compensate for the hours they were shut on Friday and Saturday.[18] To be sure, the stillness of the English Sabbath had never been known in the East End, where business as usual clattered the day long. Nor did the Jewish Sabbath subdue all business activity, except in a few streets.

[16]C. 7406, pp. 154-56.
[17]Cd. 1742, Min. 9366-77; 8891-93; 9000-07.
[18]Board of Deputies, *Minutes*, June 25, 1888, July 18, 1909; Samuel Barnett, speech to the Maccabeans, *JC*, November 3, 1893; G. R. Sims, *Living London*, 3 vols., London, 1902, I. pp. 24-35; Edward Lascelles, 'Bethnal Green and Sunday Trading,' *The Oxford House Magazine*, III, 11 (July, 1911), pp. 23-30; Cd. 1742, Min. 11657, 4283-85.

THE IMMIGRANT TRADES

Petty trade was not, however, the staple occupation of the East European immigrant in England. The great majority of immigrants sought their livelihoods in a complex of interrelated vocations which were intimately associated with immigrant life and even with its folklore. These were the 'immigrant trades', so called not only because Jewish immigrants worked at them, but in recognition of other common characteristics. In economic terms, an immigrant trade generally stood in a transitional position between factory and workshop production. The manufacture of the individual article was actually divided between the factory and the workshop, between machine and hand labour. For their part, the Jews were faithful to the workshop, and they tended to slip away from industries like tobacco, walking sticks, and boots and shoes when machinery and factory production took over. Another hallmark of the Jewish immigrant trades was extensive division of labour within the workshop. Many hands performed different tasks upon a coat or a shoe and wide gradations in wages corresponded to differences in skill. Not only was this a faster process than the old philosophy of 'one man, one garment,' but hardly any immigrant could actually produce a garment by himself.

The immigrant trades were expanding in size and also highly seasonal. They depended upon a large reserve supply of pliant Jewish and female labour to perform slightly skilled work for long, cramped, and tedious hours. The Jewish immigrant workman forewent better hours, superior working conditions, and regularity of employment of an English factory, but also Sabbath work and hostility of the native workers. He preferred to work among his own people, frequently in the employ of an old townsman or a relative. The appeal of these trades to the immigrant was clearly summarized by the Russo-Jewish Committee:

The so-called Jewish trades naturally take a large proportion [of immigrants], (1) because these were usually the only trades in which the newly-arrived immigrants could understand the language of their employers and fellow workers; (2) because these were frequently the original trades of the applicants; (3) because in certain cases of adults who had never had any handicraft occupation, these trades were found to be the most readily learnt. . . .[19]

The most important immigrant trade was the making of garments. This was true not only in England, but in the United States, Canada, and France. For a time boot and shoe making was nearly as important, but it lost ground; so did minor trades like furriery, the making of walking sticks and canes, cabinet-making, and tobacco.

The immigrant community's economy was created by, and in its turn helped to create a type known as the 'Jewish worker'. At a time when the English worker was resembling less than ever the classical Economic Man, the 'Jewish worker' was regarded as a reversion to that mythical type. He was supposedly motivated solely by personal advantage and stood ready to make any adjustment that economic necessities required, undeterred by social consequences or personal sentiment. He was the ideal worker—docile, diligent, and willing to toil interminable hours, as long as he could find work. His object was to amass experience and capital to the end that he might himself become an entrepreneur. Such a Jewish Economic Man was conceived by the civil servant and Booth investigator Hubert Llewellyn Smith:

The economic strength and weakness of Individualism form the economic strength and weakness of the East London Jewish community. Each for himself, unrestrained by the instinct of combination, pushes himself upward in the industrial scale. His standard of life readily adapts itself to his improved condition at every step. We have here all the conditions of the economist satisfied: mobility perfect; competition unremitting; modifying conditions almost absent; pursuit of gain an all-powerful motive; combination practically inoperative.[20]

Beatrice Potter, another investigator,[21] could not find a minimum standard of life among the Jews, and denied that they adhered to one. She concluded that

. . . Polish Jews and Englishwomen will do any work, at any price, under any conditions . . . the Jew . . . is unique in possessing neither

[19]Report of Location and Information Bureau, in Russo-Jewish Committee, *Report*, 1894, p. 22.
[20]*JC*, Jubilee Supplement, November 13, 1891; Llewellyn Smith gave further expression to these views in C. 7406, pp. 40–43.
[21]Beatrice Webb, *My Apprenticeship*, London, 1926, pp. 267–90, gives the background of her activities.

a minimum nor a maximum; he will accept the lowest terms rather than remain out of employment; as he rises in the world new wants stimulate him to increased intensity of effort, and no amount of effort causes him to slacken his indefatigable activity.[22]

This 'elasticity in the Standard of Life' expanded and contracted with the Jew's means, and explained to Beatrice Potter why European Jewry exhibited extremes of wealth and poverty. Here also lay, it seemed, the explanation of the ineffectiveness of the Jewish trade unions, for a union composed of a host of Jewish Economic Men could not long endure.[23] English trade unionists, dedicated to the establishment and elevation of a standard of life, sympathized with the Jews as victims of persecution yet had scant sympathy for them as workmen. The Jewish workers were accused before the Trade Union Congress of being willing to work fifteen hours a day

. . . on cold coffee and bread and cheese, and though they did not seem to earn any wages, they often in a short time were able to set up in business for themselves. (Laughter)[24]

On account of this individualism, 'these people were incorrigible; they were either sweaters or sweated.'[25] Informed opinion did not blame the Jewish worker for the conditions under which he laboured, but derogated him for being, as expressed by one trade unionist, ' . . . oh, so willing!'[26]

Few voices from the Jewish immigrants' side were willing or able to comment upon the general view which was held of them. The *Jewish Chronicle*, the main organ of the Jewish community, followed Manchester liberalism until the 1890's and saw little but good in the sober and boundlessly industrious character of the Jewish worker, even when it was disquieted by the evils of sweatshops. On the other hand, those few

[22]Sidney and Beatrice Webb, *Industrial Democracy*, 2 vols., London, 1897, I, pp. 687–88.
[23]*Ibid.*, p. 688 n. See also Beatrice Webb, *op. cit.*, p. 378, where several relevant excerpts of her earlier writings are given.
[24]Trades Union Congress, *Report*, 1894, p. 59; see also, for example, House of Commons Select Committee . . . *First Report* . . . 1888, Min. 2483.
[25]Trades Union Congress, *Report*, 1894, p. 60.
[26]Thus James MacDonald, himself a tailor and Secretary of the London Trades Council, in 'Sweating in the Tailoring Trade,' in Richard Mudie-Smith, ed., *Sweated Industries being a Handbook of the 'Daily News' Exhibition*, London, 1906, p. 66.

E

Jewish workers who spoke up were nearly unanimous in their plaint that they would gladly relinquish some of the economic virtues and work a few hours less. The strident voice of John Dyche, a Jewish trade unionist and later General Secretary of the International Ladies' Garment Workers' Union in the United States, was a rare specimen of one who took to the offensive.[27] Accepting Beatrice Potter's view that no minimum standard existed among the Jewish workers, he glorified the 'adaptibility and skill which are peculiar' to them. Dyche offered in invidious contrast the 'old, primitive, and expensive' methods of the hidebound English tailor, who supplied his prototype of the English working man. No Jewish worker, exulted Dyche, belonged to the 'great, inert mass of dull, torpid industrial slaves,' for each was instead 'always pushing his way forward.' Side by side with the grim, rigid atmosphere of the English factory, the young trade unionist eulogized the congenial, democratic climate of the Jewish workshop, and contrasted Jewish sobriety and domesticity with the hard-drinking profligacy of the English worker. As his critics justly pointed out, these contrasts are forced, and Dyche's pictures are caricatures.[28]

The Jewish workman was nevertheless a man apart from the British workman. He worked longer hours and his seasons were irregular. He did not regard himself as one endowed with a fixed station in life, and this partially explains his adaptability to the vicissitudes of his fortunes. In a new country and among natives who were more securely established in their trades, the Jewish worker's unlimited application to his work was unwelcome, the more so because there were grounds for believing that he undercut and displaced native English workers. The tension of adjustment in a new land, the insecurity of seasonal work, the desire to rise to entrepreneurship, or to bring over members of one's family, or to save up the steamship fare to America, all made their contributions to the Jewish worker's

[27]John A. Dyche, 'The Jewish Workman,' *The Contemporary Review*, LXXIII (January, 1898), pp. 35–50;——, 'The Jewish Immigrant,' *Idem*, LXXV (March, 1899), pp. 379–99.
[28]John Smith, 'The Jewish Immigrant,' *The Contemporary Review*, LXXVI (September, 1899), pp. 425–36, is a trade unionist's reply; the anti-alienist Arnold White, 'A Typical Alien Immigrant,' *Idem*, LXXXIII, (February 1898), pp. 241–50, objects to Dyche's 'sinister tone'.

fabled diligence. His individualism in part reflected the instability of the immigrant trades, where the bridge from entrepreneur to workman and back was a short one, frequently trodden many times by the same person.

If there is unanimity about Jewish labour, then it concerns the prevalence of the conditions of work known then and since as the sweating system.[29] This term has more connotations than precise meaning, for it was, in the first place, no system.[30]

[29]There is an abundance of contemporary literature upon this subject. Besides the writings and official reports of Beatrice Potter, John Burnett, H. Llewellyn Smith, already cited, see also: (Adolphe Smith,) 'A Polish Colony of Jewish Labourers,' *The Lancet*, March 5, 1884, repr. in *JC*, May 9, 1884, and E. Tcherikover, ed., *Geshikhte fun der Yiddisher Arbeter Bavegung in der Farayngte Shtatn* (History of the Jewish Labour Movement in the United States), 2 vols., N.Y., 1943, II, pp. 462–64, which was probably the first statement on Jewish sweating outside Government sources; several informative articles by David F. Schloss: *Methods of Industrial Remuneration*, 3rd ed., London, 1898, pp. 180-226; 'The Sweating System,' *The Fortnightly Review*, N. S. XLVII, No. 280 (April 1, 1890), pp. 532–51; 'The Jew as a Workman,' *The Nineteenth Century*, XXIX, No. 167 (January, 1891), pp. 96–109; 'The Present Position of the "Sweating System" Question in the United Kingdom,' *The Economic Review*, II, 4 (October, 1892), pp. 452–59, reprinted in *The Sweating System in Europe and America*, Papers of the Social Economy Department, American Social Science Association, Boston, 1892, pp. 64–72; for a diluted Manchester liberal position, see C. H. d'E. Leppington, 'Side Lights of the Sweating Commission,' *The Westminster Review*, CXXXVI, 3 (March, 1891), pp. 273–88; 5 (May, 1891), pp. 504–16. A mild Tory discussion is Arthur A. Baumann, M.P., 'The Lords' Committee on the, Sweating System,' *The National Review*, XII, No. 68 (October, 1888), pp.145–59; ——, 'Possible Remedies for the Sweating System,' *Idem*, XII, No. 69 (November, 1888), pp. 289–307. Beatrice Potter amplified her Booth report in 'East London Labour,' *The Nineteenth Century*, XXIV, No. 138 (August, 1888), pp. 161–84; 'Pages from a Work-Girl's Diary,' *Idem*, XXIV, No. 139 (September, 1888), pp. 301–14; 'The Lords and the Sweating System,' *Idem*, XXVII, No. 160 (June, 1890), pp. 885–905. (The first two articles are reprinted in Sidney and Beatrice Webb, *Problems of Modern Industry*, new ed., London, 1902.) See also 'A Tale of the Tailors,' *JC*, February 19, 1886, for a statement by a sweated worker. Typical of the international interest in the question are the reprinting of the D. F. Schloss article, *supra*; Adolph Smith, 'Das Sweating System in England,' *Archiv für Soziale Gesetzgebung und Statistik*, IX, 3–4 (1896), pp. 392–419; André-E. Sayous, 'L'entre exploitation des classes populaires à Whitechapel,' *Mémoires et documents du musée social*, Année 1902, pp. 261–319. For anti-alien protectionism, based on alleged Jewish responsibility for sweating, see such examples as Arnold White, ed., *The Destitute Alien in Great Britain*, London and N.Y., 1892, 2nd ed., 1905; ——, 'The Invasion of Pauper Foreigners,' *The Nineteenth Century*, XXIII, No. 133 (March, 1888), pp. 414–22; R. H. Sherard, *The White Slaves of England*, 2nd ed., London, 1898; Frank Hird, *The Cry of the Children*, London, 1896; at a higher level, John A. Hobson, *The Problem of Poverty*, London, 1895. The best presentations of the entire subject are: H. W. Macrosty, *Sweating: Its Cause and Remedy*, Fabian Tract No. 50, London, 1895; Edward Cadbury and George Shinn, *Sweating*, Social Service Handbooks, No. V, London, 1907, and Sayous, *op. cit., loc. cit.*

[30]'Sweating' as a term probably originated in Charles Kingsley's novel, *Alton Locke, Tailor and Poet*, London, 1850; see Charles E. Raven, *Christian Socialism 1848-1854*, London, 1920, pp. 168–179.

Its general reference, and its use in these pages, is to a cramped, dirty workshop, where long hours were worked both by master and employees in extremely insanitary conditions. However, sweating was popularly endowed with many more attributes. It was defined in terms of too much work for too little pay; of filthy outwork shops; of any work not regulated by factory legislation; of grinding the faces of the poor generally; of a supposed chain of middlemen between manufacturer and worker, each taking a slice of the wages.[31]

'Sweating dens' were extensively described by contemporaries, beginning with The Lancet's tour of the East End of London in 1884. The British medical journal's tones were more restrained than those of later writers:

In Hanbury Street we found eighteen workers crowded in a small room measuring eight yards by four yards and a half, and not quite eight feet high. The first two floors of this house were let out to lodgers who were also Jews. Their rooms were clean but damp as water was coming through the rotting wall. . . . The sink was not trapped, the kitchen range was falling to pieces, while the closet was a permanent source of trouble. A flushing apparatus had been provided, but this discharged the water *outside* the pan; the water consequently came out under the seat and flowed across the yard to the wall opposite, which was eaten away at its base. . . . the top room . . . had at times to hold eighteen persons, working in the heat of the gas and the stove, warming the pressing irons, surrounded by mounds of dust and chips from the cut cloth, breathing an atmosphere full of woollen particles containing more or less injurious dyes, it is not surprising that so large a proportion of working tailors break down from diseases of the respiratory organs.[32]

This report created quite a stir. It was followed four years later by visits to Provincial centres, where the verdict was hardly any better. Thus Manchester:

Our first visit was to a garret situated immediately over a stable. . . . There was certainly an ample supply of light, but the place was cold, draughty, and dirty. Mud had accumulated in a corner where a bucket

[31]Beatrice Webb, *op. cit.*, pp. 281–82, where several contradictory definitions are quoted; some others are in literature cited above, Note 29, and Cd. 1742, Min. 398, 11763, 11819, 14089; Lewis Lyons in *The Commonweal*, I, 3 (April, 1885), p. 19.

[32]'A Polish Colony of Jewish Labourers,' *The Lancet*, March 5, 1884, reprinted *JC*, May 9, 1884, conveniently available in E. Tcherikover, *op. cit.*, pp. 462–64.

of water is kept for damping the cloth. The paper was falling off the walls, dirt lay thick on all sides, and cobwebs hung thick on the ceiling. Though this garret has been used as a sweating shop for two years, the landlord has made no repairs, and the tenant has apparently never attempted a thorough cleansing.

At the back of this stable, under this loft, and on the ground floor, is another tailor's establishment. Here there was not such a good light. The ceiling was black with soot, and at one end there was a huge pile of dust, dirt, and scraps of cloth, which was about 3 feet wide, 12 feet long and 16 inches deep. There were twelve men and women working here, and eight in the garret above the stable.[33]

A special abomination was the toilet, of which this specimen from Leeds is perhaps worse than average:

Entering one of the houses where there are three different work-shops, employing altogether about 160 persons, we were assailed by a most appalling stench. There were three closets, the seats and floors of which were besmeared with soil. The sanitary inspector had been here and left word that the place was to be kept clean; but one of the sweaters protested that this was impossible and certainly the warning has had no effect. . . .[34]

Before the Act of 1901, factory inspection could do little to cope with sweating as such. A Factory Inspector, employed by the Home Office, could enter a workshop only in connection with the employment of women and children. As the Jewish immigrant trades were generally free of child labour, the inspector could enter only in order to discover whether women were illegally working beyond their twelve hour daily limit, past nine p.m., or upon a seventh day of the week. The law placed no limit upon the labour of adult males, except for the Sabbath restrictions. Sanitary inspection, probably the most basic need, was entrusted to negligent local authorities. The Factory Inspector's right of inspection, tenuous as it was, was further weakened by the reluctance of many Jewish women and girls to admit that they were working illegally. Although

[33]'Report of *The Lancet* Special Sanitary Commission on "Sweating" among Tailors at Liverpool and Manchester,' *The Lancet*, April 14 and 21, 1888, p. 792.
[34]'Report of *The Lancet* Special Sanitary Commission on the Sweating System in Leeds,' *The Lancet*, June 9 and 16, 1888, p. 1147. This Commission also reported upon Glasgow, June 30 and July 7, 1888, and Edinburgh, June 23, 1888. Unlike the article on London (Note 32), these reports also deal with non-Jewish sweating.

the law would not have penalized them, they were wont to pretend that they were members of the master's family or 'visitors' in the workshop-dwelling.[35] The inadequacy of the inspecting staff, the limitations of the law, the absence of even a list of workshops, the ruses to evade the Inspector's visits and queries,[36] all combined practically to nullify English factory legislation in the Jewish workshops. For all the labours of J. B. Lakeman, the Superintendent Inspector of Workshops in London,[37] and his few subordinates and the puny staffs in the Provinces, there is no sign that factory inspection exercised more than a slight deterrent upon sweating. This conclusion is emphasized by the few convictions of Jewish violators recorded in the Annual Reports of the Chief Inspector of Factories and Workshops. Most of them were punished for observing no Sabbath rest, either English or Jewish.

The Home Office set the standards at a meagre level for the workshops which they could inspect. 'Ventilation is considered satisfactory where sufficient windows exist which can be opened at will. It is insufficient where there is only one window, which is kept closed. Cleanliness is considered sufficient when there is an absence of matter likely to be injurious to health.' The inspector's demands were not onerous. One reported that water pipes had burst and that flush toilets were foul and frozen, but observed that these 'irregularities' were not 'of a very serious nature'. He found the general picture 'very good'.[37a]

The Factory Act of 1901, which required the principal manufacturer to keep a list of all his outwork contractors and their employees, was the first effective measure against sweated work. The Trade Boards Act of 1909, the first Act of Parliament in modern history to intervene in the determination of wages, expressly established a tripartite wages board in the

[35]Report of the Chief Inspector of Factories and Workshops, 1879, C. 2489, p. 16; 1880, C. 2825, p. 18; 1885, C. 4702, pp. 15–17; 1887, C. 5328, p. 47; J. B. Lakeman in *JC*, January 29, 1886.

[36](John Burnett), *Report to the Board of Trade on the Sweating System at the East End of London*, 1888, p. 9.

[37]House of Lords Commission on the Sweating System, First Report, 1888, Min. 16464–69, 16576. He is probably the 'L.' of the unflattering portrait in Beatrice Webb, *op. cit.*, pp. 270–71.

[37a]J. Redgrave, Chief Inspector of Factories and Workshops, to G. Lushington, Permanent Home Under-Secretary, January 21, 1891. H.O. 45–1508A.

clothing industry, composed of labour, employers, and Government, with power to fix a legal minimum wage. Its effect was visible before 1914, although it commenced operations only shortly before the War broke out.[38]

The disorganization of Jewish immigrant economic life is mirrored in the degrading open-air hiring which took place in Whitechapel Road.[39] It was called 'in everybody's lips', with mingled hatred and ridicule, the 'pig market' (*hazer mark*). One bitter observer suggested that

. . . when you come to London, you will want to take a stroll on the Sabbath to the honoured spot which is called in everybody's lips the h.m. [*hazer mark*]. And you will see masters (you will recognize the dealers at once by their gross bellies) scurrying about like poisoned mice among the dishevelled men. They scurry about swiftly, contemptuously, dizzily. 'Jack! perhaps you are a machinist?'

'John! I need a presser!'

'Jim! I need a hand!' (That is how they call the worker: not a whole man, but a hand, a foot). . . .

All those who remain, alas, without a master, look about with eyes full of grief . . . because it grieves them, alas, that they must remain with their poor families without work for a whole week.[40]

Exhortation and indoor hiring halls did not quell the outdoor hiring practices. To the particular distress of native and immigrant Jews, Saturday was the busiest hiring day, largely because Saturday evening or Sunday morning began a work week upon a new batch of orders. These debased practices and their quasi-public bidding were mostly for unskilled workers and 'greeners' (recent immigrants), especially during the busy season. The Poor Jews' Temporary Shelter was also a house of call for unskilled 'greeners'.[41] Various attempts to establish employment bureaus met with moderate success,

[38]R. H. Tawney, *The Establishment of Minimum Rates in the Tailoring Industry under the Trade Boards Act of 1909*. Studies in the Minimum Wage, No. II, London, 1915. See also B. L. Hutchins and A. Harrison, *A History of Factory Legislation*, 2nd ed., London, 1926, pp. 240–69.

[39]*HaEmet*, No. 3 (1877), pp. 43–46; '*Ibri 'Anokhi*, XI, 21 (February 12, 1875), p. 163; B. Spiers, *Dibrey Debash* (Honied Words), London, 1901, p. 59.

[40]Isaac Stone in *The Polish Yidel*, I, 9 (September 19, 1884).

[41]T. B. Eyges, *Zikhroines fun die Yiddishe Arbeter Bavegung in London, England* (Memoirs of the Jewish Labour Movement in London, England), Yiddish MS. in Library of YIVO, N.Y., n.p.

but had no effect on the 'pig market' because the skilled worker
was confident that he could drive a good bargain for himself,
while women, 'greeners', and the unskilled were too plentiful
to make recourse to a bureau feasible. The fluctuations of
seasonal work and the stress of foreign immigration undid
efforts to apply a measure of organization to the Jewish immigrant labour market.

The great fear of every worker was slack times, which
usually struck at the end of the summer and during the winter
months. With the earnings of most immigrant workers seldom
above the subsistence level, they could not save up for hard
times. 'Slack' also meant danger to the small master, for the
slender basis of cash and credit upon which he operated placed
his business in jeopardy with every rise and decline in the trade.
The contrast between 'busy' and 'slack' was clear to an observer:

In the busy season we see the [boot and shoe] finisher strolling
on the Sabbath, quite the whole man, very cheerful, and a bit proud.
The ink and soot are mostly washed off his face, and if God helps,
he is even wearing a piece of jewellery. In short, one sees some life
in him at this time—But in the slack season everything is dead, he
goes about with his head hanging. . . . In the very coat in which he
did his finishing upon the bench he strolls upon the Sabbath.[42]

Whatever the evils of sweating, master-workman relations
inside the workroom were at a free and easy level. A highly
informal atmosphere reigned inside the shop. The worker
often began his day in the master's workshop-dwelling before
the crack of dawn, and took breakfast coffee from the kitchen.
Drinking coffee and sewing did not always harmonize, especially
in the busy season:

. . . not without difficulty can he eat and sew in one breath; he gives
the pedal a turn and the bread a bite, a turn! a bite! The master stands
over his shoulder and cries, 'An end to it! Look sharp! Just what is
this? A coffee house? A restaurant? On Sabbath you can take enough
time to drink coffee! I won't have such a business! Quick! An end to it!
An end to it!'[43]

[42]*Die Tsukunft*, I, 18 (November 21, 1884). On slack season in Manchester
tailoring, see *Idem*, I, 22 (December 19, 1884).
[43]Isaac Stone in *The Polish Yidel*, I, 10 (September 26, 1884); another description is 'The Diary of an Investigator' in Sidney and Beatrice Webb, *Problems
of Modern Industry*, new ed., London, 1902, pp. 1–19.

There was gruelling work in the sweatshop, no matter what the trade or the job. For a clearer view, we must turn to the immigrant trades separately.

TOBACCO: THE EARLIEST IMMIGRANT TRADE

Tobacco, the oldest of immigrant trades, had a long history among the Jews in England. It was traditionally associated with the Dutch Jews who formed the main body of Jewish immigrants in the middle of the nineteenth century. At that time (1860), when the East End districts of Whitechapel and St George's contained 2,294 Dutch to only 894 Polish foreigners, tailoring lagged behind cigar-making as the major Jewish occupation.[44] In the mid-1870's it was estimated that 'between 3,000 and 4,000 industrious Jewish workmen [are] engaged in the metropolis in the tailoring and tobacco trades,'[45] and most Jewish manufacturers employing fifty or more workers were in the tobacco business.[46]

Cigar-making held a less prominent place among East European Jewish occupations than among those of the Dutch Jews. Hardly one per cent. of the arrivals at the Poor Jews' Temporary Shelter mentioned tobacco trades as their livelihood, and this proportion is corroborated by the census and the Booth survey.[47] Nevertheless, the London Jewish Guardians' annual average of some 3,200 clients included no fewer than 115 cigar-makers, probably representative of the generation then passing.[48] Of approximately 1,900 cigar-makers in London late in the 1880's, 800 were men and 1,100 were women; 251 of the men and 113 of the women were 'Russians and Poles'.[49] At the turn of the century, 342 such 'Russian and Polish' men and 331 women were at work in the trade in

[44]J. H. Stallard, op. cit., p. 5; Samuel Gompers, Seventy Years of Life and Labour, 2 vols., N.Y., 1923, I, pp. 18–22; H. Davis, 'Cigar-making in England,' The Commonweal, III, 71, 72 (May 21, 28, 1887), pp. 164, 174–75.

[45]Board of Deputies, Semi-Annual Report, March, 1870, pp. 29, 34.

[46]M. S. Oppenheim to Factory Law Commission, June 8, 1875, quoted in Board of Deputies, Annual Report, 1876, p. 53. See also Charles Booth, ed., Life and Labour of the People, London, 1893, IV, p. 221.

[47]See above, pp. 1–2; Stephen N. Fox, 'Tobacco Trades,' in Charles Booth, ed., Life and Labour, IV., pp. 219–38; House of Commons Select Committee . . . First Report . . . 1888, Min. 1200.

[48]C. 7406, p. 48.

[49]Charles Booth, op. cit., IV, p. 225; C. 7406, pp. 129, 154.

London, which by this time manufactured cigarettes as well as cigars. Among the foreign 'Dutch', 343 men and 43 women still made cigars in 1901.[50] They were mostly Jews of an older generation—that of the emigrant Jewish cigar-maker, Samuel Gompers (1850–1924).

On the other hand, East European Jews were among the first to make cigarettes in England. At a time when cigar-making was largely confined to London, the manufacture of cigarettes became an important immigrant trade in Glasgow. It was introduced there by Jacob Kramrisch, an Austrian Jew who arrived in England in 1873. He established a cigarette-making branch for Player's in Nottingham in 1882, and another for the Imperial Tobacco Company in Glasgow in 1888. Kramrisch brought 160 men, all Jews, and 150 women, partly Jews, to the Scottish city where they started to manufacture cigarettes in competition with the previously dominant American product.[51]

Although the Jewish cigarette-makers handled the same raw material, cigarettes were made quite differently from the hand work done by the cigar-makers. Considerable capital was needed in the cigarette business, both on account of mechanization and because of the structure of tobacco taxation. Before mechanization took command, the male cigarette-makers in London, were 'mostly all foreigners, and principally Russians, Dutch, Greeks, and Germans . . . most of them Jews', and earned as much as £2 and £3 a week.[52] However, machinery reduced hand craftsmanship and increased the number of cheap workers, so that it struck at the prosperity of the men. Women's pay was also affected by the machine. The supple fingers of young girls did thirteen or fourteen hours of work a day for 13s to 15s a week, and perhaps as low as 6s.[53] A decline in men's wages to £1 a week was noted with some satisfaction by a Jewish socialist writer, who blamed their

[50]*Census of England and Wales*, 1901, Cd. 875, p. 168. The nearly equal numbers of men and women among Russians and Poles suggests that they, unlike the Dutch, worked mostly in the cigarette trade.

[51]Kramrisch told his own story to the Royal Commission on Alien Immigration. Cd. 1742, Min. 21714–38; see also Min. 17863.

[52]Charles Booth, *op. cit.*, IV, pp. 232, 234.

[53]*Arbeiter Freind*, III, 4, January 27, 1888; Charles Booth, *op. cit.*, IV, pp. 234–35; Léonty Soloweitschik, *Un proletariat méconnu*, Brussels, 1898, pp. 45–46.

plight on the aloofness they had shown to their impoverished fellow Jewish workers and on their failure to pursue a vigorous trade union policy.[54] One of the workers, a Jew and a union officer, bitterly blamed the decline of his trade on free alien immigration. To him, it was mainly 'a question of the native being driven out of his means of living to make room for a foreigner who undercuts him'.[55]

The Provincial Jewish cigarette-makers were strongly enough organized to strike successfully even over matters like the job security of one or two men.[56] On the other hand, the cigar-makers' union, once a model of effective trade unionism, declined in power and membership as the machine-made product undermined the men's position.[57] The excess of women over men in the trade by the turn of the century is a reliable sign that machine-made cigars had replaced the hand product, and that factory had supplanted workshop. By then, the manufacture of both cigars and cigarettes no longer employed more than a few hundred Jews,[58] and Jewish working youth showed no tendency to seek employment in the industry. However, Jewish entrepreneurs continued to retain an important share in the tobacco business.

THE BOOT AND SHOE TRADE: THE FALL
OF THE WORKSHOP

Although the position of the skilled Jewish craftsman long held firm in cigar-making, matters were different in the boot and shoe trade. Tobacco was of much less importance in the British economy than a major industry like the manufacture of boots and shoes, which employed 202,648 males and 46,141 females in 1891,[59] a number which rose from census to census. In an

[54] *Arbeiter Freind*, III, 26, June 29, 1888.
[55] I. Pou, Letter to *JC*, September 28, 1894.
[56] *Arbeiter Freind*, X, 12, December 27, 1895; XI, 18, 20, February 7, 21, 1896.
[57] *Arbeiter Freind*, IV, 23, 24, June 7, 14, 1889.
[58] Jacob Lestschinsky's figure of 3,000 is much too high (Jacob Lestschinsky, *Der Idisher Arbayter* (*in London*) (The Jewish Worker (in London)), Vilna, 1907, p. 19. Soloweitschik's (*Un prolétariat méconnu*, pp. 47–48) figure of 9,000 is impossible. See also D. L. Munby, *Industry and Planning in Stepney*, Oxford, 1951, pp. 70–71.
[59] C. 7406, p. 67.

industry of such magnitude, the Jewish boot and shoe workers' numbers never reached 10,000, and they were thus in no position to influence the trade much. They had their stakes in a declining system of production, and it was only their deplorably sweated labour which enabled them to compete at all.[60]

Essentially the boot and shoe industry was undergoing the classic transition from domestic and outwork production to factory output, and the Jews had the misfortune to be on the wrong side. The shift to the factory depended upon technological changes mainly of American origin at the various steps of making footwear. The first of these chronologically was the sewing machine, which speedily performed the trying labour of stiching together the pieces of the upper. Although the sewing machine was scorned and fought by the skilled English shoe-maker, whose ideal of craftsmanship remained the hand-made product, it paradoxically helped to prolong the life of the outwork branch of the trade. A short scrutiny of the manufacturing process will explain this more clearly.

First, leather was patterned and cut by skilled 'clickers' in the manufacturer's shop, while junior 'clickers' cut out the 'rough stuff' for the lower part of the shoe. 'Closing' the uppers, which followed, required the shaping and stitching together of the cut leather into a recognizable upper, and was a job done by a rapidly diminishing group of skilled home workers who had never worked in their employers' premises. But the sewing machine was making inroads into hand 'closing', for by the 1890's shoe factories in the provinces were supplying London houses with ready-made uppers which needed only the next and final steps, lasting and finishing. The laster placed upper and lower upon his last and sewed them together by hand or machine, and then turned the shoe over to the finisher. The latter took the raw but essentially complete shoe and trimmed its sole, attached heels, blacked, rubbed, and polished the finished article, and generally applied the final touches.

Until the factory system impinged upon this process, the shoe worker earned well by contemporary standards. An

[60]There are good general accounts of the boot and shoe trade as a whole, and concerning Jewish participation in D. F. Schloss, 'Bootmaking' in Charles Booth, *op. cit.*, IV, pp. 69–137, and by H. Llewellyn Smith in C. 7406, pp. 67–94.

expert pattern cutter earned as high as £3 a week, and junior 'clickers' drew from 28s to 42s.[61] However, the hand-made trade centred in London began slowly to respond to the pressure from Provincial shoe factories located in Norwich, Northampton, and Leicester. Some of the London producers transferred to the provinces, leaving their displaced employees to compete with each other for inferior outwork.[62] Except when outwork was cheaper or when no machine could yet do a task done by hand, the factory did the entire job under one roof. In London in the 1880's, the making of a shoe was still divided between factory and workshop, with the latter losing ground steadily. The wholesale ready-made shoe trade, which was more adaptable to techniques of mass production than ready-made bespoke, nevertheless enabled small workshops to compete with the tide of factory production by equipping them with some of the new American machinery and using them to replace individual home workers, as Davids to the factory Goliaths. Skilled Jewish home lasters and finishers took in unskilled 'greeners' as assistants and made of their homes cramped, filthy workshops. The Jewish laster occupied his 'team' of 'greeners' with the uppers and lowers which he brought home, performing the most skilled part of the work himself and leaving the remainder to his subordinates. When this 'team' finished and the master returned the batch to the store or warehouse, the Jewish finisher took it home next to his own 'team' of family and starveling 'greeners'. Both the Jewish laster and finisher ranked as craftsman-entrepreneurs because they solicited work, recruited workers, supervised them while working alongside, and kept what profit there was.

Matters were really worse than they appear on the surface. In season, a shoe worker's labour began at dawn and lasted through half the night, but in slack times he earned only intermittently. The lasters' lot deteriorated rapidly in the early 1890's when American-made riveting machinery superseded their handwork. Many then shifted to cheap hand-sewn slipper-making.[63] The fall of the finishers followed that of the lasters.

[61]D. F. Schloss in Charles Booth. *op. cit.*, IV, pp. 86–87.
[62]*The Commonweal*, IV, 136, August 18, 1888, p. 262.
[63]Interview with Morris Stephany, Secretary of the Jewish Board of Guardians, in *JC*, July 12, 1895.

Only a few of the many small details of finishing required much skill or training, so that master finishers often discharged their 'greener' assistants as soon as they attained some skill and completed a meaningless 'apprenticeship'.[64] In spite of man-killing exertions to keep workshop labour in competition with the factory, it was a vain struggle. The position of the Jewish craftsman-entrepreneur and his 'team' steadily worsened. These petty employers were as helpless as their workers against seasonal fluctuations, and could do nothing to uphold the price they might extract from the wholesale house for their work. In one sample account, a worker-entrepreneur netted only 30s 4½d for himself and his family working at his side, just 4s 6d more than his worker.[65] The position of the diminutive manufacturer who produced a complete ready-made shoe in his workshop was no better. When busy, one of them employed ten persons to turn out four dozen pairs daily, and netted only 24s in a week.[66] Small as was this scale of production, it was rendered more complex when many shoe sizes had to be individually 'clicked'.

Even the socialist organizers of Jewish trade unions recognized that the masters' condition was no better than their workers'. One of them disregarded the usual socialist vehemence against employers to propose that the two sides unite to campaign against outwork, the common oppressor.[67] He wrote at a time when pressure against sweated outwork in the boot and shoe trade was mounting. Opposition to ready-made outwork, which had developed with so much Jewish immigrant participation, came from a more potent quarter. The National Union of Boot and Shoe Rivetters (later Operators), with a membership composed of factory and workshop workers, launched a persistent campaign against outwork which aimed to force all boot and shoe work into factories. They had the

[64]'A Practical Bootmaker,' *The Social Democrat*, II, 3, March, 1898, pp. 76–77; Isaac Stone in *Die Tsukunft*, I, 16, 17, 18 (November 7, 14, 21, 1884).

[65]D. F. Schloss in Charles Booth, *op. cit.*, IV, pp. 100–101, where details are given. The shop produced 18 dozen shoes.

[66]Computed from data of Workshop 16, in C. 7406, p. 174. The shop produced 24 dozen shoes.

[67]*Arbeiter Freind*, II, 36 (October 7, 1887); III, 8 (February 24, 1888).

sympathy of the Jewish workers and small masters, who saw a chance of improvement for themselves. Late in 1889, the National Union presented three principal demands to the manufacturers who had been giving work to outdoor shops. One was for a wage raise for all workers, indoor and outdoor, and a second demanded that outworkers be prohibited from working with anyone but their own sons—a safeguard for old-fashioned individual workmen but a fatal blow aimed at Jewish 'teams'. Finally, outwork competition with factory production was attacked root and branch by demanding that the employers provide work upon their own premises for every employee. The Union won most of its demands after a strike against some 400 employers which lasted from March to June, 1890.[68] The key point required the manufacturers to bring their out-door workers indoors 'as soon as possible'. The agreement was to be enforced by a joint board of conciliation and arbitration, composed of representatives of the two sides, who would select a neutral third party.[69] This is one of the earliest such arbitration arrangements.

It was symbolic of the downfall of Jewish sweated outwork, which was presaged by the outcome of the strike, that the Jewish masters' association merged itself with the National Union.[70] Some Jewish masters joined with their men during the strike, and many entered the new shops as ordinary workmen. Others tried to continue in the old ways, despite the vigilant enforcement of the agreement. However, the former masters and men who entered large employers' workshops did not enjoy their deliverance from the 'sweater's den'. They complained that 'they were teased and annoyed beyond endurance until the majority were driven from the large factory back to the small domestic workshops'.[71] Partly because of the disillusion with factory work, the little Jewish 'chamber masters' were the main exception to the ban on outwork. They continued to do all their work on their own premises, or sent out some of their lasting and finishing. For whatever motive,

[68] *The Commonweal*, VI, 222, April 12, 1890, p. 118; 223, April 19, 1890, p. 126.
[69] C. 7406, pp. 76–77. See also *The Commonweal*, VI, 224, April 26, 1890, p. 134.
[70] C. 7406, pp. 76–77.
[71] *JC*, March 15, 1895; Cd. 1742, Min. 20511. For complaints of the persistence of the old ways, see, for example, *idem.*, Min. 3721 ff.

probably seventy-five to one hundred Jewish boot and shoe workshops in London ignored or evaded the agreement.[72]

Although sweated outwork lingered on, the events of 1890 accelerated the movement toward factory production in the boot and shoe trade. The Lords' Commission on Sweating had reported in 1889 that 'the cheap bootmaking trade in London is that which attracts the largest number of "greeners",'[73] but by 1894 the situation changed considerably. Few 'greeners' were then gravitating to a small boot and shoe workshop where some friend or relative or even a stranger could put them to work. Where the National Union controlled employment they could not even enter the trade as 'learners' unless it had been their vocation back in Eastern Europe. With hardly a crack in the gates to admit newcomers into small shops, and with the steady advance of factory production, the number of immigrant Jewish boot and shoe workers barely remained stationary.[74] There were 1,560 'Russian and Polish' males and 31 females earning their living at the trade in East London and Hackney in 1891.[75] However, in 1911, when practically all boots and shoes were made in factories except for work of the highest quality and slippers, only 1,936 male and 74 female 'Russians and Poles' were employed at boot and shoe making.[76] Obviously, the trade was no longer the resort of 'greeners', and immigrant Jews who remained in it formed a decreasing minority of the total immigrant Jewish labour force.

Another major strike was called in 1895, with the outwork prohibition once again at issue.[77] But technological developments were continuing to eliminate outwork and thereby steadily reduced the Jewish share in the trade. There were machines for lasting and finishing, so that it was but a matter of time before these Jewish handicrafts would be squeezed out of the market. For example, a factory team of four men operating

[72]Report of the Chief Inspector of Factories and Workshops for 1894, C. 7745, p. 51.
[73]Quoted in C. 7406, p. 66.   [74]Idem., p. 78.   [75]Idem., p. 154.
[76]Census of England and Wales, 1911, Cd. 7017, pp. 221–29. See also Sidney Webb and Arnold Freeman, eds., Seasonal Trades, London, 1912, pp. 282–311.
[77]'The Crisis in the Boot and Shoe Trade,' The Labour Gazette, III, 3, March, 1895, pp. 80–81; 'A Practical Bootmaker,' The Social Democrat, loc. cit; Cd. 1742, Min. 12230 ff.

an American-made Boston laster and earning from 33s to 45s apiece, aided by a boy paid 10s, could last 860 pairs of ladies' shoes in a week of 54 hours. In a Jewish workshop, six men paid 28s each would have to toil an 84 hour week to produce as many.[78] The competition was evidently hopeless.

Important changes in the organization of the boot and shoe industry also occurred in the 1890's. Factory producers began to retail not only their own shoes but those of smaller producers, which they bought up in job lots. The slim cash margin upon which small Jewish producers operated ill fitted them to deal with such mass buyers, to whom credit had to be extended for longer periods. Perhaps this explains a rash of bankruptcies, many of them improper, and the poor commercial reputation enjoyed by the small Jewish producers at this time.[79] The decline of London's small merchant shoe-makers reduced the work available to the Jewish workshops. In 1901 there were only 149 bootmaking shops in Stepney, compared to over 1,300 shops in the garment trades.[80] Fifteen years earlier their numbers had been about equal.

The sons of immigrants did not take to boot and shoe work at all. Among the members of a young Jewish workers' club, there were no more than four boot and shoe workers among 193 working lads.[81] While the Jewish connection with the boot and shoe industry was thus becoming ever more tenuous, the share of the Jews in the tailoring trade was rapidly advancing.

TAILORING: THE STAPLE IMMIGRANT TRADE

Jewish immigrants were aligned with a declining system of shoe manufacture, but in tailoring they were becoming the symbol of a new era. The new industry of cheap, mass-manufactured, ready-made apparel came into being to meet a corresponding demand by

[78]Cd. 1742, Min. 13368–88.
[79]Cd. 1742, Min. 12209, p. 413. See also Royal Commission on Alien Immigration, *Index to Minutes of Evidence*, Cd. 1743, 1904, *s.v.*, 'Bankruptcies, Fraudulent,' 'Bankruptcy,' 'Bankruptcy of Aliens.'
[80]Cd. 1742, Min. 5803.
[81]Brady Street Club for Working Lads, *Annual Report*, 1905–1906, n.p.

F

. . . a huge and constantly increasing class . . . who have . . . wide
wants and narrow means. Luxury has soaked downwards, and a
raised standard of living among people with small incomes has
created an enormous demand for cheap elegancies . . . cheap clothes
and cheap furniture, produced as they must be by cheap methods,
give pleasure to a large number of excellent persons . . . an enormous
class of persons [is] interested in cheapness and quickness of production.[82]

The Tory writer thanked the new system for bringing to
England

. . . democracy of modern dress. It is no longer possible, as it was
even thirty years ago, [i.e. 1858] to tell with tolerable accuracy
what a man is by his dress.[83]

Ready-made clothing rose eventually to dominate the clothing market against the wishes of the traditional English tailor,
who continued to believe unswervingly that 'one man, one
garment' was the true and moral way to make clothing. The
English tailor was a workman of considerable skill, and his
handiwork was as durable a specimen of apparel as could be
bought anywhere. He had served a lengthy apprenticeship,
but the trade to which the apprentice tailor was bound was
well paid, well treated, and well organized. The clientele which
purchased the English (frequently Scottish, Irish, or German)
tailor's output was a small proportion of the population,
although its clothing needs were substantial. Very little of
what was to happen in the lower strata of the trade had much
effect upon these tailors or their union, the Amalgamated
Society of Tailors, founded in 1866. The Society had 14,352
members in 1875, and its membership stood at 12,143 in 1910,
with a very narrow fluctuation in those 35 years.[84] The rest
of England and a large colonial market had to be clad, but
that was not the work of the Amalgamated Society of Tailors.
The great English market of clothing for the lower and indus-

[82]Arthur A. Baumann, M.P., 'Possible Remedies for the Sweating System,'
The National Review, XII, No. 69 (November, 1888), pp. 292–93. See also
Beatrice Potter, 'East London Labour,' *The Nineteenth Century*, XXIV, No. 138
(August, 1888), p. 180; *The Social Democrat*, VII, 2 (February 15, 1903), p. 73;
Cd. 1742, Min. 21038.

[83]Arthur A. Baumann, *op. cit., loc. cit.*, p. 293.

[84]Sidney and Beatrice Webb, *History of Trade Unionism*, rev. ed., London, 1920,
pp. 745–47.

trial classes had been served by renovated second-hand garments and slop—a cheap, stitched-up, shoddy product. Durable, inexpensive clothes of presentable quality and appearance was a novel phenomenon of the 1840's and 1850's, one intimately bound up with Jewish entrepreneurs.[85]

The Jewish connection with the clothing business began with the second-hand clothing and rag dealers in and around Houndsditch, at the City border of the East End. The Houndsditch trading mart was antique enough to have entered the purview of Ben Jonson—'A Houndsditch man, Sir. One of the Devil's neere kinsmen, a broker.' German and Dutch Jews entered the Devil's trade in the eighteenth century and came to dominate it.[86]

By the early nineteenth century there already existed a class of 'Jews who perambulate the streets of the metropolis every morning, crying "old clothes". . . . With their whole stock, one guinea in their pockets, they sally forth from the vicinity of their lodgings in Rosemary Lane, and purchase any old clothes. . . . Those they carry to "Rag Fair", a place in the middle of a street near the Tower, and sell to a superior order of merchants, at a cent-per-cent profit, who repair them, and afterwards re-sell them, to the labouring poor'.[86a]

They sent out the garments they purchased to be 'clobbered' (renovated) and resold, or if they were past this sort of treatment they were cut up and fashioned into caps or, when even that was not possible, the tattered clothes were disposed of as rags. Henry Mayhew's East End tours of the 1860's named such emporia as Isaac's, and Simmons & Levy.[87] Although the Jews were so conspicuous as old clo' men and dealers, over a century elapsed before Jewish workmen appeared in force as makers of new clothing. Even then the old second-hand and rag market maintained a position, although transformed:

[85]D. L. Munby, op. cit., pp. 52–57; A. E. Sayous, 'Les travailleurs de l'aiguille dans l'East End vers le milieu du XIXe siecle,' Revue d'économie politique, XIII (October-November, 1899), pp. 861–77.

[86]M. Dorothy George, London Life in the XVIIIth Century, 2nd ed., London, 1930, pp. 130–31; Cecil Roth, A History of the Jews in England, 2nd ed., Oxford, 1949, pp. 199, 225–27, 286.

[86a]Robert Atkins, A Compendious History of the Israelites, London, 1810, p. 60.

[87]Henry Mayhew, London Labour and the London Poor, 4 vols., London, 1861, I, pp. 368–69; II, pp. 26 ff., John Mills, The British Jews, London, 1853, pp. 262–72.

The original, much-hatted 'old-clo" man as the Ghetto knew him in a past decade has almost vanished from our ken, ignominiously thrust aside by the march of progress. . . . Nowadays his methods are distinctly up-to-date, for he advertises in the local Yiddish paper. . . .[88]

The Jews' advent in ready-made clothing seems to be connected with the impact of the Singer sewing machine, introduced late in the 1850's and in the 1860's. The sewing machine created a place for tailors and seamstresses who were neither skilled craftsmen nor engaged in the dregs of 'clobbering' and stitching up slop work. More than anything else, it was Isaac Singer's tool which enabled the ready-made garment to capture the home market. Moreover, as 'cheap elegancies' rose on the home market the export market also rapidly mounted for the cheapness, though not the elegance, of ready-made slop apparel. The total value of garments exported rose from £3,437,410 in 1873 to £4,658,589 in 1888 and to £6,297,219 in 1902, with setbacks occurring in the late 1870's and 1886–1887. Most of this increase took place in Australia, New Zealand, and South Africa, where natives were clad in slop clothing, while the Continental and Western Hemisphere markets remained stationary between £500,000 and £775,000 per annum.[89]

With the sewing machine as the central technological feature, this steady expansion of new ready-made clothing was aided by its extensive application of division of labour. The tangled web of small clothing workshops, with their minutely specialized skills and graduated wage scales, constituted a veritable factory system without factory buildings. Yet whatever later history held in store, clothing outwork did not originate with the Jews, for it possessed a long and unsavoury history. In 1844, only seventy-two West End tailors worked exclusively upon their employers' premises compared with 270 who worked partly there and partly outdoors, and 112 who did outwork only. An estimate of all England, also in 1844, finds 3,000 indoor tailors to some 18,000 tailors working in independent outdoor workshops or at home. The outdoor

---

[88] *JC*, August 11, 1905.
[89] C. 7406, pp. 208–11; Royal Commission on Alien Immigration, *Appendix to Minutes of Evidence*, Cd. 1741–I, 1903, Table XXII, p. 30.

workers were mostly women and children who concentrated in the manufacture of uniforms, which was a major point of entry for ready-made techniques.[90] On the other hand, the fusion of sewing machine and division of labour was perhaps first used to manufacture ready-made clothing by a Jewish firm, E. Moses & Son. Moses claimed in 1860 that his was 'the first house in London, or we may say, in the World, that established the system of *New Clothing Ready Made*. . . .' He boasted that

. . . eighty per cent. of the population purchase ready-made clothing, because the prejudice against it has been conquered by the reputation of our firm. Thousands of tailors have followed our example; but we continue in the van. . . .[91]

Moses did a large bespoke (custom) business and also sold hats, boots, shoes, and other men's wear. His firm maintained three large stores at principal intersections in London and branches in Bradford and Sheffield, which were all shut on the Jewish Sabbath.[92]

To a contemporary observer, Moses' and his competitors' labour force was composed of 'unfortunates who could not find work in the "respectable" part of the trade'.[93] Charles Kingsley, writing under his own name and as Parson Lot, graphically depicted their condition.[94] As to Jews, they first appeared years later as 'young Polish Jews [who] prefer London slop-work to military service'.[95] Jewish tailoring work in 1872 was still of the ill-famed cheap and nasty sort; it was

. . . 'clobbering', a technical term for 'renovating' old garments. The better class of tailoring is but little affected in the East End, though it is adapted to a fairly considerable extent in the Western or Soho colony of Jews, with more or less success—generally with less success. . . . The number of journeymen stitchers of clothes—we can hardly call them tailors—is very large indeed: and the applications for work at our great clothing establishments are very numerous. . . .

[90]A. E. Sayous, 'Les travailleurs de l'aiguille . . .' *loc. cit.*; Wanda F. Neff, *Victorian Working Women*, 1832–1850, N.Y., 1929, pp. 129–35.

[91](E. Moses and Son,) *The Growth of an Important Branch of British Industry*, London, 1860, n.p.; D. L. Munby, *op. cit.*, pp. 52–53.

[92](E. Moses and Son,) *op. cit.*, n.p.

[93]J. G. Eccarius, *Der Kampf des Grossen und des Kleinen Kapitals oder Die Schneiderei in London*, Leipzig, 1876, p. 20.

[94]D. L. Munby, *op. cit.*, pp. 52–53; see above, Note 30.

[95]J. G. Eccarius, *op. cit.*, p. 25.

These large firms necessarily pay for labour in proportion to the supply of labour.[96]

The 'Western or Soho' colony referred to was mostly German Jews; Germans were prominent as London tailors in the mid-nineteenth century.

We have estimated that twenty-nine per cent. of the East European arrivals were in some branch of tailoring, over three times more than the next largest category, that of shoe workers.[97] The great expansion of ready-made clothing drew ever higher numbers of Jewish tailors into the trade, so that the 2,728 'Russian and Polish' male and 536 female tailors in London in 1881 multiplied to 12,344 and 2,939 respectively, in 1911.[98] At both dates, almost as many more immigrant Jews from Austria, Germany, Holland, and Rumania were also tailors. Besides, the second generation had produced a large number of English-born tailors by 1911.

To gauge the role of the Jews in the clothing industry between the 1870's and the first World War is a complex matter. Generally the Jews made ready-to-wear garments for merchants and wholesale clothiers, ranging in quality from bespoke to near-trash. As in the making of boots and shoes, the immigrant Jews tended to concentrate intensively in limited sectors of the trade, such as mantles and waistcoats, nearly to the exclusion of such apparel as shirts, vests, and trousers.[99] Not only were certain types of garment 'Jewish', but certain jobs, such as pressing or machining or basting, were also 'Jewish'. The topmost level of skill, that of a cutter or patternmaker, was seldom reached by an immigrant Jew before 1914, and the Jewish workshop usually received its work already cut. Machining (operation of a sewing machine), however, was heavily Jewish, as was pressing (of the garment at the end of the process); side jobs like buttonhole making, basting, and felling employed Jewish or Gentile girls and women and apprentice 'greeners'. The division of labour was

---

[96]'The Employment of the Jewish Poor,' *JC*, May 10, 1872. See W. G. Crory, *East London Industries*, London, 1876, pp. 92–100.
[97]See above, pp. 57–58.
[98]*Census of England and Wales*, 1911, Cd. 7017, pp. 221–29.
[99]Beatrice Potter, in Charles Booth, *op. cit.*, IV, pp. 237–38; C. 7406, pp. 105–07; Cd. 1742, Min. 20271.

elaborately detailed, and in addition to primary branches of work such as those mentioned further refinements were drawn. Thus, pressers' and machinists' pay was too high to trouble with details that cheaper labour could perform, so they were done by sub-machinists and assistant pressers. The latter were normally 'learners'—freshly arrived immigrants 'of no trade who have to be taught. . . .'[100] An an optimistic explanation has it:

They have to be treated as quasi-apprentices, i.e., placed for a short term with masters, who, in consideration of the acceptance of a very low but progressive wage, undertake to teach the trade or a department of it. In about six to nine months, the applicant, if fairly intelligent, attains sufficient proficiency to earn full wages.[101]

This fine-spun hierarchy of skill and technique, and its intimate bond with the earnings of the workmen, was accounted a revolutionary change by some contemporaries, even by one so perceptive and well-informed as Beatrice Potter (later Beatrice Webb). Actually, it did no more than refine and extend a system which had started with making slop clothing.[102]

Clothing workshops were super-abundant, especially in the East End areas of heavy Jewish settlement. In Whitechapel, at the centre of the trade, Beatrice Potter's investigation uncovered 1,015 of them in 1887-1888, of which 901 made coats and did general tailoring and the remaining 114 worked on vests, trousers, and juvenile outfits. Of the total, only twenty-one workshops employed twenty-five or more persons, and 758 employed fewer than ten.[103] The picture which emerges suggests a maze of tiny, unstable little firms, with enterprises constantly going under and new ones always being opened. Yet cogent economic reasons justified the continuance of the crazy-quilt of East London Jewish workshops, whose numbers were not diminished or noticeably consolidated in the following generation. A chronically seasonal trade, subject to the whims

[100]Russo-Jewish Committee, *Report*, 1894, p. 22.
[101]*Ibid*.
[102]Beatrice Potter, in Charles Booth, *op. cit.*, pp. 214–17. The present view is expressed most clearly by A. E. Sayous, 'Les travailleurs de l'aiguille . . . ,' *loc. cit.*
[103]Beatrice Potter, in Charles Booth, *op. cit.*, p. 239.

of fashion, could not easily support large producing units with substantial fixed costs. Many small units could sink or swim with less effect upon the trade as a whole than the fluctuations in the fortunes of a few bigger producers would have caused. Besides, the individual merchant clothier was the dominant figure in the London trade, so that the multiplication of workshops paralleled the plethora of firms which had work to give out. The existence of many small, independent workshops, and the almost trivial sum needed to set up as an entrepreneur, also made it not hard for Jews to indulge their taste for entrepreneurship.

In the provinces, much the same workshop picture can be drawn in Manchester, except for the waterproof trade, where factory production was taking over. Things were much different in Leeds, whose contrast with London is highly significant and demonstrates how little London's and Manchester's conglomerations of petty workshops owed to Jewish 'economic instinct'.[104] The Leeds trade was based on a smaller number of large workshops. The Jewish community in Leeds was not formed until the 1860's, at about the time the clothing industry arrived in the Yorkshire city, mostly from Glasgow. One of the main causes for the concentration of clothing factories in Leeds was the supply of cloth ready to hand from the Yorkshire woollen factories (those in nearby Bradford were owned by German Jews), and the supply of cheap labour.[105] From its very outset, the local clothing trade profited by being relatively without historic traditions and restrictions. Yet the immigrant Jews still did not enter the Leeds factories, but kept to their workshops. There were 101 of those in the town in 1891, which employed 1,435 male and 447 female 'Russians and Poles'.[106] These numbers had shot up during the 1880's, and included

[104]On Leeds, see *Report to the Board of Trade on the Sweating System in Leeds by the Labour Correspondent of the Board* [John Burnett], C. 5513, 1888 (hereafter cited as C. 5513); Clara E. Collet, 'Women's Work in Leeds,' *The Economic Journal*, I, 3 (September, 1891), pp. 460–73; C. 7406, pp. 116-22; *The Polish Yidel*, I, 15, October 31, 1884; 'Report of *The Lancet* Special Sanitary Commission on the Sweating System in Leeds,' *The Lancet*, June 9, 1888, pp. 1146-48.
[105]Clara E. Collet, *op. cit., loc. cit.*, p. 471. Correspondent to Leeds *Mercury*, quoted in *JC*, August 27, 1894.
[106]Clara E. Collet, *op. cit., loc. cit.*, p. 468. The author admits that the number is probably too high, despite its official source. There were only 64 Jewish workshops in 1888. *The Labour Gazette*, I, 1 (May, 1893), pp. 8-9.

the great majority of the Yorkshire city's Jewish immigrant workers.[107] While most of the Leeds clothing workshops were Jewish, all but one of the fifty-one factories were Gentile. These workshops were much larger than London's[108] and contained from twenty to thirty pieces of machinery apiece, so that steam power replaced manpower at many points,[109] and productivity was higher than in London.

This extreme contrast between London's chaotic mass of workshops and the larger establishments in Leeds is explained by the contrasting structure of the trades which they served. The London Jewish workshops took out work from the small merchant clothiers, while in Leeds the workshop received its orders in quantity from the excess backlogs of clothing factories. In spite of the larger scale of the Leeds workshops, and notwithstanding their connection with factory production, the evils of seasonal work were still rife in the earlier years of our period.[110] On the other hand, sweating in Leeds did not attain the notoriety which enveloped it in London. One writer denied the propriety of using the term in Leeds,[111] while another, more conservative and closer to the mark, declared 'without reserve that the Jewish tailors in Leeds are better off than their brethren in London.'[112] The House of Lords Commission on the Sweating System and other Government sources found little to report about sweating in Leeds. Yet Jewish tailoring in Leeds also had its lower depths.

. . . we had a lengthy conversation with the wife of a sweater, who was very unhappy because her husband had taken to sweating. It would have been better had he resisted the promptings of ambition and modestly contented himself with being sweated. Now, he had to

---

[107]A report of 1884 suggests 'without exaggeration . . . up to a thousand' Jewish workers. *The Polish Yidel*, I, 2 (July 25, 1884). C. E. Collet, *op. cit.*, *loc. cit.*, p. 468.

[108]*The Labour Gazette*, *loc. cit.* In a sample of 44, 18 employed 40 or more; 14 employed between 25 and 39; 12 employed from 10 to 24. No shop resembled the 758 in London which employed fewer than 10.

[109]C. 5513, p. 4.

[110]*Ibid.*, p. 5; *The Labour Gazette*, *loc. cit.*, *The Polish Yidel*, I, 9 (September 19, 1884). On later period, see S. Webb and A. Freeman, *op. cit.*, pp. 70–92.

[111]'There is a system in Leeds, but it is not a sweating system.' Clara E. Collet, *op. cit.*, *loc. cit.*, p. 469.

[112]C. 5513, p. 5.

pay the rent of a workshop, the cost of gas and of eight or nine machines; and he got gentlemen's coats to make, with six button-holes, for elevenpence. It was starvation for him and his workpeople; and, glancing round at the furniture and general condition of this sweater's home, it certainly looked like starvation.[113]

One branch of tailoring was indigenous to Manchester. Waterproofing, the manufacture of cloth garments treated wth rubber coating against the weather, was an industry developed by Jews in that city. The names of Mandelberg, Frankenberg, and a few other Jews, were almost synonomous with this trade.[114] It attracted workers in its early days by good wages, sometimes £2 and £3 a week, but this was before the mass influx of East European Jews.[115] In the mid-1880's the fortunes of waterproofing dropped sharply and the Jewish Board of Guardians considered the plight of 'the strangers who had been attracted here through the briskness in the waterproofing trade, which trade was now getting slack. . . .'[116] On the other hand, workers' voices were heard claiming that sweating was 'being rapidly introduced into this trade. . . .'[117] These protests were directed less against the workshops than against the rising tide of factory production which forced a more strenuous pace and lower pay upon the waterproofer in the workshops. By 1891, not more than 247 'Russians and Poles' were employed as Manchester waterproofers[118] and within three years the trade was 'almost entirely carried on in factories and large workshops'; the small workshops where the Jews worked had 'nearly died out'.[119] The garment was itself superseded by the technologically superior 'rainproof' garment, at which about 1,000 Jews were employed at the turn of the century. The

---

[113]'Report of *The Lancet* Special Commission on the Sweating System in Leeds,' *The Lancet*, June 16, 1888, p. 1210.

[114]*Die Tsukunft*, II, 7 (August 14, 1885); Manchester Jewish Board of Guardians, *Annual Report*, 1887, p. 6; Cd. 1742, Min. 17863, 20851.

[115]*Die Tsukunft*, II, 7, 8, 9 (August 14, 21, 28, 1885). This account is by a certain Rivlin, evidently a worker in the trade.

[116]Manchester Jewish Board of Guardians, *Minutes*, November 5, 1884. See also *Die Tsukunft*, II, 9, August 28, 1885.

[117]Minutes of meeting of waterproofers held in Manchester, November 23, 1889, in A. R. Rollin Archive, now in YIVO. There was a strike in 1890 which ended in a 'victory' of the workers. *Arbeiter Freind*, V, 33, 34, 35 (August 15, 22, 29, 1890). See also *Die Tsukunft, loc. cit.*

[118]C. 7406, p. 155.

[119]C. 7406, p. 130.

'rainproof' seems to have come into its own in the 1890's, when it 'displaced the waterproof garment. . . .'[120]

Manchester Jewish tailoring conformed more to the London pattern of many little workshops producing for many clothiers than to Leeds' system of fewer and larger workshops at work on substantial orders from clothing factories. Accordingly, the Jewish workshops in Manchester were small places on the scale of London.[121] 'Cottonopolis' of Lancashire sheltered 252 of these establishments in 1893 in which 1,960 Jews, including as many as 134 natives, earned livelihoods.[122] A trade union estimate of the same period suggests 1,500 Jewish tailors,[123] while the census of 1891, speaking as always of 'Russians and Poles,' found 870 men and 270 women as Manchester tailors.[124] The work they did and its effects upon traditional tailoring likewise resembled London and need not be repeated. It may be, however, that the high-class English tailors were even more adversely affected than those in London. The Manchester membership of the Amalgamated Society of Tailors declined from 600–800 circa 1890 to only 400 in 1903, and their bitterness was correspondingly acute.[125] To be sure, it is far from certain that Jewish sweatshop tailoring caused this depression, but the English had few doubts. Yet Manchester Jewish tailoring also had a side which was brighter, or at least less dark:

Manchester, as an abode for sweaters, possesses some notable advantages over London. The town is comparatively new; the streets are therefore wider and there is more air and more light. Further, it so happens that the greater number of Jew sweaters have settled in the district of Strangeways, where they have found houses in some instances built for an altogether different and higher class of tenants. Somehow the higher-class tenants did not think fit to live in this quarter, and this, so far as public health is concerned, is a fortunate circumstance, for thus many of the Manchester sweaters are located

[120]Cd. 1742, Min. 21041. On the London waterproof trade, see the testimony of Barnett Abrahams, Cd. 1742, Min. 18896 ff.
[121]*The Labour Gazette*, I, 1 (May, 1893), p. 9.
[122]Report of the Chief Inspector of Factories and Workshops for 1891, C. 6720, p. 14.
[123]*Arbeiter Freind*, VIII, 39 (September 29, 1893).
[124]C. 7406, p. 155.
[125]Manchester *Evening News*, January 28, 29, February 5, 1903.

in a better class of houses than those generally occupied by the sweaters of, for instance, London and Liverpool.[126]

Behind the pre-eminent Jewish community of London, and following the secondary communities of Manchester and Leeds, trailed an array of smaller Jewish centres—Liverpool, Glasgow, Birmingham, Newcastle, Hull. Jewish tailors came to all of them, and with the Jewish tailor came his typical system of tailoring. For these cities, which had not yet been affected by newer tailoring techniques, the advent of East European Jews meant the introduction of their characteristic manner of work. For example, the transfer of a Jewish firm named Freeman from Glasgow to Dundee in 1893, along with its staff of tailors, aroused fierce opposition from the apprehensive local tailors.[127] Jewish tailoring had come to Glasgow itself in the early 1870's, when a Scottish tailoring firm imported a group of Jewish tailors from London. However, leadership in that sort of work remained as much in the hands of Scots and Irish as in those of Jews.[128] The strongly organized Scottish tailors aired complaints of sweating upon the floor of the Trades Union Congress in the 1870's.[129] As to Birmingham, we hear of the new system as early as 1879 from an Inspector of Factories, who found it 'chiefly carried on by Polish and German Jews, who have lately immigrated in large numbers. . . . Wages of [English tailors] too, have been reduced by the competition of foreigners in the second class order trade.'[130] The rather puzzling reason given for the decline of English tailors' wages is that their time had to be spent on gratuitous alterations, perhaps of imperfectly done work. We can only surmise what this had to do with Jewish competition, although workers who made ready-made garments lost no wages for such causes. As elsewhere, 'the Jews do not keep large establishments',[131] but were found at work under crowded conditions

[126]'Report of The Lancet Special Sanitary Commission on "Sweating" among Tailors at Liverpool and Manchester,' The Lancet, April 21, 1888, p. 792.

[127]Arbeiter Freind, VIII, 26, June 30, 1893.

[128]Cd. 1742, Min. 20896; 'Report of The Lancet Special Sanitary Commission on the Sweating System in Glasgow,' The Lancet, June 30, 1888, pp. 1313-14; July 7, 1888, pp. 37-39.

[129]Trades Union Congress, Report, 1875, p. 23; 1876, p. 17; 1877, p. 29.

[130]Report of the Chief Inspector of Factories and Workshops for 1879, C. 2489, p. 16.

[131]Ibid. See also Report for 1887, C. 5328, p. 47.

in masters' attics and other undesirable locations. In 1888, the Birmingham *Daily Post* found sixty-six sweatshops in its city, where 129 men and 240 women were employed.[132]

The later 1880's were years of anti-sweating enthusiasm. Inspired by the hearings of the House of Lords Commission on Sweating, English cities became inquisitive about Jewish ready-made tailoring, which they sometimes thought identical with sweating. The main lesson learned from the various inquiries was that sweating was far from a Jewish monopoly, and that hardly a city lacked Jewish immigrant settlers who maintained at least a few clothing workshops. All the workshops were small, operated similarly, and more or less impinged on the traditional ways of the English tailor. In the case of Liverpool, the fifty-six Jewish 'middlemen' (i.e. workshop employers) enumerated in 1890 employed not only Jewish men but also Christian women and girls. They did both bespoke work for the better merchant clothiers and cheaper ready-made work for wholesale factories.[133] Hull, a smaller Jewish community, also had its proportionately sized version of the Jewish manner of tailoring. At the turn of the century, we hear of one hundred Hull Jewish tailors who struck against forty firms which employed them.[134] The ratio of tailors to employers suggests that the Hull Jewish tailor was prone to be an independent outworker, working alone in his own house or shop.

SMALLER IMMIGRANT TRADES

Fewer immigrants engaged in lesser crafts like slipper making, cap making, fur work, artificial flower work, besides other workers and petty entrepreneurs who catered to the immigrant community itself—barbers, printers, bakers, and a small but diverse host of others. No special note need be taken of the latter. The small crafts resembled the larger immigrant trades, with the Jews similarly self-confined to squalid workshops and helping to supply a growing mass market.

[132]*The Commonweal*, IV, 123 (May 19, 1888), p. 155; see 'Report of *The Lancet* Special Sanitary Commission on "Sweating" in Birmingham and the Black Country,' May 26 and June 2, 1888, pp. 1047–49, 1100–02.
[133]Report of the Chief Inspector of Factories and Workshops for 1889, C. 6060, pp. 23–25; *Idem*, 1890, C. 6330, p. 36; *JC*, September 30, 1892.
[134]*The Labour Gazette*, VII, 5 (May, 1899), p. 134.

Slipper making, which surged upward briefly in the 1890's, is a typical minor immigrant trade. Of the several hundred Jewish slipper makers many were displaced shoe lasters, victims of the suppression of boot and shoe outwork and technological innovation.[135] Perhaps 200 took to 'sewing round' (lasting) slippers of poorer quality than the English slipper maker.[136] However, the hand 'sew round' trade was 'largely disappearing' from London early in the present century, to be taken up in Leeds in a vain competition with the cheap factory product.[137]

Cap making (as distinct from hat making), a trade 'practically created' by Jews,[138] grew quickly to some importance. It branched out so rapidly that 120 little workshops were reported to have supplanted four large firms who had dominated the trade *circa* 1890. The mechanics of cap making resembled the making of other garments—patterning, cutting, sewing, pressing. However, less skill was needed at each step, and from the workers' point of view the trade was one thoroughly depressed.[139] The 320 men and eighty-six women, 'Russians and Poles', who made caps in East London and Hackney in 1891 rose to 707 and 214, respectively for all London in 1901, and remained at approximately that number in 1911.[140] A few hundred more cap makers worked in Manchester, but there were practically no others elsewhere. These figures of immigrant participation fail to reflect that English girls and women exceeded the number of Jewish male workers. Jewish girls, however, avoided cap making and preferred better paid tailoring.[141]

Furriers' work, also confined to London and Manchester, stood at a low level of skill. The Jewish furriers made cheap capes and dyed rabbit skins in imitation of more expensive furs. Because of the dyes and feathers and odours, the fur trade

[135]C. 7406, pp. 77, 88–90, 182; interview with M. Stephany in *JC*, July 12, 1895.
[136]C. 7406. p. 89,   [137]Cd. 1742, Min. 12206, 15004 ff.
[138]Manchester *Evening News*, January 28, 1903.
[139]The best discussion is in *JC*, August 9, 1895; see also C. 7406, pp. 127–29; for a socialist view of labour conditions at a leading cap maker, see *The Commonweal*, V, 188, May 17, 1889, p. 262.
[140]C. 7406, p. 154; *Census of England and Wales*, 1901, Cd. 875, p. 168.
[141]C. 7406, p. 129.

was an especially unhealthy occupation for its 400 to 500 Jewish immigrant workers.[142]

The same panorama of workshop labour and debased working conditions strikes the eye in other minor immigrant trades such as stick making, basket weaving, umbrella making, and others.

JEWISH WAGES

No aspect of the Jewish immigrant economy is harder to penetrate than that most basic to the immigrant worker—his wages and earnings. The structure of the immigrant trades and the Jews' manner of work complicate the problem of determining what the Jewish immigrant workers were paid. Did they work by the piece or by the hour? How are their earnings most accurately estimated—by the hour, the day, or the week? A wide gap between wages (rate of pay) and earnings ('take home pay') was caused by the seasonal nature of the Jewish immigrant trades. For example, 7s or 8s a day for a moderately good tailor would supposedly yield £2 2s to £2 8s a week, fair pay for a pre-World War I working man. But although the Jewish worker occasionally earned that much during busy times, he annually averaged only two to three days' work a week. While there were several full weeks of lucrative but exhausting toil in season, two days of work per week was the most to be hoped for during the slack period. Beatrice Potter estimated that four or four and a half days a week was average in large shops and for highly skilled workers, while medium sized shops and average workers worked three days a week. However, the 'great majority' of unskilled and semi-skilled workers, including the mass of Gentile women, worked an annual average of only two days or less per week.[143] Thus, the tailor's weekly average 'take home pay' of 14s to 21s

[142]Report of the Chief Inspector of Factories and Workshops for 1879, C. 2489, p. 23; *Idem* for 1887, C. 5328, p. 73; Cd. 1742, Min. 13172, 13190–92. There were 1,203 alien furriers and skinners in the United Kingdom in 1901, mostly 'Russians and Poles'. Royal Commission on Alien Immigration, *Appendix to Minutes of Evidence*, Cd. 1741-I, 1903, Table LXI, pp. 72–73.
[143]Beatrice Potter in Charles Booth, *op. cit.*, pp. 225–26; *The Labour Gazette*, I, 2 (June, 1893), p. 41. It was little different in the Provinces. On Leeds, see *The Commonweal*, IV, 124, May 26, 1888, p. 165; C. 5513, p. 5; *The Labour Gazette*, I, 1 (May, 1893), pp. 8–9.

is much lower, but certainly closer to the true picture than the wage rate alone would indicate.

Another difficulty impedes a clear view of Jewish immigrant earnings. The minute gradations of skill in the Jewish workshop had correspondingly minute gradations in the Jewish workers' wages, so that in a single workshop one or two men were paid 9s and two or three others received 7s or 7s 6d, and the remainder 5s and 5s 6d, all for much the same work. The master was recognizing their varying levels of skill and output, although he was hardly simplifying the analysis of the wage picture. No wage log effectively established a uniform rate of wages in any Jewish immigrant trade; although the Amalgamated Society of Tailors' log was referred to in disputes from time to time, it was not fashioned for ready-made work.[144] Wages also fluctuated in obedience to the price which the master bid in order to get a bundle of work from the merchant clothier or the wholesale factory.[145]

At the summit of the hierarchy in the Jewish clothing workshop both in wages and the average number of days worked, stood the head machinist and head presser. Their assistants were frequently 'greeners' who were 'learners' with the functions and earnings of apprentices. Workshops which employed many Gentile and Jewish girls and women paid them more poorly.[146] A German observer in 1876 found pressers earning £1 a week, followed by machinists at 15s or 16s, assistant machinists at 12s to 14s, buttonholers at 14s or 15s (rather high), and seamstress finishers at 7s to 10s, with the mass of workers down at the lower end of the scale.[147] It is not clear whether these figures represent West End work or East

[144]The A. S. of T. wage log was very close to the Jewish wage rate; there was no more than a ½d hourly difference. *The Labour Gazette*, I, 2 (June, 1893), p. 41.
[145]The Tailors' Improvement Association, a large but amorphous Jewish masters' group, demanded of the clothiers a 'small but proportionate rise' as the only way to meet their workers' demands for shorter hours with undiminished earnings. Their letter is in *The People's Press*, I, 11, May 17, 1890, pp. 8–9.
[146]An estimated 62.2 per cent of employees in London Jewish workshops were male. Roughly 14 per cent were pressers, with the rest about evenly divided between general tailoring and machining. There were practically no machinists or pressers among the female 37.8 per cent, of whom about one third were buttonholers and two thirds were fellers and finishers. There are slight differences between different cities and workshops. C. 7406, Table XV, p. 207.
[147]J. G. Eccarius, *op. cit.*, p. 23.

End Jewish work. A specimen of the latter, taken a few years later, indicates about the same daily rate of pay.[148]

The most inclusive and generally satisfactory table of wages in the Jewish clothing trade was compiled in 1886 and 1887 by John Burnett, Labour Correspondent to the Board of Trade. It is based upon a questionnaire to Jewish workshop employers. While it thus lacks the workers' side of the case, a quantity of related evidence generally corroborates Burnett's figures:[149]

Men's Wages, daily

Kind of work	Time or Piece	Maximum s	Maximum d	Minimum s	Minimum d	Average s	Average d	No. of Cases
Presser	time	9	0	2	6	6	5	108
Presser	piece	7	0	4	6	5	6	4
Machinist	time	10	0	2	6	6	0	188
Machinist	piece	10	0	3	4	7	0	10
General tailor	time	10	0	4	0	7	3	23
Baster	time	9	0	3	0	6	2	89
Baster	piece	7	0	3	0	5	5	5
Feller	time	6	0	3	0	4	8	12
Apprentice	time	1	2		4		8	4
Apprentice	time, per week	13	0	5	6	8	6	5
								448

Women's Wages, daily

		Maximum s	Maximum d	Minimum s	Minimum d	Average s	Average d	No. of Cases
Machinist	time	6	0	1	8	4	0	17
Baster	time	4	6		6	2	9	12
Feller	time	5	0		6	2	7	243
Feller	time, per week	22	0	9	9	14	1	10
Buttonholing	time	6	0	1	8	4	0	12
Buttonholing	piece	6	6	1	6	3	9	94
Less deductions for gimp and materials		1	3		4½		9½	
Apprentices	time	1	6		3		10	14
Apprentices	time, per week	10	0	3	0	6	10	5
								407

[148]Report of the Chief Inspector of Factories and Workshops for 1880, C. 2825, pp. 16–21. Birmingham wages at this time were reported higher than London. *Idem* for 1879, C. 2489, p. 16.

[149]This table is condensed from Burnett's data, which was printed as an Appendix to the House of Lord's Commission on the Sweating System, *Second Report*, 1889, pp. 584–88. It should be compared with J. B. Lakeman's report of 'Wages Paid to Female Operatives in the Central Metropolitan District,' Report of the Chief Inspector of Factories and Workshops for 1887, C. 5328, pp. 81–84; and with Beatrice Potter's data in Charles Booth, *op. cit.*, pp. 222–25. See also (John Burnett,) Report to the Board of Trade on the Sweating System at the East End of London, 1888, pp. 11–17; tables in C. 7406, pp. 108–25, give the impression of a 10 per cent rise in wages between 1886 and 1894. See also *The Labour Gazette*, I, 1, 2 (May, June, 1893), pp. 8–9, 41.

G

Women's wages, as is seen, were much lower than men's, and the above figures include Gentile women at work in Jewish shops. Jewish girls and women preferred better paid branches of garment work so that, unlike Gentile women, they stayed away from work in trousers, vests, and shirts and found more lucrative employment at jackets and mantles ('cloaks' in American parlance).[150]

The intricate scale of wages, and the gap between wages and actual earnings, also hold true for Manchester and other Provincial centres where Jewish tailoring so closely resembled the master pattern in London.[151] An exception must as usual be made for Leeds, even though Burnett reported that Jewish wages there were perhaps ten per cent. to fifteen per cent. lower than in London.[152] In that Yorkshire city where large workshops executed substantial orders for wholesale factories, regularity of work was gradually introduced. Toward the close of our period, a Leeds Jewish worker could expect to earn wages for a full week's work of fifty-four hours under the terms of the strike settlement of 1911.[153]

Wage rates changed little in the volatile clothing industry. Interestingly, the clothing workers' demands, when articulated, seldom stressed wages, but concentrated on better working conditions and shorter hours.[154]

Unlike the relatively plentiful data about garment work, it is hard to come by reliable information about other immigrant trades. The diligent H. Llewellyn Smith assembled only scattered, unreliable statements from boot and shoe chamber masters and small manufacturers.[155] Statements made

[150]C. 7406, pp. 125–27.
[151]On wages in Manchester, see *The Labour Gazette*, I, 1 (May, 1893), p. 9; for a cursory comparison of wages in Glasgow, Liverpool, Birmingham, and Leeds, based on evidence submitted to the House of Lords Commission on the Sweating System, see C. H. d'E. Leppington, 'Side Lights of the Sweating Commission,' *The Westminster Review*, CXXXVI, 3 (March, 1891), p. 283.
[152]C. 5513, pp. 5–6, where statements by masters and men are contrasted; C. E. Collet, *op. cit., loc. cit.*, pp. 468 ff.; *Arbeiter Freind*, XI, 17, January 31, 1896.
[153]*The Ladies' Garment Worker* (New York), III, 12 (December, 1912), p. 6; *JC*, April 7, 1911. Ninth Report by the Board of Trade of Proceedings under the Conciliation (Trade Disputes) Act, 1896, 1911, pp. 32–35.
[154]For example, the Manchester tailors, who were predominantly piece workers, demanded an advance per garment of 2d for pressers and 3d for machinists, so as not to lose earnings in a 10½ hour day. *The Commonweal*, VI, 224, April 26, 1890, p. 134.
[155]C. 7406, pp. 81–85; 171–84; *Die Tsukunft*, II, 28, 29 (January 15, 22, 1886).

by individual boot and shoe workers cannot be accepted freely because that trade was surfeited with isolated shops and individual peculiarities. Wages were declining well before the campaign against outwork in 1889-1890, because wholesale houses were lowering their prices for the work which they gave out.[156] By the time of the strike of 1890, few small masters, let alone workers, cleared £1 in a full week. We can only conjecture how closely the post-1890 outwork shops and small manufacturers adhered to the 'Uniform Statement' of wages which emerged from the strike.

Cap making, a minor immigrant trade, required less skill at most of its steps than tailoring, and the relative lightness of the work enabled girls and women to cut and press.[157] In the unequal competition with factory production, some cutters netted only 9s a week, and masters toiled alongside their employees sixteen to eighteen hours a day in busy seasons to clear 12s a week for their entrepreneurial efforts.[158]

Unfortunately, we possess no useful information concerning the incomes of a whole gamut of tradesmen—peddlers, glaziers, costermongers, shopkeepers, and the rest. However, some of them were actually tailors and boot makers who shouldered a peddler's pack or occupied a pitch in the street during the slack months of their trades.[159]

[156]Report of the Chief Inspector of Factories and Workshops for 1887, C. 5328, pp. 81, 100–03, esp. p. 102.
[157]C. 7406, pp. 127–29.
[158]JC, August 9, 1895.
[159]C. 7406, p. 63.

IV

MOVEMENTS OF PROTEST AND
IMPROVEMENT

The Jewish worker did not always mutely shoulder the burdens of the life he led. Even though he brought with him little or no experience in democratic organization and self-government, he did have a lively awareness of the evils of his position. That the social order irretrievably fixed him in his lowly estate never occurred to him, and the very idea contradicted the purpose which brought him to England. Neither did he recognize that any immutable difference stood between him and fellow Jews who attained the pinnacle of success. We see here the obverse side of the much-discussed 'elasticity in the standard of life' of the Jew; he was convinced that he could rise to the top, and that the obstacles which prevented him from advancing were man-made. Having left Russia or Poland for the purpose of bettering his lot, it was inevitable that the immigrant ask himself whether he was better off in England. There were few who could return an unqualified 'yes' to such an introspection, and the others naturally wondered what was interfering with their progress. It may well have seemed surprising that a country renowned for its economic might and political freedom should hold so poor a life for most of them.

The efflorescence of the Jewish labour and socialist movement,[1] fully equipped (perhaps too dogmatically) with a

[1] An admirable account of Jewish socialism in England until 1895 is E. Tscheri-kover, ed., *Geshikhte fun der Yiddisher Arbeter Bavegung in der Faraynigte Shtatn* (History of the Jewish Labour Movement in the United States), 2 vols., N.Y., 1943, II, pp. 76–135, by the editor, with emphasis on its intellectual development and international bearings. It supersedes the earlier Herz Burgin, *Die Geshikhte fun der Idisher Arbayter Bavegung in America, Rusland un England* (History of the Jewish Labour Movement in America, Russia and England), N.Y., 1915, which, however, reaches to 1914. Other valuable memoiristic accounts are: M. Winchevsky, *Erinnerungen* (Memoirs), Vols. IX and X of his *Gezamelte Shriftn* (Collected Works), N.Y. 1927 (another ed., Moscow, 1926); Rudolf Rocker, *In Shturem: Golus Yoren* (In Storm: Years of Exile), London and Buenos Aires,

comprehensive ideological basis, was in some ways the outcome of the immigrants' sense of deprivation of the benefits
which were expected of life in a new country. On the other
hand, it also represents the first response of Jewish thought to
an industrial and urban environment, influenced by nineteenth
century European socialism. The Jewish labour and socialist
movement in England and elsewhere represents the confluence
of two currents—socialist thought combined with a passion to
better the life of the new Jewish proletarian classes. The two
are quite distinct, and indeed, they did not always flow in the
same direction. If amelioration was the major aim of the
trade unionists in the Jewish quarter, the young[2] Jewish
intellectuals who brought socialism into the immigrant Jewish
world were by no means principally concerned with making
life physically better for their brethren.

The socialist and trade union ferment which they sought
to arouse among the Jews differed from English movements of
the same outlook. The Jewish socialists were not grounded in
utilitarianism and Free Trade; Chartism and Liberal-Labourism
were outside their experience; names like Robert Owen,
Francis Place, and Bronterre O'Brien meant little. The English
socialist seems almost taciturn beside the overflowing talk-
ativeness of the Jewish socialist, who was formed in a different
background in another country. Most Jewish socialists had a
traditional Jewish upbringing and some had even attended a
yeshibah for higher Talmudic study, or an institution which
combined such ancient learning with modern studies. But in
time they burst the trammels of their upbringing and began
also to taste the forbidden fruits of philosophy, literature,
European languages and natural science. The young children
of the Enlightenment saw a greater light when they studied
the Social Problem, whose ultimate solution lay in socialism.
This ideal could be realized only by means of a political and
social revolution. The young Jewish intellectual wrenched

1952; A. Frumkin, *In Friling fun Yiddishn Sotsialism* (In the Springtime of Jewish
Socialism), N.Y., 1940; T. Eyges, *Zikhroines fun die Yiddishe Arbeter Bavegung
in London, England* (Memoirs of the Jewish Labour Movement in London, England), (1942) MS. in YIVO, New York, and made available by its kind permission.

[2]Nearly all of the Jewish socialists who arrived in England were under thirty
years of age, like most other immigrants. Winchevsky, born in 1856, was the
oldest of the group.

himself out of his environment and sank new roots in the shifting soil of revolutionary movements.

Whether from poverty, hope of more promising fields of activity, or danger of arrest, the Jewish socialist came to England. Here he was at home only in its small Jewish quarter, alongside toiling immigrants. A common bond with English socialists, who were themselves few enough at the outset of the 1880's, was not easily forged, and socialist agitation among the English working classes was out of the question. Few of them ever entered upon the English socialist scene, although in the United States numerous Jewish socialists 'graduated' into the socialist movement. This distance helped to lend enchantment to the immigrant Jewish socialists' view of the English trade union world, to which they maintained an almost reverential attitude. How great was the contrast between the unstable, strife-ridden little Jewish unions which they organized, and the solid, secure English trade unions! Of course, this ignored the English trade unions' stubborn dedication to 'trade unionism pure and simple', the antithesis of the revolutionary principles which the Jewish socialists laboured to inculcate in the Jewish trade unions.

The two poles of trade unions as revolutionary instruments and of trade unionism for the 'pure and simple' purpose of amelioration, delimit a major theme in the history of trade unionism among Jewish workers, particularly during the generation which ended with the War in 1914. The Jewish trade unions were independent in their beginnings, but looked yearningly to amalgamation with the English trade unions as soon as possible. For the first decades, however, there was no alternative to distinct Jewish unions because of the social and cultural gulf between Jewish and English workers and the separateness of the Jewish sectors in the main immigrant trades of garment and boot and shoe making. During these years of independent existence the most articulate Jewish trade union spokesmen, chiefly socialists, talked of the day when Jewish tailors and English tailors would no longer stand apart. This partially came to pass in the decade before 1914, when techniques once deemed 'Jewish' spread beyond the Jewish workshops, and the Jewish immigrant workers' isolation from the main body diminished, because of their increased use of English. The economic and cultural factors which had discouraged amalgamation thus began to stimulate it. Yet when amalgamation became a tangible prospect some shied at it—in fact, the socialist ideologists, who now feared that all chance of Jewish socialist trade unionism would be submerged. But their voices hardly counted. The gradual dissolution of the separate Jewish economy meant *pari passu* the end of independent Jewish trade unionism, although Yiddish-speaking union locals were preserved for reasons of convenience, and independent Jewish unions survived in necessarily separate Jewish trades such as printing and baking.

The story of Jewish socialism is told here in detail although it did not take root in England. The Jewish socialist became an unimportant sectarian among his fellow-immigrants. But because England was the first centre, she led the way for the great movement which developed in the United States, and in Eastern Europe when political conditions permitted. In England Jewish socialism made its first contact with liberal society and the Jewish industrial workers. Experience and literature from England went back to Russia and on to America. The Jewish socialist and trade union movement in England therefore forms the first chapter in the general history of this movement whose latest developments have taken place in the State of Israel.

THE BEGINNINGS OF SOCIALISM

Sometime in 1875 Aaron Liebermann (1844-1880), a young writer of the Hebrew Enlightenment and formerly a student in Vilna, arrived in London. He had become interested in social problems within Jewry and in conditions of the Jewish working classes, and had been stimulated in these interests by the Russian socialist exile Peter Lavrov (1823-1900). Most of Liebermann's activity as an organizer and agitator began and ended in London in 1876, where he gathered about himself an *Agudat haSozialistim haIvrit* (Hebrew Socialist Society), which lasted for a few months of that year and carried on a programme of private lectures and discussions under his guidance.[3] In the brief duration of this pioneer Society in the Whitechapel slums, two opposing pressures can be discerned. They became clear in the group's reactions when Liebermann proposed that it refrain from meeting on the Ninth of Ab, in deference to the tragic significance of the day in Jewish history. Although Liebermann later declared that socialism was his religion, he also believed that a Hebrew Socialist Society's role was to remain within Jewry while leading the Jewish workers toward socialism, and to recognize the Jews' distinct character as a people. Liebermann's opposition held other views. It would have met on the fast day, regarding it as of no significance to a group of socialists who happened to be Jews. The latter viewpoint, which was dominant in the early years of the Jewish socialist movement, showed no special concern for the distinct character of the Jewish group, and desired to educate the Jews separately only until they could be merged into the common struggle of the working class in their several countries. Education and agitation would be in Yiddish only so long as it was the language of most of the Jewish workers; they saw no point in Liebermann's Hebrew socialist journal *HaEmet* in a language which few Jewish workers readily understood. These rival tendencies—a Jewish socialist movement versus a socialist mission among the Jews—had no opportunity to split because the Hebrew Socialist Society did not last long enough. Yet before its demise, it indicated the alternatives which faced every subsequent socialist movement among the Jews.

[3]Liebermann and his group have attracted much attention of scholars and later Jewish socialists. The basic sources are E. Tcherikover, 'Der Onhayb fun der Yiddisher Sotsialistisher Bavegung (Liebermann's Tekufeh)' (The Beginning of Socialism among the Jews (Liebermann's Period)), *YIVO Historishe Shriftn*, I. Vilna, 1929, cols. 468–594, which prints the minutes of the Hebrew Socialist Society and the call to its public meeting; translated into Hebrew (without the sources) in *Yehudim be 'Itot Mahpekhah*, (Jews in Revolutionary Periods), Tel Aviv, 1958, pp. 255–306, K. Marmor, ed., *Aaron Liebermann's Brief* (Aaron Liebermann's Correspondence), N.Y., 1951, has his letters in their original languages and Yiddish translation, with helpful notes; Z. Karl, ed., *HaEmet*, Tel Aviv, 1942, is a facsimile reprint with introduction and notes. N. M. Gelber, *Aus Zwei Jahrhunderten*, Vienna and Leipzig, 1924, pp. 185–192, esp. p. 190. (I had access to the original numbers by kind permission of Mr A. R. Rollin, London.) A hitherto unnoticed memoir is by 'K. Sh. H.' 'Kapitlekh fun der Arbayter Geshikhte,' (Chapters of Labour History), *Arbeiter Freind*, XI, 19, 26, 27, 29 (February 19, April 3, 10, 24, 1896). Peter Elman, 'The Beginnings of the Jewish Trade Union Movement in England', *Transactions of the Jewish Historical Society of England*, XVII (1951–52), pp. 53–62.

The little group started its agitation among the Jewish workers in the East End with a well-attended meeting in a hall close to the hovels of Spitalfields, on August 26, 1876. The first speakers were well received when they graphically described the lot of the Jewish worker and urged their hearers to organize. However, Liebermann's attack on the Jewish communal authorities for their stiff marriage fee of £3 provoked an interruption from a Jewish minister and the meeting broke up, like so many later ones, in quarrel and confusion.[4] At a second meeting, which ended more peacefully, the organization of a Jewish labour union was announced. It seems to have met together with the parent group, and expired with it at the close of that year.

The short-lived agitation was probably unintelligible to the Jewish community, whose journal was probably *bona fide* in stigmatizing the Hebrew Socialist Society as a 'missionary trick' to lure the Jewish poor away from Judaism.[5] However, once the communal leadership realized that socialism was really being propagated among the East End Jews, Hirsch Dainow (1833–1877), a recently arrived Maggid of some note,[6] was set to work to combat it. Dainow's task was brief, for Liebermann quit London at the end of 1876, and his Society disappeared. Some members scattered to the Provinces, others remained in London, and a few returned to the Russian revolutionary movement. Liebermann himself reappeared briefly in London in 1879, and then went on to America, where he committed suicide the following year in Syracuse, New York.

The minute, seemingly insignificant activities of Aaron

[4]This attack had some effect. The United Synagogue of London in the following year made it possible to marry in certain East End synagogues for 10s 6d, with complete remission of fees where necessary. It claimed that 'the above regulations have been adopted, in order that, as a matter of right, and without any petition, facilities may be placed within the reach of everyone desiring to marry . . . in districts immediately contiguous to the dwellings of the poor.' United Synagogue, Executive, *Minutes*, July 16, 1877.

[5]*JC*, June 23, 1876 ('Another Conversionist Trick'); September 8, 1876 ('A Warning').

[6]Zvi Hirsch Dainow (1833–1877), the Maggid of Slutsk, was well known as a preacher of the Jewish Enlightenment in Russia. He settled in London in 1876 after having been hounded out of Russia by his opponents. By the end of that year he was able to deliver an English speech. See *Jewish Encyclopedia, s.v.* Dainow, Zvi Hirsch; *Address Delivered by the Russian Maggid (The Rev. H. Dainow), at a General Meeting of the Maggid Society . . . December 30, 1876.* London, Wertheimer, Lea & Co., 1877; information from his descendants.

Liebermann's group in Victorian London were pregnant for the future. The Society was sufficiently aware of its historic significance to have left a careful protocol of all its discussions. They were the first Jewish socialist society, held the first Jewish labour meeting, published the first Jewish socialist periodical, and organized the first Jewish labour union of which there is record.[7]

Seven lean years followed Liebermann's rise and fall. When Morris Winchevsky (1856–1930)[8] came to London in 1879, he found no trace of Liebermann's work. Young Winchevsky was a talented *litterateur* with a Jewish background much like Liebermann's, and had already won some recognition as a Hebrew writer and as editor of the mildly socialist Hebrew periodical in Königsberg, *'Asefat Hakhamim* (Assembly of the Wise). Alone among the Jewish socialists, he had 'clean' and secure employment in the Seligman bank in the City, and resorted to several pseudonyms (of which 'Winchevsky' was one) in order to keep employment and agitation distinct. With all his pseudonyms and anonymous writing, the fluency and homely appeal of Winchevsky's style make his work easily recognizable, and show how well charm and irony served as propaganda for socialism. After five years' residence in England, Winchevsky and his friend E. W. Rabbinowitz (1853–1932) together published the first Yiddish socialist newspaper on July 25, 1884. The name of the new journal was *The Polish Yidel* (The Little Polish Jew), which was changed to *Die Tsukunft* (The Future), after sixteen weekly issues.[9] Winchevsky's intention in picking the first title was to emphasize the claims of the proletarian Polish Jew in England against the snobbery of the wealthy Jewish natives. The first issue humorously chided the

---

[7]There was one, and perhaps a second, earlier union. A certain Louis Smith, a refugee Paris Communard, organized a short-lived tailors' union in London in 1872 or 1874. Isaac Stone in *The Polish Yidel*, I, 3 (August 8, 1884); E. Tscherikover, ed., *op. cit.*, pp. 87–88; Z. Szajkowski, 'Yidn un die Parizer Komuneh' (Jews and the Paris Commune), in E. Tscherikover, ed., *Yidn in Frankraykh*: *Shtudyes un Materialn* (Jews in France: Studies and Materials), 2 vols., N.Y., 1942, II, p. 144. A Jewish tailors' union in Leeds possessed the banner of its predecessor, inscribed 'Founded in 1875.' *Arbeiter Freind*, V, 12 (March 21, 1890).

[8]His given name was Benzion Novochovitz, and a later American pseudonym was Leopold Benedict. 'Ben Netz' was his most frequent pseudonym in England. His memoirs (cited in Note 1) are an important source for early Jewish socialism, covering his life in detail before he came to America.

[9]M. Winchevsky, *op. cit.*, pp. 131–35.

reader for supposedly doubting that it would last longer than other Yiddish papers. In approaching socialism it was cautious:

We treat the Jew . . . as a man, as a Jew, and as a worker. . . . We wish to speak . . . about everything which concerns labour and the labouring man, because we have no hopes that our rich brethren will read *The Polish Yidel*, though we can give them a handshake, since cheques of £100 and £150 will not, God forbid, be returned (you understand, in order not to humiliate them). . . .[10]

It proposed to be a teacher of those who knew only Yiddish, a guide for 'greeners', and a source of news, while it renounced interest in religious matters or in personalities.

The Polish Yidel kept an appearance of bland neutrality even when it distinguished between four types of Jews. The 'indifferent' care only about themselves: 'assimilationists' consider Jewish separateness to be the root of Jewish troubles; 'nationalists' blame the Jews' homelessness for their sufferings; 'socialists' consider the Jewish problem to be part of the general social problem, not one apart. As to the editor, he could only 'consider it impossible . . . to decide which of the preceding four classes is right. . . .'[11] The editor of *The Polish Yidel* was a bit coy in his indecisiveness; it is clearly murder, he says elsewhere, when man kills man, but there is no objection when 10,000 die because Bismarck and Napoleon III quarrel over a piece of territory. Again, the hungry man who steals bread is jailed for theft, but one man who cheats 10,000 on the stock exchange is a businessman above reproach.[12] As a Jew, Winchevsky showed strong concern over the then rising tide of anti-Semitism. While he admitted that the Jews had freedom and opportunity in England, he also pointed to the dislike of the Jews in the East End and to the difficulty encountered by a Jew who would rent a house there. The conclusion was irrational: 'Jews, look about while there is yet time! A pogrom in Brick Lane at the crossroads of Commercial Road can be more terrible, bloodier than a pogrom in Balta. . . .' His vague counsel was to follow the ancient Hebrew adage, 'where there are no men try to be a man'.[13] Winchevsky interpreted racial

[10] *The Polish Yidel*, I, 1 (July 25, 1884).
[11] *Die Tsukunft*, I, 17 (November 14, 1884).
[12] *The Polish Yidel*, I, 4 (August 15, 1884).
[13] *The Polish Yidel*, I, 11 (October 3, 1884).

anti-Semitism in England economically: increasing population, shrinking markets, rising costs of Government. 'Charlatans' exploit these conditions by blaming everything on Jewish capitalists; they ignored or minimized the number of poor Jews, the better to pick on the world's eternal 'stepchild'. Turning to the Jews themselves, *The Polish Yidel* pointed to faults which increased their vulnerability to anti-Semitic attacks—a supposed special English dislike of foreigners, the annoyance of a trading nation with Jewish immigrant traders, and the misdeeds by individual Jews on the stock exchange, in obscene publishing, commercial scandal and gambling, and as employers of sweated labour.[14]

The press which published *The Polish Yidel* also produced the first specimens of a later torrent of socialist pamphleteering in Yiddish, Winchevsky's *Yehi Or* (Let There be Light) and Isaac Stone's *An Historical Sketch of a London Tailor*.[15] Stone's *Sketch* is the fictitious account of a London tailor's life as told by one who lies in rags and filth upon his deathbed. After unhappy vicissitudes in the Old Country, his fortunes led him to a sweatshop in London, where within ten years he alternately worked and starved to death. This testament and autobiography is a bequest to posterity. The immigrant tailor is exhorted to avoid the unfortunate's fate and awake from his slumbers:

And you, little Jew, you sleep silent
You are content with the blows everyone deals you
Your body freely given to be handled at will
Like a sin offering which bears all sins upon itself . . .
Your labour power must be your saviour
That the world and its riches may be yours.

The writer hates the sweating employer for the long hours of work, for cheating the 'greener' of his wages, for his arrogant demeanour, and hates London because it is the proper city for

---

[14]*The Polish Yidel*, I, 12 (October 10, 1884).

[15]Both pamphlets are excessively rare. I could find no copy of the London, 1884, edition of *Yehi Or*, and used its second edition, Newark, N. J., 1890. Isaac Stone's pamphlet may be partially autobiographical, and its author was a member of Liebermann's group. The YIVO Archive possesses a handwritten copy of a possibly unique copy in the Jewish National and University Library, Jerusalem, which was kindly made available to me. On Stone, see E. Tcherikover, ed., ... *Arbayter Bavegung*, II., p. 119.

'those who want their allotted span to be ended in two [years] by falling into the tailors' hands'. Finally, the ethical will:

I know that no one can help you but yourselves . . . all you Jewish workers must unite in a society, and as soon as you are united your help will then surely come . . . through your unity you will improve your bitter lot, so that you will live happier in this world, to bequeath a better future to your children. The End.'

This highly interesting work is written in popular literary Yiddish with abundant apt Hebrew puns and quotations in a bitter, ironic tone which characterizes this pioneer Yiddish journalist and pamphleteer. Basically, this is not socialism but rather a *cri de coeur* which points the way.

Winchevsky's pamphlet, which he wrote in Königsberg before coming to England, is quite different from Stone's. As befits a product of the Hebraic Enlightenment, his socialist credo is set out in thirteen Maimonidean articles, each beginning 'I believe with complete faith'!

Almost a year after the first appearance of *The Polish Yidel*, a gathering circle of ardent spirits in London decided that the time had come to issue an openly socialist newspaper in Yiddish. Winchevsky arrived at the same conclusion because he felt that *The Polish Yidel-Tsukunft* had gone as far as it could, and that the time had come to abandon pretence. He and his partner Rabbinowitz were drifting apart because the latter had developed Palestinophile sympathies and insisted on printing religious notices in the interests of business.[16] The new product was the monthly *Arbeiter Freind* (Worker's Friend). In the first issue, it set forth its programme declaring that it was published by revolutionary socialists

. . . in order to spread true socialism among Jewish workers. . . . We wish, in a word, to change entirely the present order of tyranny

---

[16]*Die Tsukunft* continued publication probably until No. 227, January 4, 1889. It left socialism and drew closer to Jewish communal affairs, and was interested in the colonization of Palestine. It termed the socialists the 'dregs' of the population and a cause of anti-Semitism. (III, 17 October 29, 1886). Rabbinowitz was consoled upon his failure by his former partner: 'Ah . . . you are a very little man with a very little head.' (*Arbeiter Freind*, IV, 6, February 8, 1889). See M. Winchevsky, *op. cit.*, II, pp. 188–93. On Rabbinowitz, see A. Druyanov, *Ketabim leToledot Hibbat Zion* (Documents on the History of the Lovers of Zion), III, Tel Aviv, 1932, col. 556 n., and the autobiographic 'Sefer Zikkaron 5640–5650,' '*Iyyim*, I (1928), pp. 66–74.

and injustice ... it must ... give way to a new and just society, which gives us and teaches us socialism. . . . But for socialism to be able to do all this, the workers must unite and organize themselves . . . in general, all questions which are connected with socialism the *Arbeiter Freind* will try to explain more clearly and significantly . . . it will try to take in all worthwhile statements concerning social questions, even if these statements do not agree with ours . . . Social-democrats, collectivists, communists, anarchists, and all men, if they but recognize the foundations, the principles of socialism, are socialists, and belong to one party, the great workers' party. . . .[17]

The appeal to readers to ponder its message 'earnestly and well' must have put both confirmed and neophyte socialists to the test, for early issues of the *Arbeiter Freind* were warmed-over history and theory, written mostly by Philip Kranz[18] in the graceless style quoted above. His Yiddish was imperfect and he had to explain to his readers that subjects as weighty as those treated in the new newspaper were not easily popularized. But with Winchevsky a regular contributor, matters improved considerably and the *Arbeiter Freind* became readable indeed. As its cause began to flourish, it changed from a monthly to a weekly, and was able to employ as assistant editor Benjamin Feigenbaum (1860–1932), a fiery and prolific writer and orator.[19]

THE MAKING OF THE
EARLY JEWISH SOCIALIST MOVEMENT

The Jewish socialist revolutionaries started off in united opposition to the existing social order, to religion in general and to Judaism particularly, and to the organized Jewish

[17]Philip Kranz (1858–1922), born Jacob Rombro, was one of the first Jewish Social-Democrats, and was trained in Yiddish writing by Winchevsky. Although not a fluent writer, he had a long career in England and, from 1890, in America as a writer, agitator, editor of the *Arbeiter Freind*, and of the *Arbeiter Tseitung* in New York. Zalman Reisen, *Leksikon fun der Yudisher Literatur un Presse* (Lexicon of the Yiddish Literature and Press), Warsaw, 1914, *s.v.* Kranz, Philip.

[18]*Arbeiter Freind*, I, 1 (July 15, 1885).

[19]Benjamin Feigenbaum, (1860–1932) reputedly a scion of an Hasidic dynasty, came to London via journalism and dock labour in Antwerp. For some three years he was the Socialists' leading orator and their most impassioned writer. When the *Arbeiter Freind* could not support him, unsuccessful attempts were made to find other employment for him. Feigenbaum joined Kranz in America. S. Cohen in *Arbeiter Freind*, VI, 28 (July 10, 1891); Zalman Reisen, *op. cit., s.v.* Feigenbaum, Benjamin.

community. When the positive doctrines of their early years are examined, one finds much less cohesiveness. Not being Marxists, if only because Marxism was just becoming well known in the 1880's, the Jewish revolutionists could not be comforted by the doctrine that inherent contradictions in the capitalist order would inevitably bring it to destruction. The main influence appears to have been Peter Lavrov (1823–1900), who had encouraged Liebermann and whom Winchevsky regarded as his spiritual father. From Ricardo via Ferdinand Lassalle (1825–1864) they fashioned a distorted 'iron law of wages' which laid down that rises in wages which trade unions might secure were always balanced by equal rises in the cost of living, so that conventional trade unionism was ultimately futile. The Jewish revolutionists therefore argued that their unions must be consecrated to socialist agitation and revolutionary strikes, to arouse the workers' class consciousness. The stormy anarchist Johann Most (1846–1906), enemy of the state and parliamentarism, helped to direct the anti-political trend which the *Arbeiter Freind* often exhibited. The physical channel by which most of these doctrines passed into the Berner Street circle was the famous Communist International Workingmen's Club in Tottenham Court Road, the centre for socialist refugees from 1848 onwards.[20] True to its programme, the *Arbeiter Freind* published pieces from every socialist point of view during these formative years of Jewish socialist thought. The Paris Commune, the Haymarket victims, and Siberian exiles were all fittingly memorialized, in addition to occasional instances of police harassment of English socialists. Despite close relations with the Socialist League in the early years (see below), it is striking that while German, Russian, French, and even Spanish and Italian contributions figure prominently in the pages of the *Arbeiter Freind*, there is hardly any instance of similar attention to an English writer. From the first, there was a cleavage between socialist and anarchist ideologies, which within a few years became two competing factions. Soon after, the remaining socialists also differentiated among themselves between Social Democrats and Social Revolutionaries;

all this parallels the evolution of contemporary socialism. By the middle 1890's, the Jewish socialists in England had lost the sense of heading a mass movement, and had time to spare for such finer matters.

The centre of Jewish socialism was its club, which was both a lounge and a beehive of socialist education and propaganda. To the distress of the earnest leaders, conviviality at socialist clubs attracted some who cared nothing for socialism, and irritated socialists maintained that food, drink, and attendant distractions were better left to the 'pub' and coffee house.[21] Taught by experience, London Jewish socialists admonished a newly opened Manchester club with their 'warmest wish that you will not satisfy yourselves with entertaining yourselves in your clubroom.'[22] (This appeal to socialist zeal met with small success, for the group in Manchester was reported at low ebb soon after).[23] The centre of the young movement was a house at 40, Berner Street in the East End, which was the home of the International Workingmen's Educational Club from 1885 to 1892. Besides the club proper, the *Arbeiter Freind* and pamphlet literature were produced from this address, and committees and causes used the premises as headquarters. A Jewish socialist was known in popular parlance as a 'Berner-Streeter.'[24]

One facet of the Jewish socialists' activities caused hard feelings in the Jewish community. Having cast off the Jewish religion on their road to socialist faith, they were convinced that the chains of religion must be struck off in order to create a truly socialist outlook. As East European Judaism was considered especially incompatible with modern enlightenment, the Jewish socialist eagerly undertook to emancipate the Jews from religion by teaching such things as science and sociology, which the immigrants could learn nowhere else because their

[21]N. B. to *Die Tsukunft*, I, 22 (December 19, 1884); *idem*, I, 23 (December 26, 1884).
[22]Letter, B. Feigenbaum to 'Dear Brethren and Friends' (Yiddish), n.d., postmarked February 8, 1889. By kind permission of Mr A. R. Rollin, London. W. W. to *Arbeiter Freind*, III, 52 (December 28, 1888).
[23]Lewis Diemschitz in *Arbeiter Freind*, IV, 51 (December 20, 1889).
[24]S. Freeman in *Arbeiter Freind*, XX, 1 (March 16, 1906). Another contemporary account is M. Baranoff in *Die Fraye Velt*, II, 5 (November, 1892), pp. 99-102; *Die Tsukunft*, I, 35 (March 27, 1885).

language was Yiddish. One experienced socialist observed that English socialism did not have to be so anti-religious because religion in England did not throttle the Englishman as Judaism did the Jew. It seemed useless to have religious Jews in socialist clubs because such attempts invariably exploded with the lighting of the first cigarette on the Sabbath.[25]

The socialists passionately attacked Judaism by means of ridicule, satire, and abuse. Typical are some *Arbeiter Freind* improvements in the Jewish prayers: the Day of Atonement's proclamation that 'Repentance, Prayer, and Charity avert the Evil Decree' was persiflaged to 'Bravery, Rebellion, and Force . . . etc.' and a doxology that 'the Lord reigns . . . has reigned . . . will reign forever' became 'Mammon reigns . . . has reigned . . . will reign BUT NOT forever.'[26] The Lamentations read on the Ninth of Ab were reproduced as *Lamentations for the Worker* upon his sorrowful lot, and the Feast of Tabernacles' historical booths in the desert were judged a trivial inconvenience compared to the hovels where dwelled descendants of the Children of Israel in England. The Seder of Passover was done over by Benjamin Feigenbaum, the author of most of these works and the most vociferous anti-religionist.[27] These quite clever performances could be read by and perhaps amuse the Jewish community, but the annual dinner-ball on the Day of Atonement from 1888, which publicly derided the holiest day of Judaism, gave mortal and enduring offence. Still, the *Arbeiter Freind* claimed 'without apologies' that nobody had been ridiculed.[28]

The disparagement of God, however, was more readily focused on such earthly representatives as the Hobebey Zion (proto-Zionist colonizers in Palestine), Delegate Chief Rabbi

[25]K. Lieberman in *Die Fraye Velt*, II, 3 (July, 1892) p. 71.
[26]*Arbeiter Freind*, III, 37 (September 14, 1888).
[27]*Seder Haggadah Shel Pesah* ('al Pi Nusah Hadash) (A New Version of the Passover Haggada), London, Worker's Friend Printing Office, c. 1888. It was also printed, as were many other socialist pamphlets, with a spurious 'Vilna, Widow and Brothers Romm' imprint, the better to deceive the Russian censorship. For the Sukkot homily, see *Arbeiter Freind*, III, 38 (September 21, 1888) Similar liturgical satires: *Arbeiter Freind*, III, 36 and 37 (September 7 and 14, 1888), and a Christmas sermon in *Arbeiter Freind*, III (December 28, 1888).
[28]*Arbeiter Freind*, III, 34, 35, 38 (August 24, 31, September 21, 1888); no source was found to substantiate Burgin, *op. cit.*, pp. 63–64, that a riot occurred.

H

Hermann Adler, and Sir Samuel Montagu. An early issue set the pattern for its generation with a discussion of Jewish prospects in Palestine

> from the pure socialist viewpoint. . . . We may say again that no colonization, no land of one's own and no independent Government will help the Jewish nation. Jewish happiness will come with the happiness of all unhappy workers, and Jewish emancipation must come with the general emancipation of humanity. . . .

It explained the embarrassing fact that Gentile worker attacked Jewish worker during anti-Semitic outbreaks as occurring because the attackers were blinded to the truth by their exploiters.[29] This was cosmopolitanism of 1886. But other, more distinctly Jewish views, were expressed: 'You must be a Jew and have no shame for it; you must be a bit of a nationalist— naturally not a kugel [pudding] patriot or a Palestine patriot. You must consider yourself equal with all socialists who preach the international idea, remaining national (not nationalist).' Therefore, Jewish socialist clubs and trade unions ought not to dub themselves 'international', since only Jews are members. The author, a certain K. Lieberman, was in a minority in 1892, but looked forward to the adoption of a national ideology by Jewish socialism about fifteen years later.

Sir Samuel Montagu was especially rank to the Jewish socialists. He was M.P. for the East End, and active in its affairs as financial patron of the Jewish Working Men's Club and the Federation of Synagogues, as sponsor of conservative trade unions, and as a labour arbitrator. Such rivalry for the attention of the Jewish public infuriated the young revolutionists, especially because Montagu was widely known for his Jewish orthodoxy and Gladstonian Liberalism. Montagu probably had a hand in the sudden quitting of the socialist journal's two printers and their departure for America forthwith. When after three months the newspaper succeeded in appearing again, upon its own printing press, it charged that Montagu and Frederic Mocatta had intimidated the printers by threatening to deprive them of their business, and had thus also succeeded in deterring other printers from accepting

---

[29] *Arbeiter Freind*, I, 7 (January 15, 1886). A later attack: *Die Fraye Velt*, II, 2 (February, 1892).

socialist business.[30] Montagu regularly took the field against the socialists and they replied lavishly in kind.

Hermann Adler was another suitable target for anti-religious propaganda, for his ecclesiastical personage attracted little sympathy in the East End. The first clash arose from his chilly answer to an appeal that he join the Anglican and Catholic Primates in speaking out against the sweating conditions which were described in Burnett's reports[31] and in testimony before the House of Lords Sweating Commission. When Adler pronounced the Burnett reports exaggerated, the *Arbeiter Freind* adjudged him a tool of sweatshop employers and thenceforward erected him as a chief target.[32] The negative impression was enhanced when Adler replied to an appeal by defeated Jewish strikers in Leeds to help them recover their jobs, by consenting to do so only if the masters would also invite him.[33] The anti-Adler campaign took such forms as the printing of a 'sermon' in which the Delegate Chief Rabbi denounced his rich friends, renounced the rabbinate, and joined the true friends of humanity at the Berner Street Club.[34]

The climactic event of the anti-religious activities was a 'synagogue parade' to the Great Synagogue early in 1889, in emulation of the 'church parades' of the time.[35] Adler responded to a request for an appropriate sermon by delivering an earlier one on sweating which offered cold comfort. The religious head of the Jewish community admitted that sweating was bad, but averred that hunger was worse; he said that if sweating meant overwork, then he and many of his wealthy congre-

[30]*Arbeiter Freind*, II, 26 (May 6, 1887); 27, 28 (August 5, 12, 1887). On alleged printers' boycott, *Arbeiter Freind*, IV, 23 (March 29, 1889). The two young printers became prominent Yiddish writers and journalists in America. On Montagu's opposition to the socialists, see *Arbeiter Freind*, III, 48 (November 30, 1888) and Religion chapter, pp. 287–88.

[31]This was the *Report to the Board of Trade on the Sweating System in the East End of London*, written by the Board of Trade's Labour Correspondent, John Burnett. This report, like a parallel one for Leeds (C. 5513, 1888) was influential in arousing public interest.

[32]*Arbeiter Freind*, III, 9–10, 16–17 (March 9, April 27, 1888).

[33]*Arbeiter Freind*, III, 26, 27 (June 29 and July 6, 1888).

[34]*Arbeiter Freind*, III, 43 (October 26, 1888); cf. also III, 28, 47, 49 (July 13, November 23, December 7, 1888); VI, 11 (March 13, 1891).

[35]The sources for the synagogue procession are the *Arbeiter Freind*, in detail with obvious bias, weekly from January 25, 1889 (IV, 4) to April 4, 1889 (IV, 14). The *JC* (March 22, 1889) eye-witness account is meticulous and hostile. See also *The Commonweal*, V. No. 167 (March 23, 1889), p. 93.

gants were equally victims with the East End immigrants. He attacked proposed eight-hour day legislation on individualist grounds: '. . . there was little that the State could do . . . to improve the lot of the working classes. . . .' While workers should organize, they should beware of the socialist agitators 'who work up their worst passions'. The Delegate Chief Rabbi concluded with a reminder to his hearers of the benevolence of the rich Jews and a hint not to offend them, besides the characteristic contemporary reminder to avoid improvident marriages.[36]

On Saturday, March 16, 1889, there took place 'a scene . . . quite unparalleled in the history of Jews in London'. The 300–400 (*Jewish Chronicle*) or 2,000–3,000 (*Arbeiter Freind*) marchers behind a German band aroused 'a reception of a mixed character . . . for the most part . . . jeers . . . and the deep expressions of dissatisfaction'. The paraders were blocked at the Great Synagogue by fifty policemen under the Superintendent and Chief Inspector of London police, and the procession counter-marched to Mile End Waste for the customary speeches and resolutions.

The outraged *Jewish Chronicle* read the leaders of the affair out of Jewry. 'It is clearly idle to talk of these persons as Jews . . . it becomes our duty to declare that they are not Jews. . . .' That evening the police visited the Berner Street Club and in the ensuing mêlée several socialists were slightly injured and one received a three months' sentence. It does not appear that any policemen were physically harmed.[37]

The synagogue procession misfired because the Jewish workers, who would follow socialists leadership in a strike, would not join an anti-religious demonstration. Thenceforward the socialists, though not the anarchists, confined themselves to more subdued educational activities and refrained from public demonstration. They did celebrate 'free marriages' to show how one could enter matrimony without

[36] *JC*, February 22, 1889.
[37] *The Commonweal*, V, Nos. 173, 175 (May 4, 18, 1889), pp. 142, 158. There was indignation on the left concerning the case; even the unfriendly Social Democratic Federation called a protest meeting. See *idem*, V, Nos. 176, 179 (May 25, June 15, 1889), pp. 167, 191. There was a similar case earlier, perhaps arising from the Pall Mall riots: *idem*, II, No. 34 (October 4, 1886), p. 183.

benefit of religious ceremony, and ridiculed 'foolish girls' who troubled with nonsensical religious forms to the disregard of the essentials of 'honour, faithfulness, and full-hearted love'.[38]

THE TRADE UNION MOVEMENT

Although the socialists' greatest efforts were spent in promoting trade unionism, trade unions were not organized by them alone, but also by upper class individuals with humanitarian inclinations, and independently by the workers themselves. Besides, the previous generation of Jewish workers, mainly of Dutch extraction, had founded its own network of friendly societies upon the model of conservative English trade unionism of the 1850's and 1860's. As material circumstances improved, these bodies tended to become associations of employers and lost whatever resemblance to trade unionism they possessed. Trade unionism on the model of a friendly society was the sort envisioned by upper-class supporters and sponsors. When Frederic D. Mocatta (1829–1905), a scholarly bullion merchant and a ranking communal worthy, addressed Jewish tailoresses he observed that they ought not to have settled in England and 'should resign themselves to small remuneration. . . .' Their organization would be social and vaguely 'protective' in nature. For its part, the *Jewish Chronicle* prodded the Jewish Board of Guardians to unionize the Jewish tailors, although it did not desire that the Board would 'try to alter those existing relations between supply and demand which are really at the root of the economic evils from which the East End tailors are suffering.'[39] The odd reliance upon such a body as the Guardians to organize the Jewish workers arose from the renewed desire to enforce factory legislation in the sweatshops, where shocking conditions had just been exposed to public gaze. In 1886, Sir Samuel Montagu assumed the role of founder and Maecenas of the Jewish Tailors' Machinists Society. The amorphous membership, guided by the millionaire and M.P., resolved to

[38]*Arbeiter Freind*, IV, 47 (November 23, 1889). T. Eyges, *op. cit.*, n.p., gives further details of anti-religious activity in the 1890's; 'Jewish Labour News', *JC*, October 7, 1904.

[39]*JC*, April 25, May 2, 1884. For an earlier attempt, see *JC*, December 9, 1881.

ask for a twelve hour day with time for lunch and tea, while also accepting its founder's advice not to ask for dinner time also. It further resolved to accomplish all of this without striking.[40] Nothing came of all these philanthropic approaches because they were too tepid and timid, and it was unclear what such unions could really do. They were not to strike; they had no funds to disburse as benefits; they had no indigenous leadership; and they depended upon wealthy patrons.

Perhaps the first recorded strike by Jewish industrial workers took place spontaneously in Leeds in May, 1885, when the workers met in a local synagogue to demand a reduction of one hour from the usual 13–14 hour day, and won it by a one week stoppage of work. Long afterwards, one of its leaders retrospectively

judged the strike merely as a protest against hard times; a sort of cry of despair! . . . We the machiners were the aristocrats. We did not strike to gain anything for ourselves. We demanded only that the basters and machinists [sic; pressers?] should work the same hours as the machiners; and after a fortnight of hardship we won (the public knew nothing about us, nor did the British unions). The masters sent agents to London for scabs, but we awaited them at the Ry. station took the arrivals to our meeting place, gave them a brotherly talk, and paid them for their tickets back to London. The strike was settled at a meeting of masters and men at the Belgrave Street Synagogue.

Old Joseph Finn (c. 1860–1946) recalled that he 'left England in January, 1886, for the U.S. as after the strike of 1885 the employers declared a boycott against me', and stayed there for some years.[41]

The early leadership of Jewish trade unionism came mainly from the socialists, even though leaders and led frequently had different goals. The worker wanted his union to give him collective strength, a higher standard of living, and an easier working life, even if it could not do much about the curse

[40]W(illiam) W(ess), in *Die Tsukunft*, II, 36 (March 12, 1886); *JC*, April 9, 1886.
[41]J. Finn in *Die Tsukunft*, I, 45 (May 2, 1885). Finn's recollections are from a letter written by him in 1943 to Mr A. R. Rollin, London, by whose kind permission I consulted it. Finn was a nephew of the Hebrew writer and scholar Samuel Joseph Finn (1819–1896).

of seasonal work. The socialist aspired to make of the Jewish worker a disciplined, class-conscious member of a revolutionary vanguard. To be sure, these two aims did not seem as contradictory in the 1880's as they later appeared, for there was a widespread conviction that revolution was near. Socialism and the revolutionary spirit made rapid strides in the 1880's in Germany, Austria, Russia, America. Even the stolid English workers were so stirred by the socialist current that the abandoned dock labourers carried on a strike to glorious victory. The revolutionary horizon shone in the late 1880's, and the Jewish socialists and trade unionists could look with self-gratification upon a rapid evolution in their own Jewish quarter from helpless apathy to a movement in full cry. Yet two or three years later they admitted their defeat and realized that they had deluded themselves. What had happened?

As trade unionists, the Jews were not inherently better or poorer than other workers. The reasons for the strength and weakness of trade unionism among immigrant Jewish workmen are to be found in the nature of their trades. The Jewish labour force was constantly shifting, for new immigrants were always arriving while others were leaving for America. Among the volatile clothing and boot and shoe workshops in London workshops were constantly opening and closing; slack seasons were periods of demoralization which sapped the ability of workers to maintain collective strength. Skilled workmen moved in and out of entrepreneurship, leaving the master-worker relation rather unsteady since either side could envision itself in the other's position. Thus, neither psychology nor economics encouraged trade unionism in the principal immigrant trades. Where there were larger and stabler producers, as in Leeds, Jewish trade unions also became effective instruments.

The multiplicity of London Jewish trade unions reveals much. An incomplete enumeration found thirteen in 1896, while a fuller survey in 1902 counted thirty-two unions, of which only four or five had been in existence six years earlier.[42] Many

[42]*Jewish Year Book*, I, London, 1896, pp. 58–59; Georg Halpern, *Der judischen Arbeiter in London*, Berlin, 1903, pp. 66–68. Other union statistics in *JC*, July 19, 1895. At least one union's books were 'very roughly kept,' *JC*, January 23, 1903, reporting as of July 10, 1891.

of these thirty-two Jewish trade unions were the outcome of renamings and fusions of other unions, particularly in the tailoring trade. Unions showed more stability in smaller trades or in skilled branches of larger trades, such as baking, butchering, Hebrew printing, and mantle-making. Few London unions ever maintained a steady membership of 300; trade unionism of such dimensions could accomplish nothing for 'green' and semi-skilled workers but call periodic and ultimately fruitless strikes. Leadership was also a problem; few unions could afford paid officers, and without a staff no organization was likely to prosper. An occasional aggravation was the presence of individuals who exploited opportunities to abscond with the treasury. The lack of leadership was made more acute by the flow of many promising leaders to America.

The report of the Hebrew Cabinet Makers' Union for the first ten months of its existence in 1887 illustrates some of these points.[43] Although its thirty charter members had grown to 120, the number of dues-paying members dropped to twenty, for the majority would pay only when benefits were actually being disbursed. In the absence of strikes, its income was £16 6s 6d, and expenses were limited to £2 17s 6d; the organizer was unpaid and served during or after working hours. The Hebrew Cabinet Makers did not long endure, and its treasury never accumulated enough to pay benefits, since its members insisted on having them before they would contribute any of their sweated pennies. On the other hand, the United Capmakers' Society supplies a specimen of a more flourishing union.[44] In the period from September 12, 1892 to October 28, 1893, its total income was £76 6s 7½d. Of this total, £40 10s 6d was realized from members' contributions, and the remainder came in equal proportions from a benefit in aid of their strike, entrance fees, and public collections for that strike. Of the expenditure, £40 17s 3d went for the strike (but only £1 13s 2½d was paid out as aid to members), and there were smaller items for subscriptions to newspapers and 'causes', to send a delegate to the Zurich Socialist Congress,

[43]*Arbeiter Freind*, II, 39 (October 28, 1887). This union followed a moderate policy. *Arbeiter Freind*, II, 24 (April 22, 1887).
[44]*Arbeiter Freind*, VIII, 48 (December 1, 1893).

and for general overhead. The Capmakers were evidently at their largest during their strike for, taking the usual 6d as entrance fee, over 300 persons paid their way into this union—a testimony to the drawing power of a successful strike. The guiding spirit of the United Capmakers' Society was the anarchist S. Yanovsky (1864–1939), who led it as a 'fighting' union, i.e. a union unencumbered by benefits, and in existence for the purpose of war on the employers.

While Jewish trade unionism in London was spasmodic, Leeds stands forth as the example of successful organization. As early as 1887, we hear of two strong garment unions. A tailors' union of 545 and a machinists' union of 232 were said to work together, and so dominated the local labour market that 'if the master will not submit, he remains without workers'.[45] Although weakened by a strike expense of £255 in that year and defeated in a general strike in the following year, they held together without a break. Thanks to the comparatively well-organized large workshops in Leeds, the Jewish trade union movement had a strength and continuity without parallel elsewhere in the Jewish immigrant communities.

Jewish trade unionism enjoyed less success in Manchester, whose Jewish immigrant trades closely resembled London's, although the Secretary of the local Trades Council praised the 'loyal union men' in the Jewish unions' ranks. At that time, the Manchester Jewish Tailors', Machinists' and Pressers' Trade Union had enrolled 900 of the 1,400 or 1,500 local Jewish tailors.[46]

---

[45]B. L. Rosenberg, Leeds, November 23, 1887, in *Arbeiter Freind*, II, 45 (December 9, 1887), also stated that the Christian workers 'are very friendly'. The Leeds Trade Council invited the Jewish unions to send delegates, although this was hardly an exceptional privilege. On the strength of Jewish unionism in Leeds, see John A. Dyche, 'My Tour in Europe,' *The Ladies Garment Worker*, V, 6 (April, 1914), pp. 1–8; S. P. Dobbs, *The Clothing Workers of Great Britain*, London, 1928, pp. 45–46; *People's Press*, I, 26 (August 30, 1890), p. 10; a contrary view is *Arbeiter Freind*, VI, 43, 44 (December 11, 19, 1891). See below, Note 98.

[46]Manchester *Evening News*, January 28, 1903; *Soziale Praxis*, VI, 4 (October 22, 1896), col. 92. On the earlier strike of 1890 see *The Commonweal*, VI, No. 224 (April 26, 1890), pp. 134–35, and V, Nos. 158, 200 (January 19 and November 9, 1889), pp. 22, 200; *People's Press*, I, 7 (April 19, 1890), p. 9; *Arbeiter Freind*, V, 16, 17, 18 (April 18, 25, May 2, 1890). A cabinet makers' strike: *Arbeiter Freind*, IV, 38 (September 20, 1889).

The main centre, however, was always London, and Jewish trade unionism stood or fell by its success in the tailoring and boot and shoe trades. In the latter trade, a problem which puzzled class-conscious trade unionism was to draw a distinction between masters and men when both were equally wretched victims of machine production. The Jewish Boot Finishers' Society, organized early in 1886, decided to invite masters as well as men to its meetings.[47] When it struck, the target was a wholesale house and its demand was an increase of 1d per pair in the price paid to the master outworker, thus enabling the latter to raise wages. The wholesaler thereupon found other Jewish finishers to take his work, which called forth the lament of the *Tsukunft*—why should Jewish masters and men do scab work which Christians had refused?[48] Such strikes were called from time to time with but slight effect. They culminated in a general assault on all outwork in 1890, by a strike which united the Jewish and Christian sections of the trade.[49] Following its success and the uninterrupted expansion of factory shoe production, outdoor work gradually disappeared and the flow of unskilled 'greeners' into the trade was stemmed.

THE CLIMACTIC YEAR OF 1889

The early Jewish trade union movement reached an emotional climax in the summer of 1889, with an unplanned and unexpected 'strike' by some 10,000 tailors in London.[50] It came about from the concatenation of a few sporadic strikes in the East End, resembling those which had been carried on for several years. At one large capmakers, 154 struck because the firm would not rehire the leaders of an earlier strike. 200 men

[47]A clear account is given in *Reports on the Volume and Effects of Recent Immigration from Eastern Europe into the United Kingdom*, C. 7406, 1894, pp. 67–94. Isaac Stone, the journalist, was secretary and organizer of this union. *Die Tsukunft*, II, 33 (February 19, 1886) ff.
[48]*Idem*, II, 45 (May 21, 1886) f.
[49]The strike manifesto is printed in *People's Press*, I, 7 (April 19, 1890), p. 8. See pp. 78–80.
[50]The main source is the *Arbeiter Freind* for the six weeks commencing August 30, 1889 (IV, 35 was in two issues, the second a strike extra). *The Commonweal* and the *JC* also gave it attention. By the kind permission of Mr A. R. Rollin, I had access to four probably unique strike placards, which practically narrate the course of the strike. They are now in the YIVO Archive, New York.

who struck at a firm of Government contractors were joined
at their meeting by workers from nearby firms in Brick Lane
and Leman Street. From such beginnings went forth a manifesto calling a general strike of 'LONDON TAILORS & SWEATERS
VICTIMS'. Addressing their 'Fellow Workers', the hastily
formed committee capitalized on the sensation being made by
the hearings of the House of Lords Commission on the Sweating
System. 'The Revelations made before the Commission by
Witnesses engaged in the Tailoring Trade are a Disgrace to
a Civilised Country. The Sweaters' Victims had hoped that
this Commission would come to some satisfactory conclusion
as to an alteration in the condition of the Sweated Tailors.'
But the Commission would not meet again for months, so 'we
have decided to take immediate action. . . . We have, therefore,
decided to join in the *General Demand for Increased Comfort
and Shorter Hours of Labour*'. Relying upon the floodtide of
popular anti-sweating sentiment, rather than upon its own
strength, the Committee issued its modest demands:

We Demand:
  1. That the hours be reduced to twelve with an interval of one
hour for dinner and half-hour for tea.
  2. All the meals to be had off the premises.
  3. Government contractors to pay wages at trade union rates.
  4. Government contractors and sweaters not to give work home
at night after working hours.

A postscript expressed an 'appeal to those engaged in the
trade to at once join either of the following Societies', and
enumerated a few among which a selection could be made!
In addition to this broadside, word of the strike was spread by
the *Arbeiter Freind* with a special edition and, no doubt the
most effective, by word of mouth throughout the Jewish district.

The chief leader of the strike was Lewis Lyons,[51] a machinist
who enjoyed the distinction of being a native of England.

[51]Lyons testified persuasively before the House of Lords Commission on the
Sweating System, and later before the Royal Commission on Alien Immigration.
He became a labour representative on the Tailoring Trade Board. Lyons split
with the socialists over his scheme to unite masters and men in opposition to the
wholesale houses. *Arbeiter Freind*, V. 26 (June 27, 1890); *People's Press*, I, 16,
17 (June 21, 28, 1890). See below, p. 129; Rudolf Rocker, *op. cit.*, pp. 228–30;
Herz Burgin, *op. cit.*, pp. 252–54, 259. 'Jewish Labour News', *JC*, October 24,
1902.

Although he had briefly published his own journal called the *Anti-Sweater* and contributed to *The Commonweal*, Lyons was an independent, not trusted by the Jewish socialists. William Wess, a self-effacing printer and anarchist, was secretary of the strike committee. Except for Charles Mowbray, an English anarchist orator, the rest of the strike committee, consisting of rank and file workers, remained in the background. As was customary in those days, the strikers paraded several miles daily to Victoria Park in Hackney, where they held demonstrations.

By mid-September, 120 shops had struck, and some masters submitted by signing the strikers' terms and posting them in their shops. The masters made no unified move until about September 10th, when a reported 300 convened in the Jewish Working Men's Club to establish their own association. They offered to shift from a daily to an hourly wage rate but at a level which would require the men to keep up the old hours in order to maintain the old earnings. Many men who depended upon the daily speeches of Lewis Lyons and the socialists for news of the strike began to drift back to work in the misunderstanding that payment by the hour meant victory. A hurriedly prepared broadside denied this, and claimed that the masters were welshing on an agreement which they had previously accepted: '. . . we found that under the pretence of an alleged dissention amongst the Strikers, the Masters' Committee refused to sign'. Although the committee promptly vindicated its authority among the strikers, '. . . they still insist in their refusal to sign the document and have therefore *broken their pledge* agreed upon at the Conference. We, therefore, declare that *The Strike Still Continues!*'

Whether through confusion or deceit the strike was deadlocked. Meanwhile, substantial aid was coming into the strikers' fund, including £100 of the unexpended balance of the Dock Labourers' Strike Committee, £10 each from the Amalgamated Society of Tailors and the London Society of Compositors, £44 from collections made in other union shops, and significant sums from some native Jews.[52] The *Jewish Chronicle* was

[52]Placard: BALANCE SHEET OF THE GREAT STRIKE OF LONDON TAILORS. Montagu's personal contribution was £30 10s and Rothschild contributed £73, mostly for the purpose of meeting the deficit when the strike was over. Nathaniel

pleased at the initiative of the downtrodden immigrant tailors:

The worm has turned at last. . . . An appreciable improvement in the material condition of the foreign tailors of the East End would do much. . . . On every ground, then, the movement is deserving of sympathy.

But it was

. . . questionable policy on the part of the poor foreigners to give an exaggerated idea of their numbers by parading through London, and thus excite further prejudice against their entire body, especially when they place themselves under the leadership of men conspicuously associated with Socialistic movements.[53]

Although they were enthusiastic organizers and agitators, the socialists did not control the strike or conduct the negotiations. They were yet further removed from control when outside intervention, which they vigorously opposed, entered the deadlocked strike.

The strike was settled through the exertions of Sir Samuel Montagu, who personally proffered his services to the men, and posted a £100 guarantee demanded by the strike committee as a token of the masters' good faith in agreeing to arbitration. The masters reluctantly agreed to a joint session under Montagu's chairmanship, and the confrontation took place at a packed meeting in the Jewish Working Men's Club, with nine newspaper reporters and Rothschild's personal representative among those present. Montagu's formula had the men abandon wage demands for one year, and the masters yield on the hours question. Exhausted by nearly six weeks of demonstrations, bargaining, and unemployment, both sides gave way. A final broadside proclaimed the terms of settlement:

After five weeks' struggle, of Machinists, Pressers, and Basters, the Master Tailors have accepted the following terms of the Men:

1. The hours of labour to be from eight o'clock in the morning until eight o'clock in the evening, with one hour for dinner and half-an-hour for tea.

2. Only four hours overtime to be worked in a week.

L. Cohen, contributed £5 5s. Total receipts were £398 15s 5d, of which £267 7s went for relief in cash and in kind. For a view of the strike's effect, see George Lansbury, *Looking Backwards—and Forwards*, London, 1935, p. 217.

[53] *JC*, September 6, 1889.

3. Not more than two hours overtime may be worked in any one day.

4. All meals to be had off the work premises.

5. The first two hours overtime to be paid for at the ordinary rate, and the second two hours to be paid for at the rate of time-and-a-half.

6. That the hour system [of pay] be not introduced.

All Men to go to Work on October 6th, 1889, on the Above Terms.
October 3rd, 1889.   *By order of the Strike Committee.*

As the strike ended, Samuel Montagu joyously declared that his arduously gained success was the 'happiest day of my life'. In reply to the employer Mark Moses' criticism of Adler's inactivity during the strike, it was authoritatively explained that Rothschild had told the Delegate Chief Rabbi not to intervene, since his Lordship was planning to do so himself. Rothschild's role, however, was an indirect one.[54]

In the flush of success, a Jewish tailors' strike in Manchester with the same objectives as in London was also pushed to a successful conclusion.

Viewing the activity of the year 1889 as it ended, the socialist Konstantin Gallop (1862–1892) enthused

But such resolution, such eagerness to organize, such steadfastness in battle, such solidarity, such firm class consciousness, as have been exhibited during the endless series of bloodless workers' struggles of the past year—such has not yet been seen or experienced by mankind. It is obvious to everyone . . . that the slumbering masses, oppressed and labouring humanity, Hercules in workmen's clothing, has come to, has awakened from its sleep . . . and was ashamed . . . of its fetters, its poverty, its dirt.[55]

Such was the view from a brief period of high tide; the ebb set in at once.

ENGLISH SOCIALISTS AND JEWISH SOCIALISTS

For all their rebellion against it, the Jewish socialists were rooted in their native Jewish environment, and developed

---

[54]*JC*, October 4, 11, 1889. The proposed arbitrators were Lords Dunraven and Rothschild, the Bishop of Bedford, the Rector of Spitalfields, and Haham Moses Gaster. The men's single proposed arbitrator was Lord Brassey, on whom see S. and B. Webb, *History of Trade Unionism*, rev. ed., London, 1920, p. 269 n.

[55]*Arbeiter Freind*, V, 1 (January 3, 1890)

independently of the growing English socialist movement. At the time the Jewish socialist movement was burgeoning, the principal English socialist groups were Henry Hyndman's Social Democratic Federation, a Marxist organization; the Socialist League, led by William Morris and preaching education towards revolution; and the gradualists of the renowned Fabian Society, the most influential English socialist group, whose best known leaders were Bernard Shaw and the Webbs. Although East London was a seedbed of the English socialist movement, two of these groups paid little or no attention to the Jewish socialists. Beatrice Potter's (Webb) studies of Jewish immigrant life in the 1880's notwithstanding, there was no significant contact between the Fabians and the 'Berner Streeters'. Of course there was wide disparity between the two groups, one foreign and the other native, one impulsively revolutionary and the other deliberately gradualist. As to the Social Democratic Federation, it was not neutral but negative towards the Jews. Hyndman, who dominated the English Marxists absolutely, was an anti-Semite, and the Federation's journal *Justice* amply expressed these views. Although the anti-Semitism of these English Marxists was ostensibly aimed only at Jewish capitalists, it bore enough animus to extend to Jews without capital and at times, to fellow-Marxists who happened to be Jews.[56] Close relations, based on personal friendship and common beliefs, existed between the Jewish socialists and the Socialist League, as seen in the pages of *The Commonweal*. Under William Morris' leadership, the League was close to the foreign socialist groups in London, especially the Germans. The Socialist League and Morris personally showed generous interest in the fortunes of their Jewish fellow-believers in the East End, whose rather diffuse revolutionism was much akin to their own. They came closer than any socialist group of the day to vindicating the fraternal ideals of international socialism.

[56]E. Silberner, 'British Socialism and the Jews,' *Historia Judaica*, XIV, 1 (April, 1952), pp. 27–52. This article concentrates on the Social Democratic Federation after 1880, to the exclusion of more important wings of English socialism. Its full evidence is not repeated here. The same author's Hebrew work, *HaSozializm haMa'aravi uShe'elat haYehudim* (Western Socialism and the Jewish Question), Jerusalem, 1955, pp. 251–68, repeats this article.

The Commonweal poured ridicule on the anti-alien movement.[57] It praised the Jewish 'teachers' of socialism in Leeds, and a new socialist society in that city 'composed of our Jewish comrades' was considered 'pleasant news to readers. . . .'[58] Socialist League members in East London met in rooms at 40, Berner Street, and lectures by Jewish socialists, both in English and Yiddish,[59] were entered in the weekly socialist calendar published in *The Commonweal*. The *Arbeiter Freind* earned 'heartiest wishes for . . . success' on account of its 'great effect in enlightening its readers on the question of Socialism'.[60] The fifth anniversary of the Berner Street club in 1890 brought such socialist eminences as William Morris and Peter Kropotkin as visitors to the Jewish socialist centre to join in the celebration.[61] Naturally, special commendations were bestowed upon every successful strike by Jewish workers, especially when, as in the shoe strike of 1890, Jewish and Christian workers acted in unison.[62] Appropriate scorn was heaped upon the anti-socialist attitude of the official Jewish community, especially when Hermann Adler and his 'Congregations of well-fed *Chosens*' interfered with the synagogue procession of March 16, 1889.[63]

The Jewish socialists who were closest to the English socialists in the earlier years were Joseph Finn of Leeds and William Wess of London, probably because of their mastery

[57]"The Blarsted Furriners,' IV, Nos. 120, 121 (April 28, May 5, 1888), pp. 130–31, 138; IV, No. 122 (May 12, 1888), p. 147; VI, No. 232 (June 21, 1890), p. 194.

[58]IV, No. 109 (February 11, 1888), p. 45. 'Sunday last we celebrated the Paris Commune. Speeches delivered in English and Jewish.' IV, No. 115 (March 24, 1888), p. 96. English and Jewish socialists shared quarters in Leeds; *Arbeiter Freind*, IV, 3 (January 18, 1889). See Ben Turner's recollections of his socialist days in Leeds with John Dyche, made in his speech as T.U.C. fraternal delegate to the A.F. of L. convention in 1910. *Ladies Garment Worker*, I, 8 (December, 1910).

[59]II, No. 14 (March, 1886), p. 24.

[60]III, No. 56 (February 5, 1887), p. 45.

[61]VI, No. 228 (June 7, 1890), p. 359. *People's Press*, I, 15 (June 14, 1890), p. 13: The Berner Street club was started 'nine years ago by one Russian Jew who wearied of the procedure of his orthodox brethren (sic). It has slowly fought its way to a membership of 200, despite the persecution of the Jews, the sweaters, and the police'.

[62]III, No. 92 (October 15, 1887), p. 334; V, No. 158 (January 19, 1889), p. 22; No. 188 (May 17, 1889), p. 262.

[63]"The Jewish Parade and Law-'N-Order,' V, No. 167 (March 23, 1889), p. 93.

of English. Wess joined nine Socialist Leaguers and three Scotsmen, including Keir Hardie, to attend the International Socialist Congress in 1889.[64] He was so popular in the League that it sponsored a concert in his aid when he was 'out of work for a long time', with a programme consisting wholly of English performers.[65]

TRADE UNION STAGNATION AND SOCIALIST FISSION

The strike of the Jewish tailors in 1889 was little more than a prolonged demonstration. It established no enforcement machinery, so that within five weeks after work officially resumed complaints were heard that unionists who insisted upon the terms of the settlement were being discharged. Mark Moses, the employers' main spokesman, admitted that the settlement had broken down, observing that his constituents 'also have to live'.[66] By April, 1890, there was talk of another general strike to abolish sweating, probably influenced by the shoe workers' strike for that purpose. The *Arbeiter Freind*, which normally leaped to the support of any mass movement, now took a dim view. It pointed to the lack of funds and leadership, and to the unsocialist concern with such publicity as letters to the Queen and the Prelates, in contrast with the failure actually to organize the workers.[67] The outcome was an interesting but short-lived attempt to unite both employers and workers to secure higher prices from the merchant clothiers for the work which the latter gave out. This would ease the common problem of Jewish masters and workers.[68]

[64]V, No. 187 (May 10, 1889), p. 250; No. 188 (May 17, 1889), p. 260.
[65]V, No. 170 (April 13, 1889), p. 119. See also Rudolf Rocker, 'Peter Kropotkin and the Yiddish Workers' Movement,' in Joseph Ishill, ed., *Peter Kropotkin*, Berkeley Heights, N. J., 1923, pp. 78–85.
[66]He suggested a campaign to lower the cost of living by reducing retail grocery prices. *Arbeiter Freind*, IV, 44, 45 (November 1, 8, 1889). See *The Commonweal*, VI, Nos. 211, 227 (January 25, May 17, 1890), pp. 30, 158.
[67]It revealingly mentions that during the 'Great Strike', a 'great part' of the strikers worked all day and attended strike meetings at night. V, 14 (April 4, 1890). See interesting observations in *People's Press*, I, 10 (May 10, 1890), p. 12.
[68]*People's Press*, I, 16 (June 21, 1890), p. 11; I, 17 (June 28, 1890), pp. 13–14; I, 20 (July 19, 1890), p. 6; I, 12 (May 31, 1890), p. 14 gives details of the agreement. *Cf.* Burgin, *op. cit.*, pp. 257–59.

I

Both Socialists and 'pure and simple' trade unionists more than once attempted to federate the East End Jewish unions under their leadership. The most significant attempt took place under socialist sponsorship, when the 'East-London Federation of Labour Unions' was inaugurated at a mass meeting on December 28, 1889, in the Great Assembly Hall.[69] James MacDonald, John Turner, Tom Mann, Ben Tillett, and Charles Mowbray all addressed the assemblage, in addition to an even longer array of Yiddish orators. The meeting was, as usual, enthusiastic, and the resolutions to federate were, as always, unanimously passed.

Although the Federation was neither Jewish nor 'international' in name, all of its constituent bodies were Jewish: the Hebrew Cabinet Makers Society, the Stick and Cane Dressers' Union, the London Tailor Machinists' Union, the International Furriers' Society, the Tailors' and Pressers' Union, the Amalgamated Lasters' Society, the United Capmakers' Society, and the International Journeymen Bootfinishers' Society. Socialism was represented by the Berner Street club and by the club's anarchist Knights of Liberty Group. With the imposing assemblage of unions under its banner, the Federation's job was practically completed and it soon disappeared. The social-democratic Proletariat Group made another fruitless attempt in 1892, with by then reduced resources.[70]

This abortive move proposed not only to combat sweating, but also determined to remedy the 'short-comings' of the Jewish workers. They were first to be enlightened in their Jewish unions and then, with the language 'shortcoming' removed, they could join the general struggle of English labour. Some measure of their strength at this time is an estimate that of 30,000 immigrant Jewish workers in

[69] *The Commonweal*, VI, No. 208 (January 4, 1890), p. 6; Federation of East-London Labour Unions, *Rules*. London, Worker's Friend Printing Office, 1890; placard in English and Yiddish announcing the meeting. (The latter two items by kind permission of Mr A. R. Rollin). On an earlier attempt, see *Arbeiter Freind*, II, 47 (December 30, 1887); III, 2 (January 13, 1888) signed 'Awake' opposes a council because it would seek mere trade union palliatives. The author was Harry Kaplansky; Burgin, *op. cit.*, p. 41. *Cf. Arbeiter Freind*, IV, 25, 31 (June 21, August 2, 1889).

[70] *Fraye Velt*, II, 4, 5 (September, November, 1892). Seven unions sent delegates to the first meeting.

London only 1,000 to 1,200 were members of Jewish trade unions. [71]

The Jewish socialists also evangelized in the Provinces, with uneven results. A new club in Manchester grew so dormant that the leaders were of a mind to close it down. [72] Liverpool's initiation into the Jewish socialist ranks took place under anarchist auspices in 1891, but brought no results of record. [73] In the small community of Hull, one Moses Kalb reported that he had recruited fifteen members in his Jewish Educational Club, and asked for help from Manchester and Leeds. [74] Such sporadic activities continued throughout the Provinces, depending on the energy and devotion of individual socialists, but only in Leeds was there a continuous history.

By 1891, the lines of division between Jewish socialists and anarchists were becoming fast. The doctrinal points at issue were esoteric, but the mood is apparent. The early confidence in imminent revolution was followed by the less exhilarating prospect of a long struggle to win over the Jewish working classes. The development of socialism in Europe and America had split the movement into sects, to whom the setbacks of the 1890's gave more time for introspection and bickering. The same phenomena were occurring in the Jewish movement; an anarchist caucus in Berner Street was countered by a quasi-social democratic group. Each faction held meetings and issued propaganda, while a group of neutrals who stood aside earned the disdain of both wings for not diving into the doctrinal maelstrom.

The anarchists were a definite minority in 1890, [75] yet within a year they became the majority. Early in 1891, the house in Berner Street was divided against itself into the anarchist

[71] *Arbeiter Freind*, VII, 39 (December 16, 1892).

[72] Letter, B. Feigenbaum to 'Brethren and Friends' (Yiddish), n.d., postmarked February 8, 1889. (By kind permission of Mr A. R. Rollin.) The complaint ends in Biblical terms (!): 'Ease and deliverance will come to us from elsewhere, and you will bear your own sins.' *Arbeiter Freind*, V, 46 (November 14, 1890).

[73] *Arbeiter Freind*, VI, 18 (May 1, 1891); there was an earlier attempt which produced no results, recorded in *Arbeiter Freind*, III, 14 (April 6, 1888). It remained a 'conservative' city; *Arbeiter Freind*, X, 4 (November 1, 1895); XI, 15 (January 17, 1896).

[74] *Arbeiter Freind*, V, 46 (November 14, 1890). On results in Birmingham, *cf. Yudisher Telegraf*, II, 59 (March 17, 1898), p. 5.

[75] *Arbeiter Freind*, V, 13 (March 28, 1890).

Knights of Liberty, the revolutionary socialist and anti-parliamentary Proletariat, and the social democratic Forward group.[76] In April of that year, the die was cast by a vote which turned over the club and the *Arbeiter Freind* to the anarchists. Yanovsky, the new editor, promised that the paper would remain an open platform. However, Winchevsky's 'Mad Philosopher' feuilleton no longer appeared and anarchist viewpoints soon predominated.

By June, 1891, the *Arbeiter Freind* admitted that it sold but 200 copies in London, many of which were not paid for.[77] The Jewish trade union leaders became alienated from the newspaper and distrusted its publishers.[78] Despite heroic efforts, both club and newspaper entered into a decline which lasted until the turn of the century. The club quit Berner Street to begin a period of wandering through the meeting rooms of the East End.

LATER SOCIALISM AND ANARCHISM

The socialists turned to a literary programme, with a new monthly, *Fraye Velt* (Free World). The spread of socialism had raised 'certain questions which the weekly agitation-papers are not in a position to answer, or can answer only superficially. . . .' The new journal reminded its readers that

. . . we are socialists but we are revolutionists besides, and we distinguish between ourselves and socialist-evolutionists and socialist-reformers . . . we recognize that socialism cannot be brought about except by a violent social revolution.[79]

The revolutionary utopianism of its full platform bears the spiritual stamp of Saint-Simon and Fourier, as well as Lavrov,

[76]*Arbeiter Freind*, VI, 1 (January 3, 1891). Gallop resigned as editor a month later for reasons 'partly personal but mostly such as do not depend on my desires'. Perhaps this means both factional pressure and the deterioration of Gallop's health (he died of tuberculosis within a year). *Arbeiter Freind*, VI, 7 (February 13, 1891).
[77]*Arbeiter Freind*, VI, 26 (June 26, 1891); Herz Burgin, *op. cit.*, p. 231 n. Earlier figures could not be found.
[78]*Arbeiter Freind*, VII, 3 (January 15, 1892). On the *Arbeiter Freind's* troubles in the 1890's, see Rudolf Rocker, *op. cit.*, pp. 200–02, 234–38, 224–32 (on Yanovsky), and 233–36 (on Wess). Wess' association with the *Arbeiter Freind* as printer and business manager appears as early as the August 5, 1887 issue.
[79]*Die Fraye Velt*, I, 1 (May, 1891), pp. 2–3.

and was probably the work of Winchevsky. A few months later, however, the *Fraye Velt* drew closer to the increasingly widespread Marxist doctrines.

The nine issues of the *Fraye Velt* which appeared between May, 1891 and November, 1892 are the high-water mark of a Jewish socialist publication in England. Many of Winchevsky's best poems appeared in it, and the theoretical or expository pieces are clearly argued. Although a vigorous polemic against the anarchists appeared in the first issue, a factional tone was avoided.[80] Of the total printing of the first three issues, 1,527 copies were sold; 569 in London, eighty-eight in the Provinces, and 870 in America. Others were doubtless smuggled into Russia, and 800 remained in stock. The average paid circulation was thus 509 per issue,[81] mainly in America, by now the movement's centre.

The *Fraye Velt* came to grips with questions which faced Jewish socialists as Jews:[82]

Remaining international and at the same time recognizing the fact that (1) our task is to work among Jews as long as the Jews still separate themselves in their language and customs from other nations, and (2) that the Jewish working masses have no one among them who shall care for their general human development and education, and there is almost no literature which could do this—we consider it our duty . . . to do the following:

(a) Through lectures, addresses and writings to educate the Jewish working masses and to bring them as far as possible to the spiritual level of the advanced working classes in the lands in which they live.

(b) To organize the Jewish workers and to make them capable, as fellow class members of the native working classes, of taking part in the class struggle of the land in which they live.

The ideal, then, was to educate the Jewish worker towards absorption into the native working class. The Jewish socialists

---

[80]*Ibid.* The *Arbeiter Freind's* attack was also mild. On Baranoff: Zalman Reisen, *op. cit.*, *s.v.* Baranoff; F. Kursky *et al.*, eds., *YIVO Historishe Shriftn*, III, Vilna, 1939, p. 296.

[81]*Die Fraye Velt*, I, 4 (September-October, 1891). Its price was 2½d and 5c in America. The small circulation contrasts with the 12,000-13,000 which was the combined printing of the *Arbeiter Freind*, and the *Arbeiter Tseitung* and the *Fraye Arbeter Shrimme* in New York, all weeklies. *Idem*, I, 1 (May, 1891).

[82]*Die Fraye Velt*, II, 5 (November, 1892), pp. 119-20. This was the platform of the Socialist Workers' Association, which fused the non-anarchist groups. See below, Note 85.

imposed a special burden upon themselves, because nobody but they could carry out their educational programme. The platform does not consider the possibility of the Jews retaining their identity, so that from a Jewish point of view it is a programme of immolation.

The dwindling strength of Jewish socialism in London was rationalized by a writer who found it 'still in the utopian period of its development . . . it is not yet in a state of maturity. . . . Its utopianism is particularly clear when we would compare it with German socialism'.[83] The German Social Democrats, who had become a flourishing political party, were looked upon as mentor and model for such struggling movements as that in London.

By the middle of 1892, various socialist factions bearing grandiose rubrics and enrolling few members, merged to form the Socialist Workers Association. The fusion was hailed by the *Fraye Velt* as 'The Beginning of a New Epoch in the Jewish Socialist Movement in London',[84] which announced its own supersession by a new journal in a 'completely new format'. This was *Der Vekker* (The Awakener), which lasted hardly more than a year.[85] The new journal pleaded for Jewish trade unionism by echoing anti-alien cries:

Do not stand afar from your English comrades, do not form a separate city within a city in which to live. Discard your Asiatic customs which you have brought with you from Russia. Cast away your wild tongue and learn the language of the land in which you live. Unite in unions. But, better yet, where possible enter English unions.

[83] *Idem*, II, 1 (January, 1892), p. 23.
[84] *Idem*, II, 5 (November, 1892), pp. 99-102. The platform: 'To improve the position of the workers as far as possible in the present society in order to prepare them for the struggle for a higher social form and to make them capable of living in that society, which will be founded on the principles of freedom, equality, and brotherhood'.—a specimen of the straddling which was necessary to unite the socialist factions. The anarchists were meanwhile grappling with the somewhat similar question of the utility of trade unionism. For example, the discussion between H(arry) K(aplansky) and Yanovsky in *Arbeiter Freind*, VII, 2 (January 8, 1892). They remained opposed to 'political, legal, centralistic trade unionism': *Vos Villen Mir* (What We Want), Broadside No. 3, 1905.
[85] Copies of *Der Vekker* are not available. The quotations from its prospectus are taken from the reminiscences of the anarchist B. Ruderman, 'Die Yiddish-Sotsialistishe Bavegung in England', (The Jewish Socialist Movement in England), *Fraye Arbeter Shtimme*, September 25, 1925. (The series begins in September, 1924).

Probably it was also *Der Vekker* which published a bitterly con-troverted article by John Burns in which the English socialist and trade unionist attacked Jewish workers for congregating in one area, and apparently also for scabbing.[86]

All this was no 'new epoch', but repetition in a frustrated tone of the old slogans within a limited sect. As Jewish socialism petered out in London and progressed in America, its leaders followed the movement. Kranz left for New York in 1890, and next year Feigenbaum accepted his invitation to join him there in socialist journalism. Gallop died of tuberculosis early in 1892. Baranoff left in 1893 or 1894, and Winchevsky, who had been the first to arrive, was the last pioneer to leave, in 1894.[87] With the last major leader gone and the last significant publica-tion at an end, Jewish socialism as a continuous and effective movement ceased. From then on it was more a matter of evanescent clubs and aid to the Russian underground movement.

While socialism decayed in the Jewish quarter there were brighter years for the anarchists as heirs to the educational and anti-religious activities of the once-united movement.[88] From their various locales came sometimes spiteful anti-religious activity, e.g. atheistic exhortations on High Holidays and Sabbath smoking in front of synagogues. Quarrels between religious and free-thinking Jews occurred and matters came to brawls at socialist clubs in London and Leeds.[89] Yet the anti-

---

[86]*Arbeiter Freind*, VIII, 8 (February 24, 1893). It is said to have appeared in a 'Jewish [*i.e.*, Yiddish] publication.'

[87]For fuller information on these Yiddish writers, see Zalman Reisen, *op. cit.*, *s.v.*

[88]There is no satisfactory account of the Jewish anarchist movement. For most of what follows, see Rudolf Rocker, *op. cit.*, *passim*, and A. Frumkin, *op. cit.*, *passim*.

[89]See Eyges, *op. cit.*; *JC*, September 23, October 7 and 28, 1904. This was not sponsored by the Jewish community, which was embarrassed by the anarchists and regarded them as pariahs. Z. H. Masliansky, 'the National Orator,' debated with them publicly, but few others did so. Z. H. Masliansky, *Sefer haZikhronot vehaMassa'ot* (Memoirs and Travels), N.Y., 1929, pp. 131, 134–35. Dr Adler himself met another parade of Jewish unemployed into the Great Synagogue early in 1894. However, the affair was a trade union demonstration and the anti-religious overtones were missing; its purpose was to 'protest their starving condition' and to demand relief. Dr Adler's sermon in the West End the following day was, in comparison with his performance five years earlier, quite socialist; the *JC* was almost respectful: 'For the first time in our history, the unemployed Jew has put himself in evidence . . . imbued with the *Zeitgeist*, they demonstrate, and demand work . . . such demonstrations ought not to be treated contemp-tuously, but . . . should be met with reasonable sympathy. . . .' The *JC* had been imbued with some '*Zeitgeist*' itself; cf. above, p. 115–16. *JC*, February 2, 1894.

religious brochures published by the anarchists had a firmer intellectual basis than the earlier passionate philippics. They reflect greater detachment from the Jewish environment, and are grounded in positivism, Darwinian thought, and contemporary research in comparative religion and folklore.[90] Many were translations from other languages.

The literary and philosophical approach of the Jewish anarchists is measured by the dominance of the attractive figure of Rudolf Rocker (1873–1958) in their movement. Rocker, a German Gentile, was a much travelled and widely read man, a master of several tongues who found his favourite anarchist movement to be that of the Jews. After some time in Liverpool, where he established the Yiddish literary monthly *Germinal*, and the short-lived *Fraye Vort* (Free Speech),[91] he came to London to edit the *Arbeiter Freind* until the War. To Rocker, anarchism was a 'freedom movement' in political and economic life and also in literature and thought, which were no less important to him. The first task of the neophyte anarchist, then, was to educate himself into freedom from the thrall of custom and law in every sphere before he could bring others to their fulfilment as anarchist free men. A visitor to a Rocker lecture might have heard him discuss Ibsen, Shaw, Havelock Ellis, or contemporary French novelists and painters, all in proficient Yiddish. Rocker and his literary collaborator Abraham Frumkin (1872–1940)[92] performed services of lasting value by enlarging the horizon of Yiddish literature with extensive translations from the literatures of many countries.

Rocker's leadership did much to focus the Jewish anarchist

[90]Some typical titles are: Johann Most, *Die Religiyezze Magefah* (The Religious Plague), London, 1901; B. Feigenbaum, *Ver Hot Ayngefirt Yom Kippur un fun Vanen Shtammt die Torah?* (Who Introduced the Day of Atonement and What is the Origin of the Torah?), 3rd ed., London, 1907; ——, *Die Idishe Inkvizitsie*, (The Jewish Inquisition), London, 1906. Wess speaks of unions' duty to develop their members' 'human feelings': *Arbeiter Freind*, X, 2 (October 18, 1895).

[91]*Germinal* appeared monthly from 1903 to 1908. It was literary and theoretical, and published many translations. *Fraye Vort* was published by Rocker in Liverpool in 1898. Zalman Reisen, *op. cit.*, cols. 686, 729, with corrections as noted. The inside t.p. of Johann Most, *op. cit.*, gives the size of the printings—from 3,000 for anarchist tracts up to 5,000 for Nordau.

[92]The two men could hardly have brought more divergent backgrounds to their collaboration. Frumkin was born in Jerusalem to a well-known family of rabbinic scholars, journalists, and pioneer Zionists. See his memoirs (cited in Note 1), *passim*, and Rocker, *op. cit.*, pp. 234–37; Zalman Reisen, *op. cit.*, *s.v.* Frumkin, Abraham.

movement more upon the international movement than upon its Jewish environment. The East End anarchist club, wherever it was domiciled, was the haven of anarchists from Russia, Spain, and Italy. Although the anarchists were let alone by the authorities, they did not escape the lurid Sidney Street affair[93] without permanent damage to their movement, which the popular mind associated with murder and wrongdoing. Rocker and the Jewish anarchists set their faces rigidly against the terrorist faction within the international movement, but they also maintained that society was to blame for conditions which provoked acts of terror, which they insisted were committed by persons who misunderstood or distorted the anarchist philosophy. When the World War broke out, the movement was dissolved by the internment of Rocker as a German alien, the suppression of the *Arbeiter Freind*, and the shutting of their club.[94]

It is a simpler story with the socialists, who by 1895 were largely in the social democratic camp, and concentrated on union organizing and publishing. Actually, there was little specifically socialist influence in Jewish trade unionism, which was itself feeble enough. Joseph Finn, the ablest trade unionist, contributed to socialist periodicals and the controversial Lewis Lyons dallied with the socialists, but both men were trade unionists first. When there were strikes, the socialists did what they could to help. They propagandized before ready-made audiences at strike demonstrations.

LATER JEWISH TRADE UNIONISM

Jewish trade unionism itself, after the lustre of its early development wore off, discouraged outsiders with its factionalism,

[93]This was one of the most sensational crimes in modern Britain. Three police officers were murdered when they surprised a band of jewellery burglars. The culprits, who were not anarchists, seem to have held their social rendezvous at the anarchist club. They were traced to and besieged by troops at a small house in Sidney Street in the East End, where all (or all but one) were killed in a holocaust. The Home Secretary, W. S. Churchill, had personal command of the proceedings. Certain aspects of the case still remain unsolved, especially the perhaps mythical 'Peter the Painter'. Rocker, *op. cit.*, pp. 462–92, esp. p. 482; J. P. Eddy, *The Mystery of Peter the Painter*, London, 1946.

[94]Rudolf Rocker, *op. cit.*, pp. 15–16, 584–96. The failure of anarchism to revive is blamed on the departure of many anarchists for Russia and Germany, together with rigorously restrictive immigration laws.

individualism, and general disorder—qualities which permanently afflicted it in England. Not long after the glories of the strike of 1889, an English trade unionist considered the Jewish Tailors' and Pressers' Union 'not worth hanging for their skins', so far were they still from firm unionism. He hoped that the time might come when 'perhaps these self-assertive individualistic Jews will learn that mutual recriminations are not the principal object of committee and general meetings'.[95] Both Jew and Gentile seconded J. B. Lakeman's pronouncement that 'trade unionism has not yet fixed itself upon the Jewish race . . .', spoken in 1894 and still true fifteen years later.[96] These ailments were particularly rife in London, which the stronger Provincial unions regarded pityingly as 'a weak centre for organization', where a ten hour day was still to be achieved long after nine hours' daily work had been won in Leeds and elsewhere.[97] Trade Unionists hopefully estimated their following at 500 in Leeds, 400 in Manchester, 100 in Liverpool, fifty in Birmingham, and twenty in Newcastle. Jewish trade unionism in the Yorkshire city presented a secure and thriving appearance, because its factories and large workshops were more fertile soil for trade unionism than London's chaotic congeries of small workshops. In 1902, the Amalgamated Jewish Tailors, Machinists, and Pressers of Leeds was a model of 'stability and success', having an income of £615, an expenditure of £533, and a reserve fund of £664.[98] Its 950 members in 1909 soared beyond 4,000 by 1913, under the stimulus of the Trade Boards Act of 1909 (see below).[99] In contrast, when a London Jewish branch of the Amalgamated

[95]*People's Press*, I, 16 (June 21, 1890), p. 11.

[96]Report of the Chief Inspector of Factories and Workshops for 1894, C. 7745, 1895, p. 49; S. and B. Webb, *Industrial Democracy*, 2 vols., London, 1897, II, p. 744 n.; J. A. Dyche, 'My Tour in Europe,' *The Ladies Garment Worker*, V, 6 (June, 1914), pp. 2–6; Anon. in *idem*, IV, 1 (January, 1913), pp. 28–30; John Burns in *idem*, V, 4 (April, 1914), p. 4.

[97]*JC*, March 7, April 7, 1911, June 7, 1912; *The Ladies Garment Worker*, III, 12 (December, 1912), pp. 5–8; *Arbeiter Freind*, X, 1 (October 11, 1895), 'Jewish Labour News', *JC*, September 12, 1902.

[98]J. A. R. Pimlott, *Toynbee Hall, Fifty Years of Social Progress*, London, 1935, p. 120. On Amalgamated Society of Tailors' efforts among Jewish tailors, J. A. Dyche, *op. cit.*, *The Ladies Garment Worker*, V, 4 (April, 1914), p. 3.

[99]R. H. Tawney, *The Establishment of Minimum Rates in the Tailoring Industry under the Trade Boards Act of* 1909. (Studies in the Minimum Wage, No. II) London, 1915, p. 93. It sent delegates to the T.U.C. regularly; Trade Union Congress, *Report* for 1904, 1906, 1909, lists delegates.

Society of Tailor's struck in 1906 it had £3 12s 9d in the till, and its membership was undoubtedly no more impressive.[100]

Summing up the frustrations of twenty-five years, an embittered trade unionist saw scant hope in London. Many strike battles had been won, and more were yet to come, but stability was as far from realization as it had been a generation earlier. Every sort of union had been tried:

independent unions, international unions, amalgamated unions, syndicalist unions, social-democratic and anarchistic unions, pure and simple, and Sabbath-observing unions. But to introduce discipline, respect for the constitution and the officers, to introduce higher dues and various benefits, to amass a large treasury, to avoid strikes so far as possible, and to learn the methods of the powerful English unions—this not.[101]

The Trade Boards Act of 1909, which provided for labour representation upon wages boards to which was given the power to fix a legal minimum wage, greatly stimulated trade unionism among the poorly paid workers in the tailoring trade. They thus helped indirectly to write the epitaph for the independent Jewish trade union movement. For under the Act's provisions, a single board for wholesale tailoring was established; this had the effect of summoning both employer and worker to organize themselves around the wages board upon which each was equally represented.[102] It raised more keenly than ever the question of the practical trade union significance of having Jewish unions, and of their relation to other unions in their trade. The alternative answers were amalgamation with some larger English union which was ready to accept them, or independent existence. Independence was feasible and even necessary so long as the Jewish tailor was a man apart, economically and linguistically, and was unwanted as a fellow-unionist by the English worker. By the close of our period, however, the stimulus of the Trade Boards Act helped to create a new union of tailors which beckoned to the independent Jewish unions in London and the Provinces. This was the Tailors' and Garment Workers' Trade Union,

[100]*JC*, March 27, 1903.
[101]Anon. in *The Ladies Garment Worker*, I, 2 (July, 1910). A more measured view: A. Rosebury to *JC*, January 9, 1903.
[102]R. H. Tawney, *op. cit.*, pp. 26, 32, 92 and *passim*.

consisting mainly of wholesale clothing workers, which arose during the turbulent years of 1911 and 1912. The Jewish unions in London were compelled to amalgamate with it by the accident of a strike which they called in sympathy with the English tailors' strike. The Jewish unions unexpectedly won all they wanted, including a wage raise, before the English strikers settled on much less favourable terms.[103]

LATER JEWISH SOCIALISM

English Jewish socialism, the parent branch of a world-wide movement, whose publications had set a pattern for a generation of socialists in Europe and America, was reduced indeed.[104] Following the demise of *Der Vekker* about 1894, none of its publications lasted longer than did its *Naye Tseit*, which appeared irregularly from 1904 to 1908.[105] These few years were probably the most fertile for Jewish socialists elsewhere, and in England they witnessed the nascent political power of the Labour Party and a revival of radical trade unionism. Russian events of 1905 also stimulated great hopes, and English shores received many socialist refugees when Tsarist reaction set in. The exiles were little interested in English affairs, however, and used London merely as a springboard for activities and propaganda directed at Russia. The Jewish groups associated with English socialists by using their meeting rooms and by occasional joint meetings. There were such

[103]*JC*, 'From the East End,' February 23, April 12, May 10, June 7, 1912; M. Walinsky, 'The New Period in the Jewish Labour Movement in London, England,' *The Ladies Garment Worker*, III, 11 (November, 1912), pp. 5–7, is optimistic, but not the anonymous writer in *idem*, IV, 7 (July, 1913), pp. 23–27. See also Rudolf Rocker, in Joseph Ishill, ed., *op. cit.*, pp. 83–84; Rudolf Rocker, *op. cit.*, pp. 492–515.

[104]The House of Lords Sweating Commission from 1888 to 1890 had heard about the Jewish socialists, but the 23,000 Q. & A. of the Royal Commission on Alien Immigration in 1902–1903 nowhere refer to the subject. Lyons' and Finn's testimony dealt solely with labour and trade unionism.

[105]Zalman Reisen, *op. cit.*, col. 717. Morris Meyer (Myer) was editor, and it was supposed to be a weekly. T. Rothstein edited the *Naye Velt*, another irregular weekly, which appeared from 1900 until 1913 or later. *Ibid.*, col. 715. The files of both are fragmentary. They also published the *Sotsial-Democrat*, of which two issues appeared in 1907–1908. *Ibid.*, col. 719. The various mastheads supply some of the organizations' names. There were: League of Jewish Social Democratic Associations of England, an East London Branch of the Social Democratic Federation, Jewish Social Democratic League of Great Britain. They were all pretty much the same circle.

occasions as a session of the Polish Socialist Party in exile with its Jewish section.[106] Yet the decade before the War, with the forward surge of British Labour and socialism, was not paralleled by English Jewish developments, despite the successes of the Jewish socialist movement abroad. An American comrade summed it up:

> Several groups still exist . . . but that is not a movement. In any case, it is so weak a movement that London has played no role in the history of the general Jewish Labour movement in the twentieth century.[107]

To be sure, there was self-diagnosis and introspection on the part of the frustrated Jewish socialists. At a conference in 1907 they surveyed the field and found it barren of accomplishment. Their whole body numbered about 200 in a Jewish immigrant community which exceeded 130,000 souls, and their largest group claimed but fifty-six members.[108] A correspondent sadly admitted that Jewish socialism in free England had 'really not more than passing luck', explaining that the class-conscious elements preferred anarchism.[109] The then Marxist Jacob Lestschinsky blamed the failure in England on the vast 'reserve army' of unskilled Jewish workers whose presence prevented effective strikes and the development of Jewish working-class consciousness.[110] Whatever the causes, by 1914 there is no longer much point in speaking of a Jewish socialist movement in England independent of Jewish trade unionism.[111]

[106]*Naye Tseit*, II, 9 (April 28, 1905). An earlier Polish-speaking socialist group of 50 was organized in Berner Street: *Arbeiter Freind*, VI, 9 (September 27, 1891). Rocker attempted, generally unsuccessfully, to interest the refugee revolutionists in England as a field for their activity. *Tsu die Yiddishe Arbayter* (To the Jewish Worker), No. 2, 1905. G. Beck, a Russian Gentile, was active in Jewish socialism in London and Paris; Herz Burgin, *op. cit.*, pp. 481–82; Rudolf Rocker, *op. cit.*, pp. 463–65.

[107]*Sotsial-Democrat*, No. 2, March, 1908. In No. 1 (November, 1907), there is a cheerless estimate of progress to date.

[108]Jacob Lestschinsky, *Der Yiddisher Arbayter* (*in London*), Vilna, 1907, pp. 31–32.

[109]Quoted in *Ibid*.

[110]*Ibid*.

V

THE FACE OF THE JEWISH QUARTER

Wherever immigrants settled—and no large English city was without them—the immigrant quarter,[1] an enclave or sometimes a few enclaves, accommodated nearly all of them. Even the hardiest, who braved the elements to make a living peddling about the countryside, made a home within the almost tangible spiritual boundaries of the immigrant quarter where their family and acquaintances lived. For the great majority, this immigrant quarter was not only the site of their dwelling, but their place of employment and the self-contained milieu which encompassed a whole range of social and cultural life. Most immigrants seldom ventured forth from it. When an immigrant's affluence and Anglicization encouraged him to move away, he did so always in the company of some of his fellows. Probably thousands of immigrant housewives and mothers spent their lives without ever really becoming familiar with more than the surrounding streets where their own people lived and the Yiddish language echoed down the narrow courts and alleys.

THE IMMIGRANT QUARTER

The immigrant's city within the city can be found in the same relative position on every city map. Whitechapel and St George's in London, Red Bank and Strangeways in Manchester, the Leylands in Leeds, and practically all the other areas of immigrant domicile stood close to the central sections of their cities. They were the acres of old residences growing increasingly shabby, which were slowly being pulled down to be replaced not by such 'downtown' fixtures as stores, offices, and theatres, but by small factories, warehouses, railway yards

---

[1]The term 'ghetto,' although widely used, is a misnomer. Historically, the word signifies compulsory residence in a segregated locality. The immigrant's domicile was in the last analysis a matter of choice.

and depots, and elementary schools for the neighbourhood children. Throughout our period, Jewish immigrant areas shifted slowly from the centre of the city as the latter claimed more and more space, and as the immigrant population increased. On the other hand, the high rents which the immigrants paid for their crammed quarters applied a brake to this process by making the maintenance of the immigrant quarter a highly profitable enterprise. Yet immigrant dwellings were never like the pestholes of Limehouse, Paddington, or Camberwell in London, or the notorious Ancoats district in Manchester. Those illfamed breeding grounds of epidemics were foul rookeries from the time they were erected, while most of the homes of Jewish settlers were slums of another type, houses once tolerable and at times even genteel which were turned into run-down and overcrowded dwellings and lodging-houses.   They were largely the remnants of decayed respectability. Occasionally Jewish settlement improved an area, such as a few streets in Spital-fields which were converted from residences of criminals and prostitutes into houses of industrious and law-abiding workers.[2] Taken together, the shanty rookeries flung together earlier in the nineteenth century were relatively unaffected by the coming of the Jews. The second category, composed of houses whose socially outcast inhabitants were ousted by Jews out-bidding them for occupancy, was of relatively slight significance. The great majority of immigrants seems to have settled in houses of sunken eminence, once inhabited by well-paid skilled workers or even by the merchant classes, who had moved else-where as the neighbourhood slowly declined.

London, the pre-eminent centre of immigrant life, displays all these characteristics most amply. Furthermore, a large quantity of writing and research concerning its history furnishes us with extensive information.[3] Jewish immigrant dwellers

---

[2]Examples are Thrawl Street and Flower and Dean Street. See Royal Commission on Alien Immigration, *Minutes of Evidence*, Cd. 1742, 1903, Min. 16250–55, 18496. (Hereinafter referred to as Cd. 1742.) *Cf.* C. Russell and H. S. Lewis, *The Jew in London*, London, 1900, p. 176–77n.

[3]See for example, on the area's historic background, including details on earlier Jewish settlement: Millicent Rose, *The East End of London*, London, 1951; D. L. Munby, *Industry and Planning in Stepney*, Oxford, 1951; Charles Booth, ed., *Life and Labour of the People of London*, 9 vols., London, 1892–97 (contains a valuable volume of demographic-economic maps); H. Llewellyn Smith, *History of*

in the East End had historic precedent aplenty for their presence. A century before the first East European Jews arrived there was a Huguenot colony of silk weavers, and other European nationalities were also represented. Jews resided at the eastern fringes of the city of London ever since Resettlement times, and in the late eighteenth and early nineteenth centuries streets in that section, e.g. Mansell Street, Leman Street, Great Prescott Street, contained the homes of wealthy and socially and communally prominent families. The Ashkenazi Great Synagogue in Duke's Place and the beautiful Sefardi synagogue in Bevis Marks were the main places of worship of these Jews, who attended together with a much larger number of poor Jews who lived in the adjoining streets.[4] The solidarity of rich and poor residing in the confines of a small enclave or even one street resembled the pattern of the old ghetto, but residential segregation based upon economic position ultimately overcame the old ways. Mainly after 1815, wealthier Jews moved to areas more becoming to their new station—at first north-east to suburban Hackney and Stamford Hill, and then across the City to the West End. Change of residence with the rise in wealth is not unusual, but in the case of the Jews, however, they constantly remained in groups and may also have delayed moving until well after their means permitted them. Still, by the middle of the nineteenth century there were several Jewish residential nuclei around the Metropolis, and a Jew who moved from a poor neighbourhood to one richer remained among Jews. Very rarely did he move completely away from his fellows. During two centuries of Jewish history in London the East End remained the starting point for incoming Jews at the foot of this residential ladder. Its evolution in the nineteenth century shows that one generation of poor Jewish immigrants practically displaced its predecessors not

East London, London, 1939; M. Dorothy George, *London Life in the XVIIIth Century*, 2nd ed., London, 1930. C. Russell and H. S. Lewis, *op. cit.*, contains an indispensable map showing Jewish population in the East End, which is reprinted (without colour) in *The Jewish Encyclopedia*, s.v. 'London'.

4'Recollections of a Veteran' (J. B. Montefiore), *JC*, September 15, 1893, partially reprinted in Lucien Wolf, *Essays in Jewish History*, ed. Cecil Roth, London, 1934, pp. 30–32; V. D. Lipman, *Social History of the Jews in England, 1850–1950*, London, 1954, pp. 11–17.

only in their synagogues and societies but also in their houses. But since the actual number of East End Jews was always growing and 'downtown' boundaries were expanding it was not enough to take over earlier Jewish houses. The immigrant quarter had to become larger. The East European Jews who crammed the historic Jewish quarter in the East End stretched it to its furthest geographical expansion and highest population, which reached a summit probably between 1905 and 1910. Besides this locality, the centre of immigrant life in every generation of Anglo-Jewish history, East European immigrants created smaller 'hives' of their own in London—Soho and Notting Hill in the west, and Hackney and Manor Park in the north-east, where accommodation was better and less cramped.

The picture of Jewish settlement in the provinces is simpler, mainly because everything was much smaller. Yet Manchester and Leeds, the two main provincial communities, each of which harboured immigrant populations of perhaps 12,000 at their zenith, had divergent situations in their immigrant quarters. In 'Cottonopolis' the Jews appeared before 1800, while the Yorkshire clothing centre hardly could muster a prayer quorum before 1840 and its community grew slowly until the 1870's.[5] As in London, the poor Jews in Manchester lived side by side with their wealthier brethren, in the northern fringe of the central city. As monied Jews moved north in a relatively straight line up the length of Cheetham Hill Road and its side streets, and built their synagogues and institutions as markers along the way, the poor Jews, including in time East European immigrants, followed them. The topographic history of Manchester Jewry is reasonably described as an ascent of Cheetham Hill, except for a sub-community which took up residence in Salford across the Irwell. Leeds Jews were practically all East European immigrants who settled in the Leylands, a dank district in that uninviting city, and slowly went forth from there partly propelled by comprehensive slum clearance.[6] From the topographic remains in other towns of significant immigrant settlement—Liverpool, Glasgow, Birmingham,

[5] *Ibid.*, p. 24; (J. Burnett), *Report to the Board of Trade on the Sweating System in Leeds by the Labour Correspondent to the Board*, 1888, p. 3; Cecil Roth, *The Rise of Provincial Jewry 1740-1840*, London, 1950, pp. 81–84.
[6] Cd. 1742, Min. 15018 ff.

K

Hull, Newcastle—we know that the picture did not differ from the larger communities. The basic phenomena were the same everywhere—concentration within one area, where earlier Jewish settlers had resided, in a location adjoining the central part of the city.

Jews and Gentiles traced the street boundaries of the ' "modern Judaea" of our Metropolis'[7] as it spread south, east, and north from its historic moorings around Duke's Place and Petticoat Lane.[8] Of the three directions, that to the north was relatively weakest, for the boundaries of the Jewish quarter first extended into Bethnal Green at the turn of the present century, and even then did not cross the Great Eastern's yards and tracks. The impetus to move south was stronger; native Jews had long resided in the Tenter Ground and Goodman's Fields. By the 1890's parts of the St George's-in-the-East parish became as thickly populated with Jews as Whitechapel and Mile End Old Town. Jewish settlement, however, kept its distance from the docks and the dock workers in the extreme south, and moved no closer to the Thameside than Cable Street. There were two spines to eastward Jewish expansion in the East End. One was Whitechapel Road (Aldgate High Street and Mile End Road at its eastern and western ends), a street of Roman origin moving east and slightly north, and the second was Commercial Road, which was hacked through courts and alleys in the mid-nineteenth century to connect the City with the docks and stretching south-east. Both slowly filled with Jewish businesses and residences. The streets branching off them were slowly infiltrated in their turn, and presently the little side turnings were also annexed into the Jewish quarter. By about 1910 the Jewish area reached its furthest extent, with the fringe of the City symbolized by Aldgate Pump as western limit, and with Cable Street to the south, the Great Eastern tracks on the northern edge, and a flexible eastern limit around Jubilee Street, Jamaica Street, and Stepney Green as its informal boundaries.

[7] *The Home and Synagogue of the Modern Jew*, London, c. 1872, p. 127.
[8] United Synagogue Visitation Committee, *Minute Book*, December 8, 1885, lists the streets 'inhabited by foreigners and by the poorest [Jews]'; C. Russell and H. S. Lewis, *op. cit.*, map; testimony of Mrs L. A. Levy and C. Barrett in Cd. 1742, Min. 17898, 2116–27.

These two square miles enclosed some of the most densely populated acres in England. This was caused not only by normal overcrowding of large families and the presence of many lodgers, but was aggravated by the razing of thousands of dwellings to make room for railway facilities, street improvements, business premises, and schools.[9] Little or no provision was made for the displaced inhabitants, who usually remained in the vicinity where they earned their livelihoods and jammed the remaining houses still further. Although wholesale demolitions for commercial purposes subsided after 1880, they continued at quite a rapid pace for such public improvements as schools and slum clearance. In other words, Jewish immigration intensified the East End's deep-rooted problem of house accommodation by preventing the population from declining as its houses were pulled down. Whitechapel's 8,264 houses of 1871 were only 5,735 in 1901, but the population pent up in the district rose from 75,552 to 78,768 in the same period, or from an average of 9.14 residents per house in 1871 to 13.74 in 1901. In the latter year, Limehouse, whose housing bore an evil enough reputation, had an average of but 7.97 per house.[10] The crowding reached its greatest extremes in the centre of the Jewish area, where it was claimed that the average density in Whitechapel of 286 per acre reached 600.[11] It must be borne in mind, however, that by 1901 many houses were actually large blocks of flats (apartment houses) sheltering dozens of families. Moreover, there is a distinct impression that the old Whitechapel houses, and houses elsewhere in the Jewish quarter, tended to be roomy. One hears of one and two room dwellings in such pristine slum areas as Lambeth, Camberwell, and Limehouse, but seldom in the Jewish quarter, where Royal Commission data suggest houses of four to six rooms.[12] To be sure, the density was still appalling, especially when it is recalled that many houses,

[9]H. J. Dyos, 'Railways and Housing in Victorian London,' *The Journal of Transport History*, II, 1 (May, 1955), pp. 11–21; 2 (November, 1955), pp. 90–100. See also *JC*, January 14 and February 17, 1902.

[10]*Census of England and Wales, 1901*, Cd. 875, 1902, Table 9.

[11]Harold E. Boulton, 'The Housing of the Poor,' *Fortnightly Review*, N.S. XLIII, (February 1, 1888), p. 280.

[12]Royal Commission on Alien Immigration, *Appendix to Minutes of Evidence*, Cd. 1741–I, 1903, Tables XXXVIII–XLV.

particularly larger ones, were fitted up as workshops. The peak
of the housing shortage was touched in 1901 and 1902, when
practically no house could be rented without key money.[13]
However, a noticeable mitigation took place directly after,
so that by 1908 several thousand houses in the Borough of
Stepney were empty and key money vanished.[14] This welcome
reversal was no result of a decline in immigration—the preceding five years were the busiest ever—but of the extension
of the new underground system with fares cheap enough to
allow workers to live beyond walking distance of their jobs. It
was not the Jews who vacated the houses. Powerful centripetal
forces still kept them in the East End *en masse* and prevented
substantial numbers from moving for some years following.

An anxiously desired goal of native Jewish efforts among
immigrants was to lure them out of the East End and to
disperse them among the smaller cities in the provinces. Few
moved, but one who did, Isaac Aryeh Rubinstein, six months
a religious functionary in so improbable a place as Penzance,
was delighted with his new home. He wondered why Jews
who were packed into the East End did not abandon their
teeming localities and settle in such towns as his, which had
contained a Jewish community earlier in the century:[15]

In the provinces there are great cities and many factories and a
variety of trades, and a man can easily learn a craft or trade which
supports its practitioner. The manufacturers are also favourably
inclined and make no distinction between nationalities and religions,
yet it is still rare to see a Jew in those cities.

To the argument that dispersion meant the loss of Judaism,
he replied that the corruptions of urban life, such as drinking
and gambling, were already the undoing of many Jews and were
far more perilous to Jewish morality:

'Were they wise, they would consider this; they would understand
their latter end', that town life is hard for them. It would be well

[13]*Idem*, Tables XLVII–XLVIII, summarizing conflicting evidence given in Cd.
1742.
[14]M. J. Landa, *The Alien Problem and Its Remedy*, London, 1911, pp. 64–73.
Report of Medical Officer of Health for Stepney, *JC*, July 22, 1904. Rates paid by
East End landlords declined between 1901 and 1904, owing to empty houses.
JC, June 24, 1904.
[15]*HaMeliz*, XXVI, 155, November 25–December 7, 1886.

for them to seek out a place to reside in Provincial cities and villages
. . . they will go forth and spread out in the land and not cramp each
other.

He was puzzled why few Jews remained in his own Penzance:

. . . They eat the good things of the land and enjoy uninterrupted,
unhindered peace. In spite of this, our brethren have left this place and
scattered. . . .

Up north in Grimsby, Joel Elijah Rabinowitz retorted that
the Jewish immigrant would continue to choose the London
slum in spite of every inducement, because employment and
fellow-Jews were to be found there.[16] The Russo-Jewish Committee, which tried earnestly to persuade immigrants to settle
away from the East End, realistically explained why the immigrants persistently ignored these blandishments:

(1) Indisposition on the part of the individual refugee to migrate
to quarters where he would be mainly among strangers.
(2) Local prejudices against foreigners, and especially against
refugee Jews, who are regarded as interlopers.
(3) The persistent objection of some of the refugees to obtaining
a knowledge of English.
(4) The objection to the schooling of the children outside Jewish
influences.[17]

Some native Jews opposed diffusion. Their fear was that the
immigrants might have 'habits and customs [which] might be
offensive and would cause injury to the name of the Anglo-
Jewish community'.[18]

Sir Samuel Montagu founded the Jewish Dispersion Committee in 1903 to continue the work of transplanting somewhat
Anglicized immigrants to smaller cities where there was employment and Jewish communal facilities existed. One instance
is Reading, where a colony of several hundred East European
immigrants established itself successfully.[19] Outsiders' wishes

[16]*Idem*, 178, December 10–22, 1886.
[17]'Private and Confidential' report to the Russo-Jewish Committee, October 12,
1892; in the Library of The Jewish Theological Seminary of America.
[18]Philip Ornstien, Secretary of the United Synagogue, address reported in *JC*,
March 20, 1903, an interesting and candid discussion.
[19]Cd. 1742, Min. 19792 ff. on Reading—testimony of J. W. Martin, former
Mayor of Reading. On the Jewish Dispersion Committee, see *Ibid.*, Min. 16776 ff.,
testimony of Sir Samuel Montagu.

to disperse the Jews are easy to explain, but the immigrants' steadfast refusal to move except to some other part of the same city at their own pace is harder to understand. Dispersion was offered on favourable terms, and painstaking efforts were made by its sponsors to ascertain that every legitimate requirement of their protégés would be met. Residential, economic, religious, educational facilities all existed. Could it have been the comfort of living in a quarter large enough to banish the physical presence of the outside world which intensified their reluctance to live elsewhere in small, exposed units? No firm evidence exists. Nor is the factor of accident in establishing an immigrant centre to be dismissed. The pioneer immigrants made their choice of homes, and those who followed them five or ten or thirty years later sought out the place where a friend or relative already resided. Thus, the bigger communities tended to grow yet bigger of their own weight. Finally, residence in a district builds up loyalties and attachments which frequently outweigh considerations of greater comfort and cleanliness to be had elsewhere.

THE IMMIGRANT HOME

In spite of all endeavours, probably ninety per cent. of the immigrants resided in the East End of London and its analogous zones in the provinces and we must examine them more closely. We have seen that the Jewish parishes within Stepney were far from being a desert of slums. Many of its streets had historic associations with London's annals, and some were adorned with homes which were charming if mostly decrepit period pieces. [20] True enough, Brady Street and Old Montague Street were noisome slums, and dozens of little courts and alleys exuded stench, but thoroughfares like Great Alie and Great Prescott Streets were lined with comfortable and well-appointed houses. It would be rash to generalize about the interior decor of the immigrant dwelling. On one hand, the furnishings of a few carefully studied households in Glasgow impressed Scottish investigators: 'the parlours are wonderful rooms, with full suites of furniture, photographs, crystal or

[20] D. L. Munby, *op. cit.*, pp. 77–79.

china ornaments, antimacassars, etc'.[21] Doubtless this was not typical, for few immigrants could or did bring substantial furnishings with them or could afford to buy them. By far the greater number of immigrants' homes were humbly, even shabbily, outfitted, many without beds enough for all inhabitants and with few articles of pleasure or beauty, and in use day and night as workrooms.

The special sanitary problems of Jewish life in the immigrant quarter are inseparable from the question of public health in Victorian London. That immense metropolitan complex was but a 'geographical expression' until 1888 and existed without effective central supervision of sanitary and health facilities until 1903.[22] Before that date, many functions of London Government were diffused among hundreds of independent petty parochial bodies. The Whitechapel Board of Works and its successor, the Borough of Stepney, were responsible for housing, water supply, and sewage inspection in the Jewish area, and fulfilled their mandate as badly as most of the corresponding bodies elsewhere in London. Thus, they employed only two inspectors to watch over all the local houses and prosecute offenders. The vagaries of water supply in the East End aggravated the sanitary problem. Private enterprise supplied London with its water until 1903, and the East London Water Works Company, a notoriously unsatisfactory public utility, was supposed to cover the East End. To a great extent because of that Company's blundering and inefficiency, the Jewish quarter, like the rest of East London, was plagued by water famines and highly irregular supply.[23] The Sanitary Committee of the Jewish Board of Guardians expressed the obvious to the local authority when it expostulated that 'until a proper water supply is laid on the dwellings of the poor,

[21]Dorothy E. Lindsay, *Report upon a Study of the Diet of the Labouring Classes in the City of Glasgow*, Glasgow, 1913, p. 23.

[22]W. A. Robson, *The Government and Misgovernment of London*, London, Allen & Unwin, 1939, in general, as well as Henry Jephson, *The Sanitary Evolution of London*, London, 1907. In the mass of fact and fantasy and prejudice upon this subject in the Minutes of the Royal Commission, the most reliable testimony is probably that of local Medical Officers of Health—S. F. Murphy (Mins. 3908 ff., 4722 ff.), Joseph Loane (Min. 4480 ff.), W. H. Hamer (Min. 17963 ff.), E. W. Hope (on Liverpool, Min. 21395 ff.), James Niven (on Manchester, Min. 21739 ff.), and D. L. Thomas (5433 ff., 7157 ff.).

[23]W. A. Robson, *op. cit.*, pp. 100–20; London County Council, *East London Water Company—Alleged Failure of Supply*, 10 March 1896.

considerable difficulty must be experienced in doing anything effective'.[24] Matters ultimately began to be set to rights only when a public water authority was established by Act of Parliament in 1903.

To an East End which was water-starved sometimes, unsatisfactorily inspected by public authorities, and overcrowded in decrepit or poorly built houses, the Jews brought not only an extra measure of overcrowding but a seeming ignorance and indifference to sanitary requirements. Accumulated and uncollected refuse lay in rotting piles inside and outside houses, while the interiors were often dank and malodorous from foul water closets, leaking ceilings, untrapped sinks, and cracked, moist walls. As it did in many fields, the Jewish Board of Guardians stepped in where Governmental bodies would not tread by undertaking to inspect and control Jewish workshops and dwellings. *The Lancet's* famous article in 1884[25] on the conditions of life and work among East End Jews stung the Board to action. It appointed its own inspector to do the parish's work among the Jews, and conducted a survey during the following six months which made some disturbing discoveries. The inspector applied only the parish standard, and 'considered houses habitable when the Roof, Walls, Floors, Yards, etc. show no structural defects, when there is no bad smell from the Drains, and when the Dustbins are provided and emptied frequently.[26] Of the first 1,332 Jewish homes visited, the habitability of 1,031 was 'found up to standard of local authority', and others had been partially or wholly repaired.[27] However, the water supply was amazingly bad. The inspector visited altogether 1,747 Jewish houses, and counted 1,621 without flushing water in their indoor or outdoor water closets.[28] Only during a cholera scare could round-the-clock water supply be secured.[29] The newly formed Sanitary Committee of the Jewish Board of Guardians carved out a

[24]Board of Guardians, *Executive Minutes*, December 4, 1884.
[25]*I.e.* 'A Polish Colony of Jewish Labourers,' *The Lancet*, March 5, 1884; repr. *JC*, May 9, 1884.
[26]Board of Guardians, *Executive Minutes*, October 1, 1884.
[27]*Idem*, October 23, 1884.
[28]David F. Schloss, 'Healthy Homes for the Working Classes,' *The Fortnightly Review*, N.S. XLIII, (April 1, 1888), pp. 533–35.
[29]Board of Guardians, *Executive Minutes*, July 24, 1883.

sizeable province of work for itself, and performed highly
meritorious service for twenty years. Between 1898 and 1903,
its inspectors visited and reported an annual average of 1,107
dwellings an average annual number of 2,899 times to remedy
sanitary defects.[30] It educated immigrant slum dwellers and
applied pressure to landlords and local authorities. Interesting
to note, the Jewish inspector's right to perform his duties
seems never to have been challenged as he entered homes,
although he had no legal coercive power. His instructions
were reportedly executed with 'utmost alacrity', not the usual
experience of sanitary inspectors.[31] The Jewish Board of
Guardians' sanitary standards were modest enough, and
seem to have carried weight with landlords and parishes.
This is due to the organization's prestige and energy, and
to important men who were profoundly concerned with this
work—Montagu, Mocatta, D. F. Schloss, N. S. Joseph.[32]

Jewish housing in Manchester, Leeds, and Liverpool left
plenty to be desired, but was in no wise the urgent problem
which the East End presented. These Midlands cities maintained efficient housing and sanitary inspection, particularly in
contrast with the chaos in London.[33] Still there was no lack of
bad spots. The Leeds Jewish quarter, as it appeared to a medical
investigator,

consists of a number of small streets with red brick cottages. The
sanitary accommodation is altogether inadequate. In one street,
where a great number of tailors live, we found only two closets for
seven houses. These were placed back to back in a little passage
between two houses. . . . The houses on this side of the street have
no back yards or windows.

Depressing as was the outside view, the investigator did not
find that the interiors of the Jews' houses are particularly dirty.
Some are dirty, but some are particularly and remarkably
clean.[34]

[30]*Idem*, October 28, 1906. For comparison with other London slum boroughs,
see Cd. 1742, Min. 17971, table.
[31]Board of Guardians, *Minutes*, July 18, 1884.
[32]Cd. 1742, Min. 15400–04—testimony of Leonard L. Cohen, President of the
Jewish Board of Guardians.
[33]See in general, T. R. Marr, *The Housing Problem in Manchester and Salford*,
Manchester, 1905, and the testimony of James Niven, Medical Officer of Health,
Cd. 1742, Min. 21739 ff., and esp. Manchester *Evening News*, January 29, 1903.
[34]Report of The Lancet Special Sanitary Commission on the Sweating System
in Leeds, *The Lancet*, June 9, 1888, p. 1148.

As in London, in Manchester also 'a certain amount of slovenliness' was charged to the immigrants, which 'tends rather to the accumulation of dust . . . than to the actual presence of filth in the house. . . .'[35] One feature of the Jewish quarter which contributed to its unkempt appearance was the fact that the Jews were 'a class, whose houses are also their workshops. . . .'[36] Bad habits prevailed notably among the newer arrivals, for

the people when they first come over have a different standard of cleanliness from what prevails in this country, but . . . they are amenable to the ordinary methods of sanitary administration. . . .[37]

Public health knowledge and enforcement in England, even in the urban slum zones, were after all far ahead of East European conditions. The immigrant had probably breathed purer air in his old town than in an English city, but it was also a place where little or nothing was known or done about garbage collection, sewage disposal, and sanitary water. It need hardly be added that medical knowledge and treatment in Russia lagged behind what even an impoverished Englishman could secure. Unlike an Englishman who moved to a large city, a new settler in England really moved into a relatively healthier environment, however his hygienic habits may have irritated nearby residents. Considerable ill-will and friction were in fact generated until the immigrant learned and practised the skills and habits necessary to life in a tightly packed city.

Because of their ignorance, the Jews had

no idea of demanding and insisting on proper sanitary accommodation . . . the Christian tenants have what is necessary, [but] the Jews must be satisfied with what is left.[38]

The Manchester Jewish Board of Guardians, like the London Board, kept its eye upon the 'dwellings of the Jewish poor' as early as 1871 to prevent epidemics.[39] A Visiting Committee inspected these homes in 1875 and observed 'a great improve-

[35]Cd. 1742, Min. 21765.
[36]Manchester Jewish Board of Guardians, *Minutes*, September 5, 1883.
[37]Cd. 1742, Min. 21810.
[38]Report of The Lancet Special Sanitary Commission on the Sweating System in Leeds, *loc. cit.*
[39]Manchester Jewish Board of Guardians, *Minutes*, September 6, 1871.

ment in the general condition of Jewish dwellings,' and requested non-Jewish critics to bear in mind that Saturday was a
better day for inspection than Thursday, the cleaning day.[40]
Years later, the City's Sanitary Committee assigned a special
Jewish lady inspector to work in 'the worst Jewish quarter in
the city, and her allotted task was to get rid of the squalor and
filth of the houses and shops'.[41] Although 'by far the majority
were found in a very dirty condition, dilapidated, and in a bad
state of repair generally', after a year's activity of inspection
and instruction 'a great improvement [was] visible over the
area'.[42] Matters cannot have been critically bad if they were so
speedily remedied.

Demolition was the surest cure for the ills found in most of
the Jewish immigrants' houses. In fact, the removal of these
dwellings and their replacement by suitable living quarters
had begun slowly to nibble away at London's immense mass
of desolate slum acreage in the 1870's. One reason for the
slowness, besides the weakness of parochial Governmental
bodies, was that model housing could not be built by public
bodies but had to be undertaken by combining public condemnation with private wrecking and new construction,
according to fixed specifications.[43] Two Jewish ventures were
prominent in the earlier years of slum clearance, the Four Per
Cent. Industrial Dwellings Company, Ltd., and the East End
Dwellings Company, Ltd. Both of these enterprises were the
outcome of the United Synagogue's inquiry into 'spiritual
destitution' in the East End in 1884, which found that physical
hardships were far more pressing.[44] The former company
assumed its title to emphasize that it was no charity and
proposed a four per cent. rate of return to investors. Objections
to the project were heard,[45] but with Rothschild as chairman

[40]*Idem*, November 3, 1875; a further report, June 27, 1884.
[41](James Niven), *Report on the Health of the City of Manchester*, 1899, Manchester, 1900, p. 172.
[42]*Idem, Report . . . 1900*, Manchester, 1901, p. 168; Cd. 1742, Min. 21779.
[43]For an antiseptic official account issued by the London County Council, see
The Housing Question in London, 1855–1900, London, 1900, which contains illus-
trations and plans.
[44]Given in *JC*, February 27, 1885. For the crypto-socialist reaction see *Die
Tsukunft*, I, 33, March 6, 1885.
[45]*JC*, March 6, 20, and 27, 1885.

and prime mover, the capital was speedily raised and the houses were opened for occupancy in 1886.

The flats in the 'Rothschild houses' were fair specimens of the quasi-public housing of their day. Each had two rooms, shared a toilet and kitchen with the adjacent flat, and opened to outdoor halls and stairways.[46] In order to reimburse investors at the promised rate, the six-storey buildings occupied no less than fifty per cent. of the ground space and tenants paid about 5s to 6s a week.[47] These grey stone houses were drab and draughty, but they were also solid and sanitary, and were probably better flats than those in other projects of the time. Although they were not restricted to Jews, all or nearly all of the inhabitants were coreligionists of the chairman. By 1894, 2,990 persons resided in the 'four percent.' houses, and perhaps 1,000 more in the East End Dwellings.[48] But many more crowded in as 'lodgers',[49] for unlike Miss Octavia Hill's housing projects, the 'Rothschild houses' did not supervise the domestic life of their inhabitants.

One of the sorest points in the relations between immigrant Jews and native English in immigrant districts revolved about the rent question. Specifically, it concerned the higher rents which Jews seemed willing to pay for houses, speeding up the displacement of English tenants. By a process of mutual cause and effect, the high rents paid by Jews invited overcrowding, which in turn further stimulated rack-renting. Nothing hindered a landlord from raising rents as he pleased or from expelling any tenant to make way for anyone whom he pleased. Matters did not improve when, as sometimes happened, the landlord was himself a Jewish immigrant. (Real estate in Jewish districts was a favoured investment for immigrants who prospered.) It is hard to learn the rents, for the abundant figures supplied to the Royal Commission reflect Stepney's years of maximum occupancy, when the 'key money' practice was rife. Yet rents probably rose fifty per cent. or sixty per cent. when a street turned Jewish, with the entire difference pocketed by

[46]*JC*, March 13, 1885.
[47]D. F. Schloss, *op. cit.*, pp. 528–29.
[48]*JC*, February 2, 1894.
[49]As alleged by the physician L. Selitrenny, 'The Jewish Working Woman in the East End,' *The Social Democrat*, II, 9 (September, 1898), p. 273.

speculating or rack-renting landlords and partially made back by tenants who took in lodgers.[50]

The Jews' alien status and the higher rents which accompanied them incited severe hostility when they settled in a new street as the Jewish quarter gradually spread out. Sensing that they would soon be submerged, some of the English and Irish inhabitants moved out at once. Others remained behind to give vent to cold or hot hostility, whether by calculated snubbing or, at times, by stones thrown and windows broken. But they too presently evacuated. In the words of a London County Councillor to the Royal Commission:

> The aliens will not conform to our ideas, and, above all, they have no sort of neighbourly feeling. . . . A foreign Jew will take a house, and he moves in on a Sunday morning, which rather, of course, upsets all the British people there. Then his habits are different. You will see the houses with sand put down in the passages instead of oilcloth or carpet. These are little things, but they all serve to make a difference.[51]

The combination of dirtiness, too-public sociability, and indifference to the English Sabbath were rank offences:

> He will use his yard for something. He will store rags there, perhaps—mountains of smelling rags, until the neighbours all round get into a most terrible state over it, or perhaps he will start a little factory in the yard, and carry on a hammering noise all night, and then he will throw out a lot of waste stuff, offal, or anything like that—it is all pitched out, and in the evening the women and girls sit out on the pavement and make a joyful noise . . . on the Sunday the place is very different to what the English are accustomed to.

[50]See above, notes 12 and 13. Evidence before the Royal Commission is voluminous and unreliable, since the rent question was in sharp dispute at the time of the hearings. Unfortunately, no Governmental body was charged with collecting data on rents, so that conclusions are necessarily tentative. The clearest general data is in Royal Commission on Alien Immigration, *Appendix to Minutes of Evidence*, Cd. 1741–I, 1903, Tables XXXVIII–XLVI. The net increase from Tables XLII to XLV is exactly 70 per cent. for the 177 houses tabulated; however, the date of the first base year is uncertain. Tables XXXIX and XL indicate a correlation between shift from Gentile to Jewish ownership of East End Jewish dwellings and rent increase. For some caustic remarks on Jewish real estate speculators see *Yudishe Telegraf*, II, 55, (February 17, 1898), p. 13; C. Russell and H. S. Lewis, *op. cit.*, pp. 16–17, 173–74; United Synagogue, *East End Scheme*, London, 1898, p. 43–44.

[51]Cd. 1742, Min. 1724. Testimony of James Lawson Silver, a leading anti-alienist. *Cf.* C. Russell and H. S. Lewis, *op. cit.*, p. xxxix–xl.

Most extraordinary sights are seen. In one place last summer there was a kind of leads to a house with other houses backing on to it, and two alien families put out their beds on the leads and two married couples slept out on the leads, much to the amusement of all the surrounding neighbourhood.[52]

The witness, a member of the energetic Housing Committee of the London County Council, succinctly put the view of perhaps thousands of his constituents:

These are little things, but they serve to show that their habits are not such as will enable them to associate.[53]

A Leeds surgeon and landlord contrasted the Jewish immigrant's home with its departed glory as 'a little palace' when English workers had lived in it:

I would go into a house twenty years ago [c. 1868] and find it a little palace, as comfortable as any man could want, with clean floor and clean windows and blinds, and nicely furnished . . .; but if I go into that same house tomorrow I should find the floor dirty, no blind at all on the windows, no fire, or what fire there is merely cinders, everything out of order. . . .[54]

Most offensive was the dirtiness, as he explained:

. . . they stop their fire-places up, and will not introduce any fresh air; I had a tenant, a Jew, and he was constantly writing to me that rats and mice abound in the house, and that there is a nasty smell in the house, and when he went away we found a whole lot of refuse fish in the house; the house had never been opened.[55]

The witness was not asked why he took in so disagreeable a class of tenants.

HEALTH

The surprising phenomenon is that such adverse conditions of life and labour did not find their usually predictable reflection in high death rates and heavy infant mortality. Reasonably full and reliable data comes only from the public authorities in

[52]Cd. 1742, Min. 1724. [53]Ibid.
[54]House of Commons, Select Committee on Emigration and Immigration (Foreigners), Second Report, August 8, 1889, Min. 1151.
[55]Idem, Min. 1134.

Manchester, and it quite conclusively proves the good health
record of Jewish immigrants. In that city, the death rate in
1901 was 21.78 per 1,000, while among Jewish immigrants
it was 16.99 per 1,000. The youthful age distribution of the
Jewish immigrant group does not explain away the difference,
for the Jewish death rate is substantially lower than the general
death rate in every age stratum except over sixty-five. In the
poorer areas of the city, whose residents were of approximately the same economic standing as the Jews, the death
rate was 33.9—exactly twice as high. We do not know the
Jewish immigrant community's birth rate, but their children's
chances of survival were better than in the Gentile environment.
The death rate for children under five was 72.50 per 1,000
in all Manchester, but 55.88 per 1,000 among the immigrants.[56]
It is not unreasonable to suppose that Jewish vital statistics
in other cities resemble Manchester's. The immigrants'
children were better fed and healthier than English children
of their economic class.[56a]

The disparity between the squalor and disorder of the
immigrants' dwellings and the physical vitality, if not robust-
ness, displayed by their inhabitants invites some explanation.
Perhaps there were sources of strength which overcame environmental hazards, but it is easier to give reasons for the
Jews' comparative health than to prove them. Did centuries
of Jewish residence in cities and towns build up a particular
immunity to the perils of urban life? We cannot tell. To be
sure, some requirements of Jewish law, such as its dietary
features, are conducive to health. Kosher meat, the only meat
eaten by an observing Jew, hedges with safeguards the health
of the animal and the freshness of the supply, no insignificant
matters in times when adulterated or diseased meat could be
marketed almost with impunity. Other religious precepts en-
join the Jew to rejoice upon his Sabbath and Festival with

[56]Abstracted from Cd. 1742, Table A, following Min. 21872, and (James
Niven), *Report on the Health of the City of Manchester, 1897,* Manchester, 1900,
p. 170.
[56a]Interdepartmental Committee on Physical Deterioration, Vol. I. Report and
Appendix, Cd. 2175. Vol. II, List of Witnesses, and Minutes of Evidence. Cd.
2210. Vol. III, Appendix and General Index. Cd. 2186. See Index, s.v. 'Jews'.
The Jewish data is also quoted in *JC,* August 19, 1904.

ample board, and were heartily fulfilled even by unobservant households. Such practices as bathing for religious purposes and a complete house-cleaning before Passover produced 'an hygienic effect', in the vocabulary of public health reformers. There seems to be some real basis for the much remarked domestic habits of the Jews, which might assure deep devotion to the rearing of the young. Finally, although Jewish law is not very direct upon this point, the Jews drank moderately: drunkenness, the bane of the poorer industrial classes, never existed in the Jewish quarter.

While these factors represent potential assets in the health ledger, even the most rigorous adherence to Jewish laws and folkways affecting hygiene could not *ipso facto* guarantee health. These practices existed, but their effects are imponderable. On the other side, there are unhealthy and even dangerous features in Jewish immigrant life, for not only was the immigrant's housing unhealthy, but so was his work. Outside the mines, hardly any occupations in England afforded such unwholesome physical settings as did tailoring and boot and shoe making in the Jewish workshops. Furthermore, the Jewish worker (when he had work) spent a larger part of each twenty-four hours at his toil than he did in eating, sleeping, and relaxation. The young woman worker especially suffered. A physician alleged that it was 'very ordinary' for her to be afflicted with 'malformation of the vertebrae, pains in the back, swelling of the veins and of the articulations, tumors at the femur and legs, malformation of the pelvis, disorder in the menses, eczema, miscarriages'.[57]

Stoop and pallor marked the physique and countenance of immigrant workers, and one characteristic immigrant disease, tuberculosis, ended the lives of many.[58] Unlike such epidemic diseases as cholera and typhus, the outcome of bad water and raw sewage, which left the Jews relatively alone, tuberculosis came about from more insidious environmental factors. A hot crammed roomful of tailors or boot-makers,

[57]L. Selitrenny, *op. cit.*, p. 274.
[58]On this problem, see the Report of the Board of Guardians Special Committee on Consumption, in Jewish Board of Guardians, *Annual Report, 1897*, pp. 24–26, and the annual reports of the Sanitary Committee (later the Health Committee) in *Idem*, 1899 ff.

inhaling and exhaling upon each other in a lint-filled smoky atmosphere for twelve or thirteen hours, admirably incubated this and other lung diseases. The perils were compounded when the worker came home and ate from the same utensils and slept in one bed with members of his family. We first learn of the incidence of tuberculosis among immigrant Jews in the late 1890's, when scientific knowledge concerning it became more accessible and its prevention rose to high priority for public health bodies. The 'white plague' was no doubt widespread before then, but the evidence is scanty. By 1909, after a decade of effort at finding, diagnosing, and preventing consumption, we learn of 1,153 known Jewish cases in London, 674 male and 474 female, of whom nine per cent. died in one year.[59] The victims were concentrated in the age stratum between twenty-five and forty-five (sixty per cent.) and were largely (sixty-five per cent.) tailors, boot and shoe makers, furriers, and cap makers, and cigarette makers. The Jewish Board of Guardians, which dealt with the cases, at first occupied itself with comforting the dying victim and disinfecting his surroundings, but it also devoted a rising proportion of its funds to consumptive care and relief. With the application of scientific knowledge and the growth of clinical, hospital, and sanitarium facilities, the stress shifted to prevention and cure. The basic problem of prevention was the same problem which bedevilled too many cases discharged as cured—they 'resume their former lives, working usually at indoor occupations and living in crowded dwellings',[60] causing a high rate of relapses and deaths. Yet not until the establishment of three Tuberculosis Dispensaries in Stepney in 1912 did the astonishing magnitude of the scourge reveal itself. As a result of the Dispensaries' practice of referring Jewish cases to the Health Committee of the Jewish Board of Guardians, that group's register of cases multiplied from 969 (517 men, 357 women, 95 children) at the close of 1911 to 1,795 in the following year, 2,698 in 1913, and 3,145 in 1914.[61] The ascent was steepest among women and children, whose proportions

[59]*Idem*, 1911, pp. 97–98.
[60]*Idem*, 1902, p. 88.
[61]From the annual reports of the Health Committee in *Idem*, 1911 ff; A. Freeman and Sidney Webb, *Seasonal Trades*, London, 1912, pp. 86–87.

L

increased by 317 per cent. and 1,010 per cent. respectively;
obviously they had been previously neglected. Besides, unlike
the early small figures the later figures include many tubercular
cases in their incipient and curable stages.

Little technical diagnosis is required to fix the responsibility
borne by living conditions in the Jewish quarter. Even when
water supply and sewage disposal were at last adequate, and
when workshops were finally subjected to a measure of supervision, the basic conditions of slum life and work contributed
an irreducible share to the deterioration of health.

WELFARE AND CHARITY

We must take note of the charities which alleviated or prevented the hardships of immigrant life. In his hour of distress
the immigrant would probably turn first to one of the in-
numerable charities of his fellow immigrants. There is no
measure of the charities which immigrant Jews did for each
other, either individually or through some sort of organization.
When thousands of young Russian Jews, unwilling to serve
their Czar as conscripts in Siberia during the Russo-Japanese
War, arrived in London, East End Jewry bustled with im-
provised arrangements. Money was raised and donations of
food and offers of shelter poured into the immigrant synagogues
where the refugees were fed. Even free steam baths were presented to them. All of this was accomplished in a few days.[61a]
In quieter times, dozens and perhaps hundreds of societies had
charitable assistance, usually mutual, as their main or sub-
sidiary motive for existence. Small congregations, trade unions,
and all manner of friendly societies stood prepared to render
their members and sometimes outsiders aid in cash, in kind,
or personal service. Not only was the immigrant a recipient of
charity, but he was also a donor—and not only among his own,
but overseas. 'Giving without a murmur'[62] was the admiring
epithet for the unusual open-handedness of the immigrants'

[61a]'Russian Refugees in the East End', *JC*, December 16, 1904.
[62]*JC*, January 2, 1903. In one unusual instance, East End Jews boarded workers'
children during the dock strike in 1912. Rudolf Rocker in Joseph Ishill ed., *Peter
Kropotkin*, Berkeley Heights, N.J., 1923, p. 91.

response to the many calls upon their miniscule philanthropic
resources. These slender amounts supported religious societies
and schools, Zionist or socialist movements, and thousands
of individuals also sent remittances to relatives in Eastern
Europe. They even continued to support some charities in the
'old home'. *Yeshibot* in Eastern Europe sent collectors to
England with a list of previous donors; it is hardly to be expected that many of them were natives in the West End.[63]

London was the seat of numerous Jewish charities, some
of eighteenth century origin, such as the Bread and Coals
Society, the Initiation Society (for circumcision), the Sabbath
Meals Society, the Soup Kitchen for the Jewish Poor, and
the Jewish Lodging House in Gun Street. Each of these worked
devotedly at its chosen service to the immigrants, and many
served as models for corresponding charities in the communities of the Provinces.

However, any discussion of Jewish charity and welfare
must consider the scope and work of the Jewish Boards of
Guardians.[64] The London Board was of course the largest and,
except for Liverpool, the oldest, and gave the lead to the
Boards in other cities. The Guardians dominated native
Jewish charity in London, for they either absorbed other
organizations or entered into close working agreements with
them, and the same practice existed in the Provinces. Although
their title was borrowed from the Guardians of the Poor
established by the Poor Law of 1834, and the 'charity organisation' concept which pervaded charity under the Poor Law
decisively influenced Jewish charitable work, the Jewish
bodies were far from dominated by the regnant Benthamism.
Whatever the supposed moral shortcomings of the English
poor, the miseries of the Jewish poor could hardly be blamed on
lack of ambition, drink, or shiftlessness. Periodic sieges of
unemployment were not due to any of these faults, or even to
business cycles, but to the hopelessly seasonal nature of the
Jewish immigrant trades. For emotional as well as narrowly

[63]*JC*, December 21, 1894.
[64]A model study is V. D. Lipman, *A Century of Social Service 1859–1959. The
History of the Jewish Board of Guardians*, London, 1959. The memoir of Kate
Magnus, *The Board of Guardians and the Men Who Made It*, London, 1909, is
now antiquated.

economic reasons the erection of a Jewish workhouse was out of the question, and it was quite unthinkable to permit Jews to enter the Poor Law workhouse. To be sure, both English and Jewish Guardians were at one in their determination to repress beggary, a nuisance which annoyed the provinces more than London.[65] Like every important Jewish charity in Western Europe and America during these generations, but unlike any English charity, the Jewish Board of Guardians derived the great majority of its clientele from East European immigrants.

The Guardians were most important to the immigrant because from its offices came relief in cash or in kind in the hour of death, illness, unemployment, or family break-up. It might give a grant towards emigration to the Empire or to America. The Board's services were available to all ages. Orphans entered the Jews' Hospital and Orphan Asylum through its good offices, and boys were apprenticed and girls were taught trades through its help and advice. A worker could secure a loan of cash or a grant of tools to start in a trade or business, and several hundred aged persons subsisted on Board of Guardians pensions. We have already seen that the work done in housing inspection and sanitary control shifted to tuberculosis prevention and treatment at the turn of the century. At about the same time, the Jewish Board of Guardians cautiously began the rudiments of social case work by giving detailed attention to the fortunes of one person or family. However, for all the great and indeed indispensable value of its activities, the Jewish Board of Guardians was respected but not loved. Although its cable name was 'Rachmonem'—the compassionate —the Guardians did not show much of this side of their character to the suppliant immigrant who could expect a 'not too effusive reception'.[66] The same facet of its corporate personality may be seen from the occasional replica of the style and tone of a Poor Law report in its Annual Reports.

Aside from Jewish charities, the East End was a classical locus of charitable endeavour in England, and Jews derived advantage from these general charities. Such organizations as

[65]See the reports of Provincial Jewish Boards of Guardians in Cd. 1742, Min. 6605, pp. 596–97.
[66]The phrase is N. S. Joseph's. *JC*, March 18, 1892.

the Children's Country Holidays Fund took children to the country and seaside for vacations, and had Jewish committees to meet the special requirements of Jewish children. In the London Hospital, which stood in Whitechapel Road from 1759, a Jewish patient could be served kosher food. Christian missionary societies also conducted medical clinics in the Jewish quarter, coupling service to the ill and ailing with a most ineffective proselytizing effort. Notwithstanding much deploring by official Jewish bodies, thousands of Jews annually attended such places as the Mildmay clinic and remained unpersuaded by the missionary lectures and hymn singing which they heard while waiting.[67] At the nadir of charity there was the Poor Law and its facilities. The Jews used the Poor Law clinic and medicines, and occasionally had to resort to its infirmary, but they practically never entered the workhouse. Despite the prominence of the Poor Law and the workhouse in the scheme of English charity, it hardly merits attention in discussing Jewish charity.[68] Agitation to the contrary, the Jewish immigrant practically never came upon the rates.

Jewish charity was extensive and generous and at times farsighted. But the Jewish immigrant stood on his own feet usually unsupported, shaky though he sometimes was.

[67] *Report . . . on . . . Medical Relief to the Jewish Poor*, June 10, 1891, in Jewish Board of Guardians, *Minute Letter Book*, p. 39.

[68] House of Commons Select Committee on Emigration and Immigration (Foreigners), *First Report*, July 27, 1888, Appendix 9, pp. 263–69; *Second Report*, August 8, 1889, pp. 85–88; Royal Commission on Alien Immigration, *Appendix to Minutes of Evidence*, Cd. 1741–I, 1903, Tables XXIV–XXXII.

VI

A SOCIETY UNTO ITSELF

Immigrant Jewry formed a society apart, with standards derived from other sources than England. In the first generation of immigrant settlement there was a great deal of mutual avoidance; even given good will on both sides, there was so little common ground between the immigrant Jew and his neighbour that it could not have been otherwise.

It is simpler to learn of social problems than to comprehend social life; easier to know of disrupted homes than of sound family life. We do not know the most important social statistics: marriages and births, children per family, and other prosaic data of social actualities. Intimate details of the home and domestic life reach us less distinctly than the evanescent society of the club and street.[1]

As in other things, immigrant life was an attempt to preserve with more or less adjustment the social standards and habits of home and communal life in Eastern Europe. To a greater extent than other migrants from rural or small town environments to the big city, the Jews maintained much of the outward appearance and even the flavour of their former way of life. To appreciate this, one must somehow look behind the impressions of street and club life and enter the home.

DOMESTIC LIFE AND CARES

The Jewish home has perhaps received an exaggerated measure of adulation, so that more detached observers are wary of accepting its catalogue of praises without demur. Strict marital fidelity, mutual affection and self-sacrifice between the generations, the home as the seat of most religious observance, patriarchal authority with a prominent role reserved for the

[1]See Jacob de Haas' suggestive remarks to the First Zionist Congress in Basel in 1897 on Jewish social characteristics in England. (World Zionist Organization), *HaProtokol shel haKongress haZioni haRishon*, (Proceedings of the First Zionist Congress), Jerusalem, 1946, pp. 30–38.

mother—all of these mark Jewish home life at its best, and can be found in countless families in high and low estate. However, the presence of domestic felicity cannot simply be assumed, yet is naturally difficult to prove. The immigrant family was larger than the average English family in the same class. In a representative sample, Harry S. Lewis found an average of 5.1 children dwelling with their immigrant parents, to 3.6 among English families.[1a] It is risky to generalize upon the character of domestic relations, and Harry S. Lewis' remarks, made in 1900, seem the most apposite:

The conjugal relations of the foreign Jews present some difficult problems, but they must be pronounced to be generally satisfactory. The Jew is a born critic, and he seldom finds fault with his wife, and he is, as a rule, blessed with domestic happiness. The Jewish husband spends most of his leisure at home, and, possibly owing to this fact, his wife's advice and influence count for much with him.[2]

The Jewish wife practically never went to work, but she assumed financial responsibility in a different way:

So far as household expenses are concerned, the wife is chancellor of the exchequer. The result is that the husband seems often more liberal in his ideas of money than the wife, who is weighted with the responsibility of avoiding a deficit in the family budget.[3]

Much attention and affection were lavished upon the children:

Jewish parents are usually indulgent and sometimes very indiscreet in the management of children, so that we need not be surprised if they sometimes lament that 'englische Kinder'—i.e. children brought up in England—are inferior to those educated abroad. . . . The zeal of Jewish parents for their children's advancement is very noticeable. For this end they will make every sacrifice.[4]

Immigration strained many such domestic fabrics severely, and the hardships of separation sundered some families permanently. As if in compensation, the scope of the family unit expanded greatly. Uncles replaced fathers, and cousins became

[1a]Based on the 1901 Case-book of the West Whitechapel Committee of the Children's Country Holidays Fund. There were 535 Jewish to 111 Christian families. While accepting Lewis' statistical accuracy, it may be that larger families were more prone to apply to the fund, thus somewhat distorting the average family size. Letter from Harry S. Lewis, *JC*, March 21, 1902.

[2]C. Russell and H. S. Lewis, *The Jew in London*, London, 1900, p. 186.

[3]*Ibid.*, p. 187.   [4]*Ibid.*, pp. 185, 182.

as brothers in the urge to maintain a semblance of familial ties in the midst of changing their countries. The struggles of immigration and settlement generated tensions and difficulties; from this 'pathology' of family life an indication of normal patterns may be derived.

The observance of Jewish laws and customs concerning marriage posed some difficult social questions. In East European Jewish society, well-nigh irresistible social habit required every male to marry; an unmarried female was fully unthinkable. Divorce, when it occurred, had to be given by the husband, although social pressure and legal adjustments in the *ketubah* (marriage document) could force the most recalcitrant of husbands to grant his estranged wife a *get* (divorce). But matters were less simple where the Jewish social order was faltering in its hold upon individuals. Husbands emigrated, leaving wives behind, often with children, to return to their parents' house until sent for. But if no word came from abroad there lay a tragic difficulty. For a deserted wife had no recourse; she had to remain an 'agunah (lit. anchored) until her husband died, of which she might not learn, or despatched a *get* to her. Sometimes the wife's family prevented the dreaded eventuality of an 'agunah by forcing a departing husband to grant a *get* before he left town, while he was yet within reach; they might remarry later. The columns of the East European press were replete with pathetic appeals from 'agunot and their families and from local rabbis pleading for news of the whereabouts of husbands who had been gone anywhere from two to fifteen years. If found, they asked, let them be exhorted to send a *get* to the woman they left behind. Husbands, when found, were often willing enough; but in a great many instances, they could not be found. Although rabbis of the day were anxious to smooth such separations by granting every possible relaxation to the woman, matters were still painfully complex. Witness a case laid before Rabbi Moses Sivitz, *circa* 1902:

A woman whose husband left her and settled in London, England, and [then] decided to leave London and cross the seas. He wrote a letter to his father and wrote thusly: 'Father, I am journeying away across the sea and I will not come again. Give my wife a *get*. . . . Let her take whatever husband she pleases and if you wish give her a *get*'.

Since then his movements are unknown, and this woman has been coming before courts for fourteen years to free her from the fetters of desertion.[5]

The rabbi's remarks suggest that in the earlier years of the separation the wife had hoped to rejoin her husband, while the rabbi for his part desired a firmer basis for a *get* than the man's letter to his father. Sivitz did not promulgate the *get* on the somewhat tenuous strength of the Yiddish letter until Rabbis Shalom Meir Schwadron and Jacob David Wilowsky-Ridvass, two outstanding authorities of the time, concurred.

The lengths rabbis would go to free the 'agunah is trenchantly illustrated by a London case submitted to Isaac Elhanan Spektor, Rabbi of Kovno.[6] Moses Shivensky had gone to London and left behind his wife and young daughter in Wishegrod. They continued to exchange letters, each asking the other to join him. Moses finally asked his wife whether it was legally safe to return to Russia; apparently he had smuggled himself out. The wife answered affirmatively. Some time later, an unidentifiable corpse was retrieved from the Thames, which contained the letters sent by the wife. Upon the strength of this circumstantial connection, and that of a deposition by an uncle who had heard Moses speak of suicide, the Rabbi of Kovno declared the corpse to be the remains of Moses. Only by virtue of this legal identification could the wife be free to remarry. If occasional remarks and personal letters sufficed to establish the identity of a decomposed body, another somewhat similar case would have posed even fewer juridical problems.[7] In this instance, a woman whose husband had been missing for some time found that a photograph of him in her possession

[5] M. S. Sivitz, *Pri Yehezkel*, Jerusalem, 1908, Part 2, p. 7. The date of the responsum may be established from Schwadron's statement (*Idem*, p. 23) that he was preparing his responsa for publication; they appeared as Part I of *Teshubot MaHaRSHam*, Warsaw, 1903. The rabbis quote the husband's letter in its Yiddish original, of which the second sentence is interpolated here from Part 2, p. 17. Considering that Sivitz was in Pittsburgh, Pa., from 1888, it is unclear why he entered the case. A similar rabbinic correspondence concerning an 'agunah of Suvalk and London whose husband was slain in the Franco-Prussian War originated with Jacob Reinowitz and was concurred in by Nathan and Hermann Adler, Sussmann Cohen, and B. Spiers, all of London; Abraham Ashkenazi and Barukh Pinto, Jerusalem; Esriel Hildesheimer, Berlin; Nafthali Zvi Judah Berlin, Volozhin; and others. *HaMaggid*, XXIII, 19 (May 4, 1879).

[6] Isaac Elhanan Spektor, *'Eyn Yizhak*, Vilna, 1889, Part III, No. 31, p. 286.

[7] *Idem*, No. 39, p. 302.

matched a photograph of a body brought up from the Thames. The similarity of the two photographs again supplied the Rabbi of Kovno with the necessary basis for legal identification, giving the wife her liberty to marry again.

However, most husbands and wives looked forward to the day of reunion, and exchanged letters during the prolonged separation. The following somewhat extended excerpt of a letter to one Moses Berman from his wife in Russia, written in April, 1888, illustrates personal feelings on both sides:[8]

To my dear and faithful Moshe Berman. I inform you that we are all, God be blessed, well. May God grant that we should hear the same of yourself. . . . your son Kirve held your letter in his hand and was very glad, continually asking, 'when will father come'. My dear Moses, you write that you are very bad off and earn very little; have I not told you before in Saulen, that you should not separate from us and leave me and the children alone; but you continually answered that wherever you will be you will be better off than in Saulen. And now you write that you repent having gone there at all. But believe me, dear husband, I and the children are worse off here than you are there.

The distressed wife gave examples of the sadness of her lot, and pressed her husband to bring her to England or to come back.

Now, my dear Moses, do write me what is to take place now. God knows when we will see each other! You are bad off there and I am bad off here, and cannot earn anything. Please let me know if there are any means for you to come back to Saulen. . . . And who knows better than I do the state of your health. . . . I send my kind greetings to Mr and Mrs Isaac for their benevolence to my husband Moses, and I pray of you to endeavour to find some means for him to enable him to find some bread for himself and his family, for besides God and yourselves I have nobody to apply to. . . .

Another sort of family dislocation took place when the

[8]Introduced in translation by Arnold White to the House of Commons Select Committee on Emigration and Immigration (Foreigners), and published in its *Report . . . 27 July, 1888* as Minute 1376. Despite the dubious auspices and unknown source of both letter and translation there seems little reason to doubt either its authenticity or the substantial accuracy of the English version. It does ring true.

husband went ahead to America, leaving the wife behind in England. This separation was not necessarily immoral or dishonourable, for a man out of work or with no visible prospect of livelihood scraped together the funds to cross the Atlantic, where he would presently send for his family. Meanwhile, the wife and children subsisted on aid from private or communal sources. The Jewish Boards of Guardians in London and the Provinces detested this practice, and periodically warned that they would refuse relief to 'deserted wives' who had acted in collusion with their husbands, and would require them to enter the hated Poor Law workhouse. However, such threats were very seldom carried out. Matters became urgent when the 'deserted wife' heard no word from her husband; there seem to have been instances when the wife and children were summarily despatched across the ocean to the husband and father, whether or not he had called for them to come.[9] Very many emigrants sent on by Jewish communal bodies were wives and children, who had to put up some of the cost themselves, just as they also constituted a goodly percentage of immigrants arriving in England. Thus, half of the arrivals at the Poor Jews' Temporary Shelter in the probably typical year of 1893–94 were the wives and children of husbands and fathers already in England.[10] In other words, nearly equal numbers of males and females among the immigrant population does not mean family units on the move together. At any given time, the immigrant quarter sheltered thousands of divided families, most of whom were probably reunited in the end.

Like practically all emigrating groups, younger people dominated the age strata of Jewish immigrants. Convincingly satisfactory demonstration is hard to come by, and S. Rosenbaum's estimate of 1905 is the best available. Of the 298,610

[9]Royal Commission on Alien Immigration, *Minutes of Evidence*, Cd. 1742, 1903, Min. 15318, 15583 ff.; C. Russell and H. S. Lewis, *op. cit.*, pp. 190–91; a rather agitated correspondence on Jewish Board of Guardians' shipment of emigrants to New York, between the United Hebrew Charities and the Guardians, is preserved in the Jewish Board of Guardians, *Minutes* and *Minute Letter Book*, April 15 to September 16, 1901. 55 per cent. of the Board's assisted emigrants were wives and children of husbands who had already crossed the Atlantic. Report of Board of Guardians Emigration Committee, in Board of Guardians, *Minute Letter Book*, August 21, 1901.
[10]Russo-Jewish Committee, *Report*, 1894, p. 27; see above, p. 46.

inhabitants of the Borough of Stepney enumerated in 1901, he classified 119,800, a shade under 40 per cent., as Jews. In this estimated total of Jews, 75.3 per cent. were under thirty-five years of age (74.4 per cent. of males, 76.1 per cent. of females); the similar figure for the non-Jews of the Borough stood at stood at 70.0 per cent. (70.2 per cent. of males, 69.7 per cent. of females).[11]

Among the consequences of fragmented family units, the lodger was one of the most ubiquitous:

Lodgers! What ghetto Jew doesn't know what a lodger is, and what ghetto Jew doesn't board a few lodgers? He himself lives in the cellar kitchen and the lodger is in the parlour.[12]

Some times the single male lodger became his landlord's son-in-law. Life was rather harder for the female lodger.[13] Actually, it is difficult to speak of home life in many houses, for with one or more lodgers, several children, and perhaps grandparents and other relatives, every Jewish immigrant household was a cramped place. Eight or nine individuals shared two small rooms, and the ratio was even higher in hundreds of dwellings. Hence a large part of home life was lived out of doors by older folk seated at their doorways, by adolescents in search of fascination and adventure, and by children at play in the courts and alleys. The immigrant Jewish quarter had in overflowing measure the communal sharing of troubles and joys found in every poor neighbourhood. Within the close confines of the Jewish settlement, kinsfolk and old townsmen tended to huddle together, and if these cozy connections had to be abandoned on account of moving elsewhere, new neighbourly intimacies soon arose to take their place. Probably thousands of next-door neighbours had a practically familial relation with each other.

---

[11]S. Rosenbaum, 'A Contribution to the Study of the Vital and Other Statistics of the Jews in the United Kingdom,' *Journal of the Royal Statistical Society*, LXVIII, pp. 526–66 (September, 1905). Census figures of aliens distort the age distribution of the immigrant community by omitting its English-born children.

[12]*Der Yudisher Telegraf*, II, 56 (February 24, 1898).

[13]L. Selitrenny, 'The Jewish Working Woman in the East End,' *The Social Democrat*, II, 2 (September, 1898), pp. 271–75, describes the Jewish working girl in exaggeratedly gloomy colours.

YOUNG PEOPLE

But in spite of such extensions and disruptions the Jewish immigrant family had tight inner ties:

Jewish children, sent for a fortnight's holiday in the country, and living for the time amongst Christians, have often told me how they miss the usual family gathering, when the Sabbath lamp is lighted, the cup of wine is drunk, and the father pronounces a blessing upon his children. It is no exaggeration to say that the happiest hours of a Jew's life are those spent within his home; and family ties in consequence much stronger amongst us than in the outside world. . . . Jewish law is very strict in requiring the utmost honour and obedience to parents. . . . Undutiful children are quite an exception. . . .[14]

The child was kept in school as much of the day as possible; not only were parents interested in his education, but there was little else for him to do.[15] The adolescent boy or girl, not yet settled in a job, represented the social dilemma of adolescence. Whether they were the relatively few who continued their schooling, or went to work bound by formal apprenticeship or as learners, or betook themselves to the volatile life of street trading, their maturing held special difficulty. They had two cultures to cope with. On one hand, there could be aid and loyalty to parents:

. . . respect for parents is preserved even after the critical age when the boy or girl goes out to work and gradually becomes self-supporting. Grown-up children, living at home and unmarried, contribute a fair proportion of their earnings to the family exchequer, sons usually giving over half, whilst daughters, who spend more money on clothing, often content themselves with paying about five shillings a week.[16]

On the other hand the younger people, more than their parents, had to harmonize Englishness and Jewishness, and on no abstract, philosophical level. Indeed, that might have been an easier personal search than that of the youth who heard one language at home, another outside; whose religious

[14]C. Russell and H. S. Lewis, *op. cit.*, pp. 181–82, 184.
[15]No corroboration could be found for L. Soloweitschik's statement that there was extensive Jewish child labour. L. Soloweitschik, *Un prolétariat méconnu*, Brussels, 1898, pp. 32–33.
[16]C. Russell and H. S. Lewis, *op. cit.*, p. 185.

upbringing, in case he wished to retain it, flew in the face of the requirements of holding a job; to whom the historic beliefs and meticulous practices of Judaism seemed stale and outdated, basically meaningless in urban, industrial, scientific civilization. Rebellion or apathy to the old way of life took several forms outside the home. While the pious and traditional went to the synagogue on the Sabbath, younger people promenaded White-chapel Road and its Provincial counterparts, often partaking of prohibited amusements.[17] To the scandal of their elders among both native and immigrant Jews, and to the surprise of many Gentiles, worship and study seemed to be cast aside for music hall and street life. What held true for boys was not greatly different for girls:

> At the most critical stage in a boy's life, when the undeveloped character is most readily susceptible to external influence, good or bad, he was left to shift for himself—His leisure hours were spent in aimless loafing about the streets, or occasional visits to low places of entertainment, proper facilities for passing his spare time in a healthy and rational manner, being virtually non-existent.[18]

The Jewish community wrestled with the apparition of prospectively wayward youth by adapting some of the techniques then coming into vogue. One of the most singular organizations for youth was the Jewish Lads' Brigade, on the model of that juvenile expression of 'muscular Christianity', the Church Lads' Brigade. It employed military trappings to infuse its young initiates with such virtues as punctuality, physical fitness, personal cleanliness, and so forth. The Brigade conducted a summer encampment on the style of army manoeuvres, and news of its activities was published in the guise of military communiqués. The highest enrolment reached by the Jewish Lads' Brigade was perhaps 1,000 to 1,500. The response of immigrant parents to the outward forms of the organization, which was preoccupied with 'ironing out the Ghetto bend', must be conjectured, yet it can hardly have been less than quizzical.[19]

[17]For example, B. Spiers, *Dibrey Debash* (Honied Words), London, 1901, p. 11.
[18]Brady Street Club for Working Boys, *First Annual Report, 1896–97*, London, 1897, pp. 5–6.
[19]Cd. 1742, Min. 818, 18273 ff. The phrase is that of the Brigade's Commander, Colonel Goldsmid, quoted in Cd. 1742, Min. 18280.

Youth clubs were more flexible in conception than the quasi-military Brigade. The first such club for immigrant youth, the Brady Street Club for Working Lads, set out

to establish a social and recreational centre for working lads fresh from school, to improve their stunted physique, raise their general tone and bearing, inculcate into them habits of manliness, straightforwardness and self-respect. . . .[20]

One principal end in view was Anglicization, under the aegis of 'men who had had the advantages of superior education and culture.'[21] Jewish concerns as such were more distant:

Although the Committee do not see their way to introduce a religious side into the work of the Club, they are particularly anxious to do all in their power to encourage Pride of Race [?] in their members.[22]

The original idea 'to encourage the mingling of Jewish and non-Jewish lads' soon faded; 'at the present moment the Jewish element so largely preponderates, that the Club may be looked upon as Jewish in all but name'.[23] Its approximately 200 boys of adolescent age controlled their own membership under the leadership of younger members of the well-to-do native Jewry. The Club offered a variety of sports, a library, indoor games, rambles and summer camping, and dramatics. The Brady Street Club, founded in 1896, was followed a few years later by the Stepney Jewish Lads' Club and the Victoria Boys' Club, and numerous others in Jewish immigrant areas. Athletics were these clubs' staff of life, but they could seldom compete against non-Jewish clubs because Saturday was the usual day for matches. The Jewish clubs therefore organized the Jewish Athletic Association in 1899 as an athletic league to sponsor Sunday sport meets. Ten years later it grew into the Association for Jewish Youth with the broader conception of its tasks which the name implies.[24]

[20]Brady Street Club . . . op. cit., p. 6.
[21]Brady Street Club for Working Boys, Eleventh Annual Report 1906–07, London, 1907, p. 6. Cf. Leonard G. Montefiore, 'Anglo-Jewry at the Cross-Roads,' The Jewish Review, V, No. 26 (July, 1914), pp. 128–35.
[22]Brady Street Club . . . , op. cit., pp. 7–8.
[23]Brady Street Club . . . , First Annual Report 1896–97, London, 1897, p. 6; cf. Cd. 1742, Min. 16632.
[24]Further material on this movement was made available by the Stepney Jewish Lads' Club, in the form of its Minutes which begin December 22, 1900, and various printed ephemera.

In both the traditional Jewish and the Victorian standards, the Jewish girl was hemmed in by a tighter code of personal behaviour than boys of her age. The well-bred young lady was properly supposed to be at home, absorbing domesticity and awaiting marriage. But such proprieties were brushed aside in a milieu where the unmarried girl did a full day's work in a shop like her father and brother, and often did not live *en famille* at all. Although it was therefore out of question to keep the maturing Jewish girl in social retirement, the organization of clubs for girls did not meet with as ready acceptance as those for boys. However, a girls' club met in a Board School as early as 1881, and the Soup Kitchen for the Jewish Poor housed a club for girls over its premises.[24a] The West Central Jewish Girls' Club was as exceptional a place as the character of its foundress, Miss Lily Montagu (1874–   ), daughter of Lord Swaythling and an originator of Liberal Judaism. Her club was run as an educational institution and was strongly religious after Miss Montagu's personal pattern. Most of its 275 girls came from the Jewish enclave in West Central London after a full day's work spent in making buttonholes, to spend an evening in a club which held religious services and concluded each evening with prayers. Its classes were approved by the Board of Education, and included such studies as artificial flower making and metal work, as well as English literature. Rather than emphasize athletics and foster the 'clubby' atmosphere as in the boys' clubs, Miss Montagu's club broadened its members' vocational skills, taught them the domestic arts and sought to expand their spiritual and intellectual view.[25] A similar attempt was not made among boys until young (later Sir) Basil L. Q. Henriques, inspired by an Oxonian social work evangelism, founded the Oxford and St George's Club in 1913.[26] No club was mixed, nor did any club undertake activities involving boys and girls together. They emphasized a sense of club intimacy to a greater extent than the larger and more amorphous Jewish social settlements in the United States.

[24a]*JC*, December 12, 1902.
[25]*JC*, February 27, 1903; Lily H. Montagu, *My Club and I*, London, n.d. (c. 1942), *passim*.
[26]Basil L. Q. Henriques, *The Indiscretions of a Warden*, London, 1937.

How young couples met, and the chain of events which culminated in both Jewish and civil ceremonies of marriage, are more than usually obscure. What we do know deals mostly with the special problems, usually legal, which arose. To be quite sure, most persons did marry. Of 94,541 alien 'Russians and Poles' enumerated for the purpose in 1911, only 2.4 per cent. of the men (1,243 of 50,601) and .7 per cent. of the women (327 of 43,940) over thirty-five years of age had not been married.[27] Nor did all of these, especially the men, remain permanently single, considering that over half of the men were yet under forty-five. Arrangements made by old-fashioned match-makers were never completely superseded. Those adaptable factotums were mostly elderly men who served as religious functionaries of some sort, and make 'a good living and something more' in what was 'long . . . a recognized institution in London'.[28] The delicate art had its international vistas as well. When a Manchester rabbi died in 1897, his community held itself responsible for marrying off its late rabbi's daughter. His brother in Russia was accordingly requested to recommend a suitable young man to become rabbi of the immigrant community and husband to his deceased predecessor's daughter. A young candidate was selected and despatched to Manchester, where he faithfully performed both duties.[29]

Three procedures were open to a couple who wished to marry. The most respectable was that contemplated under the Marriage Act of 1856 (19 & 20 Vict. c. 119), for which the couple secured a licence from the Chief Rabbi who issued the *ketubah*, and then went to a person authorized by the Chief Rabbi (usually a native Jewish minister) who would perform the actual ceremony and subsequently certify it to the Registrar's office. For reasons of convenience, piety, or economy, those who did not use this arrangement could be wed by an 'unauthorized' religious functionary and also have an ordinary civil marriage at a Registrar's office. Unlike the first type, this was recognized by law solely as a civil marriage. Third

[27] *Census of England and Wales*, 1911, Volume IX, Cd. 7017, 1913, p. 177.
[28] *JC*, January 2, 1903.
[29] *HaMeliz*, XXXVII, 146 (July 1–13, 1897); XXXVIII, 44 (February 22–March 7, 1898).

M

was the device of the unscrupulous, and of those ignorant of
the vital distinction between the public status of Jewish law in
Eastern Europe and England. In this case only Jewish marriage
was performed, and no civil notice or ceremony took place. The
couple had no legal proof of marriage; the wife lacked an en-
forcible claim on her husband's support; the children's position
was problematic. Such marriages were of a piece with *gittin*
(divorces) issued in England under Jewish law without previous
civil divorce, and were sometimes the resort of persons engaged in commercial vice. The 'clandestine marriage' (*shtille
huppah*, lit. silent wedding) was the target of impassioned
denunciations, and even of an effort to secure Parliamentary
action against it as against all 'irregular marriages' performed
outside the Chief Rabbi's provenance.[30]

CLUBS AND SOCIETIES

Long before it became the abode of multitudes of East European
Jews, the East End was the seat of a plethora of social and
benevolent associations, extending back into the eighteenth
century.[31] Their memberships were brought together on varied
bases—among the East Europeans it was usually the *lands-
mannshaft* of old fellow-townsmen, while earlier societies more
often were composed of men in the same trade.[32] We read of
groups with Birmingham in their titles, not in commemoration

[30]Board of Deputies, *Minutes*, March 21, April 21, May 23, 1888; February
25, June 19, 1889; March 19, 1890; June 22, 1896, October 21, 1896; January
27, 1907; *Annual Report*, 1901, pp. 22–23; all point to the preoccupation of the
Deputies with this question. Their efforts to enace a statute making of an 'irregular
marriage' a felony were severely censured in *JC*, March 18, 1892. See also *Official
Report of the Jewish International Conference for the Suppression of the Traffic in
Girls and Women*, London, n.d. (1910), pp. 93–104—remarks of Rabbis Adler
and Hyamson. United Synagogue Executive, *Minutes*, July 16, 1877. Royal Commission on Divorce and Matrimonial Causes, *Report*. Cd. 6478, 1912, pp. 142–45;
the Commission's *Evidence* (Cd. 6481, 1912) includes informative statements by
Adler (Min. 41363–460), D. L. Alexander (Min. 41461–507), H. S. Q. Henriques
(Min. 41508–21). See an example of 'A "Shtille Chasnah" in the Police Court'
in *JC*, May 5, 1904.
[31]B. A. Fersht, 'Chebrah Rodphea Sholom . . . the first Jewish Friendly Society
in England,' *Miscellanies of the Jewish Historical Society of England*, II (1935),
pp. 90–98; Cecil Roth, 'The Lesser London Synagogues of the Eighteenth Century,' *Idem*, III (1937), pp. 1–8.
[32]The following remarks are based principally upon an interview with I. L.
Defries in *JC*, August 9, 1912, and United Synagogue, *East End Scheme*, London,
1898, Report B, pp. 15–24, 29.

of an origin in that city but of the members' hawking of Birmingham manufactured goods ('Brummagem goods'). These associations' prosperity was equalled by that of such others as the cigar makers, and the City of London Jewish Tailors society with its 175 members and £1,112 in the till. To be sure, many societies' names are opaque as to place of origin or vocation: East London Hebrew Friendly, Sons of Jacob, Hackney Hebrew Tontine, and many more of the sort. Others chose names which are derived from Hebrew rubrics: Lovers of Justice and Peace, Harmony and Concord, Tree of Life, Sons of Judah, Righteous Path. Yet place names from Eastern Europe insistently crop up: Plotsk, Kutno, Dobrin, Lublin, Bessarabia, Cracow, Vlotslovick [sic], Poltusk. Of the 118 London Jewish benefit societies known to exist in 1898, some were divisional, i.e. at yearly intervals they divided among their members whatever funds were considered surplus. A few were tontine, meaning that dividends were paid on insurance at certain 'tontine' periods, and the last survivor of the group inherited all of its remaining assets. These devices, useful enough to attract members but financially unsound, were more popular in English lodges and benevolent organizations in earlier years of the nineteenth century than towards its end.

All benevolent societies invariably distributed one benefit: death allowances. Customarily this included grants of £2 each, at a rough average, for burial, gravestone, and confined mourning. Synagogal benefit societies also made provision for worshippers, including a rabbi, to attend during the week of mourning. Beyond this basic minimum, the widest latitude was practised. Some paid insurance from £2 2s to £20 upon the death of a member, with £10 the approximate average; smaller amounts were paid upon the death of a wife or child. Some few societies, especially well-established mutual workers' associations, granted sick pay and unemployment allowance. Fees ranged as widely as benefits, from the 1½d or 2d weekly of the Federation and Sisterhood for its modest burial benefits to 1s levied by societies with elaborate scales of grants. Many of them were thoroughly unsound fiscally, with assets far below the probable cost of the benefits which they offered.

The United Synagogue's inquiry in 1898 into the Jewish Friendly Societies established the membership of sixty-two of the 118 known groups at 10,410, but the total is extremely unreliable. Nor does an average hold much significance, for the list stretches from the Sisterhood with 1,080 subscribers and the Federation of Synagogues' 1,200 to a watchmakers' group of twenty-six. Over 3,500 belonged to societies which granted solely funeral allowances, and 800 were on the books of a mutual loan society. The oldest and wealthiest groups had the most generous allowances and therefore the highest subscription fees, which were beyond the means of most immigrants. Clearly, however, the majority of East End Jews was covered by one group or another, and many doubtless belonged to several friendly societies.

Each of these associations filled a small world of its own, furnishing members not only with a modicum of personal security, but with a sense of belonging and of participation in affairs. Every organization had a responsible committee in whose hands lay the decision to grant or not to grant, and if so, how much. Their doings were almost a byword for contentious-ness, but at least gave ample scope to their members' talents for debate and civic activity, if not always in the favourable sense. Plenty of these societies' acrimonious discords were aired before the Beth Din of the Chief Rabbi, and many more were doubtless ironed out in some other way. However, schism was one dependable source of new societies.

The sphere of immigrant life did not form one uniform social milieu. Street life in the East End and the other Jewish quarters, a sort of common denominator, displayed a vividness which fascinated many outsiders although it offended the more staid native Jewish and Gentile residents.[33] Store signs, theatrical placards, bookshops, bearded types from the old country, immigrant women wrapped in vast kerchiefs, all

[33]Henry Mayhew, *London Labour and the London Poor*, 4 vols., London, 1861, III, pp. 115–36, is part of a classic account; J. H. Clapham, *An Economic History of Modern Britain*, 3 vols., Cambridge, repr. 1950–52, III, p. 451; 'A Reminiscence of a Mid-Winter Tramp to Toynbee,' *The Social Democrat*, III, 9 (September, 1899), pp. 262–66; *The Polish Yidel*, I, 15, 16 (October 31, November 7, 1884); *Die Tsukunft*, I, 17 (November 14, 1884)—on Leeds; *Idem*, IV, Nos. 195, 196 (May 18, 25, 1888); Glasgow *Evening News*, October 11, 1902 (non vidi).

conferred an aura of exotic strangeness upon the Jewish area. Some festivals were occasions for outdoor celebration, while the Jewish Sabbath was marked by extensive promenading upon the main thoroughfare. The holidays of the autumn concluded with public merriment out in the streets during the Simhat Torah festivities. Akin to it was the Purim holiday, which maintained its old tradition of liberal imbibing and jovial masquerading from house to house. Bonfires of prohibited leaven flared all over the Jewish quarter on *Hometz Bottel* night, the evening before the Paschal Seder took place at home.[34]

Other clubs of a different sort reared their heads to provide entertainment for their habitués. Some of the coffee houses which were the Jewish quarter's equivalent of the English pubs became known resorts for gamblers in cards, dice, and horses. They catered to a well-attested passion for games of chance shared by many immigrants—something of an old weakness among Jews. Jewish moralists had enough to say upon the matter, but it is not recorded that these mis-demeaning immigrants lent them much ear. Normal social clubs, including proprietary establishments, had to contend with this persistent vice.[35] The fate of one such group tells a story typical in other ways as well:

Fifteen months ago [c. 1890] it had to be closed in consequence of its having become a resort of gambling Jews. When reopened, it was decided that the Jews could not be admitted within the building, as it was found that the English working men declined to associate with them.[36]

Nor were only Christian Englishmen reluctant to be con-vivial with immigrant workmen. The decline of the Jewish Working Men's Club demonstrates that the native Jewish

[34]George R. Sims ed., *Living London*, 3 vols., London, 1902, II, p. 31.
[35]Jacob de Haas, *op. cit.*, pp. 35–36; J. H. Brenner, *Me'Eber liGebulin*, London, 1907, is a play set in a London coffee house and conveys some of its atmosphere; *The Polish Yidel*, I, 3 (September 12, 1884), touches on Leeds; *Die Tsukunft*, IV, No. 166 (October 14, 1887). Stepney Jewish Lads' Club, *Minutes*, January 6, 1901 and January 26, 1903, show rules and measures against gambling; Cd. 1742, Min. 7648–51, 7365–68, 8304–13, 8368–84, 9363, 21253–63, all rather superficial; P. Ornstein in *JC*, January 2, 1903; C. Russell and H. S. Lewis, *op. cit.*, p. 178.
[36]H. Otto Thomas, 'The Tee-To-Tum Movement,' *The Economic Review*, II, 3 (July, 1892), p. 356.

neighbour of the immigrant was not much more cordial. This institution was founded largely by Samuel Montagu in 1876, He housed it in substantial quarters in Great Alie Street and continued as its patron for a generation along with Rothschild, Stuart Samuel, and Lionel Alexander. At its zenith late in the 1880's, the Jewish Working Men's Club enrolled about 1,400 members who benefited from its purpose of

the Anglicization of the Jews of the East End and the provision of a place of innocent amusement.[37]

Unlike similar places, this Club admitted both men and women as members and permitted neither drinking nor card playing. It was the home of a dramatic society and glee club, and accommodated chess and draughts, athletics, swimming, and much debating. No other Jewish institution provided such opportunities for adults in the East End. Yet during the 1890's its membership fluctuated around 1,000 and from about 1900 it went downhill to under 200 when it finally shut its doors in April, 1912. This decadence befell the Club during years when the surrounding streets teemed with prospective members. Why its dissolution? A spokesman complained of a

large number of removals from the district, partly due to the fact that men and women work later and are thus unable to attend, and partly to the counter-attractions of free libraries, cinematograph shows, and other clubs in which drinking and card playing are allowed. . . . Another contributing cause . . . has been the influx from abroad. The immigrants could never be induced to join the Club.[38]

The Jews who did attend were the native Jewish working-men of the East End, and when they left the area the immigrants did not replace them in the Club's quarters. The latter evidently preferred to take their pleasures in coffee shops and benevolent societies rather than in large premises, just as they turned aside all efforts to lure them away from their *hevrot* into large synagogues.

[37]*JC*, April 19, 1912; *cf. JC*, April 13, 1894; April 5, 1895, April 5, 1912; Charles Booth ed., *op. cit.*, I, pp. 99–100.
[38]*JC*, April 19, 1912.

CRIME

'Peaceful' and 'law-abiding' were terms consistently applied
to the immigrant community, but nevertheless, it had its
criminal offenders. Among the varieties of criminality, Jews
possessed certain distinctions of their own, such as the virtual
absence of crimes of violence—murder, robbery, and rape.
Most of the alien Jews who were jailed went for offences
touched with commercial dishonesty, on the style of forgery,
receiving stolen goods, fraudulent bankruptcy, adulteration of
foods, illegal distilling to avoid liquor excise.[39] However,
figures are by no means consistent, and it is quite difficult
to sort out Jewish aliens ('Russians and Poles') from aliens in
general. Some indication of the number of Jews is the presence
of ninety-nine 'Russians and Poles' among 1,982 aliens in
prison in 1894.[40] The number and proportion of Jewish aliens
in prison both rose to their peak about 1904, when the de-
portation of convicted criminal aliens commenced, and then
declined to 517 of the 2,590 alien prisoners who began to
serve their sentences in 1909. Long term convicts seem to have
been extremely few.[41] In spite of some rather alarmist anti-
alien agitation on this score, no great importance attaches to
the whole subject.

It is otherwise with the most scandalous social problem
cast up by the tides of immigration, decorously termed 'the
social evil', meaning prostitution.[42] Its full chronicle has not
yet engaged historical attention, but the evidence demonstrates

[39]Georg Halpern, *Die Juedischen Arbeiter in London*, Berlin, 1903, p. 24.
[40]*Reports upon the Volume and Effects of Recent Immigration from Eastern Europe
into the United Kingdom*, C. 7406, 1894, pp. 60–62.
[41]M. J. Landa, *The Alien Problem and Its Remedy*, London, 1911, pp. 158–68,
is a pro-alien summary of the preceding decade; Royal Commission on Alien
Immigration, *Report*, Cd. 1741, 1903, Par. 109–25, is a judicious summary of the
situation at that time, drawing upon evidence (of uneven value) given in Cd. 1742.
[42]The *Official Report of the Jewish International Conference* . . . printed as *Private
and Confidential*, is replete with information, as are the *Annual Reports* of the
Jewish Association for the Protection of Girls and Women. See also Cd. 1742,
Min. 8334–36, 8445–67, 10166–69, 12568–653 (contradicted unconvincingly in
Min. 17900–19), 13001–11; Georg Halpern, *op. cit.*, p. 24; there is a very powerful
and realistic account of the Russian end of the traffic in Mendele Mokher Seforim's
Hebrew novel *BaYamim haHem* (In Those Days), with its Yiddish version
entitled *Dos Vinshfingeril* (The Wishing Ring), many eds. It was written in the
1880's and appears to be set in the 1840's or 1850's, though the details of the
white slave trade seem contemporaneous with the time of writing.

the variety and extent of the Jewish connection with commercialized vice. The principal 'contribution' made by Jews was the supply of girls to the entrepôts of the system in Buenos Aires, Bombay, Constantinople, and elsewhere, fresh from the East European Pale and London also. There were several devices for bringing girls into the network, and a key step in the operation was often taken in London. The first steps were taken in Russia by

empty and dissolute men and also evil women who go about . . . from town to town and across the countryside . . . and deceive Jewish maidens with slippery tongue into leaving their native land and going under their guidance to distant parts, saying that there they will find good pay for their work in business firms. . . .[43]

Some likely young men would marry such girls and then take them by boat to India or Brazil or Argentina or to other American countries and sell them there to houses of prostitution.[44]

The young man might sooner turn over his 'wife' to the white slaver in England for further disposition, and return to the Pale to resume operations with another victim. A simpler trick, not requiring elaborate arrangement but riskier to execute, could be played upon the unaccompanied girls and women who arrived at the London docks, sometimes in numbers exceeding 1,000 yearly. In the chaos of landing, the recruiter could too easily entice some friendless bewildered girls to accept hospitality at a place which would turn out to be a brothel. Another source of prostitutes existed in the midst of the Jewish quarter itself, when young girls living alone or with negligent relatives were seduced by young men. In terror of the social sanctions imposed upon unchastity, and imagining that no road to respectable society lay open, they reluctantly followed the counsel of their seducers that no choice remained to them but an immoral life. False marriage was a form of ensnarement more difficult to perpetrate in London because the Chief Rabbi's vigilance and that of most immigrant rabbis erected a stiff barrier.

To surmise the number of Jewish prostitutes for whom England was a base or a transition point is entirely guesswork,

[43] *HaMeliz*, XXXVIII, 67 (March 27–April 9, 1898).
[44] *Ibid.*

but no doubt exists that it ascended steadily from the 1880's when they were yet unknown. Matters had already become serious when seven leading Western rabbis addressed an open letter in 1898 to their East European colleagues begging them to 'remove this dreadful disgrace from upon us' by warning parents and children of the imminent dangers, and by careful inquiries into the background of young men who presented themselves as bridegrooms.[45] In 1909 London was the scene of a private Jewish International Conference for the Suppression of the Traffic in Women and Girls. The situation did not go unnoticed in the interims, for the Jewish community maintained an effective Jewish Association for the Protection of Girls and Women. Its agent met every arriving boat at Tilbury, scouting about for unaccompanied girls and women while observing the movements of suspected traffickers about the dock. In one year, the Jewish Association investigated 206 cases, encompassing a wide variety of situations. There were twenty-four girls 'removed from bad or dangerous surroundings'; forty-five cases of 'houses and people suspected of carrying on, or of profiting by the trade'; nineteen had 'entered upon immoral lives (impossible to ascertain whether voluntarily or otherwise)'; fifteen girls were 'saved from being trafficked', although a larger number were trafficked or were thought to have been.[46] In the six years preceding the Conference of 1909 the Jewish Association for the Protection of Girls and Women had record of 222 'cases of girls who have taken to immoral lives and who, in many cases, have eventually disappeared from the country', and forty-four others were so suspected, while 198 'people and houses [were] suspected of being concerned in the Traffic'. And this was not all, for it admitted that

it is more probable that we merely touch the fringe. There must be scores of cases undiscovered to every one that we get to know of.

In the same six years 151 'Russians' and 'Roumanians' ('probably nearly all are Jews and Jewesses') were convicted

[45] *Ibid.* Signatories were H. Adler (London), Zadoc-Kahn (Paris), M. Guedemann (Vienna), M. Horovitz (Frankfurt-am-Main), M. Hirsch (Hamburg), E. Hildesheimer (Berlin), M. Ehrenreich (Rome).
[46] Jewish Association for the Protection of Girls and Women, *Annual Report*, 1902, p. 21.

of keeping brothels, and 521 who were found guilty of soliciting customers.[47] Yet it seems that comparatively few of the Jewish girls who entered prostitution in London actually practised the trade there, although one or two streets in the Jewish quarter were a known red light district. It was to remain thus almost until the War, an embarrassment to the Jewish community, and a source of corruption and degradation to more than a few.

Viewing the social life of the Jewish immigrant community as a whole, one is struck by its self-centredness, its utter autonomy from the rest of the population. Currents of anti-alienism and hostility might swirl about them, but their personal and group life proceeded obliviously. The only effect of hostility would have been to consolidate them yet more closely and to heighten their mutual dependence. To the native Jew was left the task of defending the Jews' civil status and reputation; the newcomers had to labour an entire generation to build a material foundation for themselves and had little time to consider their relation to a Gentile world which was as alien to them as they were to it.

[47] *Official Report of the Jewish International Conference* . . . pp. 30–31. Probably many individuals were convicted more than once.

VII

THE RELIGION OF THE IMMIGRANT

The Jewish immigrant's form of personal expression was rooted in the Judaism of his fathers, for where so much else in his new land was alien and beyond his control, at least there he could feel at home. It was natural, if not instinctive, that a newly arrived Jew seek out his relatives and former townsmen not only for employment and material aid but to join them in an effort to recreate the social and religious life which they had left behind. In the *hebra* (pl. *hebrot*, lit. society) a Jew associated himself with fellow Jews not only for purposes of regular worship and study and conviviality, but also for the basic needs of distress—illness, burial, and confined mourning. For thousands of Jews, after their immediate family such a religious *hebra* was the 'primary cell' of their social life. With its flexibility and continuity with a seemingly infinite past, the *hebra* could sustain them in a determination to withstand the corrosion of a foreign land. Ties with the old country and the old religion were maintained not only by this typical institution, but also by that peculiarly Jewish way, queries addressed to eminent East European rabbinic figures for adjudication according to Jewish law. It might be the rabbi of the old town or such international personages as Isaac Elhanan Spektor, Rabbi of Kovno (1819–1896), or Nafthali Zvi Judah Berlin (1817–1893), Head of the *Yeshibah* at Volozhin, and some few others, who received the issue for decision. Their views far outweighed the opinion of any rabbi of the new country.

A firm characteristic of every Jewish immigrant quarter is the proliferation of *hebrot* occupying small houses of worship in dwellings, small stores, or occasionally in converted churches left behind by a departed Christian population. The immigrants' *hebrot* commenced and usually remained small, clangorous, and often dirty. The passion, length, noise, and frequency of the services held there were quite incomprehensible to Englishmen and to most English Jews, though some were drawn to it by curiosity and half admiration.

Such a *hebra*, composed mostly of the sort of workers whom she had observed at their toil, was reported by Beatrice Potter:[1]

Here, early in the morning, or late at night, the devout members meet to recite the morning and evening prayers, or to decipher the sacred books of the Talmud. And it is a curious and touching sight to enter one of the poorer and more wretched of these places on a Sabbath morning. Probably the one you choose will be situated in a small alley or narrow court, or it may be built out in a back-yard. To reach the entrance you stumble over broken pavement and household debris; possibly you pick your way over the rickety bridge connecting it with the cottage property fronting the street. From the outside it appears a long wooden building surmounted by a skylight, very similar to the ordinary sweater's workshop.

Probably these surroundings were somewhat exceptional. Some older *hebrot*, especially, were prosperous enough to present a more inviting appearance. But the order and style of worship were nearly identical everywhere:

. . . the heat and odour convince you that the skylight is not used for ventilation. From behind the trellis of the 'ladies' gallery' you see at the far end of the room the richly curtained Ark of the Covenant, wherein are laid, attired in gorgeous vestments, the sacred scrolls of the Law. Slightly elevated on a platform in the midst of the congregation stands the reader or minister, surrounded by the seven who are called up to the reading of the Law from among the congregation. Scarves of white cashmere or silk, softly bordered and fringed, are thrown across the shoulders of the men, and relieve the dusty hue and disguise the Western cut of the clothes they wear. A low, monotonous, but musical-toned recital of Hebrew prayers, each man praying for himself to the God of his fathers, rises from the congregation, whilst the reader intones, with a somewhat louder voice, the recognized portion of the Pentateuch. Add to this rhythmical cadence of numerous voices, the swaying to and fro of the bodies of the worshippers—expressive of the words of personal adoration: 'All my bones exclaim, Oh! Lord, who is like unto Thee!'—and you may imagine yourself in a far-off Eastern land. But you are roused from your dreams. Your eye wanders from the men who form the congregation, to the small body of women who watch behind the

[1]Beatrice Potter, 'The Jewish Community,' in Charles Booth, ed., *Life and Labour of the People*, 9 vols., London, 1893–1902, I, pp. 567–69.

trellis. Here, certainly, you have the Western world, in the bright-coloured ostrich feathers, large bustles, and tight-fitting coats of cotton velvet or brocaded satinette. At last you step out, stifled by the heat and dazed by the strange contrast of the old-world memories of a majestic religion and the squalid vulgarity of an East End slum.

The synagogue, large or small, was historically a centre of devout study and charitable benevolence. Beatrice Potter was impressed by what she saw of intellectual and eleemosynary activity:

. . . if you could follow the quick spoken Judisch, you would be still more bewildered by these 'destitute foreigners' . . . the men are scattered over the benches (may-be there are several who are still muttering their prayers), or they are gathered together in knots, sharpening their intellects with the ingenious points and subtle logic of the Talmudical argument, refreshing their minds from the rich stores of Talmudical wit, or listening with ready helpfulness to the tale of distress of a newcomer from the foreign home.

The observant immigrant in the East End and the Provinces did not usually derive his religious pleasure and instruction from Talmudic learning. He could not look to the somewhat aloof figure of the rabbi nor to the more commonplace *shammash* (sexton) for edification. Rather would he joyously welcome the musical ministrations of a visiting *hazan* (cantor), who usually passed through England en route to or from the greener fields of America. An appearance by a fine East European *hazan* to conduct services would strain the walls of the largest synagogues in the East End, and cause commotions by those who could not enter. With rapt attention the Jew would allow the masterful officiant to evoke the fit emotions of solemnity, ecstasy, and delight, and go home to remember the great day unto his grand-children's time. Almost as exciting to the pious immigrant was the oration of the *maggid*, the popular religious preacher who sometimes talked throughout an entire Sabbath or holiday after-noon dispensing a 'verie livelie worde of God'. Crowded into a large synagogue, as many as a thousand Jews heard the *maggid* proclaim, exhort, and even chant his message to them—wholehearted compliance with Jewish law, trust in God and Providence, and, from those employed by the official com-munity to use their techniques for its purposes, Anglicization and circumspect deportment in the new land. Like the *hazan*, the *maggid* had a highly personal style, and employed the tools of popular eloquence—stories, parables from the animal and human kingdoms, appeals to the personal experience of his hearers, as well as an astonishingly fertile skill at homiletic exposition of sacred literature. While visiting *maggidim* like Zvi Hirsch Masliansky (1856–1943), the 'National Orator', were enthusiastically received,[2] the most distinguished among English *maggidim* was Rabbi Hayyim Zundel Maccoby (1856–1916) (some *maggidim* possessed rabbinic ordination), known as the Maggid of Kamenitz.[3] This unusual man, whose unofficial title was Anglo-Judaized to 'the Rev. C. Z. Maccoby', served from his arrival in London in 1890 until 1894 as preacher to a group of *hebrot*, and was then absorbed into the communal religious structure as 'Chief Preacher' to the Federation of Synagogues until his death. His truly wondrous abilities as a *maggid* and the force of his personality were dimmed by the tedium of the many parochial duties which were laid upon him. Rabbi Meir Berlin (1880–1949), depressed by the 'total ruin' of the personality of the Maggid of Kamenitz, whom he recalled from Russia, blamed 'the destructive power of Jewish life in London'.[4]

The great majority of the *hebrot* could not afford to support a rabbi. As they understood the rabbinic office, it was not pastoral, but concentrated upon the older responsibilities of resident scholar, communal arbiter, and teacher of advanced students. Few *hebrot* could maintain a rabbi for the performance of his traditional rôle, especially because it was largely superseded by the services of the organized Jewish community. The Hasidic rabbi and his retinue, with its emotional and mystical atmosphere, did not settle in England before 1914.

The *hebra*, then, had to be satisfied with the services of its

[2]On the Maggid of Kamenitz, *cf.* H. Z. Maccoby, *'Imre Hayyim* (Homilies) ed., M. Mansky, Tel Aviv, 1929, pp. vii-xiii; Meir Berlin, *MiVolozhin 'ad Yerushalayim* (From Volozhin to Jerusalem), 2 vols., Tel Aviv, 1939; II, pp. 43–44. Z. H. Masliansky, *Sefer haZikhronot veha Massa 'ot* (Memoirs and Travels), N.Y., 1929, pp. 137–38.

[3]*JC*, December 21, 1894, January 4, 1895: 'The Russian Preacher, Mr H. Masslainski.' Z. H. Masliansky, *op. cit.*, pp. 130–46; On the Maggid of Kelm in England, see the hostile report in *HaMeliz*, xxv, 74, 95 (October 19, 1885, January 1, 1886).

[4]Meir Berlin, *op. cit.*, p. 44.

shammash for the general oversight of its activity, and so much the better if he or some able layman could fill the scholarly role which was usually the rabbi's. In general, the religious vocations within the immigrant community furnished precarious livings. The average *hebra* functionary held his job among as many others as he could. The trouble was that, except for the work of a *shohet*, thousands of Jews were more or less competent, so that a recognized vocation could not be established. A man would try to eke out a sustenance as a combined *shammash*, *hazan*, and *melammed* (elementary Hebrew tutor). He might try his hand at business, particularly at something like scribe, matchmaker, book dealer, or wine merchant, all of which had a synagogal bearing. One successful preacher became yet more successful as proprietor of a Russian steam bathhouse. Hundreds of men floated in and out of these callings and few of them made a living, fewer yet without some self-abasement. This does not take into account the honourable phenomenon of rabbis, by no means few, who scorned to put their rabbinic learning up for sale, as they saw it, and chose to work like anybody else with occasional exercise as unpaid teachers and preachers.

The combination of *hebra* poverty and the near absolutism of the Chief Rabbinate in the religious sphere, made the status of the London immigrant rabbi a sorry one. The social and legal conditions of English life inevitably stripped him of most of his traditional functions, such as judicial services and control of marital affairs. He was no longer the central figure of his community, for many functions which still remained, like dietary laws, were the exclusive province of the Chief Rabbinate. An ultimate indignity required that an immigrant rabbi who entered under the communal canopy surrender his very title, and in return be designated 'the Reverend Mister'. Young Rabbi Meir Berlin, remembering the high standing of the East European rabbi and perhaps also bearing in mind the prestige of his illustrious forbears in his native *yeshiva* town of Volozhin, was perhaps too melancholy over the fate of the immigrant rabbis whom he saw in London. These men, he declared, were 'robbed . . . both of their rabbinates and their self-respect. It was a great tragedy to see a rabbi in London.

Poverty was discernible in his dress and manner'. Some were required to preach so frequently that it seemed as though they hardly realized what they were saying.[5] It is to be noted, however, that the sway of the Chief Rabbinate was more moderate in the Provinces (see below).

IMMIGRANT RELIGIOUS PRACTICE

The taciturn round of religious life and practice can easily be lost in the swirl of organized activity and its discords. The immigrants, absorbed in simple observance at home or in their *hebrot*, did not leave much material about the humble routine of religious life. So our main problems are unsolved, and perhaps cannot be solved. What did the Jewish immigrant discard and what did he retain of the traditional religious mode of life? What accounting is there for his selections in keeping one area of his heritage while casting another away? How many Jews attended the synagogue daily or weekly or yearly or not at all? What effect did the new environment have upon their religious life and attitudes? Above all, how fared the old religion in the hands of a new English generation? We have but scraps of knowledge on these fundamental issues.

For example, we know that Jewish business in the Jewish quarter was normally shut during the Jewish Sabbath—from sundown Friday to nightfall Saturday—but we also know that during the busy season Jewish workers worked late into Friday night. If the Jewish worker did not report for work on Saturday, it is no proof that he was in the synagogue, for the open air labour market was in full operation in Whitechapel Road.[6] The many small synagogues possessed a capacity far below the total immigrant population, but still complained of many unsubscribed seats.[7]

The best estimate is that about half of the eligible Jews belonged to *hebrot* of some sort. It seems reasonable that this

[5] *Ibid.*, p. 42.

[6] 'In Whitechapel there was a tendency not to go to synagogue. The Jews had to work hard all the week, and their inclination was to remain in bed on Saturday.' Sir Samuel Montagu to Council of the United Synagogue, *JC*, May 5, 1893.

[7] Montagu complained that the twenty *hebrot* in the Federation of Synagogues, of which he was President, had 1,500 unsubscribed seats. However, many of these were probably used by non-subscribing worshippers. *JC*, May 5, 1893.

proportion is somewhat higher among heads of families than among single young men, and higher in the Provinces than in London. Those unaffiliated were a subject of some concern. Said Dayan B. Spiers in a Sabbath homily:

My spirit grieves that many of them have not joined and do not join any synagogue or hebra, and they thus do not come throughout the year to worship, to hear the service of song and prayer, or to hear words of Torah or ethical edification. Transgression thereby leads to further transgression, and they transgress the precepts of God and His Holy Torah, in matters between man and God, and between man and his fellow, thus causing, God forbid, desecration of God's Name, etc.[8]

The clearest overt measure of Jewish observance is probably the observance of the Jewish Sabbath. It is therefore, symptomatic that laments upon its lax observance or non-observance were heard from all sides, immigrant, native, and Gentile. The declining standard of Sabbath observance was recorded by J. B. Lakeman, the Superintendent Inspector of Workshops in London, who was

. . . sorry to chronicle the fact that many Jews, who twelve months ago, were strictly orthodox in their religion have been compelled under penalty of losing their trade to work during their Sabbath, because the Christian (i.e. the West End) employer requires his work to be completed not later than four o'clock on Saturdays.[9]

That the fault really lay with Christian employers is not so certain, for such an immigrant as Samuel Jacob Rabbinowitz (1857–1921), Communal Rabbi in Liverpool, looked closer homeward for the cause of declining Sabbath observance, a situation which he bitterly regretted.

In the first place, the decision when to work and how many hours of the day to work does not lie in the worker's hand . . . if they [the Jewish tailoring employers] demand nothing less than to work on the Sabbath, it forces the Jewish worker, who had wanted to rest on the Sabbath, to work. . . . On the other hand, the Jewish worker was also ashamed, and afraid to make his Jewishness too conspicuous [by objecting] . . .[10]

[8]B. Spiers, *Dibrey Debash* (Honied Words), London, 1901, p. 5.
[9]Report of the Chief Inspector of Factories and Workshops for 1894, C. 7745, 1895, p. 48.
[10]S. J. Rabbinowitz, *Menuhat Shabbat* (*Shabbos Ruhe*) (Sabbath Rest), Liverpool, 1919, p. 4.

N

The forthright rabbi did not hesitate to blame his fellow Jews, including those who were personally observant but kept their shops in operation and their Jewish employees at work on the Sabbath.[11]

Whether it was the fault of compelling circumstance, which ultimately made a virtue of necessity, or of growing religious indifference, many 'greeners' found themselves working on the Sabbath, a thing unthinkable to most of them in the milieu which they had left behind. Rabbi Rabbinowitz expressed the greeners' dilemma in poignant terms:

The poor worker, for the most part the foreigner, who came here . . . to earn his morsel of bread honourably . . . stands before a great trial. In his heart a terrible life and death struggle takes place between body and soul, between hunger and faith. . . .

Although he might try every means in order 'to live as a Jew as did his father and grandfather, and as his brethren do,' his new environment was making that impossible. He could find no job, even in the Jewish immigrant trades, where the Sabbath might be observed, and 'is conquered by need and hunger and goes to work on the Sabbath like an ox to the abbatoir'.[12]

Both native and immigrant sources addressed numerous pleas to the Jewish immigrant to observe his immemorial day of rest, whether in deference to its sanctity or for the honour of Jewry. We hear of a Sabbath Observance Society which aimed 'to lessen the great and unfortunately growing evil of Sabbath desecration'.[13] Machzikei HaDath proclaimed that one object of its establishment was 'to prevent the Sabbath desecration which is much on the increase, there being seemingly, nobody able to put a stop to it'.[14] Spiers, preaching to an immigrant audience on behalf of the native Jewish community, did not fail to emphasize the importance of the Sabbath in Gentile eyes:

For what will the nations say if they see the Jews walking about in streets and markets in large groups? They do not do such things on their day of rest. . . . Where is the sanctity of the Sabbath if you go

[11] *Ibid.*, pp. 22–24; I. H. Daiches, *Derashot MaHaRYaH* (Sermons), pp. 120–21.
[12] S. J. Rabbinowitz, *op. cit.*, p. 16.
[13] *JC*, January 18, 1895.
[14] See below, p. 211.

about in such large groups in the markets, spending the Holy Day in such manner?[15]

The religious dislocations produced by immigration were succinctly defined by Spiers. Back in Eastern Europe 'it is easy to be pious and it is no great matter to observe and uphold the Divine Commandments. But here, in this country, it is a great thing and a very great test. . . .'[16] This larger issue was analyzed with admirable clarity by Harry S. Lewis (1861–1947), a Toynbee Hall resident and Jewish minister, a man of great spiritual sensitivity. He estimated that 'more than half of the Jews of London go to work on the Sabbath', although 'the observance of the holidays is much more general'. The causes had as much to do with psychological attitudes as with economic necessities.

It is a common saying amongst the foreign Jews that England is a 'freie Medinah'—a country where the restrictions of orthodoxy cease to apply. . . . A friend of mine, who refused to work on the Sabbath and suffered on account of his staunchness, told me that he was reproached with being like a 'greener'. . . .[17]

Rabbi Rabbinowitz severely censured this class of transgressors:

Some . . . of our foreign ignorami think that in England one may do anything, that in England there is no God at all, that as soon as one crosses the Russian border everything becomes anarchic [hefker], that one is free and excused from everything. Others . . . suppose also . . . that to be a Sabbath violator and to do away with Jewishness is a species of wisdom, some kind of progress. . . .[18]

The immigrant's first critical neglect of religious observance often influenced his later practices in a decisive fashion. Lewis believed that 'it may well be that the Jewish workman begins unwillingly to follow his employment on the Sabbath, but . . . the first steps in such matters soon involve indifference to obligations which were regarded as sacred'. Sabbath observance was sometimes possible in the Jewish trades, and it was the

[15]B. Spiers, *Dibrey Debash*, p. 11.   [16]*Ibid.*, p. 54.
[17]'East End Judaism: The Possibilities of Reform,' a paper delivered to the West End Synagogue Society, in *JC*, February 20, 1903. (The quotations given below come from this lecture).
[18]S. J. Rabbinowitz, *op. cit.*, p. 25.

conviction of both Lewis and Rabbinowitz that many Jewish workers and employers neglected these opportunities to keep the Sabbath. Observance would be reinstated when both sides were 'impelled to do so by strong conviction', which, however, was lacking in many cases.

Although there was a gathering wall of indifference and laxity, Lewis did not find resentment or rejection by the immigrant of his religious heritage, except in radical anti-religious circles, whose external influence was small. The immigrant 'is not out of sympathy with the service of the synagogue, which is endeared to him by early associations, so that even those parts which are unintelligible are not less beloved'. However, 'many consider it sufficient to attend on the High Festivals'.

On the High Holidays a great reservoir of Jewish feeling welled up, which has been largely submerged during the year. A dramatic illustration is afforded by the annual free services in the vast Great Assembly Hall sponsored by the United Synagogue. In 1894, 8,000 persons had crammed into the Hall by 5.30 a.m. for services which were not to start until 7 a.m., and many more had to be turned away. The Rev. B. Schewzik, who directed the worship of the immense congregation during the long prayers, claimed that 'whole congregations . . . deserted their little hebras to join the larger multitude'. He claimed that

some seventy-five per cent. [were] young men between the ages of eighteen and twenty-five, many of whom have been won from the ranks of socialism, and have not attended a place of worship, as they confess, for years.[19]

Other *ad hoc* congregations were organized for the High Holidays in the Jewish Working Men's Club, in meeting halls,

[19] *JC*, October 12, 1894. Services had been sponsored by the United Synagogue for some years before. In 1891, 4,500 persons were said to have attended services at the Jews' Free School. The Rev. B. Spiers preached in 'English and German' and the Rev. J. Kohn-Zedek spoke in 'Judaic German'. Letter, Alfred L. Cohen to P. Ornstein, October 18, 1891, in United Synagogue Council, *Minutes*, October 27, 1891. The attendance at services in the rooms of the Jewish Working Men's Club was smaller than it might have been because the services were conducted in the English style. The Rev. B. Schewzik preached to 'a vast throng' at services held in Beaumont Hall. Letter, Benjamin L. Cohen to P. Ornstein, October 15, 1891, in *Ibid*. The Westminster Jews' Free School also arranged such services in its West London district, United Synagogue Executive, *Minutes*, May 24, 1888.

and in some less savoury places, frequently by private pro-
moters.[20]

Only a minority of adult male Jews attended synagogue
once a week or oftener, besides a much larger proportion who
attended on holidays.[20a] One census of synagogue-goers, taken
as part of a newspaper census of religious worship in the Metropolis, gives some clue of normal attendance at services. On
the first day of Passover, 1903, enumerators counted 15,157
men, 4,375 women, and 7,080 children who passed through
the portals of sixty-five native and immigrant houses of
worship in London.[21] This total of 26,612 worshippers, upon
a day whose attendance generally ranks second to the High
Holidays, represents not more than twenty-five per cent. of
London Jewry at that time. We may estimate that about
20,000 were members of the immigrant community. A minority
it is, but its size is clear demonstration that Jewish religious
practice is the most widespread communal phenomenon in the
social and cultural life of immigrant Jewry. Even the religiously
indifferent remained unswervingly within the Jewish fold;
despite the exertions of numerous Christian missions, cases of
apostasy are nearly infinitesimal.

THE LONDON HEBROT AND THEIR BACKGROUND

Although Beatrice Potter was not alone in her romantic conception of the *hebra* as an exotic oriental import, the *hebra's*
small town environment could not be imported. Where *hebrot*
existed in the larger cities of Eastern Europe, they were the

[20]These 'mushroom congregations' advertised in the Yiddish press in the High
Holiday season. A more critical survey of the Day of Atonement in the East End
is in *JC*, September 23, 1904.

[20a]*JC*, September 16, 1904. The London Society for the Promotion of Christianity
among the Jews, with an annual income of £30,000, issued constant 'progress
reports.' No credence can be placed in its absurdly exaggerated claims of achievements in England or elsewhere. The same holds true of other missionary societies.
However, cf. the closing chapters of P. Smolenskin's famous novel *HaTo'eh
beDarkhey haHayyim* (Astray on the Path of Life), many eds., written in the 1870's;
and the Rev. W. H. Davies' defence of the missionaries, *JC*, November 11, 1904.

[21]R. Mudie-Smith, *Religious Life of the People of London*, London, 1905, pp. 5,
265. There were certain inconsistencies in the figures, *e.g.* the attendance at
Duke's Place and the Spitalfields Great Synagogue were twice their respective
capacities, and a few congregations were omitted. The *JC* (April 24, 1903) thought
that the synagogues were 'splendidly attended'.

satellites of a quasi-official communal synagogue and accepted
the religious leadership emanating from that synagogue and
its rabbi. On the other hand, there were also some conventicles
of dissenters from the established communal order who kept to
themselves, like the Hasidim in Lithuania. The United Synagogue of London and the Chief Rabbinate of England had
reached their contemporary forms by precisely this process
of growth from their historic nuclei, the Great Synagogue in
Duke's Place and its presiding rabbi.[22] The Jews who migrated
to other parts of London and to the Provinces created a small
network of synagogues and *hebrot* in the new areas, yet continued to recognize the primacy of the Great Synagogue and
its rabbi. By the time this development had come to full fruition
in the 1870's, the Great Synagogue at the City border of the
East End was nearly bare of its old native worshippers, whose
descendants were now members of a prosperous periphery
elsewhere in London. They were replaced by new immigrants,
who worshipped in the Great Synagogue but were not
members thereof.[23] Instead, most of the immigrants were
members of some *hebra* or were not members anywhere, and
came to Duke's Place to hear a *maggid* on a Sabbath or for some
other temporary attraction. The ability of the Great Synagogue, appropriately called the Cathedral Synagogue of Anglo-
Jewry, to secure a hold on the loyalty of immigrants and
ultimately to incorporate them into the official community,
had been proven in earlier generations. It might have again
succeeded in establishing itself as the Cathedral Synagogue
for the new immigration from Russia and Poland, but the
edifice in Duke's Place and the leadership of the United Synagogue never quite tried. Several efforts, which are described
below, did not recover the spiritual primacy which had been
lost by failure to take positive interest in the independent

[22]For the origins of the Anglo-Jewish ecclesiastical system, *cf.* Cecil Roth, *A
History of the Jews in England*, 2nd ed., Oxford, 1949, pp. 227–28; ——, *A History
of the Great Synagogue*, 1690–1940, London, 1948, pp. 125–32; 246–49, 266–70.
——, 'The Chief Rabbinate of England', in I. Epstein, E. Levine, C. Roth, ed.,
Essays in Honour of the Very Rev. Dr J. H. Hertz, London, 5703, pp. 371–84; C.
Duschinsky, *The Rabbinate of the Great Synagogue, London, from 1756 to 1842*,
London, 1921.
[23]Cecil Roth, *A History of the Great Synagogue*, 1690–1940, London, 1948, pp.
277–82, 289–92.

hebrot. These places of worship did not cramp one another in the hundreds of villages of the Pale, but were squeezed together in the few acres of the East End and the immigrant settlements in the Provinces. German Jews maintained their own *hebra* in Spital Square in the East End. With prosperity, many of them left the old vicinity to settle in the Canonbury Road area where the North London Synagogue stood. This enclave became the London bastion of the German Jewish orthodoxy expounded by Rabbi Samson Raphael Hirsch of Frankfurt (1808–1889), which remained independent of both native and immigrant Judaism, except for a few members who participated in the Machzikei HaDath struggle (see below).

On the other hand, some of the English *hebrot* were on the scene long before their Russian and Polish clientele, left over by the earlier German and Dutch Jewish immigration of the later eighteenth century and the first half of the nineteenth century. Some of that earlier membership had prospered and joined more affluent City and West End synagogues, while others remained with a *hebra* and pushed it up the ladder to synagogal wealth and prestige. However, a residue of *hebrot* remained stationary, and new generations of immigrants in their precincts followed upon the steps of departed forerunners. For example, what was called the Polish Synagogue of Cutler Street in Edwardian England started in the East End in 1790, over two generations before the substantial advent of Polish Jews. The Little Scarborough Street *hebra* started in Gun Yard in 1792, and the large *hebra* in Great Prescott Street originated as early as 1748. The Dutch *hebra* of Sandy's Row, founded in 1860, and the German Synagogue in Spital Square, founded in 1870, both remained important well after German and Dutch Jews had receded to a small minority in Whitechapel.[24] Whatever the changes of character and locale which these venerable *hebrot* underwent, it is plain that they and others existed long before the latest and largest wave of Jewish immigrants arrived in England. The latter revived nearly as many somnolent *hebrot* as they founded.

A Gentile observer like Beatrice Potter could look upon the

[24]The factual basis is in an historical memoir in *JC*, March 24 and April 11, 1911; Cecil Roth, *A History of the Jews in England*, 2nd ed., Oxford, 1949, p. 198.

hebra with sympathy and generous use of Oriental imagery.
To the native Jew, the *hebra* was a problem because it was
foreign to the ecclesiastical system of his community, alien
in language and appearance, and seemed even to be a 'clandestine religious society'.[25] More balanced views were expressed
in the 1880's in the *Jewish Chronicle*, when the matter came to
irritated communal attention, which were an improvement
upon earlier, sharper antagonism.[26] The communal journal
expressed conflicting views on the *hebrot*, yet also educated its
readers on the peculiarities of immigrant religion. Although
most English Jews know nothing about them, 'there are few
amongst us whose immediate ancestors were not members of
a Hebra'.[27] Having dealt with this psychic bruise, it undertook
to explain how it happened that the *hebrot* 'hold their
[members'] affection as in a vice'.[28] It observed that

. . . the hebrot, or minor places of worship . . . originate partly in the
aversion felt by our foreign poor to the religious manners and customs
of English Jews. . . . The sooner the immigrants to our shore learn
to reconcile themselves to their new conditions of living, the better
for themselves. Whatever tends to perpetuate the isolation of this
element of the community must be dangerous to its welfare.[29]

The principle of unity within the established community was
categorically affirmed:

To form 'wheels within wheels', or little communities within a
great one, is to weaken the general body. They have no right, if
permanent residents, to isolate themselves from their English coreligionists. . . . They should hasten to assimilate themselves, completely, with the community amongst whom they dwell. . . .[30]

[25]Manchester Jewish Board of Guardians, *Minutes*, January 9, 1878.

[26]The Sandy's Row *hebra* was snubbed by the Chief Rabbi at the consecration
of its building in 1870, but was received more hospitably in 1886. Its building was
a former chapel. Most of its members were 'working men of the humblest class'
and 'nearly all natives of Holland'. *JC*, May 20, 1881. A *JC* report of May 20,
1881 placed its membership at 420, income at £517, and expenditure at £464.
It had been £1,140 in debt a few years earlier, but was now £100 in the black.
Typical names mentioned are Van Staveren, Reed, Levy, de Vries, Solomons,
Loesen, Porten, Winkel, Bronkhurst, Limburg, Davids, Hond, Kattenburg,
Loafer. This Dutch *hebra*, apparently in transition to a full synagogue, did not
reach that level because the Dutch Jews moved away from Spitalfields, and the few
who remained were submerged, as was their *hebra*, by the East European tide. A
later report (*JC*, June 15, 1883) gives 350 members and income of £391, so it
was still 'undoubtedly one of the largest Chebroth.'

[27]*JC*, February 25, 1881.   [28]*JC*, November 21, 1884.
[29]*JC*, January 23, 1880.   [30]*JC*, February 6, 1880.

Although they were 'willing to welcome' new immigrants, there was a clear stipulation:

. . . if they intend to remain in England, if they wish to become members of our community, we have a right to demand that they will show signs of an earnest wish for complete amalgamation with the aims and feelings of their hosts.[31]

It was not yet recognized that the *hebrot* and their members had little wish 'to become members of our community'. To join an established English synagogue cost £3 10s,[32] and very few could afford so astronomical a charge, assuming that they desired to join at all. Although by their very existence they 'deliberately manufacture material for unfavourable and unjust opinions about ourselves', the *hebrot* had 'far more virtues than are observable on the surface'.[33] Indeed, 'the system is to some extent not without its uses'. For instance, the benefits which the *hebra* distributed were 'a great negative assistance to the [Jewish] Board of Guardians'.[34]

The least charitable view of the *hebrot* came from a certain 'Aaron, Minister in a large provincial town'. His complaints articulate what others probably thought but hesitated to say:

It is because Jews have lived within themselves in other countries on the 'Hebra' principle that they have made the existence of Jews in those countries intolerable . . . your suggestion [to federate the *hebrot*] . . . would help foreign Jews to do for England what they have done for Russia . . . the sooner the Hebra movement is crushed out of existence the sooner we will remove from our midst the only draw-back to the advancement of Jews in this country.[35]

This strikingly unfair view was sharply rebuked in several letters, and its writer partly recanted, but there is interest in a view which associates the persecutions in Russia with the failings of *hebrot*, and implies that the sufferings of Russian Jewry would be visited upon English Jewry if the *hebrot* take root.

[31]*JC*, February 25, 1881.
[32]This was the charge at the New Synagogue in the City, which lost 50 of its members between 1881 and 1883. *JC*, May 18, 1883.
[33]*JC*, February 25, 1881.
[34]The subject is discussed in detail in a series on 'Judaism at the End End,' *JC*, December 12 and 19, 1884; January 2, 1885.
[35]*JC*, December 5, 1884, ff.

When Nathaniel de (soon first Lord) Rothschild, as President of the United Synagogue, proposed that the organization look into 'spiritual destitution' in the East End, the *Jewish Chronicle* expressed admiration for the religious fervour of East End Jewry, explaining that the phrase referred only to so much of the *hebra* atmosphere as was not 'pure religion'. It defended Rothschild's use of a term denoting pauperism by correctly noting that many immigrant Jews were 'destitute' of any *hebra* connection, and therefore required the ministrations of the United Synagogue. However, a proposal apparently unfavourable to the *hebrot* which bore the magical name of Rothschild excited alarm in the East End, so that the foremost magnate of the community had to assure all that he did not intend to close the *hebrot*.[36] The report itself found nothing spiritually destitute in the East End, but recommended that something be done about housing conditions.

Since the immigrant Jews steadfastly preferred their *hebrot*, the *Jewish Chronicle* proposed that the *hebrot* attach themselves to larger but slowly decaying Jewish synagogues, following the example of the Hayye Adam *hebra* and the venerable but declining Hambro' Synagogue.[37] A less preferable course was a federation of *hebrot*, 'analogous in some way to the United Synagogue',[38] as Hermann Adler desired in order to 'try to break down the territorial principle [i.e. *landsmannschaft*], which is at the root of the multiplicity of Hebras. . . .'[39] To federate required English Jews, for the separatist nature of *hebrot* and their close little quarrels made it unlikely that they could do so alone.[40] A danger not overlooked by the native community was that a federation of *hebrot*, if formed through immigrant initiative, might result in a separatist immigrant community.

[36]*JC*, January 2, 1885; 'pure religion' is explained on December 19, 1884, and Rothschild clarified his intentions on the following January 2. The entrance of the United Synagogue into questions of housing and material destitution is probably a result of the small furore generated by the report in *The Lancet*, March 5, 1884, on Jewish conditions in East London.

[37]*JC*, February 25, 1881.

[38]*Ibid*.

[39]*JC*, November 21, 1884.

[40]*JC*, February 25, 1881, in encouragement of an abortive attempt, and April 29, 1881

THE FEDERATION OF
SYNAGOGUES AND THE UNITED SYNAGOGUE

The initiative in bringing the *hebrot* together came from sympathetic native Jews in the fall of 1886 and early 1887, led by Sir Samuel Montagu (1832–1911), the pious millionaire bullion broker (later Lord Swaythling), who was then M.P. for Whitechapel. Montagu's assets, spiritual and tangible, were strengthened by his willingness to take time off from his business in Old Broad Street to attend to tedious *hebra* bickerings, hardly a mile to the east. He was a member of forty synagogues. But however great his means and abilities for communal leadership, Montagu's rise to the summit was permanently baulked by the hereditary rule of the Rothschilds. Communal gossip made the rivalry between the two bankers a cause for the organization of the *hebrot* apart from the United Synagogue, where Rothschild ruled.[41] Close to Montagu was Hermann Landau (1844–1924), also a banker and the first immigrant from Poland to become a part of proper Anglo-Jewry, and Mark Moses, another Polish Jew, a prosperous clothing contractor and man of affairs in the East End. These leaders emphasized their intention not to intervene in *hebra* internal affairs, but merely to help them by financial stabilization, sanitary guidance, and settlement of disputes. The benefits which might accrue from following the lead of the pious millionaire were not directly mentioned, but such silence hardly betokened indifference.

To the hostile native community, Montagu argued that *hebrot* had come to stay, and that if left to themselves they would continue to embarrass the native Jews by remaining numerous, noisy, and dirty—places into which English influences would not penetrate.[42] They might even band together on their own and break away from the established community. The United Synagogue remained unpersuaded:

[41]Although this subject was not directly mentioned in the communal press, it was widely known then and now. The *Arbeiter Freind's* discussions of the strike negotiations of 1889 mockingly refer to Montagu's desire to outdo Rothschild by effecting the settlement himself.
[42]For example, *JC*, February 25, 1881.

. . . at a time when the desire of the community is to unite as much as possible its various organizations, and to make further provision for the religious requirements of the poor in the East of London, it surely seems inopportune to create and extend a body whose policy must inevitably tend to disunion and disintegration. . . .[43]

Hermann Landau reminded these opponents that

in the latter part of 1887 great dissatisfaction was expressed in the East End with existing ecclesiastical arrangements and meetings were actually held to organize a new Schechita Board, etc. The Federation was called into existence to prevent any development of this movement, and has, therefore, been the means of preventing communal disunion.[44]

But schism, averted once, boiled over a few years later.

Montagu's role in settling the strike of 1889 convinced him that danger lay in wait for Judaism from another quarter: 'the influence of a few Atheists over Jewish Working Men can no longer be ignored'. It was therefore for the Federation of Synagogues, 'comprising so large a number of observant Jews, to take the lead in combating this most serious evil'. Rabbi M. Lerner of Alsace was employed from 1890 until 1894 as

. . . a gentleman well acquainted with Judisch-Deutsch and able to lecture in English as a Maggid, or Minister (not Dayan), salary £300 per annum . . . in religious matters . . . under the jurisdiction of Dr Adler.[45]

He was followed by Rabbi Avigdor Chaikin from 1901 to 1911, who by that time did not need to bother much with the socialist menace. He came from the Jewish immigrant community in Paris, and also sat as a Dayan upon the Beth Din of the Chief Rabbi. Rabbi Meir Jung, originally from Hungary, succeeded him. The Federation also employed the eloquent Hayyim Zundel Maccoby as its 'Chief Preacher'.

Once he succeeded in assembling enough *hebra* representatives, Montagu soon formed the Federation of Minor Synagogues (the qualifying 'Minor' was dropped within two years)[46] over which he reigned in benign despotism until his

[43]United Synagogue, Council, *Minutes*, February 18, 1890.
[44]*JC*, May 24, 1889. A correspondent reports that disaffection still existed.
[45] Joseph E. Blank, *The Minutes of the Federation of Synagogues*, London, 1912, pp. 20–21.
[46]The elimination of this modest modifier was attacked as a token of aspirations to rival the United Synagogue. *JC*, June 7, 1889. To Montagu's explanation that

death. Financially, the Federation amalgamated the burial and benefit societies which were part of each *hebra*. Ten years after its foundation, the Federation Burial Society counted 1,200 members who paid 1½d weekly for their own or a dependant's interment, and for an additional ½d per week survivors received £1 to tide over the week of confined mourning.[47]

One year after its birth, the Federation of Synagogues enrolled thirty synagogues with 2,120 members, and its secretary supposed that 'eight or ten or twelve more' very small *hebrot* outside its embrace could claim about 400 members more.[48] The Federation of 1903 had 4,391 seatholders in its thirty-nine constituents, which rose to about 6,000 in fifty-one constituents at Montagu's death in 1911.[49] Montagu's restraining hand is evident in keeping new *hebrot* from arising while doubling the membership; he also succeeded in amalgamating some *hebrot*. An architect's services were made available to *hebrot* who intended to build or were beleaguered by health or sanitary authorities.[50] Montagu's largesse was substantial. In the first two years of the Federation's existence, his gifts exceeded £2,000, an amount probably equal to the better part of a year's expenditures by all of them.[51]

Montagu energetically pushed the Federation onto the councils of sundry communal bodies. The Jewish Board of Guardians granted it a seat readily, hoping that the Federation would exert desirable influence upon the Board's clientele.[52]

---

it was done to meet the objection of the Dalston Synagogue to being deemed minor, the Editor retorted that that synagogue was neither minor nor in the East End, and was therefore 'filched' from the United. *JC*, June 14, 1889.

[47]United Synagogue, *East End Scheme*, London, 1898, p. 21.

[48]Testimony of Joseph E. Blank to House of Commons Select Committee on Emigration and Immigration, *Report*, 1889, Min. 2699. However, as many as fifty or sixty *hebrot* were believed to exist in 1883. *JC*, September 28, 1883.

[49]Testimony of Sir Samuel Montagu to Royal Commission on Alien Immigration, *Minutes of Evidence*, Cd. 1742, 1903, Min, 16674. Joseph E. Blank, *op. cit.*, p. 26.

[50]The Jewish Board of Guardians also inspected the premises of unsanitary *hebrot* and took appropriate action. For instance, its *Minutes*, April 14, 1890, and prolonged correspondence between it and the *hebra*, in *Idem, Minute Letter Book*, April 20, 1890, ff.

[51]*JC*, November 15, 1889. To this could be added a £300 loan to a *hebra* and the support of the Federation's preacher at £300 per annum. See above, Note 45.

[52]Jewish Board of Guardians, *Minutes*, February 12, March 12, May 13, 1888. The Federation responded by conducting synagogue appeals for the Board. *Idem, Minute Letter Book*, July 8, 1889.

However, the powerhouse of the Jewish community, the Executive of the United Synagogue, denied an application to seat the *hebrot* upon its Shechita and Flour [for Passover] Committees.[53] At this period the United Synagogue was desultorily planning a major project in the East End, whose keystone was the erection of a synagogue to accommodate 1,000 men and 200 women, as well as some lesser features. However, the well-heeled membership of the 'United' showed no inclination to undertake such expenditures, and they may also have inwardly felt that a costly building might only be a white elephant—a rather well-founded premonition. Montagu and the Federation fought the plan vehemently. When Rothschild and Sir Julian Goldsmid informed the Council of the United Synagogue that nobody in East or West London showed much interest in the plan, the whole matter was thereupon dropped.[54] Native Jewry, which deplored the *hebrot*, had nothing to put in their place. The United Synagogue did make a number of more modest efforts in the East End. It moved as early as 1877 to place its marriage fees within the reach of poor immigrants,[55] and generally took charge of *shehitah* supervision. In seeking to gain the adherence of the East End, it usually placed a representative East End rabbi upon its Beth Din although denying the title of Rabbi to everyone but the Chief Rabbi. Later Dayanim sitting for the East End were held in decent respect, but the first, Jacob Reinowitz (1818–1893), was neither supported nor appreciated. He had come to England in 1875 to visit his son-in-law, Rabbi Sussman Cohen in Manchester, and was persuaded to remain in England to preside over the *Hebra Shass* (Talmud Study *Hebra*) in London. That he 'gradually took up a position as a member of the Beth Din' originated in the need for a third member to make a judicial quorum alongside Chief Rabbi Adler and the Rev. Bernard Spiers (1827–1901). Rabbi Reinowitz was a gentle and much-loved figure in the immigrant community, and is the prototype of Reb Shmuel in Zangwill's *Dreamers*

[53]*JC*, June 7, 1889.
[54]*JC*, May 8, 1891. At that meeting, Benjamin L. Cohen, President of the Board and Montagu's brother-in-law, attacked the *hebrot* and the Federation for deterring rapid Anglicization.
[55]United Synagogue, Council, *Minutes*, August 16, 1877.

of the Ghetto. In an obituary expressive of a pang of communal remorse at the treatment meted out to him, the *Jewish Chronicle* regretted that he had been

but little understood and appreciated by the community, and he was allowed to subsist on a miserable pittance grudgingly given by the United Synagogue.[56]

The United Synagogue could well lament the death of its sole rabbinic representative in the East End. For the next twenty years, rabbinic leadership of the East End's orthodox Jews was in the hands of the rabbi of Machzikei HaDath, Aba Werner (1837–1912), who was not within the communal structure and until 1905 refused to recognize its authority. During his life tenure at Machzikei Ha Dath, there is less reality to the frequent discussions of giving the Beth Din a role which could command the devotion of the immigrant community. A further reason lay in the person of the Chief Rabbi who, supported by the communal magnates, was loth to surrender a particle of his authority. Adlerism, as hostile contemporaries termed it, had as its corrollary that a Beth Din, in comparison with the Chief Rabbi, would be wholly decorative in powers—a situation hardly conformable to Jewish law.

The refurbishing of the Beth Din was a part of the United Synagogue's comprehensive East End Scheme,[57] formulated in 1898 and partly executed. Its goal was 'a practical and workable Scheme for ameliorating the condition, socially, intellectually, spiritually, and otherwise, of the poorest Jews in the East of London. . . .'[58] More or less, the Scheme was an omnibus of suggestions that had wandered in and out of the communal agenda for fifteen years. This time there was no recommendation for a large central synagogue, but instead a series of measures to expand greatly social services and educational facilities in the East End—less broad than a Toynbee Hall, but more than a synagogue or a typical American 'Jewish Centre'. The East End planners proposed a benevolent society, a 'thrift society' (savings bank), a youth club, mothers' education groups,

[56]*JC*, May 19, 1893, November 16, 1894.
[57]United Synagogue, *East End Scheme*, London, 1898. There is much data in the reports.
[58]*Ibid.*, p. 1.

encouragement of vocational education, interpreters for the courts of justice in the East End, a free Jewish library, arbitration services by the Beth Din, and public lectures on matters of religious and general interest. A large hall was to be built to house all these activities.

Some of this wide periphery of public services and benefits was adopted, including the appointment of two Dayanim. The expectation that the two young English rabbis would be the hoped-for surrogates of immigrant interests was jarred by a meeting which inveighed against

those who mean to appoint for us East End Jews as Rabbis, persons whom we by no means can recognize as such, as by the word Rabbis we understand well known and highly educated men in Talmudical learning.[59]

Their threat to repudiate the community upon this occasion was evidently not taken very seriously, for Moses Hyamson (1863–1948) and Asher Feldman (1873–1948) were elevated as planned. A mollifying letter assured the protesters of the intention to appoint only men 'of strict orthodox principles' who 'will command the confidence of Jews in that district [the East End]. . . .' Its tone reveals some evaporation of the old haughty condescension for it was the 'earnest desire' of the Council of the United Synagogue

to respect the religious sympathies and feelings of the Jews of foreign birth who dwell in the East of London and to keep in close touch with them so that they may feel they are all members of the same community as their English brethren. They have always been, and will ever be, ready to listen to any suggestion which may be thought desirable in the interests of any section of Jews in London. . . .[60]

Although Lord Rothschild refused to consider an East European rabbi as a regular Dayan, the Beth Din and the Chief Rabbi coopted such a man, Rabbi Moses Avigdor Chaikin of the Federation of Synagogues. This conciliatory attitude had not always been visible, but the rupture which occurred a few years earlier with Machzikei HaDath taught its lessons.

[59]The protest is in United Synagogue, Council, *Minutes*, March 4, 1902. P. Ornstein, Secretary, replied on March 10; *cf. infra*. A deputation waited upon Rothschild to no avail. *JC*, March 28, 1902.
[60]*Ibid.*

THE MACHZIKEI HADATH SCHISM

The most categorical challenge from immigrants to established English Judaism came from the Machzikei HaDath (Upholders of the Religion) synagogue-community.[61] Their outlook may tersely be summarized as a rejection of the official Judaism of England as a heterodoxy to be combatted, and with which truly pious Jews ought not to be associated. They were convinced that Judaism as practised by native Jews was not true Judaism, and that its pretence to orthodoxy was false. With this passionate conviction, it is not remarkable that a *casus belli* speedily appeared. When it came in 1892, Machzikei HaDath precipitated the bitterest religious conflict in a generation. The movement began a few years earlier among members of two distinct groups acting together—the North London Synagogue of pious Anglicized German Jews, and a high orthodox *hebra* in Booth Street named Machzikei Shomrei Shabbath (Upholders of Sabbath Observers). They formed a society named Machzikei HaDath to agitate for stricter communal orthodoxy, particularly in the sphere of *shehitah*. Men like the pious Yiddish journalist-printer Isaac Wolf Metchik (1849–1953 [sic]) consistently advocated the repudiation of official Judaism and the establishment of a rival community in the East End, to be supported by the income of an independent *shehitah* system. Metchik's views evoked a flurry of friendly and hostile responses, but his opponents pointed to the newly founded Federation of Synagogues as an omen of pious intentions on the part of the native community.[62] The situation quieted until 1891.

Matters came to a head when the Machzikei HaDath, with its German and East European elements, failed to impose more stringent supervision upon the unwilling butchers. They thereupon established an independent *shehitah* system. Chief Rabbi Adler, however, touched off the explosion by publicly pro-

---

[61]A strongly pro-Machzikei HaDath memoir is Bernard Homa, *A Fortress of Judaism in Anglo-Jewry*, London, 1953. Dr Homa's recollections as a grandson of Rabbi Werner and son of a late warden are valuable, if partisan. I am indebted to him for permission to see and use the extensive materials in his possession.
[62]*Die Tsukunft*, IV, No. 168, October 28, 1887; IV, 172, December 2, 1887.

claiming the new *shehitah* to be *trefah*—not *kosher* and hence inedible by observant Jews—because they were in rebellion against the recognized religious authority. He strengthened his case by a supporting letter from Isaac Elhanan Spektor, Rabbi of Kovno (see below). Machzikei HaDath responded to the Chief Rabbi by declaring the entire communal *shehitah* to be *trefah* likewise, on the grounds that it was incorrect in Jewish law. Each side thereupon appealed to the East End with handbills and broadsides stating the merits of its case, until the Board of Shechita requested Adler to cease.[63] Thus, the food a Jew ate was a declaration of allegiance to one side or the other.

Nothing could have presented a graver threat to the historic unity of the community than this relatively small group of highly orthodox Jews who were summoning the immigrant Jewry of England to establish itself as an independent community. The Chief Rabbi, who had to deal with native Jews who wanted to move towards Reform was now confronted with a movement which repudiated the religious integrity of English Judaism's 'Victorian Compromise'. Early in 1893 the Machzikei HaDath as a *shehitah* system officially coalesced with the Shomrei Shabbath *hevra* in Booth Street to form a self-recognized independent Jewish community. The pious Germans receded into the background of the movement. The new body published a manifesto which expressed their dissatisfaction with the state of English Judaism:[64]

The objects . . . are . . . to uphold the Jewish Religion in this country, where to our great regret, the foundations of our law have become weakened, and the whole structure of Religion is threatened (as evidence the unsatisfactory state of the provision of Kosher meat, Passover food and other requisites), and to prevent the Sabbath desecration which is much on the increase, there being, seemingly, nobody able to put a stop to it. Some even favour the reform sects, who try to do away with the oral law altogether, retaining only

[63]Homa, *op. cit.*, ch. 1, *passim*; JC, March 11, 1892, ff; August 19, 1892.
[64]Machzikey Hadass and Shomre Shabboss, *Laws*, London, 5653; 2nd ed., 1905. The second edition adds a note: 'P.S. It ought not to be overlooked that according to an agreement . . . peace and harmony has been restored between the Machsikey Hadass and the Kehilah'. For a typical view of English Judaism by a leading figure, see [Jacob Zinkin] *Heshbonot Shel Mizvah*, London, 1920, pp. 101–13.

such precepts of the written law which suit their personal inclinations, rejecting other, even principal laws of the Torah, which do not find favour with them—Who knoweth how much further this may lead to? [sic.]

In view of the unworthiness of the existing community, Machzikei HaDath resolved to pursue the path of separatism:

And in order not to be mixed up with such people we have established this holy community in order that every one individually may be encouraged and strengthened by the union, to walk in the path of the law as revealed to us on Sinai and as explained by our teachers, the Rabbis of the Talmud and later authorities, the wells whose water we drink, viz. the Shulchan Aruch and not to deviate from that path either to the right or to the left.

Such orthodox fundamentalism was accompanied by the selection of a rabbinic head of sovereign religious authority, consciously following the older European pattern:

But to be sure to follow the right course we have to choose and elect a Rabbi great in wisdom and religious fervour whose authority, competence and sanctity must be testified to by the great Rabbinical authorities of Russia and Poland. Such a one will be our Teacher, our Judge, he will select our Shochtim, he will licence our butchers. Let us build our own synagogue, our own house of learning where every one is free to learn and to teach, so that the knowledge of the law may be spread. Sabbath breakers shall not intermix with us. The following rules, if strictly observed, will protect us against being swallowed up by outsiders, and with the Almighty's help, we shall so fortify our position that our children after us will be able to follow in the path we have trodden out for them, even as our forefathers have done for us. Thus shall we preserve our sacred religion for generations to come. And may the Almighty bring the redeemer speedily in our days, AMEN.

The ordinances of the synagogue-community emphasized the reaction against an Anglicized form of Judaism: 'The ritual of the Synagogue services must be strictly in accord with the Shulchan Aruch [standard legal code] and same as adopted by the Communities in Russia and Poland'. A special point was noted that the 'Reader's Desk (amud) must be close to the Ark', and that the 'Bimah [platform for reading the Torah] must be in the Centre of the Synagogue', both traditional

212 JEWISH IMMIGRANT IN ENGLAND 1870–1914

rules which English synagogue architecture had allowed to lapse in favour of a more stage-like arrangement of worship. Finally, no officiant might wear 'such canonicals which may appear as if imitating christian clergy at church services', a pointed slur at contemporary native Jewish practice. Great authority was vested in their Rabbi, Aba Werner, who had had a distinguished career as Dayan in the *yeshibah* town of Telz and as Rabbi of Helsingfors before his arrival in England in 1891.[65]

Chief Rabbi Adler, realizing that the immigrant rebels would heed neither his threats nor his defence, turned to rabbinic luminaries upon the continent for public letters of support. Prominent among them stood Rabbi Isaac Elhanan Spektor (1819–1896) of Kovno, a frequent spokesman for his people before the Russian regime and an experienced persecutor of dissidents. It was an extraordinary letter which the Chief Rabbi sent. He stated simply that a group of rebels was circulating a canard as to the reliability of the *shehitah* supervised by him. A letter of support was requested because

Your Excellency knows how abundant is the charity amongst us. If the controversy should spread, then the members of the community will turn their back on them [East End Jews] and will no longer help them or our unfortunate Jewish brethren.[66]

No record survives to bear witness to the Rabbi of Kovno's opinion of this hint, although he duly responded with a condemnation of the schismatics. The embattled Machzikei HaDath combatted this missive and others such by sending its own letters and a brochure which presented its version of the affair, so that some Continental rabbis did withdraw earlier condemnations and assured the rebels of their confidence in the esteemed Rabbi Werner.[67]

[65]On Rabbi Werner, cf. Homa, *op. cit.*, ch. 2, *passim*; JC, December 27, 1912.
[66]Hebrew text in Homa, *op. cit.*, pp. xvi, 37, 104–105, where it is printed for the first time. However, there is not definite proof that this is the letter which was sent, since it is only a letter-press copy of a draft. We assume that this letter or one very similar was actually sent.
[67]There is a collection of such documents in Homa, *op. cit.*, pp. xiv–xxxv, 121–27. Cf. Israel Meir Kahan, *Nidhey Yisrael* (The Dispersed of Israel) (Hebrew and Yiddish), Warsaw, 1894, reprinted with English translation, New York, 1951, pp. 170–71, obviously referring to the struggle; pp. 118–22 and 263–64, which seem to be influenced by it.

An added embarrassment was the ½d reduction per pound of Machzikei HaDath meat, which compelled the Board of Shehitah to follow suit, to the delight of consumers. The communal journal, pleased by this unexpected benefit, said that the Board had suffered this 'unkindest cut of all' because of their habit of 'mixing up finance with questions of *kashruth*'.[68]

The bare-knuckled nature of this religious battle is intimated in Metchik's complaint that because of association with Machzikei HaDath, a Hebrew teacher had lost his job, a *hazan* had been discharged, and a printer no longer received communal patronage.[69] Later communal tradition corroborates the animosity of the struggle on both sides.

In 1898, the separatist community acquired a fine, venerable Huguenot church in Spitalfields. Under the popular rubric of the Spitalfields Great Synagogue it became the principal synagogue of the East End, both in worship and study—a position which the Great Synagogue in Duke's Place might have filled had it been more foresighted.

Thenceforward, the official community and Machzikei HaDath, with its fervidly pious immigrants, left each other alone in mutual disdain. After the bouquets of endorsements and the hails of condemnation, the two sides gradually relaxed their attacks; but the independent *shehitah* remained in operation. Imminent financial ruin was the force which ultimately brought the pious separatists to terms in 1905.[70] The outcome was that the institutions connected with Machzikei HaDath—synagogue, school, rabbi, *shehitah*—were preserved, but the conception of an independent community was surrendered. The jurisdiction of the Chief Rabbi was recognized, 'provided that he acts in accordance with the Shulchan Oruch'. Rabbi Werner's position as 'minister' of the synagogue was confirmed in return, but he ceased the exercise of rabbinic functions concerning marriage and divorce. As to the tender issue of *shehitah*, the rebels maintained only part of their system, and had to recognize the authority of the Board of Shehita over the remainder. The synagogue also became a constituent of the

[68] *JC*, August 11, 1892.
[69] *Ibid.*, cf. [Jacob Zinkin,] *op. cit.*, p. 151.
[70] I am indebted to Dr Homa for permission to consult these contracts.

Federation of Synagogues, from whom it received a loan of £1,000; the Board of Shehita, of which Montagu was also President, granted a subsidy to maintain its fallen rival system. A violation of the terms by Machzikei HaDath, such as renewed aspirations to independence, would give legal cause for cancellation of the subsidy and recall of the entire loan on short notice. Thus did the insurgents yield their contentious separatism in favour of a position within the fold as the leading synagogue of the East End.

IMMIGRANT RELIGION IN THE PROVINCES

The East European immigrants who settled in the Provincial cities were in a situation in some respects different. The total population of Provincial Jewry barely reached one-third of London's by the beginning of the present century, and its historic career began at a considerably later period than the London community's. The complex ecclesiastical arrangements in London were far simpler in the Provinces, where there was no United Synagogue and the control of the Chief Rabbinate in religious life was weaker. Hence the comparative absence of decadent *hebrot* awaiting the reviving touch of new immigrants, and a more autonomous position for both native and immigrant rabbi. Perhaps there was also a greater rapport between native Jews and immigrants in religious and communal matters, especially in small communities. Still, the immigrants founded their own religious institutions, although not before some of them joined the synagogues of the native Jews and found them not to their taste. Naturally enough, the English members of such congregations were for their part vigorous enough in resisting the mass incursions which might overwhelm them numerically. No actual conflicts arose, for the Provincial immigrants resembled their compatriots in London in keeping to their own *hebrot*. Information concerning immigrant Judaism in the Provinces is scantier than that for London, but some contemporary references may be gleaned.

Foremost among Provincial communities stood Manchester, whose Jewish population almost quadrupled between 1870 and 1890. At the latter date, the city had nearly 20,000 Jews and the number of *hebrot* was reported at a minimum of two dozen.[71] The line of separation between the Sefardi, Reform, and native orthodox on one hand, and the immigrants' *hebrot* on the other, was a clear one. However, the *hebrot* themselves were far from united. A reporter found them split into adherents of two rival rabbis;[72] perhaps this is an instance of competing supervisions of *shehitah* and other functions which conferred more than prestige alone. A few years later, Rabbi Abbi Reiness of Kovno appeared briefly upon the scene, with an authorization from Chief Rabbi Adler to issue responsa to religious questions 'and to act as Moreh Horoho [rabbinic guide] to the large Jewish community resident in Strangeways and Hightown, Manchester'.[73] Such an arrangement would have been unthinkable in London, and the reasons for the authorization are uncertain. However, it foundered upon the unwillingness of the *hebrot* to accept Reiness' leadership, despite his high qualifications. The institution of a Communal Rabbi for both native and immigrant Jews was to come later.

Jewish religious life in Leeds, second in size among Provincial communities, developed in a straight line which contrasts with the bickersome congeries of bethels in every larger Jewish community. The Leeds community was substantially the creation of Russian and Polish Jews. In the early 1860's, there were barely the ten Jews required for a *minyan*, but by the end of the 1880's, an estimated 6,000 to 8,000 Jews lived in the city.[74] The principal immigrant synagogue—to describe it as a *hebra* would not be justified—was the Beth HaMidrash HaGadol (The Great House of Study), which was founded in the early 1870's and moved to successively larger premises in 1877, c. 1880, 1886, 1895, and 1907. The Beth HaMidrash HaGadol could afford to send to Russia for an important rabbinical figure, Israel Hayyim Daiches (1850–1937), who assumed his duties in 1901.[75] He became to a large

[71]Manchester Jewish Board of Guardians, *Annual Report*, 1889, p. 5; *Jewish World*, July 12, 1889; N. Berlin in *Die Tsukunft*, IV, 195, May 11, 1888.

[72]*Die Tsukunft*, IV, 195, 196 (May 11, 18, 1888).

[73]*JC*, September 29, 1893.

[74]*Report to the Board of Trade on the Sweating System in Leeds*. C. 5513, 1888, p. 3. The source is the Rev. Moses Abrahams of Leeds.

[75]*Jewish World*, September 14, 1906; I. H. Daiches, *Derashot MaHaRYaH* Leeds, 1920, p. viii–ix, gives the background of Daiches' coming to England.

extent the communal rabbi of the immigrants, and was soon generally regarded as the leading East European rabbi in the Provinces. Rabbi Daiches' Hebrew periodical *Bet Va' ad la Hak-hamin* (Meeting House of the Wise) is the sole repository of rabbinic learning published in England in that generation.[76]

Leeds was also the scene of successful efforts to unite the synagogues in *shehitah* matters, and upon this beginning a recognized local Beth Din was established in 1913, with both immigrant and native rabbinic members.[77]

Liverpool contrasts with Manchester and Leeds, both as to the early beginnings of its community and the vigour of native religious institutions. The native synagogues, which remained in areas abandoned by native Jews and occupied by immigrants, seem to have met the religious wants of many of the 4,000 to 6,0000 immigrant Jews in the city. An uncertain report in the 1880's, classified seventy per cent. of the membership of an English synagogue as immigrants,[78] while another contemporaneous observer was impressed by the relative scarcity of *hebrot* and their functionaries. With a reasonably cohesive community, it was possible to employ a philosophical East European rabbi and Zionist, Samuel Jacob Rabbinowitz, as rabbinic leader of the immigrant community.[79]

According to a contemporary statement, Glasgow Jewry was already three-fourths Polish-Jewish by 1881, although the Jews were supposedly well Anglicized (Caledonized?)[80] The fresh immigration took its first independent step by opening a hall for separate worship, thus bringing the *hebra* to Glasgow.[81] Near the end of our period, one communal worthy reported that 7,000 immigrant Jews on the South Side were served by a large *hebra* and three smaller ones.[82] This immigrant

[76]Eleven copies were published in Leeds between 1902 and 1904. He is also the author of several legal and homiletic works. See pp. 247–48.

[77]*JC*, January 20, 27, February 3, 1911; I. H. Daiches, *op. cit.*, p. ix.

[78]*Arbeiter Freind*, IV, 6, February 8, 1889. The reporter is the anarchist J. Jaffe who was in Liverpool awaiting his boat to America.

[79]*Die Tsukunft*, IV, 182, July 8, 1887; I. Raffalovich, *Ziyyunim veTamrurim*, Tel Aviv, 1952, pp. 107–108; *HaMeliz*, XXV, 92, December 21, 1885.

[80]*JC*, August 19, 26, 1881.

[81]*The Polish Yidel*, I, 10, September 26, 1884; *HaMeliz*, XIX, 102, January 9, 1885.

[82]Interview with Michael Simons, 'Glasgow's Foremost Jew', *JC*, March 24, 1911. See also *Jewish World*, June 22, 1906.

community was led by a vigorous East European rabbi, Samuel Isaac Hillman, (1863–1948), an important member of the Provincial rabbinate, and in later years a London Dayan.

Rather typical of the smaller communities is Hull, the major port of entry for transmigrants. It counted 'as many as 600 Jewish families' at the end of the 1880's, a figure which did not exceed 800 or 900 by 1914. As though by agreement with the native synagogue, the immigrants established their own 'Central Synagogue' in the 1870's, and two smaller *hebrot* later served those who did not join the parent *hebra*.[83]

Every town where immigrants settled—Cardiff, Newcastle, Swansea, Gateshead, Sunderland—sheltered one or more *hebrot*. With due allowance for local variations, their conditions were essentially the same. The little immigrant communities probably enrolled a larger proportion of the local immigrant population than did the major centres. An unaffiiliated immigrant Jew would feel unbearably isolated in a smaller city, where the protective immigrant milieu of London and Manchester and Leeds was comparatively lacking.

THE CLOSING YEARS

Immigrant Judaism began to mature organizationally at the close of our period. Side by side with the ever more vocal discontent with 'Adlerism' expressed by many native Jews and ministers under the thumb of the ageing Chief Rabbi, came the first tentative moves to convene England's immigrant rabbis. These efforts aimed partially at filling the vacuum which was created in 1911 by the death of Hermann Adler at the age of 72, after a reign which began *de facto* in 1880 and *de jure* in 1892. While promising to remain within the communal framework, the approximately thirty rabbis who gathered in Leeds in 1910 insisted upon meeting apart from the native ministers so that they might hold their discussions in the 'rabbinical manner', without the presence of men who did not possess rabbinic ordination.[84] Some opponents of the Chief Rabbinate,

[83] *JC*, May 17, 1889; information from members of the Hull Jewish community.
[84] Rabbis Yoffey of Manchester and Hurwitz of Sunderland stated when interviewed that the Chief Rabbi had 'expressed his warm approval'. They enumerated twenty-two rabbis in the Provinces and six in London, figures which are probably

such as the Zionists, placed high hopes in the outcome of the meeting in Leeds. It was thought that these would be real rabbis, truly representative of the sunken mass of pious immigrants, and not tainted by imitations of Anglican clergy. Only the high hopes can explain the bitter reaction to the Leeds meeting.

The rabbis, most of whom were from the Provinces, debated with vigour and some disorder and show of emotion. But the discussions and the subsequent resolutions disheartened the hopeful observers in the native community. The conference hotly argued matters like phylacteries, prayer shawls, ritual baths, and the dangers of the theatre. One of the resolutions admonished every married woman to shave her head and don a wig, while another called on Jews to stay away from dance halls and theatres. The assemblage attacked modern methods in Hebrew education, and specifically any method not received from their forefathers. Thus, when it was expected that the rabbis would present a workable platform for the orthodox Jews of England, the sum of their debates and resolutions was a protest against England itself. They could only fall back upon the Jewish piety of Eastern Europe in which they were nurtured and which was their true spiritual milieu.

The *Jewish Chronicle*, which had favoured the conference, blazed away:

. . . narrow-minded, dark asceticisms . . . parasitic growths, dank mould . . . ridiculous proposals . . . obsolete barbarisms . . . some of their remedies were well-nigh as disgraceful as the disease they sought to attack. . . .[85]

After the Chief Rabbi's death, there was a feeling that 'the Chief Rabbinate, which Dr Adler and Lord Rothschild built up, has gone to pieces'.[86] However, after the Leeds conclave the ruling oligarchy no longer had to fear that native malcontents would look to immigrant rabbis. When the terms

---

limited to those exercising rabbinic functions. *JC*, January 27, 1911. They replied to a ministerial attack upon the plan of their conference by objecting to the presence of an alleged heretic at the ministerial conference, but this was the only sour note before the meeting was held. *JC*, February 17, 1911.

[85]*JC*, March 10, 17, 1911; I. H. Daiches, *op. cit.*, p. ix.

[86]*The Zionist*, Vol. II, No. 1 (April, 1911).

of the prospective Chief Rabbi's authority were under discussion, a memorandum from the immigrant side proposed in essence that the new incumbent be stripped of the old powers and be made first among rabbinic equals. It received no attention. Although it seemed that something had to be done to integrate the immigrant community into the communal system, the oligarchs had their own way entirely in the selection of the new Chief Rabbi. He was Joseph Herman Hertz (1872–1946), Hungarian by birth, American in education and residence, and a very forthright Uitlander before the Boer War. The advent of this zealous and commanding figure in many ways opens a new chapter, which was soon followed by the War crisis; all another story.

VIII

EDUCATION:
A MATTER OF ORIENTATION

While the adult immigrants were largely left to their own devices, their children were vigorously taken in hand by the State, by parents, and by native Jewry, for the purpose of making them English, Jewish, or Anglo-Jewish. The State, which was then erecting a national system of elementary education beginning with the Act of 1870, could absorb Jewish children with millions of other little Englishmen into the new State (Board) schools. For its part, the native Jewish community had long supported a system of elementary schools which were, by contemporary standards, excellent. The Jewish immigrant who sent his children to one of these schools also had educational goals of his own which found expression in special schools which met after regular school hours.

Education in England,[1] although not yet comparable to the highly developed national systems of France and Germany, was infinitely ahead of any the immigrants had experienced. Eastern Europe knew nothing yet of universal compulsory education at public expense. While the Czars had earlier flirted with educational reform for the Jews, their efforts smacked of insincerity and were the nub of bitter internecine Jewish conflicts. By the 1870's and 1880's new policies swept away the Government schools in favour of more direct oppression. The exertions of the Hapsburgs in this field had been more important, but they terminated earlier and affected an area from which relatively few Jews came to England. The Jews who arrived in England had generally been educated in a *heder*[2] (lit. room)—the one room schoolhouse of East European

[1] On English education in this period, see E. Halevy, *History of the EnglishPeople in the Nineteenth Century*, V and VI, 2nd ed., London, 1951–52, V, pp. 143–75, 189–210; VI, pp. 64–73, 81–93; also J. W. Adamson, *History of Education in England*, 1789–1902, London, 1926. There is no work on Jewish education in-England.

[2] On the *heder*, *cf.* Zevi Scharfstein, *HaHeder beHayyey ʿAmenu*, (The *Heder* in the Life of Our People), N.Y., 1941.

Jewry. This perpetually decrepit institution met in the dwelling of the schoolmaster, where the elements of prayer, Bible, and other religious subject matter were taught, with the occasional addition of some arithmetic and letter writing. All this was learned by rote in Yiddish, the mother tongue, under conditions which made the *heder* nearly synonomous with inefficiency, squalor, and disorder. Here and there a *melammed* (schoolmaster) earned a reputation for efficiency and ability, but most of them were poor specimens. More gifted pupils might be educated privately before they were sent off to a *yeshibah* for intensive Talmudic study. From the outset of our period noticeable inroads were being made in the *heder* system, but it was still prevalent. Thus, not the least striking transformation in the immigrant was the alacrity with which he turned over his children to the educational system of his new land, whether Board or Jewish denominational (voluntary) schools which were the antithesis of all he had experienced in the *heder*. At the same time, the immigrants preserved the *heder* in spite of every effort by outsiders to root it out.

MAKING ENGLISHMEN

The voluntary schools arose at a time when only the religious bodies of England undertook to educate the mass of English children. Native Jewry had long distinguished itself for the schools it had erected, some of which originated as *hadarim* in the eighteenth century. The desire to Anglicize a continuous flow of immigration supplied a special reason for maintaining these schools. Pre-eminent among these institutions was the Jews' Free School in Spitalfields, whose remote origins date to the eighteenth century, but whose actual foundation was in 1817. In its early days it was a Talmud Torah, i.e. an enlarged *heder* for poor children. However, the effect of westernization upon early English Jewry was to fuse Jewish education with general elementary education under one roof. That the Jews' Free School was able to multiply its capacity many times was largely due to the support of the Rothschilds, who regarded it as a special charity of their own. Wings and annexes were added to the main structure, so that the sprawling institution soon resembled several schools under one administration. By the turn of the twentieth century it held about 4,300 children, being the largest elementary school in England. Its hulk, no longer a school, stands in Spitalfields today, stretching out unwieldy limbs to the streets around. As the citadel of Anglicization, the very bulk of the Jews' Free School could impress every immigrant with what England and its Jews proposed to do for his children.

In 1870,[3] the 1,600 boys (aged six to fourteen) who attended the school were taught by sixteen certificated teachers and assistant teachers and thirteen pupil teachers under Headmaster Moses Angel. For the 1,000 girls there were forty women, including staff in training. This staff, which must have been weighed down by the vast number each had to teach, was somewhat augmented by Government aid granted under the Act of 1870. In 1880, there was a staff of seventy-three, of whom forty-two were pupil teachers not much older than their pupils. (One pupil teacher was young Israel Zangwill, who was surrounded by the human environment he was later to describe.) The Act of 1870 also shifted the ratio of English to Hebrew studies from eighteen to twelve hours per week to twenty-two and seven and a half hours per week, respectively. School met on week-days except Friday from 9 a.m. to 1 p.m. and 2 p.m. to 4 p.m., and on Sunday mornings.

The Jews' Free School taught the elements of Judaism and almost everything else by catechism, rote labour, and grammar grinding. Such a routine reflected the accepted pedagogical practice of the time, and indeed could hardly have been avoided with so many pupils under one teacher. Not only did the institution teach its pupils, but it presented every boy with a full suit of clothing annually, and even more to the girls. In later years, a child could eat breakfast or lunch free at any Jewish or State school; however, this came from the State.

The head of the School for fifty-one years was Moses Angel (1819–1898), a meticulous man who daily set and wound all

---

[3]The following data are from 'Official Minutes of Evidence taken by the Scheme of Education Committee of the School Board for London. Professor Huxley, Chairman. Testimony by Moses Angel, Master of the Jews' School', in 'Elementary Education in England, No. 111', *The School Board Chronicle*, Vol. 21, No. 2 (July 8, 1871), pp. 242–44.

the clocks in school. His views on problems peculiar to his school and to Jewish education are of interest. Despite the variations in the age of the pupils, Angel said that 'any boy who attended fairly could go over six standards in three years' which completed the course of study. He believed it well for a boy to leave school at eleven years of age, when he could earn four shillings per week, as 'it would be cruel to keep him at school to cram his head till he arrived at the age of fourteen, merely to earn four shillings a week then, instead of being able to earn more'. (His school was later to pioneer in vocational and mechanical education.) Nearly all the children were 'very regular or very irregular', and he would have liked to divide his school on that cleavage with separate programmes for each group. Angel also testified that

. . . jewish children were more vivacious and less amenable to the natural laws of discipline than the English children were. . . . For keeping up discipline, he punished the bad and rewarded the good. . . . There were many offences in school for which children must be punished immediately; sometimes they met a boy having the instincts of a tiger, and they must put him down.

While realizing that the rod was sometimes necessary 'only through the fault of the teacher', his teachers could 'tap' but not 'flog' a pupil.[4]

Considering the immigrant composition of the Jews' Free School's children, Angel's views on immigrants bear mention. He educated children who

. . . were ignorant even of the elements of sound; until they had been Anglicized or humanized it was difficult to tell what was their moral condition, and many of them scarcely knew their own names.

He was distressed by children

. . . who knew neither English nor any intelligible language. . . . Their parents were the refuse population of the worst parts of Europe, whose first object in sending the children to school was to get them out of the way . . . the population among whom his school was placed lived a quasi-dishonourable life [hawking]. . . .[5]

[4] *Ibid.*
[5] *Ibid.* There was an unfavourable communal reaction to Angel's reference to 'refuse population' and especially the 'quasi-dishonourable life' of the population

The glaring harshness of these comments is slightly mitigated by the truth that in 1870, when Angel spoke, many East European immigrants were indeed near-paupers who drifted to England, sometimes with the aid of communities who wanted to be rid of them.

The Jews' Free School was gigantic, but the smaller Jewish voluntary schools were also substantial in size. The two Jews' Infant Schools for children from four to seven years old, with a capacity of 1,240, sent its finished products into the Jewish school system. The Spanish and Portuguese School in the East End took 350; the Stepney Jewish School, 392; and the Westminster Jews' Free School for poor Jews in the West End, 358. These figures, with the addition of a few smaller institutions, give a total of 5,687 places in London Jewish schools in 1880, to which must be added schools in Manchester (1,276), Liverpool (512), and Birmingham (389).[6] Leeds, with more Jews than either Liverpool or Birmingham, had no Jewish school. The absence is accounted for by the late growth of Leeds Jewry, by which time a State school system existed to accommodate Jewish children. The Jewish schools remained relatively static after 1880; from almost 5,700 in 1880 they ascended to a maximum of 8,200 at the turn of the century.[7]

Each of the schools had a pattern of its own. Thus, the mammoth Jews' Free School specialized in the Anglicization of the young. Of its enrolment of 3,573 in 1894, forty-seven per cent. were born abroad, forty-one per cent. were born in England to foreign-born parents, and only twelve per cent. had native parents.[8] Four years later, the same categories yield proportions

around his school. His defence was that both statements were true, that many immigrants were 'refuse population' deported by police from their native lands, and that hawking is 'quasi-dishonourable' because it requires misrepresentation. Angel claimed that in any case the reference was not to Jews but Irish, who were the hawkers around the Jews' Free School. While the apologia was accepted, Angel had to remark how 'violently' this matter had been taken. Board of Deputies, *Minutes*, January 30, February 28, 1872. Letter, Moses Angel to the President and Committee of the Jews' Free School, February 13, 1872 (a copy is in *Minutes*, loc. cit.).

[6] Report of Privy Council Committee on Education, 1880, quoted in *JC*, October 1, 1880.

[7] *Jewish Yearbook*, 1901–1902, p. 74. Idem, 1902–1903, pp. 75–77.

[8] Joseph Jacobs, *Statistics of Jewish Population in London*, 1873–1893, London, 1894, n.p.

of thirty-nine per cent., fifty-two per cent., and nine per cent.[9] The growth of the second group reflects the birth of an English generation to the East European immigrants, while the drop in the natives implies the departure of native Jewry from the neighbourhood, as was happening at the time. The decline in immigration after the passage of the Aliens Act in 1905 shrank the number of foreign-born children, while more and more children were born in England to foreign-born parents. It was too early to speak before 1914 of a third generation, i.e. children of native parents, attending Jewish voluntary schools.

In contrast to the Jews' Free School, the Stepney Jewish School was the most native in its pupil composition. It had been founded in 1863 at the initiative of the Adler family as part of the effort to attract Jewish families to move farther east, out of crowded Whitechapel and Spitalfields.[10] Till the turn of the century it remained predominantly a school for English Jews. Of its 893 children, only four per cent. were born abroad, thirty-two per cent. were born in England of foreign parents, and sixty-four per cent were third generation.[11] Four years later, in 1898, the respective proportions were almost the same: four per cent., thirty-seven per cent., fifty-nine per cent.[12] To maintain so high a percentage of native children, the Stepney Jewish School discouraged the enrolment of less Anglicized types. However, when an imperfectly Anglicized immigrant Jewry followed native Jewry eastward into Mile End and Bow, the native percentage probably diminished nevertheless.

The venerable Spanish and Portuguese School in Heneage Lane educated native Jewish children, and particularly the children of its own dwindling group. However, historic Sefardi Jewry had pretty well disappeared from the vicinity of Bevis Marks synagogue and its school. Of 276 children on the books in 1894, fifteen per cent. were foreign-born, thirty-one per cent. were born in England of foreign parents, and fifty-four per cent. had native parents.[13] Of the 440 children in 1898, the

[9] *Jewish Yearbook*, 1898, p. 67.
[10] Letter from Marcus N. Adler in *JC*, January 9, 1891.
[11] Joseph Jacobs, *op. cit.*, n.p.
[12] *Jewish Yearbook*, 1898, *loc. cit.*
[13] Joseph Jacobs, *op. cit.*, n.p.

P

same categories show eight per cent., twenty-four per cent., and sixty-eight per cent.[14] It may be surmised that the main stock among the native pupils was Dutch Jews, long resident in Spitalfields.

Before the Education Act of 1870, only in Jewish schools were Jewish children not exposed to some form of Christian religious instruction. From that year, a tax-supported State school system, religiously neutral, could look after the education of Jewish children just as the rest of the children of England. The burden of elementary education gradually shifted off the shoulders of the Jewish Community, which was aided by Government grants to its schools. In spite of the Jews' Free School as an imposing witness to the earlier order of things, the education of native and immigrant children of the poor and lower middle classes gradually left the hands of the Jewish community. Government control over Jewish schools increased, and a diminishing proportion of Jewish children attended them. Financial aid was doled out on the notorious 'pass' system—so much cash per passing pupil in each subject in which an examination was prescribed. These faults aside, the Jewish schools did well by the 'pass' system, for the proportion of passing pupils in any subject rarely fell below ninety-five per cent. For example, the State provided £3,295 of the £14,000 budget of the Jews' Free School in 1891.[15] The controversial Education Act of 1902, which met the demands of the Church of England, altered the customary names to 'provided' and 'non-provided' schools, referring to schools whose buildings had or had not been originally provided by the State. For the Jews, the cost of practically all but religious instruction and physical maintenance was thenceforward defrayed by the State.

As the distinctions between Jewish and State schools gradually dissolved, it made little difference to Jewish parents where they sent their children to school. State schools gradually

[14] *Jewish Yearbook*, 1898, *loc. cit.*
[15] *JC*, June 12, 1891. The Jews' Free School collected 'school pence' of 1d per week from pupils who could afford it. This amounted to £357 in 1890, an average of 2s for each of the 3,400 pupils. An Act of 1891 abolished pupils' fees in return for a grant of 10s per pupil per annum. For the Jews' Free School this would have amounted to some £1,700. Halevy, *op. cit.*, v, p. 144.

made common cause to educate Jewish children in Jewish areas. Sixteen State schools in the East End, which had 15,056 children on their rolls in 1902,[16] were practically run by the Jewish community at the desire of the London School Board and its statutory successors. According to the supervisor of schools for the East End, such schools

. . . are practically Jewish—that is to say, we observe the Jewish holidays . . . very few children in these schools are of the Christian persuasion . . . so that the schools are practically run as Jewish schools. . . . the Board's plan has been, when the larger number of children has become Jewish to add the school to the list of Jewish schools. Practically they run it on Jewish lines.[17]

To run a school 'on Jewish lines' also meant early closing on winter Friday afternoons, a substantial proportion of Jewish teachers, and possibly also a Jewish headmaster.[18] Its pupils would receive about five hours' weekly Jewish religious education. Gentile children were very few; they would usually enrol in a nearby Church of England school. Experience at the Old Castle Street school, the first Board school in the East End, guided all the rest. Before 1880 it enrolled few of the Jewish children who even then formed the majority in its district, because it conducted the non-denominational Christian teaching prescribed in the Cowper-Temple clause of the Education Act of 1870. (Compulsory school attendance was barely beginning at the time). When the school's managers voted to hire a Jewish headmaster and to introduce Hebrew studies for the Jewish children, the situation changed quickly.[19] Although the Jews' Free School was practically adjacent, the Old Castle Street Board school had 1,273 children by 1882, of whom ninety-five per cent. were Jews.[20]

Other Board schools opened in succession while the Jewish schools remained the same in number and rose comparatively little in enrolment. From 6,929 Jewish children at school in

[16]Royal Commission on Alien Immigration, *Minutes of Evidence*. Cd. 1742, 1903, Min. 10284. (Hereafter referred to as Cd. 1742).
[17]Cd. 1742, Min. 10283, 10310.
[18]Cd. 1742, Min. 10308.
[19]Cd. 1742, Min. 10291; also House of Commons Select Committee on Emigration and Immigration (Foreigners), *Second Report*, 1889, Min. 1674–80.
[20]*Ibid.*; Jacobs, *op. cit.*, n.p.

London in 1882, of whom 2,592 (thirty-seven per cent.) were already in Board schools, the total in 1894 reached 15,964, with 8,114 (fifty-one per cent.) in Board Schools.[21] The total increase was 230 per cent., but for the Board schools it is 313 per cent. and for the Jewish schools only eighty-one per cent. In terms of the increase alone, Board schools absorbed sixty-one per cent. and the Jewish schools' share was thirty-nine per cent.

The total of children at school constantly rose. In 1901, there were 13,052 Jewish children in London Board schools to 8,246 in the Jewish voluntary schools for a total of 21,298.[22] There were 17,712 Jewish children in elementary schools in Stepney in 1902, of whom some 6,200 attended Jewish schools.[23] In 1911, Stepney and the contiguous Bethnal Green and the City of London had 28,779 Jewish children at school, of whom only 5,684 were at a Jewish school.[24] Thus, the Jewish schools' share, which had been sixty-three per cent. in 1886 (all of London), dropped to forty-nine per cent. in 1894 (all of London), to thirty-seven per cent. in 1900 (Borough of Stepney), and barely twenty per cent. (for the City, Bethnal Green, and Stepney) in 1911. Although these are not uniform areas, the picture is clear enough.

Besides the entirely Jewish State schools, another group of State schools, usually on the fringes of the Jewish quarter, educated a sizeable minority of immigrant children. There were seven such schools at the margins of the immigrant quarter which had 2,601 (twenty-six per cent.) Jewish children among their 9,908 pupils.[25] The most unusual case is the Jewish children who attended National, i.e. Church of England schools. Parents showed extreme reluctance to send their children to Christian schools:

. . . we have to drive them into the National schools; we have to compel them to go there. When the other schools are filled up, we must have them in a school; and so we have to drive them in there.[26]

[21]Jacobs, op. cit., n.p.   [22]Jewish Yearbook, 1901–1902, p. 74.
[23]Cd. 1742, Min. 10281–82.
[24]Jewish World, November 10, 1911. The figure of Jewish school children in the entire county of London was 37,419. S. Levy, 'Problems of Anglicization', in The Jewish Annual, VI, 1943–1944, London, 1943, pp. 80–82. The paper dates to 1911.
[25]Cd. 1742, Min. 10297, 10303.   [26]Cd. 1742, Min. 10316-17.

Eight National schools in East London enrolled 1,628 Jewish children among their 3,231 pupils, just fifty per cent. One school, St Stephen's of Spitalfields, counted sixty-three per cent. of its children as Jews. Thus developed the interesting arrangement that Jewish religious teaching was given under the roof of an English church.[27]

The existence of a special Jewish sub-system within the State school system was regarded with some justice as a sound solution to the problem of schooling immigrant children. No serious question was raised of the propriety of having State schools 'distinctly set aside for Jewish children'.[28] Denominational education had been the historic foundation of English education, and Jewry was content with equality for its children within the framework of religious teaching given in State schools. General sentiment considered that

. . . the Elementary Education Act of 1870 . . . removed the need of the establishment of any new Jewish voluntary schools . . . there is not the slightest reason why we should not participate in the general benefits which the State is able to confer impartially on all its citizens.[29]

Specifically Jewish education in State schools was entrusted to the Jewish Association for the Diffusion of Religious Knowledge, which managed matters rather unsatisfactorily owing to poor financial support. As cumbersome in action as in name, the Association recruited and paid elementary schoolmasters for a few extra hours' work weekly, although many of them were hardly qualified. It was presently converted into the Jewish Religious Education Board under the United Synagogue with representation for other groups. At its height in 1911, it taught about 8,000 children of about 20,000 children eligible for its services.[30]

What was the sort of child who is here represented by so many figures and ratios? The verdict of the school teachers upon their immigrant pupils was highly favourable. Headmasters spoke well of their 'keen and intelligent interest in

[27]Cd. 1742, Min. 10303–07.
[28]Cd. 1742, Min. 10310.
[29]S. Levy, *op. cit., loc. cit.*
[30]*Ibid.*; Norman Bentwich, 'Jewish Educational Disorganization in London', in *The Jewish Review*, III, No. 16 (November, 1912), pp. 355–66.

all that concerns the welfare of our country'. They were found to be 'bright',[31] 'superior intellectually',[32] 'excellent workers in school',[33] 'anxious to learn',[34] 'superior . . . in facility, in industry, and in perseverance'.[35] The immigrant Jew was invariably characterized as devoted to the care of his children. In a period when a pioneer generation of public educators had to struggle hard to draw children to school from indifferent or unwilling parents, they could well be delighted by the consuming eagerness with which Jewish children were sent to school in neighbourhoods where neglect of children and hostility to schooling were rampant. Some educators, however, seemed disturbed at the ease with which Jewish children over-took and overcame native English children in the classroom.[36] There is a less favourable aspect to the schoolmaster's testi-mony. Jewish juvenile 'smartness, especially in commercial things'[37] exceed that of Christian children, and 'they have a perfect want of moral sense'[38] in respect of truthfulness.

At a time when English elementary education was coming under closer State control, the *disjecta membra* which composed secondary education had barely been touched. It seems a fair conjecture that eighty-five per cent. or ninety per cent. of immigrant children attended no secondary school, unless in the evenings. Many did attend vocational courses of various types at the People's Palace in Mile End and at the Polytechnic in Regent Street and smaller institutions for a low fee or free; not to be overlooked are the educational activities of Toynbee Hall and its counterparts of lesser fame. Yet in spite of the gradual broadening of educational opportunities for the lower classes during late Victorian and Edwardian times, education must still be understood as elementary schooling. Except for little Jews' College, which prepared students for the Jewish ministry, the Jewish community did not maintain higher

[31]Cd. 1742, Min. 18329.   [32]C9. 1742, Min. 18861.
[33]Cd. 1742, Min. 18868.   [34]Cd. 1742, Min. 10337.
[35]Cd. 1742, Min. 18822–23.
[36]Charles Booth, ed., *Life and Labour of the People in London*, 9 vols., London, 1892, III, pp. 207–25. See also 'The Child of the Alien', *The Social Democrat*, VII, 8, August 15, 1903, pp. 473–76—gushily sympathetic. G. A. N. Lowndes, *The Silent Social Revolution*, London, 1937, pp. 3–44, gives insight into the social background of English elementary education.
[37]Cd. 1742, Min. 10359.   [38]Cd. 1742, Min. 10361.

educational institutions. Jewish immigrant students at British universities seem to have been very few, mostly at the University of London. To be sure, there was the fiery Reader in Rabbinic at Cambridge, Solomon Schechter (1847–1915), a Rumanian Jew by origin. There was also Selig Brodetsky (1888–1954), a young Talmudist, and son of a poor *shammash*, who was bracketed Senior Wrangler in 1908 after a dazzling school career which gave considerable pride to the immigrant community. These were, of course, the rare exceptions.

MAKING JEWS

Jewish parents displayed no discernible preference for Jewish schools over the State system so far as concerned general education. Immigrant Jewry did not greatly care who made Englishmen of their children, but they jealously guarded their right to make Jews of their children in their own way. While willingly yielding up what England required of their children, they simultaneously clung to the forms of Jewish education which were familiar to them. The objectives were as of old: the inculcation of the elements of Jewish prayer, Bible, and law, for the perpetuation of what had been perpetuated thus far. With something of the spontaneity which brought *hebrot* into existence wherever immigrant Jews settled, the *heder* mushroomed. Abetted by the ancient tradition that every possible moment ought to be devoted to sacred study, and by the more immediate desire to keep the children out of the house and somehow occupied, the *heder* was in nearly continuous session at the dwelling of the *melammed*.[39] Physically, it was usually a sorry place. The 'class-room' was the size of an average room in the slums—nine by nine by seven or eight feet high. From five to fifteen children might be in it at once, depending on the weather or the ability of the *melammed* to round up his scholars. Children attended early in the morning, at noon during school recess, and late in the afternoon into the evening. They came as young as four and up to thirteen to attend the formless lessons given by their *melammed*. He would

[39] S. Levy, *op. cit.*, *loc. cit.*; on parental preference, Cd. 1742, Min. 10315–16.

take a few at a time, and the rest would play about outside awaiting their turn.

The *melammed* kept busy. Up at dawn to take some pupils to morning services, he taught others during noon hour. His real work began later in the afternoon. 'At four-thirty come the pupils who live at a distance. They receive instruction in reading, and then march home again . . . the business of the day commences at [five o'clock]. For an hour and a half there are reading lessons, together with such simple things as the Berochoth [benedictions]. At six-thirty the translation class starts work—usually on the Sedrah [Pentateuchal synagogue lesson] of the week—and continues until seven o'clock or seven-thirty. At seven-thirty exit the younger children and enter the older ones. Chumish [Pentateuch], Rashi [commentary thereon], and even Shulchan Aruch [code of law] and Mishna-yoth [sections of the Mishnah] are the subjects till nine. Maariv [evening prayers] is said at each class'.[39a]

The *melammed* personally did not cut much of a figure. He might be a religious functionary who wanted to improve his income, or an elderly individual who could not do hard work, and some *melammedim* were even temporarily unemployed workers. Like masters of one room English schools whom the new State school system was pressing out of existence at the time, no standards were asked or imposed.

Little was taught in the *heder* that was not better done either in a Jewish or a Board school. Thousands of Jewish immigrants, trusting enough in sending their children for a general education, were uneasy with this official religious education. If they could do nothing about making Englishmen of their children, the immigrants still wanted to make Jews of them in their own way in the pattern they recognized.

Heder education was regarded with aversion by native Jewry. The mention of dirty *hadarim* roused the *Jewish Chronicle* to express hope that the District Board of Works (the local authority in London before 1888) would shut 'this and similar nuisances' which 'abound' in spite of their 'appalling' conditions and standards. It did hit upon the main reason for the *heder's* continued existence—despite religious education

[39a] *JC*, October 21, 1904.

given in Board and Jewish voluntary schools, the immigrant Jews still wanted to be 'independent' and desired 'convenience'. It was distressed to see the schools maintained by native Jewry 'passed by in contempt' because the Jewish immigrant poor would not trust 'the religious instruction imparted by intelligent Englishmen'.[40] Yet the *Chronicle* admitted that Hebrew teaching in England was of a very poor standard compared with the reformed teaching of Greek and Latin. 'Hebrew instruction among Jewish children in England is very little more than a waste of time as at present conducted. . . .'[41] The Rev A. L. Green (1821–1883), a native Jewish minister who could speak in Yiddish, explained to an immigrant audience that

England was not famous for its *Yeshibot* because Hebrew learning did not pay in this commercial country, and therefore it was incumbent upon them to do something more than to educate their children solely in Hebrew and Rabbinical teachings.[42]

Hadarim were detested because in them was sensed a barrier to the full Anglicization of the coming generation. Headmasters were displeased, even slighted, by the second school which so many children attended, and Moses Angel urged the Jewish Board of Guardians to take general measures against all *hadarim*.[43] There was, in short, far more animus against *hadarim* for the children than against the *hebrot* of their parents.

The *heder* setting was shabby. A sanitary inspector in Whitechapel found a *heder* in use eighteen inches below street level, nine by nine and six feet high, with thirteen children within, aged five to seven.[44] A year later, twenty-five children were reported using a room nine by eight and nine feet high.[45] Such exposures, and especially those made by the *Lancet* in 1884 stirred the Jewish Board of Guardians to despatch its own Sanitary Inspector to inquire into the sanitary aspects of

---

[40]*JC*, January 30, 1880.
[41]*JC*, August 12, 1881. Cf. Israel Meir Kahan, *Nidhey Yisrael* (The Dispersed of Israel) (Hebrew and Yiddish), Warsaw 1894, reprinted with English translation, New York, 1951, p. 106.
[42]*JC*, April 1, 1881.
[43]Jewish Board of Guardians, *Minutes*, May 17, 1886; *Minute Letter Book*; however, a Christian Headmaster of a Jewish Board school was not unfavourably disposed to *heder* education. Min. 18846–49, 18856–57.
[44]*JC*, January 23, 1880.
[45]*JC*, December 9, 1881.

the *heder*. He found twenty-three of them, and probably as many escaped his notice. In spite of preconceptions, nearly all the *melammedim* qualified as 'respectable', and some even earned the brevet of 'gentleman'. Every *heder* was in session from five p.m. to eight p.m., and some had noon hours as well; still others simply reported 'all day and evening'. The twenty-three places listed had about 550 children 'enrolled', and attending about two hours daily. As for the severest accusation against the *heder*, the inspector found 'cases of overcrowding . . . quite exceptions'.[46] The Jewish Board of Guardians thereupon dropped the matter.[47] A survey in 1891 found 'considerably more than 200 *hadarim* in the East End', with an attendance of 'at least 2,000 boys' aged five to fourteen, who paid fees anywhere from 6d to 1s 6d per week. To meet the evident desire for fuller Hebrew instruction, it was suggested that the Jews' Free School arrange an evening class for older boys at an extra fee,[48] but nothing came of this proposal.

The *Jewish Chronicle*, which yielded to few in its aversion to *hadarim*, realized that it was useless to argue the matter with the immigrant; 'what can be done is to improve the *hadarim*'.[49] Improvement came from within, when various *hevroth* sponsored their own *hadarim*. There could then be communal responsibility and supervision, however haphazard, and the *heder* might become a school with a graded course of study.[50] Thus, a group of women maintained an independent Hebrew school and clothed its pupils as a charitable project; from such beginnings grew the Manchester Talmud Torah, which taught between 600 and 700 children in 1910.[51] In accord with pious custom, the benefactors attended the public distribution of their largesse, and the investigation of the recipients' merits 'was carried on in the course of the dis-

[46]The Inspector's notes are in the Jewish Board of Guardians, *Executive Minute Book*, n.p., n.d.
[47]D. F. Schloss, Hon. Sec., Sanitary Committee, to L. L. Alexander, Hon. Sec. of the Board, December 5, 1884, in *Minute Letter Book*, December 5, 1884.
[48]*JC*, April 10, 1891.
[49]*JC*, November 21, 1884.
[50]The Steward Street *hebra* maintained a *heder* with four teachers and 100 children. *The Polish Yidel*, I, 8, September 12, 1884.
[51]I. W. Slotki, *Seventy Years of Hebrew Education*, 1880–1950, Manchester, 1950, pp. 9–14.

tribution'.[52] Hardly more attractive were the vanishing customs of sending children to recite Psalms at the bedside of a woman in confinement or in a room with the dead before interment.

Like the hours of the *hadarim*, those of the Talmud Torah were very long, with the difference that children in a Talmud Torah came there and stayed on until dismissal. At the Manchester Talmud Torah pupils came daily from noon to one p.m. and four-thirty p.m. to eight p.m., and from ten a.m. to one p.m. and three p.m. to five p.m. on Sunday.[53] While the children did not attend school on Friday or Saturday, they were expected to be in synagogue. Nineteen hours a week of extra school is explained by cramped dwellings and the absence of recreational facilities which made it advisable for families to despatch willing or unwilling children to *heder* or Talmud Torah. Talmud Torah instruction proceeded with an unchanged curriculum and with Yiddish the language of instruction. Acceptable teachers who knew English were not to be found, and parents earnestly wanted children to be fluent in the language of their home. However, the alleged anti-Anglicizing influence of Yiddish was so sore a point with the native Jewry that the elimination of the 'jargon' was sometimes made a condition of financial aid. Teachers' wages probably varied widely, to judge by the proud statement of the Manchester Talmud Torah that it paid £1 or 25s to teachers, where other schools paid 8s to 14s.[54] It would be interesting to know how promptly these salaries were paid.

A Talmud Torah such as that in Manchester, or Machzikei HaDath in London with about 850 children,[55] was an improvement and a refinement but not a break with the *heder* and the Jewish outlook it represented. However, the new currents which brought to life the Zionist movement and an Hebraic revival also flowed into the educational field. The new Hebraists cherished the progress of the new Palestine, and joined modern Hebrew to the study of Bible and rabbinic literature; Jewish history and Hebrew songs shared time with liturgy and customs as subjects of study in a pedagogic reflection of the new ideals. The essence of the new approach was Hebrew as the language

[52] *Ibid.*, pp. 2–21.
[53] *Ibid.*, p. 35.
[54] *Die Tsukunft*, IV, No. 184, February 17, 1888.
[55] *Jewish World*, July 20, 1906.

of the classroom—the 'natural method' by which the revived ancient tongue replaced the grind of translation into Yiddish or English. The movement in England is inseparably bound up with the name of J. K. Goldbloom (1872–   ) founder and headmaster of the Hebrew Talmud Torah in Redman's Road, East Stepney, for fifty-three years.[56] Among the most significant achievements which flowed from Redman's Road was the recognition of Hebrew teaching as a separate profession which required special knowledge and training. The teachers received the unheard-of pay of £3 and £4 per week, while tuition at 2s per week was relatively high.[57]

The new ideals and methods in the stagnant field of Jewish education did not make their way without sharp opposition. There was, on one hand, the unconquerable apathy of native Jewry, to most of whom Jewish education meant speedy Anglo-Judaization into the Victorian cast. They correctly supposed that the new education had much to do with 'Zionistic schemes'. Private *melammedim* were disturbed at the thought of another bite taken off their daily bread, while many of the high orthodox deemed it impious to use the sacred tongue for mere secular speech and surmised some heterodox intent. In spite of the orthodox Judaism taught in the Hebrew Talmud Torah, charges concerning the religious propriety of Hebrew as the language of instruction were aired before the Beth Din of Chief Rabbi Adler in 1903. Although a clean bill of health was given, there were further disputes and secessions before the new approach carried all organized opposition before it.[58] The Redman's Road Talmud Torah commenced a notable career of wide significance. It had over 600 pupils by 1914, and some 350 at an annex in Bethnal Green.[59] 'Hebrew-in-Hebrew' schools were also opened in Leeds and Glasgow, and the Manchester Talmud Torah went over to the 'natural method' of Hebrew study for some years.[60] The Hebrew

---

[56]Much of my information has come from Mr Goldbloom, to whom I am indebted. *Cf.* also *Talmud Torah Ivrit beIvrit* . . . 1901 to 1951. Fifty Years of Its Existence. London, 1951. (In Hebrew, English, and Yiddish.)

[57]Statement of Mr J. K. Goldbloom.

[58]*Talmud Torah* . . . pp. 5–6 (English section); 30–32 (Yiddish section); 5–6 (Hebrew section).

[59]*Ibid.*, p. 6 (English section); statement of Mr J. K. Goldbloom.

[60]*Ibid.*, pp. 6–7 (English section); I. W. Slotki, *op. cit.*, pp. 68–70.

journalist J. S. Fuchs operated a Hebrew Higher Grade School in Liverpool for some years.[61]

The new system slowly earned the approbation of the community, even of those neither Hebraist nor Zionist, including Chief Rabbi Adler. On the other side, Rabbi Werner, the aged leader of high orthodoxy in the East End, endorsed the Talmud Torah.[62] The Zionists, led by the *Jewish Chronicle* (in Zionist hands from 1907) were enthusiastic in their support.

All the improvements notwithstanding, the educational institutions of immigrant Jewry were in perpetual financial distress. It seemed that

the rank and file of the Anglo-Jewish community have determined that they [the Talmud Torahs] are not to be encouraged . . . they perpetuate those evils [because of which they would not give help] by their refusal to assist the institutions.[63]

The only significant outside support of the Talmud Torahs was the Talmud Torah Trust, founded in 1905 by the two partners in communal individualism, Sir Samuel Montagu and Hermann Landau. It granted the three largest Talmud Torahs in London about £500 per annum and the services of an architect.[64]

APPRENTICESHIP AND EVENING CLASSES

The years of adolescence were less distinctly patterned than the more ordered age of childhood. For the vast majority of the young the completion of elementary education meant the termination of their formal schooling, and entry into the workaday world. Most boys left school at thirteen or fourteen, and quit Jewish studies posthaste at the age of thirteen. Further study was largely vocational training, and under the declining but still prevalent system this required a term of apprenticeship in order to enter a skilled handicraft or trade. Apprenticeship usually lasted seven years, with a premium at the outset

[61]J. S. Fuchs, *An Hebrew Centre. A Critical View of English Judaism*, London, H. Ginzburg, 1909. (In Hebrew).
[62]*Talmud Torah* . . . pp. 19–25 (Hebrew section).
[63]Bentwich, *op. cit.*, p. 452.
[64]*Ibid.*

and nominal pay which was earned only in the last year of the term. For a Jewish youth, apprenticeship was enveloped in difficulties, especially in the many cases where the family could not pay any premium, but urgently required the cash contributed by a grown son. In addition to whatever reluctance existed to employ Jewish boys, there was the extra problem of maintaining religious observance. Furthermore, few Jews themselves worked at trades which could employ apprentices from among their own people.[65] But the deepest problem in guiding the sons of immigrants into apprenticed trades was psychological. Few Jews really aspired to remain skilled wage-earners, but instead preferred to think of themselves and their children as clerical and professional persons, or as independent entrepreneurs, so that the path leading to life-long wage-earning held fewer attractions than its sponsors hoped. A formal term of apprenticeship was not needed for tailors in the Jewish sector of that trade; thousands of boys and grown 'greeners' entered workshops as 'learners' at a minimal wage and advanced informally as they increased their skill.

Jewish Boards of Guardians throughout England sedulously fostered apprenticeship, mainly in the effort to draw Jews out of tailoring and boot and shoe making. It was also hoped that if Jews diversified their economic basis, they might also leave the East End. Earnest appeals and sermons were directed at the Jewish immigrant for his sons' sake, advancing the attractions of the apprentice's indenture. The Guardians laboured to find suitable trades and masters and also advanced money for premiums, not in such 'overstocked' trades as tailoring but rather in vocations like watchmaking, cabinet making, printing, bookbinding, and leather work. For the girls, modest careers were available as bookbinders, feather dressers, and artificial flower makers. By the mid-1880's 264 boys were bound to indentures in sixty-nine trades and crafts, while public technical training came to supplement or replace the centuries-old training by apprenticeship.[66] However, the number of boys apprenticed through the aid and encouragement of the London

[65]The subject is regularly discussed in the Reports of the Apprenticeship Committee in the Jewish Board of Guardians, *Annual Reports*.
[66]*JC*, February 29, 1884; *cf. JC*, May 10, 1872, and Board of Guardians, *Minutes*, May 6, 1873.

Jewish Board of Guardians did not go above 500, and similar efforts in the Provinces were not crowned with greater success.[67] When the London Board inquired into the apprentices' problems—premiums, wages, hours, religion—it could see no way to make any essential change to enhance the desirability of an indenture.[68]

No form of Anglicization was more advantageous to the immigrant than learning English, or more devoutly desired by native Jews than the disappearance of the despised Yiddish. Little direct schooling was open to adults or could be widely used by them for the burden of the working day made it a trial to attend a class at night. There was not only a problem of time and fatigue in learning English but perhaps some reluctance to part with so intimate a part of one's old milieu as its language. This was mainly true of older people. In any case, the sponsors of the Russo-Jewish Committee's Free English Evening Classes felt certain that

. . . a certain prejudice which was experienced to a limited extent when the classes were first started has now entirely passed away, and any illusory ideas as to any possible religious decadence . . . from the preliminary step of learning English . . . are no longer entertained.[69]

Classes first convened in 1892 in order to 'impart a knowledge of the English language, habits and usages to adult Russian Jews and Jewesses. . . .'[70] The Russo-Jewish Committee also commissioned Joseph Jacobs, the historian and folklorist, and Hermann Landau, the immigrant banker, to prepare the first Yiddish-English lexicon, which went into many editions from its first publication in 1894.

The course of study lasted about two years, and at its conclusion the student could 'read and understand, say, an average newspaper article'.[71] Classes were generally held in Board school rooms, usually each Monday, Tuesday, and Wednesday evening from seven-thirty to nine-thirty p.m.,

[67]*JC*, June 27, 1884.
[68]Board of Guardians, *Minutes*, November 11, 1901.
[69]Russo-Jewish Committee, *Annual Report*, 1897, p. 29.
[70]Board of Deputies, *Annual Report, 1893–1894*, pp. 44–45.
[71]Russo-Jewish Committee, *Annual Report*, 1894, p. 39.

with an average nightly attendance of 500 to 600 persons—
not the same persons regularly, however. Reading and writing
was the main emphasis; 'specific instruction in speaking
English [was] given only incidentally as part of the regular
curriculum'.[72] The students were 'mostly under thirty years
of age' [73] and were about five-eighths men.[74] This modest
training opened the doors of English life and culture, broadened
economic opportunities, and probably helped to fasten a bond
between the immigrant generation and its children.

Several thousand adult immigrants took part in traditional
study of sacred literature. However, no *yeshibah* for advanced
Talmudic study took firm root in this period, although the
Ets Hayyim (Tree of Life) in London struggled hard and did
survive. Largely due to the efforts of immigrant rabbis in the
Provinces, little *yeshibot* opened modest premises in Man-
chester and Liverpool and maintained an unsteady existence.[75]
A number of young Talmudists did attend *Yeshibot* on the
Continent.

The Anglicization of the young was effective, as was probably
inevitable with or without conscious effort by immigrant or
native Jews. In fact, it was so successful that after 1918 the
Jewish communal anxiety was to promote Judaization before
its Anglicized generation drifted out of reach.

---

[72]*Idem*, 1894, pp. 39–40.
[73]*Idem*, 1892–1893, p. 28.
[74]*Idem*, 1897, p. 29.
[75]An unsuccessful attempt was made at opening a *yeshibah*, by the untiring S. Cohen ('Simcha Becker'), in 1886. Despite an imposing list of sponsors it did not last long. *Die Tsukunft*, II, No. 45, May 21, 1886 and II, No. 50, June 25, 1886.

IX

VARIETIES OF CULTURAL EXPRESSION

Jewish cultural life in England had little distinction, especially in comparison with the intellectual lustre of the emancipated Jewries on the Continent. English art, literature, and scholarship heard much more about the Jew than from him. 'This is a commercial country', explained a Jewish minister to an immigrant audience, and therefore the immigrant ought not to expect much scope for whatever learning he possessed, nor make the mistake of educating his son 'solely in Hebrew and rabbinical teachings'.[1] The warning was justified. Rabbinic learning had but a fleeting tradition of study in England, and the heyday of the western *Wissenschaft des Judentums* in the mid-nineteenth century passed by with practically no participation by English Jews.[2] Immigration from Eastern Europe did not change the situation much. Although rabbinic culture in East European Jewry had developed to one of its highest peaks in the history of Judaism, the emigrants whom those lands sent forth were not rabbinic scholars. We lack precise data, but it is clear that those who left, especially before 1900, were not the pious and learned. Nor, on the other hand, were the emigrants much influenced by the ideals of the *Haskalah*, the Europeanizing movement in Jewish social and cultural life, and they were surely not associated with the Russified Jewish intelligentsia. The emigrants came mostly from the small cities and villages of the Pale of Settlement, places where the traditional way of life was slowest to weaken. Their language was Yiddish, not Polish or Russian, and their spiritual and intellectual environment was pretty well circumscribed by traditional

[1]The Rev. A. L. Green (1821–1883), quoted in *JC*, April 1, 1881.
[2]An exception might be made for the Bodleian Library and the British Museum, both Meccas for Jewish research. See Schechter, 'The Hebrew Collection of the British Museum', *Studies in Judaism*, I (Phila., 1896, repr. 1938), pp. 252–69; 'Four Epistles to the Jews of England', *Idem.*, II (Phila., 1908, repr. 1938), pp. 193–201; B. Spiers, *Divrei Hefez (Acceptable Words)*, London, c. 1878, pp. 35–36; *JC*, August 12, 1881; Ismar Elbogen, 'Briefwechsel zwischen Leopold Zunz und Frederic David Mocatta', *Gaster Anniversary Volume*, London, 1936, pp. 144–54.

Q

Jewish religious life and thought. Even with the broad diffusion of Jewish cultural interests among the Jewish masses of all social classes, there is little indication of any learned element among the emigrants who departed. Just as the arriving Jewish immigrant was generally not a student of Talmudic tractates,[3] neither did he read Hebrew poems and stories by Judah Loeb Gordon and Peretz Smolenskin with their Haskalah blandishments and moralizing. If Hebrew literature be called upon to supply a prototype of the Jewish immigrant, the product might resemble the characters created by Mendele Mokher Seforim (1836–1917). The Jewish immigrant's cultural background was almost wholly Jewish, unmixed with Russian or Polish Gentile components, and it was compounded of Jewish folk elements and normative rabbinic Judaism. His 'enlightenment' came all at once when he landed in England, unguided by intellectual leaders and without any programme, simply as an inevitable consequence of migration to a western country.

Nevertheless, small but distinct numbers of persons who represented some principal trends in the cultural life of East European Jewry did arrive in England. Traditional Talmudic study and its ideals were rather well represented, especially when one considers England's unreceptivity to them. Rabbis like Aba Werner (1837–1912), Israel Hayyim Daiches (1850–1937), and Samuel J. Rabbinowitz (1857–1921) figured with some distinction in the well-endowed rabbinic world of Eastern Europe, and in England their rabbinic scholarship of the older type greatly outshone that of any English rabbi. The burgeoning milieu of Hebrew and Yiddish letters touched English shores in the persons of Hebrew and Yiddish writers who came to England, even though that usually happened by accident or indirection. However, once in England, the interest of figures so notable as Ahad HaAm (Asher Ginzberg, 1856–1927), Joseph Hayyim Brenner (1882–1921), and Uri Nissan Gnessin (1878–1913) in English affairs was slight. Even more than the East European rabbi resident in England, they lacked the requisite audience for their creative production, and the environment which supplied their subject matter was also gone.

[3]See Rabbi S. I. Hillman's eulogy of R. Eliezer Gordon, in 'Or HaYashar (The Just Light), London, c. 1930, p. 109.

As to the Russified or Polonized Jew, of whom some few arrived in England, he had little choice indeed. He had either to revert to the Jewish environment or pass on to the English, since no middle ground existed for him. Such was the experience of Philip Kranz, who left his Russian socialism in Paris to become the editor of the Yiddish *Arbeiter Freind* in London, and of numerous later socialists. However, a man like Stanislaus Mendelson led the Polish Socialist Party in exile from London, and had nothing to do with the community of Polish and Russian Jews. Such cases were few in number, and they regarded England as but a haven until times brightened for them in their native lands. Rudolf Rocker, the Gentile leader of Yiddish-speaking anarchism, vainly appealed to them to consider England a fruitful field for revolutionary activity.[4]

RABBINIC CULTURE

Without attempting to describe the cultural level of the mass of Jewish immigrants with any precision, it is evident that their basic roots were in historic rabbinic Judaism as expounded and practised in Eastern Europe, and their living ideal of wisdom and sanctity was in the persons of East European rabbis, the religious, intellectual, and sometimes political leaders of their communities. Yet in England, the mature wisdom, profound learning, and unassuming piety which characterize East European rabbis at their best conveys itself poorly. The transformation of scene and the severe diminution in authority and prestige which these rabbis suffered more or less, made them sound notes which attracted little sympathy. It is rather revealing of the disharmony of their position when one contrasts the immigrant rabbis in their English and Hebrew garbs; in speaking English words or to a non-immigrant audience, their words suggest an attitude of querulousness and arbitrary insistence, and they seem defensive and ill at ease. The main conclave of immigrant rabbis in Leeds in 1910 met a disastrous public reception by its bald, literal assertion of the

---

[4] R. Rocker, *Tsu die Yiddishe Arbayter*, No. 2, 1905. See pp. 140–41.

supreme authority of Jewish law and its rather gratuitous dwelling on the more unpalatable aspects to emphasize the point.[5] On the other hand, their Hebrew works are more abstracted from the English environment, or they analyze the conditions of life in the new land through the classic techniques of Jewish homiletic thought and exposition. Even where the lesson of a lengthy printed sermon is jejune, the hearer or reader can derive enjoyment from a learned use of Biblical and rabbinic texts, or from an ingenious or poetic use to which a passage is put. The composition of novellae or commentaries or super-commentaries or textual notes to sacred literature, or responsa concerning *halakhic* matters, restore the rabbi to the position he wished to occupy. One may study page on page of erudite, technical discussion of Jewish law, which display mastery of sources and judicious weighing of views in the classic manner. Like much of rabbinic literature, the style is crabbed, alternating between diffuseness and knotted brevity; the organization is as chaotic as the Talmudic text itself, and is pock-marked with sometimes bewildering abbreviations— reading for no one but the thoroughly schooled initiate. However, the composition of such rabbinic studies on the immense corpus of Jewish oral tradition links the new environment with its historic past.

In his primary capacity of authoritative judge and interpreter of Jewish law, the rabbi was in demand for decisions upon small and large matters as they arose. Although the scope of such queries (*she'elot*) could be as universal as the scope of Jewish law,[6] in practice they tended to be limited to matters of synagogal practice, *kashrut*, and, most important and complex, marital life and domestic affairs. Moreover, a learned and respected rabbi rendered abundant services of mediation, arbitration, and personal and moral advice. As indicated elsewhere, the rabbis who figured most prominently as *posekim* (decisors) in the immigrant community were Jacob Reinowitz and Aba Werner in London, and in the Provinces, Israel Hayyim Daiches of Leeds. However, the decision to consult a

[5] See pp. 217–18.
[6] See in general Solomon B. Freehof, *The Responsa Literature*, Philadelphia, 1955; the bio-bibliographical S. N. Gottlieb, *'Oholey Shem*, Pinsk, 1912, pp. 449–71, 539.

rabbi, and the decision which rabbi to consult, were individual and voluntary. It was not uncommon, especially in complex matters, for the rabbi who had been asked or for the originator of the query to place his problem before an eminent East European rabbi for decision or for assent to a decision which had already been taken. Thus, in spite of a rabbinic jurisdiction coextensive with Queen Victoria's domains, Chief Rabbi Hermann Adler and his Beth Din addressed themselves to East European rabbinic authorities, probably to gain support for their rulings in the immigrant community. A prominent respondent to *she'elot* in his generation was Isaac Elhanan Spektor of Kovno,[7] and others more or less contemporary were Joseph Saul Nathanson[8] and then Isaac Schmelkes[9] of Lemberg, Naftali Zvi Judah Berlin,[10] Head of the Academy at Volozhin, Shalom Meir Schwadron of Brzezany,[11] and, for moral and personal counsel, Israel Meir Kahan[12] of Radom. Somewhat out of this milieu, but of equal stature, stood David Hoffmann[13] of Berlin (1843–1921), the principal *posek* for German orthodox Jewry and its loyal offshoots. Withal, there is no sizeable body of responsa to queries from English immigrant Jewry, including both responsa issued in England and those referred to Continental authorities. Unfortunately for the historian, the rabbis generally preferred to publish fewer elaborate responsa to a large number of briefer ones, and, largely owing to their principally juridical interests, they often neglect to indicate either the source or date of the queries which they received. However, the adherence to the principle of the responsum

[7]See his *'Eyn Yizhak* (Well of Isaac), Vilna, 1889, Part III (Eben Ha'Ezer), Nos. 31, 39.
[8]See his *Sho'el uMeshib* (Questioner and Answerer), Lemberg, 1859.
[9]See his *Beth Yizhak* (House of Isaac), Prszemsyl, 1901, Part I, No. 145.
[10]See his *Meshib Dabar* (The Answerer), Warsaw, 1894, No. 17. This query was referred to him by R. Jacob Reinowitz; perhaps also No. 74, addressed to R. Sussman Cohen.
[11]Although he wrote many responsa to American queries, no responsa to England were found in his large collection: I (Warsaw, 1903), II (Pietrikov, 1917) However, see below, note 14.
[12]See, for example, his counsel to Jacob Zinkin concerning Machzikei HaDath in Bernard Homa, *A Fortress of Judaism in Anglo-Jewry*, London, 1953, pp. 132–34, xxiii–xxvi.
[13]See his *Melammed le Ho'il* (Helpful Teacher), I (Frankfort-a-M., 1924), No. 40. However, very few of his 'constituency' would have been East European immigrants in England.

could not but strengthen the cultural and religious ties between the Jewries of Eastern Europe and England.[14]

The paucity of responsa by immigrant rabbis in England is a tell-tale sign of the decline of the culture and its values which these scholars symbolized. Historically, rabbinic responsa proliferate in periods and areas of cultural and demographic change, when problems in Jewish law are deepest. That immigrant rabbis, men of undoubted scholarly competence, had so few opportunities to come to grips with the profound social and religious issues which arose from the mass movement of Jews to a new country portends that their moral authority no longer possessed decisive sway in large areas of Jewish life.[15]

London, and sometimes the Provinces, were occasionally visited by rabbinical luminaries from Eastern Europe, although the purposes of such visits were usually unconnected with immigrant life. Samuel Mohilever came in 1886 to solicit aid for the struggling Palestine colonies,[16] while Isaac Reines and a few other rabbis appeared in 1900 for the Fourth Zionist Congress, which was held in the Metropolis.[17] Hayyim Berlin's visit in 1886 was for an undetermined purpose, but Eliezer Gordon died in London in 1910 during a visit to raise funds for the yeshiva in Telz of which he was head.[18] Only Jacob David Wilowsky (Ridvass) had much concern with immigrant affairs, although the quite accidental presence of Abraham Isaac Kook in London in mid-1914 endowed Machzikei HaDath

[14]There is a particularly interesting set of three responsa upon one query by J. D. Wilowsky-Ridvass, S. M. Schwadron, and M. S. Shivitz, in M. S. Shivitz, *Pri Yehezkel* (The Fruit of Ezekiel), Jerusalem, 1908, Part II, pp. 7–36, 45. A probably rare instance of a responsum to the Continent from England is by I. H. Daiches concerning a divorce, sent to Zagiersh in 1907. I. H. Daiches, *Mikveh Yisrael* (The Hope of Israel), Leeds, 1912, pp. 30–32. Benjamin Schewzik, *Teshubah 'al debar 'Efer haNisrafin* (*Responsum with regard to the ashes of cremated bodies . . .*), London, 1888, prohibits cremation but is an academic exercise.

[15]Israel J. Yoffey, *Keneset Yisrael*, Manchester, 1910, p. 151; S. J. Rabbinowitz, *Yashresh Ya'akob* (Jacob Will Strike Root), Jerusalem, 1925, p. 126; S. B. Freehof, *op. cit.*, pp. 41–45.

[16]Alter Druyanov, *Ketabim leToledot Hibbat Zion*, II (Tel Aviv, 1925), cols. 98–99, 115, 119, 121–22, 140–42. The visitors' book at the Jews' Temporary Shelter, London, contains his signature, and also that of Hayyim Berlin.

[17]Bernard Homa, *op. cit.*, pp. 60, 149.

[18]He signed his approbation of the ordinances of Machzikei HaDath in 1910, noting that worship in that synagogue made him 'not feel that I was in . . . London but . . . in the communities of Eiseschock, Volozhin, or the like. . . .' *Ibid.*, pp. 79–80, 143.

with a presiding rabbi of exalted standing for the duration of the War.

The English career of Israel Hayyim Daiches represents a specimen of rabbinic cultural activity. He came to Leeds in 1901 at the invitation of its well-organized immigrant community, although he would probably have remained in Russia but for the danger that a son would be conscripted into the Czar's army.[19] He soon published, and wrote the larger part, of a Hebrew rabbinic periodical *Bet Va'ad laHakhamim* (Meeting House of the Wise), and succeeded in producing eleven numbers between 1902 and 1904. The contributors who foregathered in his Meeting House created an atmosphere of somewhat westernized rabbinic learning, although the contents were well weighted with rabbinic studies in the traditional manner. Daiches' two sons, Salis and Samuel, who both attained later prominence as rabbis and scholars, were placed among the contributors by their proud father. Perhaps the most noteworthy name among other writers is David Hoffmann, besides whom some East European rabbis offered fruits of their learning. But *Bet Va'ad laHakhamim* was not a viable enterprise, for, as its editor recalled, 'in this country it was also impossible to sell a few hundred copies of a rabbinic monthly which was full to overflowing with novellae in Torah, worthy responsa, and wonderful homilies. I had to withdraw from its publication after I found that I had not the ability to stand the loss. . . .'[20] Daiches also participated actively in convening a group of fellow East European rabbis in Manchester in 1903, when a concerted effort was undertaken to establish *yeshibot* in English cities on the East European model. He was a central figure in the varied but unsuccessful efforts of the immigrant rabbis to play a significant role in the larger community.[21]

As a scholar, Daiches' principal works include the notable responsum *Mikveh Yisrael*[22] (The Hope [or Baths] of Israel)

[19] *Derashot MaHaRYah*, Leeds, 1920, p. viii. See also David Daiches, 'My Father, and His Father,' *Commentary*, XX, 6 (December, 1955), pp. 522–33.
[20] *Mikveh Yisrael*, Leeds, 1912, pp. 1–2.
[21] *Derashot MaHaRYaH*, Leeds, 1920, pp. ix–x.
[22] 'An Halachic Discourse Concerning the fitness for use of Ritual Baths supplied by modern Water-Works.' Leeds, 1912.

and its supplement *'Eyn Yisrael*[23] (The Well of Israel), which deal with the suitability of using the public water supply in ritual bathhouses. Drawing on both a variety of precedents and views in rabbinic literature, and an extensive knowledge which he acquired of the engineering techniques in municipal water works, Daiches authorized the use of piped water after a lengthy and technically erudite discussion which ranged over many side issues as well. It is a noteworthy specimen of the application of the classic query-responsum technique to a problem of concern to observant Jews, and the authorization was accepted by most of them. The learned world, including that part of it which was indifferent to the practical urgency of the problem, accorded its plaudits.[24] Daiches' most notable achievement was *Netibot Yerushalayim*, a commentary on several tractates of the Palestinian Talmud, most of which he completed as a young man in Russia. The last, on Tractate *Baba Mezia*, appeared in London in 1926. The commentary follows the principles of Talmudic study of Rabbi Elijah, the Gaon of Vilna, and occupies a place of distinction in the literature on the relatively neglected Palestinian Talmud.[24a] The Leeds rabbi also published his *Derashot* (Homilies) in 1921. Their points, it must be admitted, are nearly borne under by the mass of learned discussion, inspiring to the Talmudically proficient but baffling to others.

Rabbi Daiches' elaborately learned sermons do not at all resemble the direct popular appeal of the sermons of a *maggid*. Unfortunately, we have few such popular sermons; when the *maggid* went into print, he preferred to give the skeleton of his homiletic approach, or to present a formalized reproduction of rabbinic literature.[25] Thus, to judge a man from his book, Rabbi Israel Yoffey of Manchester was a more fluent preacher, for his *Keneset Yisrael*[26] (Congregation of Israel) abounds in references to personal and group problems of Jewish life in

[23]Leeds, 1912.

[24]Israel Abrahams in 'Books and Bookmen', *JC*, March 8, 1912; quotes David Hoffmann in *Idem*, April 12, 1912. See below, note 36.

[24a]Louis Ginzberg, *Commentary on the Palestinian Talmud* (Hebrew), 3 vols., New York, 1941, I, p. 131.

[25]H. Z. Maccoby, *'Imre Hayyim*, ed. M. Mansky, Tel. Aviv, 1929, contains only the homiletic material but not its development or applications.

[26]Manchester, 1910.

and out of the immigrant world. Rabbi Samuel Rabbinowitz of Liverpool reached higher in his books, which he composed under the flail of adversity in his family and public life.[27] He was a pioneer thinker of the religious Zionist movement, and his most interesting contributions to it arose from his profound concern with the Jewish social ethic. To him, the reality of Jewish exile lay not only in political and social oppression and spiritual self-abasement, but also because Judaism itself was in exile since it would never be able to mold a society in the ethical cast which the Torah requires. Rabbinowitz taught that the realization of the Zionist ideal of an independent Jewish homeland in Palestine is prerequisite to the full realization of Judaism, because only in Palestine can a Jewish social order be created and a just harmony between personal and social Judaism be attained. In a state of exile, the observance of Judaism in a Gentile environment becomes too much a matter of individual observance, which can too readily pervert itself to self-centred and formal Jewish piety. Rabbinowitz directed some strictures at his fellow pious Jews for their indifference to the social import of Judaism in spite of all their devoutness, and even questioned their ultimate religious integrity—an astonishing piece of moral and pragmatic courage.[28] Many of Rabbinowitz' writings come to grips with some of the fundamental issues in the philosophy of Judaism—the existence of God, the Divine attributes, revelation, moral questions, and more. Of all rabbinic literature produced in England, Rabbinowitz' works are the most fertile and stimulating, and deserve better than the permanent neglect which has been their lot.

In estimating the effect of the English environment upon the outlook of the traditional religious and intellectual leadership of the Jewish community, we must recall that these men arrived in England between the ages of thirty-five and about fifty—long past their formative years and ten or more years older than the average immigrant who debarked. The habit

[27]His principal works composed in England are *LiTekufot haYamim* (For the Appointed Days), Liverpool, 1917; *Yashresh Ya'akob* (Jacob Will Strike Root), Jerusalem, 1925.
[28]This is but a general summary of his thinking; a convenient kernel of much of it is contained in *LiTekufot HaYamim*, Liverpool, 1917, p. 92.

of unrestricted free inquiry was no characteristic of their life and thought, and the dangers to their form of Judaism in England helped to fortify their profound conservatism. However, certain emphases tend to occur in their thinking, perhaps because of the new land. They particularly stressed the historic reality of Jewish exile anywhere but in Palestine, and the duty of Jewish ethnic loyalty in the English crucible. To the conception of Jewish exile, heretofore interpreted principally in religious terms of Jewish sinfulness and ultimate Divine redemption, they added a social dimension by their melancholy over the downtrodden Jewish immigrant and the vanishing of Jewish life in the land of freedom.[29] Although the rabbis were well aware of the immeasurable difference between Czarist tyranny and English democratic constitutionalism,[30] they also experienced manifold examples of the communal and religious disintegration which seemed unavoidable in any emancipated Jewry. Besides, enough flies stuck in the ointment of English freedom, especially the Aliens Act of 1905, to make some of its fragrance appear exaggerated. The rabbis supported the Zionist movement, not only because of the historic hope for national restoration, but because the apparent alternatives of English freedom combined with religious disintegration, or Czarist oppression combined with full religious life, made reborn Palestine seem the last best hope on earth for amalgamating Jewish freedom with full religious life in the land bequeathed by God to His people. Once they observed it at close quarters, English Judaism stirred the wrath and contempt of the immigrant scholars. They shared the feeling of the immigrants that it was cold and formal, and were most affronted by its indifference to Jewish learning.[31] In their view, the English Jew was ultimately more concerned with being English than Jewish.

[29]I. J. Yoffey, op. cit., pp. 20, 23, 62, 74–5, 101 f.; I. H. Daiches, Derashot MaHaRYab, Leeds, 1920, p. 168; on the religious bearing of Jewish social conditions see S. J. Rabbinowitz, Menuhat Shabbat (Shabbos Ruhe), Liverpool, 1919.
[30]Eulogy on Edward VII by Rabbi S. I. Hillman in op. cit., esp. p. 96; H. Z. Maccoby, op. cit., p. xii; Aaron Hyman, Bet Va'ad . . . London, 1902, p. viii–ix; Jacob Zinkin, Jubal Shai . . . on the Occasion of the Queen's Jubilee, London, E. W. Rabbinowitz, 1887, p. 5, a sermon preached when the author had just landed in England.
[31]For one example among many see Aaron Hyman, op. cit., loc. cit.

THE HEBREW AND YIDDISH MILIEUX

This tradition of rabbinic intellectualism, perhaps the most pervasive spiritual current in post-Biblical history, was the point of departure for the Hebrew humanists and belletrists. New generations of Hebrew and Yiddish writers, nurtured in European Judaism, developed a Western literature in these Jewish languages by importing genres and expanding the range of literary subjects. This literature, the child of Enlightenment and also its vehicle, served a didactic purpose by holding up the mirror to Jewish life and thought and by sketching the outlines of a new, enlightened Jewish society. In the flowering of modern Hebrew literature, and during its creative summits between 1845–1870 and 1890–1920, England's role, like those of Western countries, was negligible. The Hebrew literary centres were in Galicia, Vilna, Warsaw, or Odessa, and beyond that cultural sphere only in New York did a struggling circle gradually achieve some note after it reached an unsteady adjustment with American life. London and the rest of England stood midway between the established centre in Eastern Europe and the centre being born in America, trying and hoping, but powerless to come to life as a Hebrew or Yiddish literary magnet. The basic desiderata of audience and livelihood were lacking for anyone who desired to live as a serious writer. That in spite of severely inhospitable conditions a miniscule Hebraic world was maintained, a Hebrew weekly journal was published, and the banner of the Hebrew national literary and philosophic renaissance was lofted, are phenomena to be admired.

There were Hebrew-speaking groups and associations of enthusiasts for the new literature already met in the early 1880's. These activities were sometimes displeasing to the straiter orthodox because of their worldly use of the Holy Tongue.[32] Native Jews, who revered the sanctity of a language which very few of them understood, were also wanting in

---

[32]An early example is reported in Manchester in *HaMaggid*, mentioning a still earlier group. *HaMaggid*, XXVI, 11 (March 14, 1883). There was also an early Hebrew periodical (of which no copy has been located) called *HaZofeh LeBet Yisrael*, mentioned in *Die Tsukunft*, IV, No. 157, August 12, 1887.

sympathy for secular Hebrew, although this attitude gradually changed. On the other hand, the natives' dislike of Yiddish was tantamount to abhorrence and that language symbolized all that they found strange and distasteful about the new English Jews. No Yiddish press, poetry, or theatre could overcome this unconquerable aversion. Yiddish was also the language of immigrant radicalism, although among the revolutionaries were competent Hebrew writers like Morris Winchevsky and Abraham Frumkin. However, they too devoted themselves to Yiddish.

The general tone of immigrant Hebrew culture was expressed by its central repository *HaYehudi* (The Jew), published weekly with interruptions by Isaac Suwalsky (1861–1913) from 1897 until his death. The tenuous enterprise was conducted by the dauntless man from his little flat in Whitechapel, surrounded by his family and nearly pushed out of doors by the mass of equipment.[33] From the available numbers, one must conclude that the heroic editorial effort of publishing *HaYehudi* was not matched by distinguished literary content. Suwalsky was an earnest but second-rate writer, and he was not novel or stimulating in discussing his guiding premises of Zionism, the revival of Hebrew culture, and moderate orthodox religion. The news of the Jewish world in *HaYehudi* added little to what the *Jewish Chronicle* reported, and the little Hebrew environment in London and the Provinces could hardly stop the presses with its activities. Other men who typified this conservative Hebraic spirit were Joseph Kohn-Zedek (1827–1903),[34] a rabbinic *maskil* who had published Hebrew periodicals in Galicia, but was enveloped by the Jewish communal system in England, and Aaron Hyman (1863–1937),[35] at home in the older milieu of rabbinic learning

[33]M. Berlin, *MiVolozhin 'ad Yerushalayim* (From Volozhin to Jerusalem), 2 vols., II, pp. 44–45. Suwalsky also wrote *Hayyey haYehudi 'al pi haTalmud* (Jewish Life According to the Talmud), Warsaw, 1899; *Ma'amar Betelin uMebutalin* (Discourse on Null and Void), London, 1900, a defence of the Zionist bank project.

[34]See Zalman Reisen, *Leksikon fun die Yiddishe Literatur un Presse*, Warsaw, 1914, col. 326–27; M. Winchevsky, *Erinnerungen*, 2 vols., N.Y., 1927, II, pp. 310–12.

[35]His principal works in England are *Bet Va'ad la Hakhamim* (Meeting House of the Wise: A Key to All Rabbinic *Agadoth*), London, 1902; *Toledot haTannaim vehaAmoraim*, 3 vols., London, 1910, a detailed biographical encyclopedia of the

but with a foot in modern Hebrew studies through his Hebrew handbooks and biographical dictionaries of rabbinic literature. The same may be said of Isaac Last (1847–1912), who published numerous editions of medieval Hebrew manuscripts under considerable material difficulty.[36]

Despite their common cause, factional jealousy and personal strife often rent the ranks of the Hebrew platoons, and bubbled on the surface of *HaYehudi*. The Hebrew Conference in Manchester in 1909, the most ambitious effort to concert the forces of Hebrew culture, almost foundered on the shoals of individual quarrels and self-aggrandizement.[37] Although interest in Hebrew by this time extended beyond these circles, it was too diffuse and incoherent to be capitalized upon. An eloquent appeal in 1912 to create an 'Hebrew Centre' in England for the centralization of Hebrew light and leading as part of a new world Hebraic organization, met the trivial response which its most distinguished signatory predicted it would.[38]

The uncrowned leader of Hebrew forces was Ahad HaAm, who arrived in London from Odessa in 1907 to take charge of the Wissotsky tea and wine interests in London. This man, the pre-eminent Hebrew essayist, editor, and philosopher of his generation, spent fifteen unhappy years in England. The unrivalled Hebrew milieu of Odessa, where he was the central figure, had barely the feeblest shadow in London, and his creative brilliance was dimmed by the press of business, deterioration of health, and the misery of being a fish out of water. Like the lesser luminaries, Ahad HaAm was mordant and sarcastic about English Jewry in which he had had to settle, and kept aloof from the London Hebraists—although the latter

Talmudic rabbis. The former work sold 3,000 copies in eight years, a good sale for a rabbinic work. *Ibid.*, I, p. vii.

[36]For example, *Magen 'Abot* (The Shield of the Fathers . . . by R. Menahem b. Solomon haMeiri), London, 1909. It includes (pp. 161–67) learned notes by I. H. Daiches.

[37]See *HaYehudi* for May, 1909; J. S. Fuchs, *Merkaz Ivri* (*An Hebrew Centre*), London, 1909, an address delivered at the conference. The author (1868–1938) had been a Hebrew journalist of some note on the Continent and editor for a time of *HaMaggid*; he settled in Liverpool and conducted an advanced Hebrew Higher Grade School.

[38]*JC*, March 8, 1912; Ahad HaAm to S. J. (Ish) Horowitz, April 7, 1912, in Ahad HaAm (Asher Ginzberg), *'Igrot* (Letters), 6 vols., Berlin, 1923–25, IV, p. 271.

were delighted to honour him whenever possible.[39] His sole contribution upon English matters was 'Upon Two Thresholds', an attack on Claude G. Montefiore's conception of Jewish and Christian ethics. The essay used the ideas of his opponent as a point of departure for some wide-ranging observations upon that subject and for a few stinging remarks about Judaism in England.[40]

Far to the left was the self-tormented Joseph Hayyim Brenner (1882–1921), the quasi-nihilist and revolutionary who turned passionately back to Jewish survival and pioneering struggle in Palestine. His four years in London, from 1904 to 1908, were lived nearly in self-isolation. From a small room he wrote most of his periodical *HaMe'orer* (The Awakener), which he printed and distributed himself. Even though the scene of one of his plays and some of his stories is set in London, Brenner's spiritual and intellectual orientation were far away. Like his friend Uri Nissan Gnessin (1878–1913) and Ahad HaAm, Brenner regarded London as but a wayfaring station, and proceeded to Palestine via Eastern Europe in 1909.[41]

A tragically short-lived predecessor of these two impressionists was Jacob Samuel Katzenellenbogen (1877–1902), who drowned in Switzerland where he had gone to mend his body from tuberculosis contracted in London. His short lifetime was marred by bitter poverty, like that of another sojourner in England, the future Hebraist and Arabist Benzion Halper (1884–1924).[42] Katzenellenbogen's narrative 'A Winter's

[39]*Ibid.*, IV, pp. 2–5, 15–16, 25–26, 42, 60–61, 150, 236–37. A Urinovsky (Ben-'Or), *Toledot haSifrut Ha'Ivrit laHadashah* (History of Modern Hebrew Literature), 3 vols., Tel Aviv, 1948, II, p. 148; Chaim Weizmann, *Trial and Error*, N.Y., 1949, pp. 106–108.

[40]*'Al Parashat Derahim* (At the Crossroads), 3rd ed., 4 vols., Berlin, 1921, IV, pp. 38–58.

[41]J. H. Brenner, *Me'Eber liGebulin* (Beyond the Boundaries), London, 1907, is a four-act play on the socialist and emigre milieu in London; the scene is laid in a London restaurant. It is rich in incident and individual characterization and conflict but lacks unity of theme and plot. See also A. Beilin, 'Y. H. Brenner beLondon', *HaTekufah*, XIV–XV (1922), pp. 646–71; J. H. Brenner, 'Igrot (Letters), ed. M. Poznansky, 2 vols., Tel Aviv, 1941, I, pp. 115–391, II, pp. 345–46, esp. I, pp. 121, 248, 340; A. Urinovsky (Ben-Or), *op. cit.*, II, pp. 429–31. On Gnessin in London, see his *Ketabim* (Works), 3 vols., Merhaviah, 1946, III, pp. 135–40; L. S. Kraditor, 'Ven U. N. Gnessin iz Geven in London', *Yiddish London*, II (Winter, 1939), pp. 70–74; A. Beilin, *op. cit.*; A. Urinovsky, *op. cit.*, II, p. 391.

[42]Cyrus Adler, 'Benzion Halper', *American Jewish Year Book, 1924–25*, pp. 459–60, 462.

Night in the Streets of East London'[43] is a vignette, pathetic and acidulous, of a man evicted by an impatient landlady for arrears of rent. The abandoned and lonely man (by no coincidence, a writer) wanders in the cold from street to street and stops at the warm, well-provisioned houses of friends who had flattered his talent, pretending only to visit them because shame constrains him from revealing his plight. They are hospitable enough, although he is too bitter to admit it. He is sure they know what is wrong, yet they refrain from showing real sympathy by offering him shelter. So he must roam the courts and alleys until, too weary to walk any more, he eludes the policeman and sinks to sleep in a doorway, to rise achingly next morning to another aimless, helpless day. The young author of 'A Winter's Night' probably wrote from personal history, and it is not far-fetched to suppose that he allegorized the state of Hebrew letters in England, homeless but too proud to beg from its half-hearted friends.

Like serious literature in Hebrew, that in Yiddish was also at sea in London. A writer's chance to earn his livelihood as a Yiddish journalist was always imperilled by the instability of the Yiddish press, and it was impossible to make a living from serious writing. Although the mass of poor immigrants did speak Yiddish, few of them regarded it as the language of elevated thought and expression—that was a level reserved for Hebrew, even by those who did not understand the Holy Tongue. The literary ferment in the Yiddish milieux of Eastern Europe was unknown to them, and a literary and esthetic ideal was slow to develop in a language whose function for some centuries had been the transmission of popularized religious and ethical teachings to semi-educated Jews, especially women. Like thousands of immigrants, many writers dallied in England before proceeding on to America. Morris Rosenfeld (1862–1924) was twice in London in the 1880's but could not free himself from sweatshop work, and was unsympathetically treated by Kranz and Winchevsky in the *Arbeiter Freind*. He moved permanently to America in 1888, where recognition

[43]Jacob Samuel Katzenellenbogen, *Leyl Horef*, '*al peney Rehobot Mizrah London*, London, 1908; see preface for biographical information.

was still painfully slow.[44] There is an air of transience to the Yiddish literary scene in London and the Provinces; in short, Yiddish literature of merit did not flourish.

Yiddish literature first appeared in England in the service of the socialist movement.[45] Winchevsky's English period, when his talents were consecrated to socialism, were among the most productive years of his career. For its part, Jewish socialism and anarchism, by rejecting Jewish tradition and its Hebraic mould, probably helped to lay some of the foundation for belle-tristic creativity in the traditionally subordinate language. Yiddish stories, poems, and tracts were addressed to the new Jewish industrial working class, offering moral edification and exhortation in the newer manner, upon the sins of society and their social rights and wrongs. Yiddish socialist literature and socialistic bellelettres flourished early in England, but, like the socialists, its sceptre departed by the mid-1890's. Under the subsequent leadership of the anarchists, the Yiddish literary scene in England is characterized by abundance of translation and paucity of meritorious original work. This is because the anarchists broadened the cultural scope of the Jewish masses by translating the best of contemporary European literature into their vernacular, but did not wish to make of Yiddish itself anything more than a vehicle.

By its position as the language of the masses of Jews, Yiddish early became the language of a press. London was one of the first European cities to possess the requisite sizeable audience, freedom of expression, and competent personnel necessary to publish Yiddish newspapers with unbroken regularity. Of the Yiddish newspapers published in England, those dedicated to socialism take first place in quality on account of their earnestness and their over-riding sense of responsibility to their readers. Their critical sense in probing the affairs of Jewry and the world and their high literary standard entitle them to favourable comparison with the contemporary press in England. Unfortunately, only fragments exist of the rest of the Yiddish press in England and not of all newspapers which were published, so that we are reduced to a

[44]Jacob Shatzky, *Morris Rosenfeld in Licht fun Zayne Briev*, N.Y., 1936, pp. 6–9, 22–23.
[45]See Chapter IV, esp. pp. 108–10, 137.

bibliographic enumeration of some of them from contemporary records.[46] Yiddish journalistic enterprises came and went; editors went off to try their hands at newspapers of their own; factions of socialists published their own periodicals to spread a specialized version of true enlightenment;[47] trade unions, religious groups, and Zionists pleaded their causes in fleeting *flugblätter*;[48] emigre revolutionists printed journals in London for furtive circulation in Russia.[49]

We know of five attempts to publish Yiddish newspapers before 1890, none of which survived the year of its debut. These were in 1867,[50] 1874,[51] 1878,[52] 1884,[53] and 1889,[54] and

[46]The Yiddish press in England is a practically uncharted field. Bibliographical information is available in Zalman Reisen, *op. cit.*, Part II; Cecil Roth, *Magna Bibliotheca Anglo-Judaica*, London, 1937; the catalogues of YIVO and the Jewish Division of the New York Public Library. J. Shatzky, ed., *Zamlbukh leKhoved dem Zvey Hundert un Fuftsikstn Yovel fun der Yiddisher Presse, 1686-1936*, N.Y., 1936, contains no comprehensive information on England. See also E. Wortsmann's caustic survey, 'Die Iddishe Presse in England', *Der Iddisher Kemfer*, II, 11, 12, 15 (June 14, 21, July 12, 1907).

[47]*E.g. Die Frayhayt* (anarchist factional), weekly, 1902 to?; *Dos Naye Tsayt*, (socialist) fortnightly, at times weekly, 1904–1908; *Der Sotsial-Demokrat*, (socialist) monthly, 2 issues, 1907–1908; *Fraye Arbayter Velt* (anarchist, factional), 1906.

[48]*E.g. HaZofeh* ('A Strictly Orthodox Organ for Judaism'), weekly from March 2, 1894 to December 6, 1895, ed. Isaac Wolf Metchik (Meczyk), listed in Reisen and Roth as 'Jewish Observer'; *Dos Naye Leben* (Zionist-socialist-territorialist), monthly, 1906; Reisen lists *Der Trayd Yunionist*, a fortnightly, and *Der Shnayder-Arbayter*, without dates—probably strike publications.

[49]*E.g. Der Arbayter*, ed. M. Rubinstein, 1899-1902, for the Polish Socialist Party.

[50]*London Yudish-Deitshe Tseitung*, ed. Nafthali Levy, 1867, listed in Reisen, Roth; *non vidi*. The first Yiddish newspaper in an English-speaking country. Levy's editorship is dubious, as he seems to have come to England only c. 1876; J. Kohn-Zedek, *Eleh Posekekha Yisrael*, (These Be Thy Decisors, O Israel!), London, 1884, p. 101. On Levy, see his correspondence in *HaMeliz*, XIV, 2 (July 24–August 5, 1878) ff., and Morris Winchevsky, *op. cit.*, II, pp. 29–32.

[51]*HaShofar* (*The Trumpet*), 9 issues commencing January 21, 1874. See *HaMaggid*, XVII, II (March 10, 1874). Only a photostat of the first page of the first issue is available, in *Der Hammer*, V, 5 (May, 1931), p. 40. E. R. Malachi, 'Ver iz Geven der Redaktor fun HaShofar?' in Jacob Shatzky ed., *Zamlbukh le-Khoved* . . . N.Y., 1937, pp. 315–17, is unconvincing in arguing that, contrary to the sources he cites, H. D. Eliashevitz was not the editor because he is otherwise unknown as a Yiddish writer. The title page suggests a learned Maskil, which he was; furthermore, the Yiddish press owes a large part of its foundation to Hebrew Maskilim.

[52]*Londoner Izraelit*, ed. Nafthali Levy, weekly, 1878; listed in Reisen, Roth, *non vidi*. J. Kohn-Zedek (*op. cit., loc. cit.*) states that it was a Yiddish supplement to Levy's *HaKerem* (in Hebrew; listed in Roth; *non vidi*) of which five issues appeared.

[53]*HaShulamit*, ed. J. Leep-Brill (1835–1886), frequently controverted in *The Polish Yidel*, and mentioned in 1890 (Jewish Board of Guardians, *Minutes*, December 8, 1890) and 1902 (Cd. 1742, Min. 1451 ff.). The editor (see Zalman

R

there may well have been others unknown. Yiddish newspapers first appeared regularly in the later 1890's, and not until the turn of the century did they reach a measure of permanence and stability. Some newspapers were published with a high sense of their mission, expressed in the manifesto of *HaShofar* (*The Trumpet*) to its readers in 1874:

The need of a newspaper for every people has been described in many books. . . . A newspaper is food for the souls of men as bread is for their bodies. . . . The more a people is educated, the more they require newspapers. . . . An educated people cares for the spirit not less than for the body; we see very often here in England that even those Englishmen who did not attend school at all in their youth are still civilized. . . . [Newspapers] make up the lack of their education in their youth . . . therefore all editors, although they are mostly the most educated people, try to write their newspapers simply, so that everyone, even the ignorant, shall understand. . . .[55]

The Haskalah didacticism of *HaShofar* was followed by the socialist didacticism of the *Polish Yidel* and the *Arbeiter Freind* beginning in 1884. The pious Isaac Wolf Metchik's (1849–1953 [sic] earnestness flowed in the channels of religious orthodoxy, as befitted one of the founders of Machzikei HaDath. His *HaZofeh* (The Observer), published in 1894 and 1895, surveyed the Jewish scene from its religious vantage point, exhorting readers to maintain Jewish religious life in its fullness.

The loftier purposes of enlightenment were not the only ends pursued by Yiddish newspapers. As early as 1886, the *Tsukunft* was practically converted into political campaign propaganda for Sir Samuel Montagu's successful effort to be returned as Whitechapel's M.P.[56] The *Yudisher Ekspres* was founded in Leeds in 1895 for a similar purpose, and was then transferred to London in 1899, where it appeared daily for several years.[57] Moise Bril (1860–1921) was one of the more

Reisen, *op. cit.*, col. 133) was a scholar and editor of a Hebrew paper in Jerusalem and a German paper in Mainz.

[54]Ozer Blaustein (1840–1899) is said to have come to London in 1889 or 1890 as editor of *Die Epokhe* during its short existence, acc. to Reisen.

[55]I, 1, January 21, 1874; see above, note 51.

[56]*Die Tsukunft*, III, 1 (July 1, 1886).

[57]Zalman Reisen, *Leksikon fun der Yudisher Literatur Presse un Filologie*, 4 vols., Vilna, 1926–30, *s.v.* Bril, Isaac Loeb. The Leeds name was the *Jewish Recorder*. *Non vidi.*

active journalistic entrepreneurs who aimed more directly at giving his public what he supposed they wanted. His weekly *Idisher Telefon* disclaimed any desire to deal in personal or institutional rivalries. It would 'not preach religion, and not propagandize for atheism', but would 'be a Jewish newspaper only so far as concerns Yiddish language and writing, but in every other connection it will be a general, neutral, non-partisan newspaper'.[58] The *Idisher Telefon* became one of several Yiddish newspapers which eschewed partisan issues and served their readers a diet of sensational news from London and elsewhere, and devoted a large proportion of each number to the 'roman'—usually a melodramatic tale of Jewish or non-Jewish provenance. When this newspaper staggered under the expenses of a libel suit, Bril brought out another weekly besides *Bril's Speshel* (*Bril's Jewish Special*), which appeared from 1902 until 1907 and perhaps later. Beginning in 1906, the *Yudishe Velt* was published as a supplement to the *Jewish World*, and possessed some of the excellences of that native Jewish newspaper. It offered its readers such contributors as Isaac Loeb Paretz, David Frishman, and Nahum Sokolow, and it espoused an Anglicizing mission which was more self-conscious than that of newspapers rooted in the immigrant world. The most prominent and long-lived of all the Yiddish newspapers was the *Yudisher Zhurnal* (*Jewish Journal*), which Anshel Levy founded in 1907 and edited until 1913, when Morris Myer (1879–1944) took over. Myer possessed ample experience as a writer, translator, and former socialist, and had worked for Levy in the latter's short-lived popular 'literary' weekly, *Der Roman-Zhurnal*, in 1908–1909. Myer's journal came to dominate the Yiddish journalistic milieu, and Myer became the central figure in that sphere for many years.[59]

In the absence of a full sample, it is difficult to analyze the Yiddish press, or to estimate its position in the immigrant community. From the endless strictures which they heaped upon each other and the contempt which the socialist press displayed for them all, we may suppose them to have been 'klal Yisrael' in their basic outlook—traditionally religious

[58]I, 1 (February 4, 1897), p. 1.
[59]Zalman Reisen, *op. cit.*, *s.v.* Myer, Morris.

to a greater or lesser degree, usually pro-Zionist, devotedly
concerned with the social and organizational life of the immigrant community, in turn defending and reproving the Jews
and very well larded with 'romanen'. The Yiddish press kept a
prudent distance from contentious social and economic questions,
except the defence of Jews against anti-Semitism and in favour
of free immigration to England. However, we do not know
much about their circulations, their staffs, or their influence as
leaders or followers of opinion.[60]

London was also a cradle of the Yiddish theatre, one of the
principal glories of modern Yiddish literature and art, but it
showed scant interest in the mature product.[61] In the 1880's
Morris Winchevsky had the opportunity to write theatrical
criticism of the crude productions of the little Yiddish theatrical
troupe in the East End, and at the International Hall in Holborn,
where the young Jacob and Sarah Adler were embarking on
eminent careers with such vehicles-to-be as 'Shulamith',
'Uriel Acosta', and 'Bar Kokhba', all by Goldfaden. There
was also a 'Russian Jewish Opera Company' which presented
musical productions ranging in quality from quasi-opera to
low vaudeville.[62] Hardly anyone in the English or Yiddish
speaking Jewish communities was aware of the significance of
what was developing, or appreciated the difference between
the then embryonic Yiddish theatre and the coarse entertain-
ments available in East End Jewish coffee shops. In any case,
the Yiddish theatre did not settle in England, for the pioneer
troupe went on to make its home in New York. In the following
twenty years, wandering troupes and celebrated players performed fairly continuously in London and the Provinces, but a
permanent theatre of a high standard did not evolve. Various

[60]Other Yiddish papers, non-socialist, non-anarchist, non-Zionist, include the
following listed in Reisen: *Yudishe Tsaytung* of Glasgow, weekly and daily,
1902–1903; *Der Yunger Dor*, periodically in 1911; *Der Londoner Yud*, weekly,
1904 (not Poale Zion, however); *Londoner Yudishes Tageblatt*, daily, 1909–1910;
Pipifoks (*Illustrated Jewish Bits*), humorous Jewish weekly, 1899–1901; *Der
Fonograf*, short-lived, n.d.; *Die Koöperativeh Tsaytung*, one issue, n.d.
[61]M. J. Landa, *The Jew in Drama*, London, 1926, pp. 284–97; Jacob Shatzky
ed., *Arkhiv far der Geshikhte fun Yidishn Teater un Drameh*, Vilna-N.Y., 1930, has
nothing on England, except *passim*, pp. 487–88; J. Rodker, 'The Theatre in
Whitechapel', *Poetry and Drama*, I, 1 (March, 1913), pp. 43–44.
[62]Regularly noticed in *Polish Yidel*, I, 1 (July 25, 1884), ff.; *Die Tsukunft*, I,
30 (February 13, 1885), f. *JC*, June 17, 1904.

music halls in and near the East End mounted Yiddish shows—sketches, songs and comedians.[62a]

The most ambitious effort was made in 1912, with the erection of the Feinman Yiddish People's Theatre in the East End—an excellent house with a capacity of 1,500.[63] It opened 'amid scenes of unbounded and unprecedented enthusiasm' with a performance of an opera *King Ahaz* by Samuel Alman, based upon Abraham Mapu's Hebrew novel *The Guilt of Samaria*.[64] The Feinman theatre outdid itself with a production of Rigoletto in Yiddish which earned a remarkable tribute from the London *News Chronicle*:

Nowhere, except in grand opera, at Covent Garden, could one hear, in England, a company of such brilliant talents as in this Yiddish Theatre, in the very heart of the East End, which has been founded by the subscriptions of rich and poor Jews, and has been built to fulfil a great racial ideal among these people . . . [it] stands by itself as one of the most notable operatic triumphs in this country . . . performed by both the company and the orchestra, with an accuracy, a precision, and a perfect mastery, astonishing in its excellence.[65]

The Feinman Theatre lacked only money to pursue its triumphant careêr, but it lacked it more and more, for the expense of building the theatre left hardly anything as working capital. It presented the standard repertory of the Yiddish theatre, but its box office seems to have run a poor second to the cheaper Yiddish operettas at the Pavilion Theatre. Religious Jews, many of whom were but little attracted to the idea of a theatre at all, were especially wroth with the Feinman's performances on the Sabbath. The initial burst of enthusiasm faded, and help did not come from the West End, so that the Feinman Yiddish People's Theatre closed its curtains permanently in the same year they were first opened.[66] The field was left thenceforward to touring repertory companies from abroad, and music hall performances trod the boards in the lengthy interims.

[62a]The Orient Theatre, built in the East End in 1905 was a mainly Yiddish theatre. *JC*, May 2, 1902; October 31, 1902 (quoting the *Standard*); June 10, 1904.
[63]*JC*, March 8, 1912.
[64]*JC*, March 22, April 19, 1912.
[65]Quoted in *JC*, April 19, 1912.
[66]*JC*, August 2, 1912.

ZIONISM IN THE IMMIGRANT MILIEU

Jewish mass settlement in Western countries took place at the time that the Zionist analysis of the Jewish position and its proposed solution were making rapid headway in men's minds. That analysis, briefly put, denied that the Jews were ever secure anywhere but in their homeland. It asserted that Jewish emancipation, the hope of Jewry for the past century, exacted as its price the effacement of Jewish identity and the dilution of historic Judaism to the vanishing point, and that even such abasement would still not win the Jew acceptance into Western society. Instead, let a Jewish society be created in the ancient Jewish land, where the very act of entry would constitute emancipation, and where Judaism would need to seek no external tolerance for its full realization. While the balance of learned and publicistic opinion in Eastern Europe preferred Palestine as a destination, the torrent of emigration flowed not thither but to the New World and Western Europe. In the immigrant's view, while his own salvation lay in a Western country, national salvation lay either with revolution in Eastern Europe or national renewal in Palestine. Thus, he agreed with articulate opinion, and felt no personal contradiction between Zionist convictions and the choice he made of settling in England.

The immigrants were stirred by the vision of an independent national future like that of a Western nation, but not unalloyed with messianic overtones, in a land where the oppression more or less inevitable in exile would be unthinkable. Although Jacob Lestschinsky, writing from afar, saw immigrant Jewry in London as a potential emigration reservoir, there is little indication that such Zionist enthusiasm meant 'aliyah. The immigrants' Zionism could give little financial support for Palestine projects, while their lack of position in English society dismissed any thought of their exercising influence upon the British Government for the Zionist political programme. Zionism drew its political and intellectual leadership from the West End, although mostly from men like Israel Cohen, Harry Sacher, Leon Simon, Herbert Bentwich, and Leopold Greenberg, who were the second and third generation of early East European immigration.[67]

Here is not the place to discuss the position of England in the Zionist movement, nor the origins of the Balfour Declaration and Palestine mandate—but it may be noted that the immigrant community played no role in any of this.[68] Rather is it sought to understand Zionism's 'place in life' in the immigrant world.

Before Herzl's appearance on the scene in 1896, Zionism as an organized movement consisted of a number of 'Lovers of Zion' associations. The first branch was established in London early in 1885, on the heels of the organizing conference of the movement in Kattowitz.[69] High hopes were cherished for English help by the East European leaders; in fact, they thought briefly of establishing the main office in London.[70] The new branch's chairman was a certain Mr Berg, and its secretaries were two Hebrew writers and communal functionaries, Joseph Kohn-Zedek and Jacob I. Hirschbein. Sir Samuel Montagu, then parliamentary candidate for Whitechapel, agreed to be Treasurer. The little group sought to establish colonies in Palestine for persecuted East European Jews, and thus 'in time, to win back Palestine for the Jews'.[71] It aimed to connect its activities with the recent centenary honours paid to Sir Moses Montefiore, the patriarchal champion of Palestine Jewry. The London Lovers of Zion's early activities were

[67]Paul Goodman, *Zionism in England, English Zionist Federation, 1899–1929*, London, 1929; Marvin J. Goldfine, *Early Zionism in England*, Master's essay Columbia University, 1939 (typescript).

[68]Chaim Weizmann, an immigrant in 1904, was, as a chemist and university lecturer, hardly typical of immigrant life. His activities as a Zionist were in the native Jewish milieu, and his contacts with the immigrant world were relatively slight. Chaim Weizmann, *Trial and Error*, N.Y., 1949, pp. 93–120.

[69]*HaMaggid*, XXVIII, 2, (January 8, 1885); *Die Tsukunft*, I, 25, 31, (January 9 and February 20, 1885); E. W. Rabbinowitz, 'Sefer Zikkaron 5640–5650', '*Iyyim*, I (1928), p. 74. On Rabbinowitz' combination of Haskalah, social consciousness, and Zionism, see his letter to J. L. Levin (YaHaLaL), in *HaMaggid*, XXVI, 20 (May 23, 1883), repr. with additions in Alter Druyanov, *op. cit.*, III, cols. 555–60. There was an earlier immigrants Zionist society in Manchester. *HaMaggid*, XXVI, 40 (October 10, 1883). Perhaps the London group was the same as the "B'nei Zion" Association for the Propagation of Jewish Nationalism & Colonization of the Holy Land', which published M. L. Lilienblum, *The Regeneration of Israel on the Land of His* [sic] *Fathers*, London, n.d. (c. 1882 to 1885). This translation from Hebrew is one of the the the first, and perhaps the first, Zionist pamphlets in English.

[70]Alter Druyanov, *op. cit.*, III, cols. 716–18.

[71]*Die Tsukunft*, I, 25 (January 9, 1885).

blemished by a jurisdictional quarrel with an unscrupulous Palestinian messenger, which contributed to its early demise.[72] Lovers of Zion groups also emerged in other communities, including Liverpool, Manchester, and even Tredegar, Wales.[73] A new London society in 1888 interested itself more personally in Palestine colonization. It was to consist of fifty worthy men who would subscribe 5s weekly apiece, and when £200 had thus been raised, 'our big brothers in London' would be invited to contribute the balance required to purchase a plot in Palestine for them to undertake co-operative farming.[74] For reasons which are evident enough, nothing came of this plan.

The Lovers of Zion, who formed a national federation under native Jewish leadership in 1891, continued their work of education and small-scale philanthropy until the revolutionary change wrought by the appearance upon the scene of Theodor Herzl. One of the extraordinary episodes in the early career of the Zionist prophet was his nearly Messianic reception in Whitechapel on July 13, 1896, where he went to deliver his first public address upon political Zionism. Herzl's charismatic presence and flowing speech strikingly affected the popular mind, and his progress through the streets became an astonishing personal triumph.[75] The World Zionist Congress which he convened in 1897, and the World Zionist Organization which the Congress thereupon established, sprouted branches with unusual speed in the immigrant world.

In spite of their initial hesitancy, the Lovers of Zion were also swept into Herzl's new movement, and the English Zionist Federation was founded in 1898.[76] With little to aspire to but to render its meagre aid and comfort to the few Palestine

[72]*Idem*, II, 16, 18, 20 (October 23, November 6, 20, 1885); III, 2, 3 (July 8, 15, 1886); E. W. Rabbinowitz, *loc. cit.*

[73]S. L. Citron, *Toledot Hibbat Zion*, Odessa, 1914, p. 294; Liverpool Jewish Board of Guardians, *Minutes*, October 23, 1892; *HaMaggid*, XXVIII, 22 (June 5, 1884); *HaMeliz*, XXVIII, 256, (November 23–December 5, 1888).

[74]*Die Tsukunft*, IV, No. 207 (August, 10 1888).

[75]Alex Bein, *Theodor Herzl*, Philadelphia, 1940, pp. 205–207.

[76]Paul Goodman, *op. cit.*, pp. 6–7; *Palastina*, No. 20 (June 1897), p. 1 ff.; see Jacob de Haas' report on England presented to the First Zionist Congress, in *HaProtokol*, Hebrew trans., Tel Aviv, 1946, p. 38. Hayyim Zundel Maccoby, the *maggid*, was the principal moral force behind immigrant Zionism in the 1890's. However, his influence waned when he did not enter the reorganized movement. See H. Z. Maccoby, *op. cit.*, pp. vii, xii.

colonies, the movement had rather stagnated in the 1890's. All this changed completely in the following decade, between the foundation of the Zionist movement in 1897, the death of Herzl in 1904, and the victory of Czarism in Russia in 1906. In these years, the rapid flowering of Zionism as a movement of hope and redemption moved more Jews than had ever before been touched by a mass movement. As to its effect upon the immigrants, an English rabbi observed that at its height

. . . Zionism has become a strong factor in East End life. It has rallied round it the intellectual forces of East End Jewry. The national ideal—the ideal of the Jewish spirit—has taken a strong hold upon the greater bulk of the Jewish population. It has attracted the flower of Jewish youth. The ideal has given rise to numerous associations, nearly every one of which has its literary programme, its lectures and debates, its reading parties and Hebrew talks, whilst some have started, on a very modest scale, reading rooms and circulating libraries.[77]

The movement also suffered from some typical failings of immigrant organizational life—splintering and aimless turmoil. The outsider's picture of thriving societies was sharply modified by an insider's closer look:

The societies mostly consist only of committees and the latter have very little connection with the members. . . .[78]

The two or three members which every group has are often torn away from other groups. . . . They simply made the most of all passable Biblical phrases to give names to their associations, all of which exist only on paper. . . .[79]

To an extent, these groups expressed the Jewishness of many who were not cosmopolitan socialists yet were alienated by the forms of immigrant religious life. To the advantage of Zionist agitation, the principal immigrant rabbi in London, Aba Werner, was a Zionist, and so were other immigrant rabbis like S. J. Rabbinowitz, I. J. Yoffey, and I. H. Daiches. This helped to counteract the suspicions of the religious admissibility

[77]Dayan Asher Feldman, *JC*, December 24, 1903.
[78]*Die Tsionistishe Korrespondents*, No. 3, n.d., quoted in K. Marmor, 'Die Elyen Bill fun der English Zionist Federation un Irer Entshtehung', *Die Yudishe Fraybayt*, I, No. 2–3 (May–June, 1905), p. 15. This article is valuable for its extensive quotations from unavailable sources.
[79]*Die Yudisher Ekspres*, November 5, 1902, quoted in *Ibid*.

of Zionism which were entertained by many pious Jews. On the other hand, leadership was not 'clerical', but was vested mostly in younger people. The content of East End Zionism consisted mostly of affirmation of basic principles expounded by such founders as Lilienblum, Pinsker, and Herzl, while some younger intelligentsia stressed Ahad HaAm's Hebraic and spiritual emphasis. The call to Zionist Shekel Day summed it up:

. . . Every son of Jewry who buys the shekel thereby shows that 'his nation is the Jewish' and that 'all Jews from all parts of the world are closer to him than his non-Jewish fellow-citizens of the same country and of the same class', and his 'national coin is not the shilling and not the franc but the Hebrew shekel'.[80]

Parelleling developments on the Continent, there was also a trend to synthesize the hitherto opposite ideals of socialism and Zionism, to amalgamate the struggles for working class and Jewish national emancipation. The early Socialist Zionists in England attempted to build trade unions with a Zionist programme. But they abandoned trade unionism in favour of Socialist Zionist societies, affiliated with similar groups on the Continent.[80a] Dr Nahman Syrkin, intellectual leader of the movement, addressed his 'Call to Jewish Youth' in London in 1901, but its effects were greater among Russo-Jewish academic youth than in England. An early Poale Zion (Workers of Zion) platform was adopted in Leeds in 1905:

Poale Zion is a national movement of Jewish workers which undertakes the following tasks:
(1) To create a national-political centre in Palestine for the Jewish people.
(2) To lead a struggle for civil and national rights in the Diaspora.
(3) To struggle against the present economic order equally with other proletarian organizations.[81]

This rather forced composite of socialist and Zionist aims is the English counterpart of the deeper stirrings in Eastern Europe which produced the Second Aliyah and its vital con-

[80]Placard for Shekel Day, 1903, quoted in K. Marmor, *op. cit.*, p. 19–20.
[80a]'Jewish Labour News', *JC*, February 26, 1904.
[81]*Die Yudishe Frayhayt*, I, No. 2–3 (May–June, 1905), p. 38; Nahman Syrkin, *Geklibene Tsionistish-Sotsialistishe Shriften*, 2 vols., N.Y., 1925, I, pp. 35–46.

sequences in the pre-history of the State of Israel. However, the second and third points of this platform meant little in the English environment and had little effect on the English Zionist scene, while a 'national-political' centre is political Zionism at its lukewarmest.

Intellectually, the most vigorous group in immigrant Zionism was the 'democratic fraction', a loose caucus which emphasized practical work in Palestine and the fostering of Hebraic culture. Its leader in England during his few years' residence was the publicist Dr Ezekiel Wortsmann.[82] Rejecting the mass appeal and the messianism which were current in the Zionism around them, the 'democratic fraction' selected some basic points for emphasis: 'We must know that to revive a people and not to revive its national tongue along with it is an impossible thing. . . . We consider ourselves as strangers everywhere, even where we have been given complete civil rights, because we want to have a home of our own. . . .'[83] Only those who accepted these principles were to be admitted into the group. The West End leadership of the movement, which was unquestioningly accepted on all hands, drew the strictures of the 'democratic fraction' for what seemed its cavalier assumption of the right to lead the Zionist forces.

Actually, the relations between East End Zionist and West End Zionist were warmer than in other areas of communal activity. Both strove in the same cause, both affirmed the unity of Jewry in culture and in fate, and held in the same disdain the Anglicized Jews, and the oligarchic communal structure which they could not master. Yet not all was harmony. We hear the immigrant Zionists allege that fellow-Zionists of the West End prevented them from sending delegates of their own choice to the Congress, specifically Dr Wortsmann as spokesman of the 'democratic fraction'.

[82]1878–1938. His *Vos Villen die Tsionisten?*, London, 1901, is one of the first political Zionist tracts in Yiddish. He was an active Hebrew and Yiddish journalist, editor, and publisher in several countries. See Zalman Reisen, *Leksikon fun der Yudisher Literatur*, 4 vols., Vilna, 1929, *s.v.* Vortsmann, Yehezkel.

[83]*Kosel Ma'arovi*, No. 1, c. Summer, 1902, quoted in K. Marmor, *op. cit.*, p. 15.

THE LARGER PICTURE

In sum, the main currents flowing in Jewish cultural life were secularization and Anglicization. The synagogue and its auxiliaries, representing traditional religious life and thought, lost their place as the hub of communal and cultural life, particularly among young immigrants and immigrants' children. Independent forms and agencies of cultural life filled in the vacuum, and the synagogue, far from dominating them, became merely one among many competing groups. It was further disadvantaged because it had yet a long and painful process of accommodation to endure, while the others sprang up newborn.

Anglicization, the second current, would have happened with or without the diligent efforts of native Jewry to hasten it and to mould it in the cast which seemed most becoming. It reached deeper, involving the transformation of the economic life of the immigrants, the change of their language, the modification of their social habits, and the metamorphosis of their communal life. Nor was Anglicization solely a process of passive cultural absorption, as the acceleration of immigrant cultural effort throughout the period of immigration shows.

There was hardly any cultural life among the immigrants during the 1870's and early 1880's, except for the miniscule circles of the Enlightened Hebraists. The latter 1880's were highlighted by the burgeoning of Jewish revolutionary socialism and the speedy laying of its basic institutions and patterns— the press and literature clubs, public agitation. However, socialism moved to America after 1892 and 1893, leaving the movement in England reduced to the status of a sect. Anarchism became instead the major force in this area, but it was isolated from immigrant Jewish life even though it nested in its midst, spoke its language, and performed valuable services for Yiddish literature. The foundations of independent immigrant cultural life are in the later 1890's, when the renewed Zionist movement also became its main guiding star. These were years of concerted efforts by native Jewry to establish English Jewish social and cultural footholds in the immigrant quarters, culminating in Whitechapel with the opening of the Jewish Institute (later Adler House) in 1905.[84] Within its walls, both lecturer and *maggid* held the platforms on Friday evenings, Jewish ministers aided their voluntary clients with guidance and advice, and the venerable communal *Beth Midrash* was housed for pious study. The Whitechapel Public Library and Free Art Gallery (where J. L. Cahan sat from 1901 to 1904 recording the folklore of arriving immigrants), and Toynbee Hall's and other settlements' facilities, established for the welfare of the East End, had substantial Jewish immigrant participation.[85] After some early flickerings, the Yiddish press came to life and the seeds of Zionism sprouted at the close of the 1890's, and quasi-autonomous cultural life reached its peak. Rabbinic culture enjoyed a mild flourishing with the presence of East European rabbis of some note, and Hebraic interests secured a firm if small niche. Yiddish cultural life at a higher level did not fare quite so well. Its press expanded consistently until 1914, but the results of fostering Yiddish bellelettres and theatre were less encouraging.

[84] *JC*, March 22, 1912.
[85] Jacob Shatzky, *Yehuda Leib Cahan (1881–1937)*, N.Y., 1938, pp. 12–14; (Henrietta Barnett), *Canon Barnett His Life, Work, and Friends*, London, 1921, pp. 397–460, 563–69; there is also a Yiddish broadside advocating the establishment of a public library in the collection of Mr A. R. Rollin.

X

CONCLUSION: JEWISH IMMIGRATION IN MODERN ENGLISH AND JEWISH HISTORY

Jewish migrations are a complex but convincing example of the relations between Jewish and general historic phenomena. Between the earlier years of the nineteenth century and 1930 occurred the heaviest voluntary migration of people known in history. The preferred destination of the 62,000,000 persons who crossed international frontiers in this age of relative 'free trade' in human movement was the American Union, but areas in both hemispheres felt deep effects.[1] South America, South Africa, and Australia were invigorated by the tides of immigration hardly less than the United States. On the other hand, migration, even of such dimensions, was itself partly an aspect of such pervasive nineteenth century trends as industrial development, urban growth, and strivings for personal freedom. Under the heading of migration one may well include tens of millions more who crossed no political boundary, yet traversed an economic frontier by pulling up stakes from a farm or village community and settling in an industrial city within their own country. The social consequences of these immense movements are too diverse for neat summary, but one immediate outcome of entry into mobile social structures was the disintegration of the patriarchal family and fixed personal status, as part of a profound disruption of venerable habits of life.

Each of these considerations applies with intensity to contemporaneous Jewish migrations. The number of migrating Jews, nearly all European, attained a total over 3,000,000 between 1840 and 1914.[2] Furthermore, Jewish migration

[1]Maurice R. Davie, *World Immigration*, N.Y., 1936, pp. 11–12; Walter F. Willcox, ed., *International Migrations*, National Bureau of Economic Research, 2 vols., N.Y., 1929–1931, I, pp. 81–88.

[2]Arthur Ruppin, *Die Soziologie der Juden*, 2 vols., Berlin, 1930, I, pp. 130–36; ———, *The Jewish Fate and Future*, London, 1939, pp. 44–45.

within national frontiers is important in order to appreciate the significance of the international movement, for it too is an integral part of the migration and of the related trends to urbanization and industrial growth. Hundreds of thousands of Jews populated such new East European Jewish metropolises as Warsaw, Odessa, and Lodz in the nineteenth century without leaving Russia, at the same time as even greater numbers crossed seas and borders to settle in New York, Chicago, London, Paris and Buenos Aires. These millions of people profoundly transformed the economic and social face of Jewry in the nineteenth and early twentieth centuries by transferring the majority of their people from small cities and villages to metropolitan centres. The immediately visible result of urbanization was a rather foul slum zone and a knotty problem of health and housing for the new city dwellers, and a need to acclimate them to the unfamiliar routines of large city life. The physical problems of the Jewish quarters did not vanish until the areas were torn down (or, as in London, bombed out) or the Jews abandoned them. Further under the surface, the withdrawal of the traditional socio-religious controls opened a cultural and psychological void not easily filled, although at the same time the persistence and vigour of a wide range of religious and cultural life is noteworthy.

However, the differences between Jewish and general migration are no less significant than some of the similarities already mentioned. Unlike typical migrants, the Jews were not peasants or illiterates; the cultural baggage which they carried contained folklore but was basically a conscious historic culture; and migrations were common experience, if not in their own lives, then in the historic experience of the Jewish people. The ratio of males to females is more nearly equal than among any other migratory group in England, clearly suggesting a migration by families (although often split up), with no intention to return to the 'old home'. European Jews did not live in metropolitan centres, of which in any case there were few before the nineteenth century, but they were nonetheless a town-dwelling people. Although we may seek causes of Jewish migration among general factors, there is an irreducible residue of distinctly Jewish motives.

MIGRATION'S IMPACT UPON JEWRY

Basic changes confronted every Jew who moved from East to West as soon as he set foot upon the new soil. Some goals which had been the object of generations of struggle were automatically realized and others were rapidly achieved. In Eastern Europe, the movements to emancipate the Jews from old and new disabilities, to westernize their social and cultural life, to dissolve the millenial identity of the synagogue and the Jewish community, inched forward with painful slowness. The multitude of legal, residential, economic and educational restrictions officially ended in Eastern Europe only at the close of the first World War, but they all vanished with the first breath of English air. The *Haskalah*, a pervasive current in Jewish life beginning with the European Enlightenment, reached Eastern Europe early in the nineteenth century to expound its doctrine of social and cultural westernization— adoption of the language and dress of the non-Jewish environment, economic diversification, a Hebraic humanistic education with general studies instead of Talmudic scholasticism, elevation of the status of women. In contrast to the relatively slow progress of the Russian *Haskalah*, which had hardly reached the small towns where most of the immigrants originated, change came rapidly in England, at least externally, with an immigrant's arrival. Dress changed and then language, at least among those who were young enough to convert painlessly; the economic and educational position of women rose. Moreover, all of this occurred without exhortation or literary didacticism. With so much gained at a stroke, a *Haskalah* programme as a means to secure emancipation became outdated, while life in England imposed requirements which made further preaching of Westernization quite superfluous. Once in England, however, East European Jews moved speedily in the direction of Anglicization and assimilation into English culture, not toward enlightened Hebraic rationalism. Not Hebrew but halting English replaced Yiddish even in many inner Jewish matters, while immigrant life was disconcertingly unwilling to mend its ways even in matters so slight as a decorous religious service. Awareness soon came that not Westernization but erosion was the problem affecting Judaism in England.

Nor is this yet a full reckoning of the transformations brought about by settlement in a Western country where the Jews had been emancipated. Officially or unofficially, the old East European Jewish communities still exercised powerful influence over personal life, especially in such older cities as Vilna and Cracow and in the small towns. All such forms of communal constraint vanished with settlement in England, where also none of the Jewish community's financial cost was obligatory. Judaism in the West became secularized as the synagogue declined from its central dominant role to become one Jewish institution among many, and as 'Jewishness', i.e. consciousness of being a Jew, and even active communal participation, flourished without 'Judaism', i.e. personal observance of the religious tradition. This evolution was very slow among England's native Jews; indeed, a secular form of communal organization took hold quicker among the immigrants with their multiplicity of independent associations which existed for many diverse purposes.

The personal relations between native and immigrant Jews were distant, and feelings of mutual disdain were heard from both quarters. Yet there remained considerable fellow-feeling, enough to preserve the sense of being a single community in law and in fate. However, the native oligarchs remained determined that despite the numerical preponderance of foreign Jews, the official Jewish community would remain thoroughly English, and in this they were signally successful. On the other side, pious Jews were disturbed by this community's infirm orthodoxy; Hebraists and Zionists took offence at its indifference to their cause; immigrants on the left assailed its ruling class; all disliked its patently condescending air toward them. Notwithstanding frictions and occasional eruptions, the Jewish community maintained itself as one body and slowly made peace with the immigrant element whose children largely assumed control in the 1930's and 1940's.

The effect of urban life upon former small town residents must not be overemphasized. The Jews did not abandon their old workshop scale of labour to enter the English industrial

s

system, but found a place for its continuance within their special trades. For these and other reasons, the Jewish immigrant group formed its separate sub-economy, although making contact at every point with the general English economy. But the distinctness has not disappeared to this day, when the Jews possess no separate economic life but are distinguishable from the population at large by certain trends as a group.

ENGLAND AND THE JEWISH IMMIGRANT

England was not a country of immigration but of emigration. Quite aside from the impoverished masses who fled the Irish countryside in the nineteenth century, England herself sent forth millions of able-bodied emigrants throughout the nineteenth century. Despite preachers of imperialism vaunting the duty of populating the 'outposts of empire', they generally made their way to Canada or the United States.[3] The English view never regarded the mother country as a land of open spaces and unlimited opportunity, but rather as a place of restricted possibilities and fairly fixed social position, with emigration the alternative for the restless and ambitious. The English trade union, while making what improvements it could in the condition of its members, also sponsored an emigration fund to finance its members' movement to other lands. Churches, friendly and other societies, colonial Governments and the Home Government, local parish and Poor Law authorities, granted aid to emigrants from time to time. This outward balance of emigrant farmers and artisans far outweighed the Russian and Polish Jews who settled in London and the Midlands cities. The some 120,000 Jewish immigrants who settled in England provoked such public attention that they became a leading English political question.[4]

[3] S. C. Johnson, *A History of Emigration from the United Kingdom to North America*, London, 1913, passim; Walter F. Willcox, *op. cit.*, II, pp. 239–260.

[4] In addition to tracts on sweating, cited elsewhere, the following are some fairly typical statements: Robert Anderson, 'The Problem of the Criminal Alien', *The Nineteenth Century and After*, LXIX, No. 408 (February, 1911), pp. 217–24; 4th Earl of Dunraven, 'The Invasion of Destitute Aliens', *The Nineteenth Century*, XXXI, No. 184 (June, 1892), pp. 985–1000, by the Chairman of the House of Lords Commission on the Sweating System; W. Evans-Gordon, 'The Stranger Within Our Gates', *The Nineteenth Century and After*, XLIX, No. 408 (February, 1911), pp. 210–216; 'Foreign Undesirables', *Blackwood's Magazine*, CLXIX

Two attitudes seem to determine the attitude towards immigration. On one hand, unfeigned sympathy existed for the Jews under the Czar's rule in their sufferings. The English humanitarian tradition detested Czarist absolutism, and the constellation of international relations, at any rate before the Anglo-Russian rapprochement of 1907, implied no restraint upon Russophobia in England. Libertarian views and sympathy for Jewish sufferers inclined the English public to gaze pityingly upon the 'victims of persecution' who settled in England, and to accept tolerantly their peculiarities. All went well enough so long as economic conditions were not too unfavourable, and immigrant workmen did not appear as competitors but as refugees. The uncomplaining tolerance of immigrants varied from decade to decade with social conditions. They became an issue when social reform became a dominant concern in English politics. Thus, at a Guildhall meeting protesting new persecutions in Russia in 1890, the Rev. Hugh Price Hughes, a leading Dissenter and advocate of imperialism, denounced Russian oppression while observing that it brought to England 'a great number of Jews to take the bread out of our citizens' mouths'. As the 1880's closed, the position of the lower classes penetrated the public consciousness more than at any time after Chartist days forty years earlier. This time, however, attention focussed not on the factory workers but on the 'outcast classes'—widows, broken families of the poor, casual labourers, and working women and children.

(February, 1901), pp. 279–89; H. Hamilton Fyfe, 'The Alien and the Empire', *The Nineteenth Century and After*, LIV, No. 319 (September, 1903), pp. 414–19; James D. Whelpley, *The Problem of the Immigrant*, London, 1905. The writings of Arnold White are of interest: *Problems of a Great City*, London, 1886, new ed., London, 1895; 'The Invasion of Pauper Foreigners', *The Nineteenth Century*, XXIII, No. 133 (March, 1888), pp. 414–22; ed., *The Destitute Alien in Great Britain*, London and N.Y., 1892, 2nd ed., London and N.Y., 1895; 'Alien Immigration—a Rejoinder', *The Fortnightly Review*, N.S. LVII, No. 389 (March 1, 1895), pp. 501–07; 'Europe and the Jews', *Contemporary Review*, LXXII (November, 1897), pp. 733–742 (on Herzl's views); 'A Typical Alien Immigrant', *Idem*, LXXIII (February, 1898), pp. 241–250; *The Modern Jew*, London, 1899. Writings in the aliens' defence are: Geoffrey Drage, 'Alien Immigration', *The Fortnightly Review*, N.S. LVII, No. 337 (January 1, 1895), pp. 37–46; Stephen N. Fox, 'The Invasion of Pauper Foreigners', *Contemporary Review*, LIII (June, 1888), pp. 855–67; M. J. Landa, *The Alien Problem and Its Remedy*, London, 1912. Representative of more impartial study are W. Cunningham, *Alien Immigration to England*, London 1897; E. Manson, 'The Admission of Aliens', *The Journal of the Society of Comparative Legislation*, N.S. IV (December, 1902), pp. 114–27.

[5]*Persecution of the Jews in Russia*, London, 1890, pp. 97–8.

It was the decade of Charles Booth's voluminous examination of London life and labour (in which the Jews received considerable attention), and of efforts to elevate the 'outcast' by such movements as the Salvation Army, university settlements, and housing reform. The 'new unionism' and the rebirth of English socialism dazzled or worried the public with their meteoric ascent. Much of the concern with social problems was illustrated by examples drawn from the East End of London, so the Jews of that district received unprecedented publicity. The evils of sweated work which agitated the public were quickly associated with the Jews, although sweating in the Jews' special trades preceded the Jews, and infested industries where no Jewish worker was to be found. Thus, a misleading nexus between the Jews and sweating became fixed in the public mind which endured for many years. As soon became clear, an attack on sweated work required detailed legislation and enforcement, while to single out the most conspicuous and least popular segment of the sweated labour force and prevent their immigration held greater political appeal.[6] The various programmes of social reform which jockeyed for position before the people from 1885 to 1905 necessarily had to decide on the significance of immigration, and what if anything they proposed to do about it.

On the far left of the politics of the day, all socialist groups rejected anti-alien measures out of hand as quack medicine for far greater ills. Some, like William Morris in the heroic years of the movement, were converts to the inevitability of world revolution, and derided the barriers between the worker-revolutionaries in every country. Socialists of the Fabian persuasion, engaged in plans for comprehensive social reform, condemned restriction of immigration as an absurd palliative for problems which the dominant classes would not touch. Some socialists' acceptance of poor Jews' entry was perversely coupled with anti-Semitic views in general.[7] However, the

[6]Elie Halevy, *Imperialism and the Rise of Labour* (*A History of the English People in the Nineteenth Century*, V), 2nd ed., London, 1951, pp. 371–72, 374.

[7]Edmund Silberner, 'British Socialism and the Jews', *Historia Judaica*, XIV, 1 (April, 1952), pp. 27–52; John Burns' remarks on the Aliens Bill of 1904 in *Parliamentary Debates*, 4th series, vol. 133, cols. 1149–50, 1158–60 (April 25, 1904). On Hyndman, see 'Jewish Labour News', *JC*, April 1, 1904.

early Labour Party minimized nationalist appeal and scorned racism, while the approach to foreign affairs in these early years of its career was marked by near-pacifist idealism. The Labourites refused to allow aliens to bear the onus for the East End's perennial social problems, with which many early leaders were intimately familiar as residents or social workers.

The Liberal Party, especially its Gladstonian traditionalists, regarded free access to England as an unshakable aspect of Free Trade, and were not to be convinced that any harm was incurred by the unobstructed settlement of immigrants. Sir Charles Dilke, most leftward of Liberals, held the general opinion of social reformers that 'the prohibition of alien immigration is a sham remedy for very grave evils in the labour market'.[8] A younger man who shared the same conviction, C. P. Trevelyan, studied the relation between alien immigration and sweating, and felt 'thankful to them [aliens] for turning the searchlight of public reprobation on a system which our own people suffer in common with them'.[9] Young Winston Churchill, then M.P. for a considerably Jewish constituency in Manchester, concluded, in common with general sentiment in his Party, that there were not

. . . any urgent or sufficient reasons, racial or social, for departing from the old tolerant and generous practice of free entry and asylum to which this country has so long adhered and from which it has so greatly gained.[10]

It was among the Tories that immigration restriction ultimately made headway, particularly in Disraeli's most direct intellectual descendants, the Chamberlain wing of the Party. This group took interest in moderate social reform and vigorously promoted imperialism; its conservative, social, national outlook was analogous to such parties on the Continent to an extent seldom found among English political

[8]*Idem*, vol. 8, col. 1080 (February 11, 1893).
[9]*Idem*, vol. 133, col. 1080 (April 25, 1904).
[10]Letter to Nathan Laski, printed in *The Times*, May 31, 1904, repr. *JC*, June 3, 1904 and Oskar K. Rabinowicz, *Winston Churchill on Jewish Problems*, London, 1956, pp. 50–53, which contains full information on his views in the matter. For the Liberal leaders' views, see Henry Campbell-Bannerman, *Speeches . . . 1899–1908*, London, 1908, pp. 165–67; Asquith's remarks in *Parliamentary Debates*, 4th series, vol. 133, cols. 1094–99 (April 25, 1904).

278 JEWISH IMMIGRANT IN ENGLAND 1870-1914

groups.[11] The Chamberlain wing of the Conservative Party was indifferent to Free Trade, and its attitude gradually grew into an inclination to scrap entirely this cornerstone of finance and politics. This supplied the most hotly fought political issue in the first years of the century and brought defeat to the Conservative Party in an historic election in 1905. Although Chamberlain's conservatism was quite unalloyed by the Christian overtones of cognate Continental movements, it was rather influenced by the vogue of racial theory such as diffused by Houston Stewart Chamberlain's writings. Racism's pragmatic meaning, anti-Semitism, was hardly transplanted to England, but the concept of racial differences and an ardour to preserve the 'purity' of a racial stock did become elements in the climate of opinion, even in Liberal Imperialist circles.[12] It also cast somewhat of a spell over Sidney and Beatrice Webb.[13] Some thousands of unprepossessing-looking Jewish immigrants making shabby homes in England constituted the main racial threat from within to Anglo-Saxondom, especially because 'the best Blood of the country' was flowing out among native emigrants.[14] The full depths of racism, requiring not mere anti-alienism but anti-Semitism towards all Jews, including apostates and their children, were never plumbed. England no less than the Jews resisted such movements. The influence of racial thinking in public affairs (aside from a feeling of diplomatic kinship with Germany because of supposed racial community)[15] did not penetrate much beyond anti-alienism, whose advocates, be it noted, seldom wearied of reiterating that they bore no animus against the Jews as such.[16] The origins of the Aliens Act of 1905 lie in the search for politically profitable protectionism and in the modern superstition of race.

[11]Elie Halevy, *op. cit.*, pp. 226–36, 243, 286–87, 302, 322–28.

[12]Caustically treated by J. A. Hobson, *Imperialism*, 3rd ed., London, Allen & Unwin, 1948, pp. 153–285; but the same author's *Problems of Poverty*, London, 1891, pp. 59–62 is anti-alien verging on anti-Semitic. Arnold White's writings are anti-alien at their outset, but shift to anti-Semitism; for his views at their ripest, see Cd. 1742, Min. 329-32, 920–24, 1134–51.

[13]Sidney and Beatrice Webb, *Industrial Democracy*, 2 vols., London, 1897, II, pp. 698 n, 744 n.

[14]James Lowther's phrase, in *Parliamentary Debates*, 4th series, vol. 8, col. 1165 (February 11, 1893).

[15]Elie Halevy, *op. cit.*, pp. 41–52.

[16]See Chaim Weizmann's sympathetic remarks on Major Evans-Gordon in his *Trial and Error*, N.Y., 1949, pp. 90–91.

There is an interaction between English and American thinking about immigration. Before the Aliens Act of 1905, English advocates of restriction pointed to the United States, an ampler land, as a country which nevertheless saw the need for prudent limitation of immigration.[17] With the Act on the books, the shoe was on the other foot. Americans dissatisfied with the very moderate forms of immigration control in their country praised the English example, which granted wide powers to officers and *ad hoc* immigration tribunals of private citizens to exclude immigrants from landing. As western countries heightened the barriers to immigration, the United States' policy ended by being sterner than England's. The effects of the Aliens Act itself were more psychological than legal; discussion of emigration in Eastern Europe seems to have practically excluded England from consideration as a destination, and the decade before the outbreak of war is marked by the complete preponderance of America. The diminution of immigration to England after 1906 was greater than the terms of the Act warranted.

Political history aside, the Jewish immigrants made no unique contribution to the English economy. Fields other than tailoring were too minor or the Jews' numbers too few, save perhaps the early Jewish start in the cigarette industry, to be of moment. As to tailoring, the dominant immigrant trade, the cheap ready-made garments with which the Jews were so intimately associated would have clothed the people, though not so rapidly as they did, thanks to the labour of thousands of industrious Jewish tailors. Just as the Jews quickened one industrial process, they held back another—the shift to factory production in such trades as boot and shoe making, in which they concentrated only as long as they could work in shops, and left when alternatives to factory employment fell away. The Jews created no social problem not already existing, such as urban slums and congestion, even if their presence added to them in a few areas. The high rents which were the price of the immigrants' inclination to settle together

17Reports to the Board of Trade on Alien Immigration, C. 7113, 1893. The reports are the product of D. F. Schloss and John Burnett's study of immigration in the United States, conducted in 1892.

diverted the probable course of real-estate history by delaying
the conversion of their districts from residential to commercial
purposes. The swelling of urban Jewish quarters mildly
exacerbated Jewish-Gentile relations on the shifting fringes of
Jewish neighbourhoods, but nothing serious came of this
friction.

The immigrant cannot be said to have contributed to the
main stream of English cultural life. The immigrant community
conducted its cultural affairs autonomously, largely in Yiddish
and Hebrew, with its roots in Jewish history and its background in Eastern Europe; it was more in England than of it.
Gradually, however, the English experience, at first expressed
in the immigrant's tongue, was expressed in the English
language. The shift to English took place first on the plane of
cheap journalism and sometimes vulgar theatrics before it
ascended to a higher level. In considering the cultural vista
as a whole, it seems remarkable that so economically dis-
favoured a group could have had so much truck with sophisti-
cated forms of cultural expression. The children of immigrants,
or youthful immigrants educated in England, contributed
figures of some note to English arts and sciences, such as Louis
Golding (1895-1958), Harold Laski (1893-1950), Joseph
Leftwich (1894-   ), Maurice Samuel (1895-   ), Selig
Brodetsky (1888-1954), John Yudkin (1910-   ), Sir Lewis
Namier (1888-   ), Solomon (the pianist) (1903-   ),
Sir Jacob Epstein (1880-1959). The genius of Isaac Rosenfeld
(1892-1918), nurtured in the Jewish quarter, whose poems
began to reap recognition when their author was cut down in
the War, demands particular mention. These men started in
the immigrant environment and crossed the threshold of the
English literary and scientific and artistic worlds, and many of
them were consciously and creatively influenced by their background.

NATIVES, IMMIGRANTS, AND THE
JEWISH COMMUNITY

The immigration of Jews to England decisively altered the
Jewish community. In the forty years from 1880 it approximately quintupled from its original 60,000 not only by direct

addition from the dock-side but from the immigrants' high birth rate. Although the official community showed no basic structural change, the community as remade by immigrants profoundly revised the inner spirit and approach of the traditional bodies during the generations in which the great majority of Jews in England were foreign-born or the children of foreign-born parents. In external affairs the old community found itself out of joint also. English Jewry, so important in the nineteenth century concert of world Jewry because of its emancipated status and its wealthy and influential oligarchy at the centre of a great Empire, assumed a somewhat different aspect in the twentieth century. Now neither the Empire, the Jewish mercantile and financial oligarchy, nor the old manner of transacting Jewish business of international concern by private discussion and special intervention on the part of humanitarian powers, was any longer the pivotal fact it had been. A new factor replaced these outmoded forms of importance when Great Britain undertook the Government of Palestine under a mandate of the League of Nations. It contained the unprecedented commitment to aid in the development of the Jewish National Home, as had been promised in the Balfour Declaration. English Jews therefore became particularly important in the Zionist movement, which scorned nineteenth century methods of Jewish diplomacy in favour of a democratically organized mass movement, and naturally cast its lot with the mass of immigrants instead of the wealthy natives. The outlook of most of the latter left much to be desired from the Zionist standpoint. Between the Wars, the leadership of the movement which established the State of Israel was vested, outside of Palestine itself, in England.

Materials do not exist to construct a psychological inventory of the Jewish immigrant's view of England. No less a person than Ahad HaAm derided the English Jewish community as 'a cemetery with pretty gravestones',[18] and lesser figures were scarcely more complimentary. The philosopher's expectations and interests, however, were not those of a struggling immigrant, preoccupied with making a living and reuniting his

[18]Ahad HaAm, '*Igrot*, 6 vols., Jerusalem and Berlin, 1923–1925, IV, p. 15.

family, or with saving money to go to America. The latter remains the true hero and subject of any study of migration. His painful migration moved the geographical moorings of the Jewish people, and his hard life laid a firm foundation for large scale Jewish life in lands of freedom.

APPENDIX

		Russians	Russian Poles	Rumanians	Total
	M	1,724	4,385	Not	63,025
	F	789	2,671	Listed	37,613
1871		2,513	7,056		100,638
	M	2,639	6,097	64	74,097
	F	1,150	4,582	27	43,934
1881		3,789	10,679	91	118,031
	M	13,732	11,817	437	115,886
	F	9,894	9,631	297	82,227
1891		23,626	21,448	734	198,113
	M	34,013	11,562	1,850	151,329
	F	27,776	9,493	1,446	96,429
1901		61,789	21,055	3,296	247,758
	M	33,312	17,289	1,992	167,762
	F	29,550	15,390	1,730	117,068
1911		62,862	32,679	3,722	284,830

ESTIMATES OF CHRISTIAN POLES IN ENGLAND AND WALES, 1871-1911

1871	1,500
1881	2,000
1891	3,500
1901	3,200
1911	3,500

Jerzy Zubrzycki, *Polish Immigrants in Britain*, The Hague, 1955.

For discussion of statistical problems, see Lloyd P. Gartner, 'Notes on the Statistics of Jewish Immigration to England, 1871-1914', *Jewish Social Studies*, XXI.

GLOSSARY OF HEBREW TERMS

'agunah: pl. *'agunot*, a deserted wife.

'aliyah, lit. ascent: migration to Palestine.

Ashkenazi, pl. *Ashkenazim*: German and East European Jews.

Beth Din: Jewish court.

Beth Midrash: a place for study of sacred literature, often serving as a synagogue or adjunct to one.

Dayan: judge, member of a *Beth Din*, q.v.

get, pl. *gittim* or *gittin*: Jewish bill of divorce, given by man to woman.

halakhah: Jewish law.

Haskalah: the westernizing enlightenment movement in European Jewry, which reached Eastern Europe in the mid-nineteenth century.

Hazan: a synagogue cantor.

heder, pl. *hadarim* (has various corruptions), lit. room: one room school, usually the teacher's house.

hebra, pl. *hebrot*: association, usually religious or charitable.

Hometz Bottel, corruption of *Bittul Hamez*: ceremonial removal of leavened foods, the day before Passover.

ketubah, pl. *ketubot*: Jewish marriage document, given by man to woman.

maskil, pl. *maskilim*: devotee of *Haskalah*, q.v.

melammed, pl. *melammedim*: teacher in a *heder*, q.v.

Minyan: quorum of ten men for public worship.

posek, pl. *posekim*: decisor, rabbinic respondent to a *she'elah*, q.v.

Sefardi, pl. *Sefardim*: Spanish Jew or descendant of a Spanish Jew.

shammash: synagogue sexton.

maggid, pl. *maggidim*: preacher.

she'elah: question in Jewish law submitted to a rabbi; cf. *posek*.

shehitah: slaughter of animals for food according to Jewish law.

shohet, pl. *shohetim*: slaughterer of animals for food according to Jewish law.

trefah: inedible meat according to Jewish law, owing to inherent nature (e.g. pig, shellfish), disease, or improper *shehitah* (q.v.) and handling.

yeshibah, pl. *yeshibot*: academy for Talmudic study.

BIBLIOGRAPHY

Archival Sources

Board of Deputies of British Jews, *Minute Books, 1871–1914.* At the offices of the Board, Woburn Square, London, W.C.2. (Add little to published records but occasionally contain details and correspondence.)

Board of Guardians and Trustees for the Relief of the Jewish Poor, *Minute Books.* 1859–1914. *Executive and Other Committees Minute Book.* 1869–1894. (Of great value.) (Similar records of the cognate bodies in Manchester and Liverpool yielded little of value.)

Eyges, T., *Zikhroines fun die Yiddishe Arbeter Bavegung in London, England* (Memoirs of the Jewish Labour Movement in London, England). MS. in Library of the YIVO Institute, New York. Covers the author's immigration to London c. 1887 as a boy of 14 or 15 and his activities in the local socialist milieu until c. 1895. Written c. 1942.

Homa, Bernard, M.D., L.C.C. Archive of the history of Machzikei HaDath, London. Broadsides, pamphlets, correspondence, 1892– .
Examined by Dr Homa's kind permission. Some of the material is published in his book, cited below.

Poor Jews' Temporary Shelter. *Minute Books.* 1885–1914. *Visitors' Book,* 1885– . At the Shelter, Mansell Street, London, E.1. (Occasional useful sidelights on immigration.)

Public Record Office   Home Office paper, file 45/B 1508A. Sweating, 1891.
Public Record Office.   Foreign Office papers, file 65. Consular Reports, Russian, 1886–1901.

Rollin, A. R., Archive of the Jewish labour and socialist movement. Periodicals, broadsides, a few letters, c. 1884–1895. Of indispensable importance. Examined and transcribed by kind permission of Mr Rollin; much of it now deposited in Library of the YIVO Institute, New York.

Stepney Jewish Lads' Club. *Minute Book.* 1900–1904. At the Club, Stepney Green, London, E.1. (Serviceable for youth work.)

United Synagogue. Council *Minute Book.* Executive *Minute Book,* 1871–1914. (Some Executive Minutes are valuable, but most add little to published records.) At the United Synagogue, Woburn Square, London, W.C.2.

Official Reports

Chief Inspector of Factories and Workshops. Annual Report for Year Ending 31st October . . . 1878–1914. (Occasional references to Jewish workshops.)

Medical Officers of Health. Annual Reports, 1880–1914. (Based on parish reports, but little Jewish material.)

Statistical tables relating to Emigration and Immigration from and into the United Kingdom, and Report to the Board of Trade thereon. 1876–1908. (Because of inadequate distinction between immigrants 'en route' and 'not stated to be en route' the figures are without value, except to the extent of illustrating fluctuations in the volume of immigration. Comments are sometimes useful.)

Reports of H.M. Inspector, with Statement as to the Expulsion of Aliens, 1907–1914.

Report on number and nationality of passengers leaving the United Kingdom, and destinations, 1905–1906. Net balances for previous years, 1907–1914. (Possesses the same deficiency as the earlier tables of emigration and immigration.)

Special Reports,
in Chronological Order

Report to the Board of Trade on the Sweating System in Leeds by the Labour Correspondent of the Board. [John Burnett] C. 5513, 1888. (S.P. 1887, LXXXVI, p. 561.)

Report to the Board of Trade on the Sweating System at the East End of London by the Labour Correspondent of the Board. [John Burnett] February 17, 1888. (S.P. 1887, LXXXIX, p. 253.) (Both of considerable value.)

House of Commons Select Committee on Emigration and Immigration (Foreigners). Report . . . Proceedings . . . Minutes of Evidence, and Appendix. I: July 27, 1888. II: August 8, 1889. (S.P. 1888, XI, p. 419; 1889, X, p. 265.) (Valuable appendices. Evidence is of some use.)

House of Lords Select Committee on the Sweating System. Report . . . Proceedings . . . Minutes of Evidence, and Appendix. I: August 11, 1888. II: December 20, 1888. III: May 24, 1889. IV: August 17, 1889. V: Appendix . . . Proceedings. 1890. (A mass of fact, autobiography, and fantasy, with useful appendices. Valuable but chaotic.) (S.P. 1888, XX, XXI; 1889, XIII, XIV; 1890, XVII, p. 257.)

Board of Trade. (Alien Immigration.) Reports on the Volume and Effects of Recent Immigration from Eastern Europe into the United Kingdom. C. 7406, 1894. (S.P. 1894, LXVIII, p. 341.) (Of the highest merit.)

Memorandum by Dr Theodore Thomson concerning arrival of Immigrants and Transmigrants in England, as to measures taken to prevent . . . cholera, and other infectious Diseases, 1896. (S.P. 1896, LXVII, p. 729.) (Informative.)

Census of England and Wales, 1901. County of Lancaster. Cd. 1002, 1902. County of London. Cd. 875, 1902. General Report; with Appendices. Cd. 2174, 1904. (S.P. 1902, CXIX, p. 389; CXX, p. 1; S.P. 1904, CVIII, p. 1.)

House of Commons and House of Lords. Reports from the Joint Select Committee of . . . on Housing of the Working Classes, 1902. (S.P. 1902, V, p. 801.)

Royal Commission on Alien Immigration. I: Report. Cd. 1742, 1903. II: Minutes of Evidence. Cd. 1742, 1903. III: Appendix. Cd. 1741–I, 1903. IV: Index and Analysis to Minutes of Evidence. Cd. 1743, 1904. (S.P. 1903, IX.) (Massive, with much information and considerable opinion. Fundamental.)

Interdepartmental Committee on Physical Deterioration. I: Report and Appendix. Cd. 2175, 1904. II: List of Witnesses and Minutes of Evidence. Cd. 2210, 1904. III: Appendix and General Index. Cd. 2186, 1904. (S.P. 1904, XXXII.) (Contains material on Jewish immigrant children).

Regulations, etc. Made by the Secretary of State for the Home Department with Regard to the Administration of the Aliens Act. Cd. 2879, 1906. (S.P. 1906, XCVI, p. 729.)

Report of an Enquiry by the Board of Trade into the Earnings and Hours of Labour of Workpeople of the United Kingdom. II: Clothing Trades in 1906. Cd. 4844, 1909. (S.P. 1909, LXXX, p. 325.) (Statistical. Difficult to extract Jewish material.)

Expulsion of Aliens. Correspondence between the Secretary of State for the Home Department and His Honour Judge Rentoul, K.C., March 11, 1909. (S.P. 1909, LXX, p. 527.) (The jurist exaggerated the ineffectiveness of deportations and H. J Gladstone challenged him.)

Census of England and Wales, 1911. Volume IX. Birth-places. . . . Ages and Occupations of Foreigners. Cd. 7017, 1913. (S.P. 1913, LXXVIII, p. 1.)

Report of the Departmental Committee on the Establishment of a Receiving-House for Alien Immigrants at the Port of London. I: Report and Appendix. Cd. 5575, 1911. II: Minutes of Evidence. Cd. 5576, 1911. (S.P. 1911, X.) (On the effect of the Aliens Act of 1905.)

Royal Commission on Divorce and Matrimonial Causes. Report. Cd. 6478, 1912. Minutes of Evidence. Cd. 6479, 6480, 6481, 1912. (S.P. 1912-1913, XVIII, XIX, XX.) (On the problem of Jewish 'Irregular divorces'.)

London County Council. East London Water Company—Alleged Failure of Supply. 10 March, 1896.

London County Council. London Water Supply. Report of the Water Committee. 1900.

London County Council. The Housing Question in London, 1900. (Official account of housing improvements, 1855–1900)

(City of Manchester.) Report on the Health of the City of Manchester, 1899; 1900; by James Niven (Medical Officer of Health). (Contains studies of Jewish areas.)

Organizations and Institutions

Brady Street Club for Working Boys. Annual Reports, 1895–1896 ff. (Not all available. On youth work.)

Board of Guardians for the Relief of the Jewish Poor. Annual Reports. 1859 ff. (Informed evaluations and precise data.)

Russo-Jewish Committee. Annual Reports, 1882 ff. (Only a few available. Its Conjoint Committee with the Jewish Board of Guardians published separate reports which are contained in the Annual Reports of the latter body.)

Poor Jews' Temporary Shelter. Annual Reports, 1885 ff. (Not all available. The Shelter had its finger on the pulse of immigration, perhaps more than any other organization.)

Jewish Association for the Protection of Girls and Women. Annual Reports. 1885 ff. (Only a few available. On travellers' aid and struggle against white slave trade.)

Trades Union Congress. Reports. 1875–77; 1894–95; 1904; 1906; 1909. (Complaints about sweating; anti-alien discussions; delegates from Jewish unions.)

Major Periodicals

Arbeiter Freind. Weekly with interruptions, London, 1885–1915. Socialist to 1892; anarchist thereafter.

Bet Va'ad laHakhamim. (Meeting House of the Wise). Monthly, Leeds, 1902–1904, ed. I. H. Daiches. Journal of rabbinic scholarship.

The Commonweal. Weekly, London, 1885–1890. William Morris pioneer socialist journal. Informative and sympathetic on Jewish 'comrades'.

HaEmet. Monthly, Vienna, 1877. The first socialist publication, ed. Aaron Liebermann. Largely written in London.

Die Fraye Velt. Monthly, London, 1891–1892. Socialist.

The Jewish Chronicle. Weekly, London, 1841–   . The organ of the Jewish community; inexhaustibly informative on Jewish communal affairs and hardly less so on other Jewish concerns.

The Jewish Year Book. Annual, London, 1896–   . Jewish communal almanac. L. J. Greenberg reviewed the aliens question annually, 1899–1906.

HaMaggid. Weekly, Lyck, Berlin, Cracow, London, 1856–1903. Extensive but not very good correspondence from England.

HaMeliz. Weekly and daily with interruptions, St Petersburg, Odessa, 1861–1904. Extensive but not very good correspondence from England.

MaMe'orer. Monthly, London, 1907–1908. J. H. Brenner's organ, important in Hebrew literary history.

Die Naye Tsayt. Weekly and fortnightly with interruptions, London, 1904–1908. Socialist.

The People's Press. Weekly, London, 1890–1891. John Burns' organ of the 'new unionism'. Attentive to Jewish labour.

The Polish Yidel. Weekly, London, 1884. After sixteen issues changed to *Die Tsukunft* (s.v.). The first Yiddish socialist publication, though somewhat furtive in its convictions.

Die Tsukunft. Weekly, London, 1884–1889. Continuation of *The Polish Yidel,* without its socialism after c. 1886.

HaYehudi. Weekly with interruptions, London, 1897–1913. The voice of the Hebraists.

Idisher Telefon. Weekly, London, 1897–1899(?). Popular.

Der Yudisher Emigrant. Fortnightly, St Petersburg, 1907–1914. The East European background to immigration.

T

Yudisher Ekspres. Weekly and daily, Leeds, 1896–1899; London, 1899– ? non vidi.

Die Yudishe Frayhayt. Monthly, London, 1905. Socialist-Zionist.

Yudisher Zhurnal. Daily, London, 1907–1944. Non vidi.

Zherminal. Fortnightly and monthly, London, 1900–1908. Anarchist literary journal, ed. R. Rocker.

Printed Books and Articles

Adamson, J. W., *History of Education in England, 1789–1902*, London, 1926.

Ahasverus, pseud., 'Baiting the Jew Baiter. By One Who Did It', *To-day*, I, 1 (January, 1884), pp. 55–57.

'The Alien Immigrant', *Blackwood's Magazine*, CLXXIII (January, 1903), pp. 132–41.

American Social Science Association. Social Economy Department. Papers. *The Sweating System in Europe and America*, n.p., n.d. (Boston, 1892).

Anderson, Robert, 'The Problem of the Criminal Alien', *The Nineteenth Century and After*, LXIX, No. 408 (February, 1911), pp. 217–25.

Aronides, pseud., 'The Problem before Anglo-Jewry', *Contemporary Review*, CII (July, 1912), pp. 57–65.

Aronfeld, C. C., 'Jewish Enemy Aliens in England during the First World War', *Jewish Social Studies*, XVIII, 4 (October, 1956), pp. 275–83.

Atkins, Robert, *A Compendious History of the Israelites*, London, 1810.

Baernweither, J. M., 'Die Statistik ueber die Arbeitslose in England', *Archiv fuer Soziale Gesetzgebung und Statistik*, I, 1 (1888), pp. 43–68.

(Barnett, Henrietta,) *Canon Barnett His Life, Work, and Friends . . .* London, 1921.

Barnett, Lionel D., ed. and trans., *El Libro de los Acuerdos Being the Records and Accompts of the Spanish and Portuguese Synagogue of London*, Oxford, 1931.

Baumann, Arthur A., 'The Lords' Committee on the Sweating System', *The National Review*, XII, No. 68 (October, 1888), pp. 145–59.

———, 'Possible Remedies for the Sweating System', *The National Review*, XII, No. 69 (November, 1888), pp. 289–307.

Beer, M., *Fifty Years of International Socialism*, London, Allen & Unwin, 1935.

———, *History of British Socialism*, new ed., repr. London, Allen & Unwin, 1948.

Behrman, S.N., *Duveen*, New York, 1952.

Beilin, A., *In die Shvartse Teg* (In the Black Days), London, 1907.

———, 'Y. H. Brenner beLondon' (J. H. Brenner in London), *HaTekufah*, XIV–XV (1922), pp. 646–71.

Bein, Alex, *Theodor Herzl*, Philadelphia, 1940.

Benjamin, Lewis S. (Lewis Melville), 'The Passing of the English Jew', *The Nineteenth Century and After*, LXXII, No. 427 (September, 1912), pp. 491–504.

Bentwich, Herbert, *The Administration of the Aliens Act*, London, 1906.

Bentwich, Margery and Norman, *Herbert Bentwich, The Pilgrim Father*, Jerusalem, 1940.

Bentwich, Norman, 'Jewish Educational Disorganization in London', *The Jewish Review*, III, No. 16 (November, 1912), pp. 355–66.

Berlin, M., *MiVolozhin 'ad Yerushalayim* (From Volozhin to Jerusalem), 2 vols., Tel Aviv, 1939.

Berlin, Nafthali Zvi Judah, *Meshib Dabar* (Responsa), Warsaw, 1894.

Bernstein, Eduard, 'Einige Bemerkungen ueber die Juedische Einwanderung in England', A. Nossig, ed., *Juedische Statistik*, Berlin, 1903, pp. 336–44.

Besant, Sir Walter, *East London*, New York, 1901.

Black, I. I., *Shebiley haYahadut be'Angliah. The Paths of Judaism in England*, Manchester, 1903.

Blank, Joseph E., *The Minutes of the Federation of Synagogues*, London, 1912.

Bloom, Herbert I., *The Economic Activities of the Jews of Amsterdam in the Seventeenth and Eighteenth Centuries*, Williamsport, Pa., 1937.

Board for Administering the Affairs of Shehitah, *Laws*, London, 1880.

Booth, Charles, 'The Inhabitants of Tower Hamlets (School Board Division), their Condition and Occupations', *Journal of the Royal Statistical Society*, L. 2 (June, 1887), pp. 326–91.

———, ed., *Life and Labour of the People of London*, 9 vols., London, 1892–1897.

Boulton, Harold E., 'The Housing of the Poor', *Fortnightly Review*, N. S. XLIII, No. 254 (February 1, 1888), pp. 279–86.

Brenner, Joseph Hayyim, *Me'Eber liGebulin* (Beyond the Boundaries), London, 1907.

———, *'Igarot* (Letters), ed., M. Poznansky, 2 vols., Tel Aviv, 1941.

Buechner, Ludwig, *Die Entshtehung un Entwiklung fun Religion* (The Origin and Development of Religion), London, 1909.

Burgin, Herz, *Die Geshikhte fun der Idisher Arbayter Bavegung in America, Rusland un England* (History of the Jewish Labour Movement in America, Russia and England), New York, 1915.

Cadbury, Edward and Shann, George, *Sweating* (Social Service Handbooks, No. V), London, 1907.

The Case of Henry Simons, A Polish Jew Merchant . . . London, 1753.

'The Child of the Alien', *The Social Democrat*, VII, 8 (August 15, 1903), pp. 473–76.

Chotzinoff, Samuel, *A Lost Paradise: Early Reminiscences*, New York, 1955.

Chotzner, Joseph, *Zichronoth; or Reminiscences of a Student of Jewish Theology . . .* London, 1885.

Clapham, J. H., *An Economic History of Modern Britain*, 3 vols., Cambridge, repr. 1950–1952.

Cohen, J. M., *The Life of Ludwig Mond*, London, 1956.

Collet, Clara E., 'Women's Work in Leeds', *The Economic Journal*, I, 3 (September, 1891), pp. 460–73.

Colquhoun, P., *A Treatise on the Police of the Metropolis*, 6th ed., London, 1800.

Connell, Brian, *Manifest Destiny*, London, 1953.

'The Crisis in the Boot and Shoe Trade', *The Labour Gazette*, III, 3 (March, 1895), pp. 80–81.

Crory, W. Glenny, *East London Industries*, London, 1876.

Cunningham, W., *Alien Immigration to England*, London, 1897.

Daiches, David, 'My Father, and His Father', *Commentary*, XX, 6 (December, 1955), pp. 522–33.

———, 'Trebbler, Bleggages, Persians', *The New Yorker*, XXX, 18 (June 19, 1954), pp. 78 ff.

———, *Two Worlds*, New York, 1956.

Daiches, Israel Hayyim, *Derashot MaHaRYaH* (Sermons), Leeds, 1920.

———, *Mikveh Yisrael . . . Concerning the fitness for use of Ritual Baths supplied by modern Water-works*, Leeds, 1912.

———, '*Eyn Yisrael* (The Well of Israel), Leeds, 1912.

———, *Netibot Yerushalayim* (Commentary on the Palestinian Talmud), London, 1926.

Dainow, H., *Address Delivered by the Russian Maggid . . . December 30th, 1876*, London, 1877.

Davie, Maurice R., *World Immigration*, New York, 1936.

Dobbs, S. P., *The Clothing Workers of Great Britain*. (Studies in Economics and Political Science No. 96), London, 1928.

Drage, Geoffrey, 'Alien Immigration', *The Fortnightly Review*, N.S. LVII, No. 337 (January 1, 1895), pp. 37–46.

———, 'Alien Immigration', *Journal of the Royal Statistical Society*, LVIII (March, 1895), pp. 1–35.

Druyanov, Alter, *Ketabim leToledot Hibbat Zion* (Documents on the History of the Lovers of Zion), 3 vols., Odessa, Tel Aviv, 1919, 1925, 1932.

Dubnow, S. M., *History of the Jews in Russia and Poland*, 3 vols., Philadelphia, 1916–1918.

Dunraven, 4th Earl of, 'The Invasion of Destitute Aliens', *The Nineteenth Century*, XXXI, No. 184 (June, 1892), pp. 985–1000.

Duschinsky, Charles, *The Rabbinate of the Great Synagogue, 1756–1842*, Oxford, 1921.

Dyche, John A., 'The Jewish Workman', *Contemporary Review*, LXXIII (January, 1898), pp. 35–50.

———, 'The Jewish Immigrant', *Contemporary Review*, LXXV (March, 1899), pp. 379–99.

———, 'My Tour in Europe', *The Ladies Garment Worker*, V, 4 (April, 1914), pp. 1–4; 6 (June, 1914), pp. 1–8.

Dyos, H. J., 'Railways and Housing in Victorian London', *The Journal of Transport History*, II, 1 (May, 1955), pp. 11–21; 2 (November, 1955), pp. 90–100.

Eccarius, J. G., *Der Kampf des Grossen und des Kleinen Kapitals oder Die Schneiderei in London*, Leipzig, 1876.

Eddy, J. P., *The Mystery of 'Peter the Painter'*, London, 1946.

Elbogen, Ismar, 'Briefwechsel zwischen Leopold Zunz und Frederick David Mocatta', *Gaster Anniversary Volume*, London, 1936, pp. 144–54.

'Elementary Education in England, No. III', *The School Board Chronicle*, XXI, 2 (July 8, 1871), pp. 242–44.

Elman, Peter, 'The Beginnings of the Jewish Trade Union Movement in England', *Transactions of the Jewish Historical Society of England*, XVII (1951–1952), pp. 53–62.

Emden, Jacob, *Megillat Sefer* (Autobiography), ed., David Kahana, Warsaw, 1896.

Evans-Gordon, W., *The Alien Immigrant*, London, 1903.

———, 'The Stranger Within Our Gates', *The Nineteenth Century and After*, LXIX, No. 408 (February, 1911), pp. 210–16.

'The Evolution of the Boot and Shoe Trade' by A Practical Boot-maker, *The Social-Democrat*, II, 3 (March, 1898), pp. 75–76.

Federation of East London Labour Unions, *Rules*, London, 1890.

Feigenbaum, B., *Elisha ben Avuyah, Lives of Jewish Free-thinkers of Ancient Times*, London, n.d.

———, *Fun Vanen Shtamen die Hayntige Iden?* (What is the Origin of Today's Jews?), London, 1910.

———, *Fun Vanen Shtamt der Mensh?* (What is the Origin of Man?), London, 1888.

———, *Die Idishe Hilf, oder: Vos iz die Makkeh un Vos iz die Refueh?* (The Jewish Aid, or: What is the Illness and What is the Cure?), Leeds, n.d. (c. 1890–1893).

———, *Die Idishe Inkvizitsie, Kedass Rakhmonim bnei Rakhmonim* (The Jewish Inquisition, According to the Religion of 'Merciful Children of Merciful Fathers'), London, 1906.

———, *Vie Kumt a Yud tsu Sotsializmus?* (How Comes a Jew to Socialism?), London, 1899, 2nd ed., London, 1900.

———, *Ver Hot Ayngefirt Yom Kippur un fun Vanen Shtamt die Torah?* (Who Introduced the Day of Atonement and What is the Origin of the Torah?), London, 1907.

Fersht, B. A., 'Chebrah Rodphea Sholom. . . . Notes upon the first Jewish Friendly Society in England', *Miscellanies of the Jewish Historical Society of England*, II (1935), pp. 90–98.

(Finn, J.,) *A Voice from the Aliens. About the Anti-Alien Resolution of the Cardiff Trade Union Congress*, London, n.d. (c. 1896).

Fischer, Paul, *Das Ostende von London. Ein soziales Nachtbild*, (Berliner Arbeiterbibliothek. II Serie), 2 vols., Berlin, 1891–1895.

'Foreign Undesirables', *Blackwood's Magazine*, CLXIX (February, 1901), pp. 279–89.

Fox, Stephen N., 'The Invasion of Pauper Foreigners', *Contemporary Review*, LIII (June, 1888), pp. 855–67.

Freehof, Solomon B., *The Responsa Literature*, Philadelphia, 1955.

Friedmann, Philipp, 'Wirtschaftliche Umschichtungsprozesse und Industrialisierung in der polnischen Judenschaft', *Jewish Studies in Memory of George Alexander Kohut*, New York, 1935, pp. 178–247.

Frumkin, Abraham, *In Friling fun Yidishn Sotsialism* (In the Springtime of Jewish Socialism), New York, 1940.

Fuchs, J. S., *An Hebrew Centre. Merkaz Ivri. A critical view of English Judaism*, London, 1909.

Fyfe, H. Hamilton, 'The Alien and the Empire', *The Nineteenth Century and After*, LIV, No. 319 (September, 1903), pp. 414–19.

Gartner, Lloyd P., 'Jewish Immigrants in London in the 1880's', *Essays on Jewish Life and Thought in Honour of Salo W. Baron*, New York, 1959, pp. 231–49.

———, 'Statistics of Jewish Immigration to England, 1870–1914', *Jewish Social Studies*, XXI.

Gelber, N. M., *Aus Zwei Jahrhunderten*, Vienna and Leipzig, 1924.

George M. Dorothy, *London Life in the XVIIIth Century*, 2nd ed., London, 1930.

Ginzberg, Asher, (pseud., Ahad HaAm), *Al Parashat Derakhim* (At the Crossroads), 4 vols., Berlin, 1921.

———, *'Igrot* (Letters), 6 vols., Berlin, 1923–1925.

Gnessin, Uri Nissan, *Ketabim* (Works), 3 vols., Merhaviah, 1946.

Goldfine, Marvin J., *The Growth of Zionism in England up to the World War*, Master's essay, Columbia University, 1939.

Gompers, Samuel, *Seventy Years of Life and Labour*, 2 vols., New York, 1923.

Goodman, Paul, *Zionism in England: English Zionist Federation, 1899–1929*, London, n.d. (c. 1929).

Gottlieb, Samuel Noah, *Sefer Oholey Shem* (Tents of Shem: bio-bibliographic directory of rabbis), Pinsk, 1912.

Greenberg, L. J., *Report upon the Status of the Jews in England* [to the Fourth World Zionist Congress], London, 1900.

Halevy, Elie, *A History of the English People in the Nineteenth Century*, V, VI, 2nd ed., London, repr. 1952.

Halpern, Georg, *Die Juedischen Arbeiter in London*, Berlin, 1903.

———, 'Die juedische Einwanderung-Bevoelkerung Londons', A. Nossig, ed., *Juedische Statistik*, Berlin, 1903, pp. 322–35.

Hansen, Marcus L., *The Atlantic Migration* 1607–1860, Cambridge, Mass., 1940.

Harris, Joseph, *Random Notes and Reflections*, Liverpool, 1912.

Henriques, Basil L. Q., *The Indiscretions of a Warden*, London, 1937.
Henriques, H. S. Q., *Jewish Marriages and the English Law*, Oxford, 1909.

Hillman, Samuel I., *'Or haYashar* (The Just Light), London, n.d. (c. 1926).

Hird, Frank, *The Cry of the Children*, London, 1898.

Hobson, J. A., *Imperialism*, 3rd ed., London, Allen & Unwin, repr. 1948.

———, *Problems of Poverty*, London, 1891.

Hoffman, David, *Melammed le Ho'il* (Responsa), 3 vols., Frankfurt-am-Main, 1926–1932.

Homa, Bernard, *A Fortress of Judaism in Anglo-Jewry*, London, 1953.

The Home and the Synagogue of the Modern Jew, London, n.d. (c. 1872).

Huldermann, Bernhard, *Albert Ballin*, London, 1922.

Hutchins, B. L., *Home Work and Sweating. The Causes and the Remedies* (Fabian Tract No. 130), London, 1907.

———, and A. Harrison, *A History of Factory Legislation*, 3rd ed., London, 1926.

Hyman, Aaron, *Bet Va'ad laHakhamim* (Key to Rabbinic Agadot), London, 1902.

———, *Toledot Tannaim vaAmoraim* (Biographies of Talmudic Teachers), 3 vols., London, 1910.

Jacobs, Joseph, *Statistics of Jewish Population in London*, 1873–1893, London, 1894.

———, *Studies in Jewish Statistics*, London, 1891.

Jaffe, Joseph, *'Alim liTerufah haSekhel vehaYezer* (Leaves for the Cure of Mind and Conscience), Manchester, 1895.

Jephson, Henry L., *The Sanitary Evolution of London*, London, 1907.

(Jewish Association for the Protection of Girls and Women,) *Official Report of the Jewish International Conference on the Suppression of the Traffic in Girls and Women*, held April 5th, 6th, and 7th, 1910, in London. 'Private and Confidential'. London, 1910.

'The Jewish Workman', *The Social Democrat*, II, 1 (January, 1898), pp. 19–20.

'The Jews in East London', *The Social Democrat*, VII, 2 (February, 1903), pp. 72–83.

Johnson, S. C., *A History of Emigration from the United Kingdom to North America, 1783–1912*, London, 1913.

Jones, Ernest, *The Life and Work of Sigmund Freud*, I, New York, 1953.

Joseph, N. S., *The 'New Departure' in Jewish Charity. An Address at the Inaugural Meeting of the Visiting and Bureau Departments of the Russo-Jewish Committee January 26th, 1893*. London, n.d. (1893).

Kahan, Israel Meir, *Nidhey Yisrael* (The Dispersed of Israel), Warsaw, 1894, reprinted with English trans., New York, 1951.

Kaplan, Stanley, 'The Anglicization of the East European Jewish Immigrant as seen by the London *Jewish Chronicle*, 1870–1897', *YIVO Annual of Jewish Social Science*, X (1955), pp. 267–78.

Katzenellenbogen, J. S., *Leyl Horef 'al peney Rehobot Mizrah London* (A Winter's Night upon the Streets of East London), London, 1908.

Kingsley, Charles, *Alton Locke, Tailor and Poet*, New York, 1850.

Kingsley, Charles (Parson Lot, pseud.), 'Cheap Clothes and Nasty', *Works*, London and New York, 1899, II, pp. 69–100.

Kissman, Joseph, *Studies in the History of Rumanian Jews in the 19th and the Beginning of the 20th Centuries*. (Yiddish). New York, 1944.

Kohn-Zedek, Joseph, *HaTorah vehaMizvah, Eleh Posekekha, Yisrael!* (Law and Commandment. These Be Thy Decisors, O Israel!), London, 1884.

Kraditor, L. S., 'Ven U. N. Gnessin iz Geven in London' (When U. N. Gnessin Was in London), *Yiddish London*, II (Winter, 1939), pp. 70–74.

Kranz, Philip, *Got, Religion un Moral* (God, Religion and Morality), London, 1906.

Landa, M. J., *The Alien Problem and Its Remedy*, London, 1911.

———, *The Jew in Drama*, London, 1926.

Lansbury, George, *Looking Backwards—and Forwards*, London, 1935.

Lascelles, Edward, 'Bethnal Green and Sunday Trading', *The Oxford House Magazine*, III, 11 (July, 1911), pp. 23–30.

Last, Isaac, ed., Menahem ben Solomon Meiri, *Magen Abot* (Shield of the Fathers), London, 1909.

Leppington, C. H. d'E., 'Side Lights of the Sweating Commission', *The Westminster Review*, CXXXVI, 3 (March, 1891), pp. 273–88; 5 (May, 1891), pp. 504–16.

Lestschinsky, J., *Der Idisher Arbayter (in London)*, Vilna, 1907.

Lewis, H. S., 'Jewish Education in London', *Jewish Education*, X, 2 (April-June, 1938), pp. 70–76. See also C. Russell.

Levy, A. B., *East End Story*, London, 1951.

Levy, Arnold, *History of the Sunderland Jewish Community*, London, 1956.

Levy, Nafthali, *Nahlat Naftali . . . Kodesh Naftali* (Responsa and Novellae), Pressburg, 1891.

Levy, S., 'Problems of Anglicization', *The Jewish Annual*, VI (1943–1944), pp. 80–88.

Lifschitz, Jacob, *Zikhron Ya'akob* (Memories of Jacob), I, Frankfurt-am-Main, 1924; II–III, Kovno, 1927–1930.

(Liebermann, A.,) 'HaYehudim beLondon', *HaEmet*, I, 3 (1877), pp. 43–46.

Lilienblum, M. L., *The Regeneration of Israel On the Land of His* (sic) *Forefathers*. Published by The 'B'nei Zion' Association for the Propagation of Jewish Nationalism and Colonization of the Holy Land. (N.p., N.d.) [London, c. 1882–1885].

Lindsay, Dorothy E., *Report upon a Study of the Diet of the Labouring Classes in the City of Glasgow*, Glasgow, 1913.

Lipman, V. D., *Social History of the Jews in England 1850–1950*, London, 1954.

———, *A Century of Social Service 1859–1959. The History of the Jewish Board of Guardians*. London, 1959.

———, 'Synagogal Organisation in Anglo-Jewry', *Jewish Journal of Sociology*, I, 1 (April, 1959), pp. 80–93.

Lissack, M., *Jewish Perseverance . . . : An Autobiography*, 2nd ed., London, 1851.

Lowndes, G. A. N., *The Silent Social Revolution: An Account of the Expansion of Public Education in England and Wales, 1895–1935*, London, 1937.

Maccoby, Hayyim Zundel, *'Imrey Hayyim* (Homilies), ed., M. Mansky, Tel Aviv, 1929.

Machzikey Hadass and Shomre Shaboss, *Laws*, London, 5653 (1893), 2nd ed., London, 1905.

MacDonald, J. Ramsay, 'Sweating—Its Cause and Cure', *The Independent Review*, II, 1 (February, 1904), pp. 72–85.

MacDonald, James, 'Government Sweating in the Clothing Contracts', *The New Review*, XI, 5 (November, 1894), pp. 471–74.

Macrosty, H. W., *Sweating: Its Cause and Remedy*, (Fabian Tract No. 50), London, 1895.

Magnus, Kate, *The Board of Guardians and the Men Who Made It*, London, 1909.

Malachi, E. R., 'Ver Iz Geven der Redaktor fun "HaShofar"?' (Who Was the Editor of HaShofar?), J. Shatzky, ed., *Zamlbukh liKhoved dem Zvey Hundert un Fuftsikstn Yovel fun der Yiddisher Presse, 1686–1936* (Collection in Honour of the 250th Anniversary of the Yiddish Press, 1686–1936), New York, 1937, pp. 315–317.

Mansion House Relief Fund, Liverpool Commission, *Memoir of Proceedings*, Liverpool, n.d. (1882).

Manson, E., 'The Admission of Aliens', *The Journal of the Society of Comparative Legislation*, N.S. IV (December, 1902), pp. 114–27.

Marmor, Kalman, *Der Onhayb fun der Yiddisher Literatur in America, 1870–1890* (The Beginning of Yiddish Literature in America), New York, 1944.

(———,) 'Die Elyen Bill fun der English Zionist Federation', (The Alien Bill of the English Zionist Federation), *Die Yudishe Frayhayt*, I, 2–3 (May-June, 1905), pp. 13–26.

———, 'Der Ershter Idisher Sotsialistisher Farayn' (The First Jewish Socialist Society), *Der Hammer*, V. 5 (May, 1931), pp. 36–41.

———, ed., *Ahron Liebermanns Brief* (Aaron Liebermann's Correspondence), New York, 1951.

Marr, T. R., *The Housing Problem in Manchester and Salford*, Manchester, 1905.

Masliansky, Zvi Hirsch, *Sefer haZikhronot vehaMassa'ot* (*Kitbey*, III) (Memoirs and Travels), New York, 1929.

Massel, Joseph, ed., and trans., *Shimshon haGibbor* (Milton's *Samson Agonistes*), Manchester, 1890.

Mayhew, Henry, *London Labour and the London Poor*, 4 vols., London, 1861.

Mew, James, 'Yiddish Literature and Drama', *Contemporary Review*, XCI (February, 1907), pp. 260–69.

Meyer, Mrs Carl, and Clementina Black, *Makers of Our Clothes: A Case for Trade Boards*, London, 1909.

Milne, William P., 'Selig Brodetsky', *The Journal of the London Mathematical Society*, XXX, 1 (January, 1956), pp. 121–25.

Mills, John, *The British Jews*, London, 1853.

'The Modern Jew', *Quarterly Review*, CLXXXIII, No. 365 (January, 1896), pp. 29–57.

Mohilever, Samuel, *Hikrey Halakhah uShe'elot uTeshubot* (Halakhic Studies and Responsa), ed., J. L. Fishman (Maimon), I, Jerusalem, 1944.

Montagu, Lily H., *My Club and I. The Story of the West Central Jewish Club*, London, n.d. (c. 1942).

Montefiore, Leonard G., 'Anglo-Jewry at the Cross-Roads', *The Jewish Review*, V, No. 26 (July, 1914), pp. 128–35.

Moore, Samuel, 'Das Sweating System in England', *Archiv fuer Soziale Gesetzgebung und Statistik*, I, 4 (1888), pp. 642–46.

(Moses, E., and Son,) *The Growth of an Important Branch of British Industry*, London, 1860.

Most, Johann, *Der Komunistisher Anarkhizmus* (Communist Anarchism), London, 1906.

———, *Die Aygenthums Bestie* (The Property Beast), ed. and trans., B. Feigenbaum, London, 1888.

———, *Die Religiyezze Magefeh* (The Religious Plague), London, 1901.

Mudie-Smith, Richard, *Religious Life of the People of London*, London, 1905.

———, ed., *Sweated Industries being a Handbook of the 'Daily News' Exhibition*, London, 1906.

Munby, D. L., *Industry and Planning in Stepney*, Oxford, 1951.

Myer, Morris, *Yiddish Theatre in London* 1902–1942, London, n.d. (In Yiddish).

National Anti-Sweating League, *A Short Bibliography of 'Sweating and . . . the Legal Minimum Wage'*, London, 1906.

————, *Report of Conference on a Minimum Wage*, London, 1907.

Neff, Wanda F., *Victorian Working Women . . . 1832–1850*, New York, 1929.

Nossig, Alfred, ed., *Judische Statistik*, Berlin, 1903.

Oesterley, W. O. E., *Walks in Jewry*, London, 1901.

Pasquet, D., *Londres et les ouvriers de Londres*, Paris, 1913.

Pearson, Karl and Margaret Moul, 'The Problem of Alien Immigration into Great Britain, Illustrated by an Examination of Russian and Polish Jewish Children', *Annals of Eugenics*, I (October, 1925), pp. 5–127.

Pépin, Ernest, *La question des étrangers en Angleterre*, Paris, 1914.

Pimlott, J. A. R., *Toynbee Hall. Fifty Years of Social Progress*, London, 1935.

Poliakoff, D., 'Tsionizmus fun a Sotsialistishen Shtandpunkt' (Zionism from a Socialist Standpoint), *Yudishe Frayhayt*, II, 3–4 (May-June, 1905), pp. 28–36.

Potter, Beatrice, 'The Sweating System, II', *The Charity Organisation Review*, IV, No. 37 (January, 1888), pp. 12–15.

————, 'East London Labour', *The Nineteenth Century*, XXIV, No. 138 (August, 1888), pp. 161–84.

————, 'Pages from a Work-Girl's Diary', *The Nineteenth Century*, XXIV, No. 139 (September, 1888), pp. 301–14.

————, 'The Lords and the Sweating System', *The Nineteenth Century*, XXVII, No. 160 (June, 1890), pp. 885–905.
See also Webb, Beatrice; Webb, Sidney and Beatrice.

Rabbinowitz, E. W., 'Sefer Zikkaron 5640–5650' (Memoirs, 1880–1890), *'Iyyim*, I (1928), pp. 66–74.

Rabbinowitz, Samuel J., *LiTekufot haYamim* (At the Appointed Seasons), Liverpool, 1917.

————, *Menuhat Shabbat (Shabbos Ruhe)* (Sabbath Rest), Liverpool, 1919.

————, *Yashresh Ya'akob* (Jacob Will Strike Root), Jerusalem, 1925.

Rabinowicz, Oskar K., *Winston Churchill on Jewish Problems*, London, 1956.

302   BIBLIOGRAPHY

Raffalovich, Isaiah, *Ziyyunim veTamrurim* (Notes and Embitterments), Tel Aviv, 1952.

Raven, Charles E., *Christian Socialism* 1848–1854, London, 1920.

Reisen, Zalman, *Leksikon fun die Yiddishe Literatur un Presse* (Lexicon of the Yiddish Literature and Press), ed., S. Niger, Warsaw, 1914. Second ed., 4 vols., Vilna, 1929.

Robson, William A., *The Government and Misgovernment of London*, London, Allen & Unwin, 1939.

Rocker, Rudolf, *In Shturem. Golus Yoren* (In Storm. Years of Exile), London and Buenos Aires, 1952.

———, 'Peter Kropotkin and the Yiddish Workers' Movement', Joseph Ishill, ed., *Peter Kropotkin, The Rebel, Thinker and Humanitarian*, Berkeley Heights, N. J., n.d. (c. 1923), pp. 78–85.

Rodker, J., 'The Theatre In Whitechapel', *Poetry and Drama*, I, 1 (March, 1913), pp. 43–44.

Rogers, William, *Reminiscences*, Comp. R. H. Hadden, 3rd ed., New York, 1888.

Rollin, A. R., 'The Jewish Contribution to the British Textile Industry', *Transactions of the Jewish Historical Society of England*, XVII (1951–1952), pp. 45–51.

Rose, Millicent, *The East End of London*, London, 1951.

Rosenbaum, S., 'A Contribution to the Study of the Vital and Other Statistics of the Jews in the United Kingdom', *Journal of the Royal Statistical Society*, LXVIII (September, 1905), pp. 526–66.

Roth, Cecil, *The Great Synagogue, 1690–1910*, London, 1948.

———, *A History of the Jews in England*, 2nd ed., Oxford, 1949.

———, *Magna Bibliotheca Anglo-Judaica*, London, 1937.

———, *The Rise of Provincial Jewry . . . 1740–1840*, London, 1950.

———, 'The Chief Rabbinate of England', *Essays in Honour of the Very Rev. Dr J. H. Hertz*, London, 5703 (1943), pp. 371–84.

Roth, Cecil, 'The Court Jews of Edwardian England', *Jewish Social Studies*, V, 4 (October, 1943), pp. 355–66.

———, 'The Lesser London Synagogues of the Eighteenth Century', *Miscellanies of the Jewish Historical Society of England*, III (1937), pp. 1–8.

————, 'The Portsmouth Community and Its Historical Background', *Transactions of the Jewish Historical Society of England*, XIII (1936), pp. 156–86.

Ruderman, B., 'Die Yiddish-Sotsialistishe Bavegung in England' (The Jewish Socialist Movement in England), *Freie Arbeter Shtimme*, weekly from September, 1924 to September, 1925.

Ruppin, Arthur, *The Jewish Fate and Future*, London, 1939.

————, *The Jews of To-day*, London, 1913.

————, *Soziologie der Juden*, 2 vols., Berlin, 1930.

Russell, C. and H. S. Lewis, *The Jew in London, a Study of Racial Character and Present-day Conditions* . . . London, 1900.

(Russo-Jewish Committee), *The Persecution of the Jews in Russia*, London, 1891.

(————,) *Russian Atrocities, 1881. Supplementary Statement*, London, 1882.

Samuelson, James, *The Lament of the Sweated*, London, 1908.

(Sandy's Row Synagogue), Society Hebrath Menahem Abelim Hesed veEmeth. Kindness and Truth. Sandy's Row Synagogue . . . *Rules and Regulations*, Revised 1867 . . . 1879, London, 1879.

Sayous, André-E., 'L'entre-exploitation des classes populaires à Whitechapel', *Mémoires et documents du musée social*, Année 1902, pp. 261–319.

————, 'L'immigration en Angleterre', *La Grande Revue*, IV, 1 (1900), pp. 229–44.

————, 'Les travailleurs de l'aiguille dans l'East End vers le milieu du xixᵉ siecle', *Revue d'économie politique*, XIII (October-November, 1899), pp. 861–77.

————, 'Whitechapel', *Revue économique internationale*, Année 20 (1928), III, 3, pp. 503–37.

Scharfstein, Zvi, *HaHeder beHayyey 'Amenu* (The *Heder* in the Life of Our People), New York, 1941.

Schechter, Solomon, 'Four Epistles to the Jews of England', *Studies in Judaism*, II, Philadelphia, repr. 1938, pp. 193–201.

————, 'The Hebrew Collection of the British Museum', *Studies in Judaism*, I, Philadelphia, repr. 1938, pp. 252–69.

Schewzik, Benjamin, *Teshubab 'al debar 'Efer HaNisrafin. Responsum with regard to the ashes of cremated bodies in which are explained some laws referring to this strange practice*. London, 1888.

Schiff, David Tebele, *Leshon Zahav* (Responsa and Novellae), Offenbach, 1822.

Schloss, David F., *Methods of Industrial Remuneration*, 3rd ed., London, 1898.

———, 'The Sweating System, I', *The Charity Organisation Review*, IV, No. 37 (January, 1888), pp. 1–12.

———, 'Healthy Homes for the Working Classes', *The Fortnightly Review*, N.S. XLIII, No. 256 (April 1, 1888), pp. 526–37.

———, 'The Sweating System', *The Fortnightly Review*, N.S. XLVII, No. 280 (April 1, 1890), pp. 532–51.

———, 'The Jew as a Workman', *The Nineteenth Century*, XXIX, No. 167 (January, 1891), pp. 96–109.

———, 'The Present Position of the "Sweating System" Question in the United Kingdom', *The Economic Review*, II, 4 (October, 1892), pp. 452–69.

———, 'The Dearness of Cheap Labour', *The Fortnightly Review*, N.S. LIII, No. 313 (January, 1893), pp. 54–63.

Schmelkes, Isaac, *Bet Yizhak* (Responsa), Przemsl, 1901.

Sekon, G. A., *Locomotion in Victorian London*, Oxford, 1938.

Selitrenny, L., 'The Jewish Working Woman in the East End', *The Social Democrat*, II, 9 (September, 1898), pp. 271–75.

Shatzky, Jacob, *Morris Rosenfeld in Likht fun Zayne Briev* (Morris Rosenfeld in the Light of His Letters), New York, 1936.

———, *Yehuda Layb Cahan* (1881–1937), New York, 1938.

———, ed., *Arkhiv far der Geshikhte fun Yidishn Teater un Drameh* (Archive for the History of Jewish Theatre and Drama), Vilna, New York, 1930.

———, ed., *Zamlbukh liKhoved dem Zvey Hundert un Fuftsikstn Yovel fun der Yiddisher Presse*, 1686–1936 (Collection in Honour of the 250th Anniversary of the Yiddish Press, 1686–1936), New York, 1937.

Shaw, William, *To the Right Honourable the Lords Spiritual and Temporal, and to the Members of the House of Commons*, London, 1847.

Sherard, Robert H., *The Child-Slaves of Britain*, London, 1905.

———, *The White Slaves of England*, 2nd ed., London, 1898.

Shinwell, Emanuel, *Conflict Without Malice*, London, 1955.

Silberner, Edmund, *HaSozialism haMaʻarabi uShe'elat haYehudim* (Western Socialism and the Jewish Question), Jerusalem, 1955.

———, 'Friedrich Engels and the Jews', *Jewish Social Studies*, XI, 4 (October, 1949), pp. 323–42.

———, 'British Socialism and the Jews', *Historia Judaica*, XIV, 1 (April, 1952), pp. 27–52.

Silverstone, Gedalia, *Pirhey Abib* (Talmudic Notes, Dialectics, Novellae, Exegesis), London, 1901.

Sims, George R., ed., *Living London*, 3 vols., London, 1902.

Sivitz, Moses Simon, *Pri Yehezkel* (Talmudic Novellae, Responsa), Jerusalem, 1908.

Slotki, Israel W., *Jewish Education in Manchester and Salford*, Manchester, 1928.

———, *Seventy Years of Hebrew Education, 1880–1950*, Manchester, 1950.

Smith, Adolphe, 'Das Sweating-System in England', *Archiv fuer Soziale Gesetzgebung und Statistik*, IX, 3–4 (1896), pp. 392–419.

Smith, H. Llewellyn, *History of East London*, London, 1939.

Smith, John, 'The Jewish Immigrant', *Contemporary Review*, LXXVI (September, 1899), pp. 425–36.

Smolenskin, Perez, *HaTo'eh beDarkhey HaHayyim* (Astray on the Path of Life), Tel Aviv, 1951 (other editions).

Soloweitschik, Leonty, *Un prolétariat méconnu. Etude sur la situation sociale et economique des ouvriers juifs*, Brussels, 1898.

Spektor, Isaac Elhanan, '*Eyn Yizhak* (Responsa), Vilna, 1889.

Spiers, B., *Dibrey Debash. Part I. Eighteen Ethical Sermons delivered to the Working Classes. . . . Part II. Talmudic and Medrashic Dissertations and Biblical Exegesis*, London, 1901.

———, *Divrei Hefez* (Acceptable Words), London, n.d. (c. 1886).

Stallard, J. H., *London Pauperism amongst Jews and Christians*, London, 1867.

Stone, Isaac, *Eyne kurtse lebens beshreybung fun a Londoner Shnayder. An Historical sketch of a London Tailor*, London, 1884. (Hand-written copy in Library of YIVO Institute, New York).

Sussmann, Abraham, *Barukh miBanim* (Talmudic Proverbs, Ethical Discourses), Vilna, 1869.

———, *Bet Abraham* (Commentary on the Shulhan Arukh), Koenigsberg, 1853.

———, *VaYa'as Abraham* (Homilies and Responsa), Vilna, 1879.

v

Suwalsky, Isaac, *Ma'amar Betelin uMebutallin* (Discourse on Null and Void), London, 1900.

Syrkin, Nahman, 'An oifruf tsu der Idisher Yugnt' (A Call to Jewish Youth), in *Geklibene Tsionistish-Sotsialistishe Shriften* (Collected Zionist-Socialist Writings), 2 vols., New York, 1925, pp. 35–46.

Szajkowski, Zosa, 'Yidn un die Parizer Komuneh', in E. Tcherikover, ed., *Yidn in Frankreich* (Jews in France), 2 vols., New York, 1942, pp. 93–154.

———, 'How the Mass Migration to America Began', *Jewish Social Studies*, IV, 4 (October, 1942), pp. 291–310.

———, 'Jewish Emigration Policy in the Period of the Rumanian Exodus, 1899–1903', *Jewish Social Studies*, XIII, 1 (January, 1951), pp. 47–70.

———, 'The Attitude of American Jews to East European Jewish Immigration (1881–1893)', *Publications of the American Jewish Historical Society*, XL, 3 (March, 1951), pp. 221–80.

———, 'The European Attitude to East European Jewish Immigration (1881–1893)', *Publications of the American Jewish Historical Society*, XLI, 2 (December, 1951), pp. 127–62.

Talmud Torah Ivrit be Ivrit . . . 1901 to 1951, London, 1951.

Tawney, R. H., *The Establishment of Minimum Rates in the Tailoring Industry under the Trade Boards Act of 1909* (Studies in the Minimum Wage, No. II), London, 1915.

Tcherikover, E., 'Der Onhayb fun der Yiddisher Sotsialistisher Bavegung (Liebermanns Tekufeh)' (The Beginning of the Jewish Socialist Movement (Liebermann's Period)), *YIVO Historishe Shriftn*, I, Vilna, 1929, cols. 469–532.

———, 'Pioter Lavrov un die Yiddishe Sotsialistn Emigrantn' (Peter Lavrov and the Jewish Socialist Emigrants), in E. Tcherikover, A. Menes, F. Kursky, A. Rosen, eds., *Die Yiddishe Sotsialistishe Bavegung biz der Grindung fun 'Bund'* (The Jewish Socialist Movement until the Founding of the 'Bund' [1897], (*YIVO Historishe Shriftn, III*), Vilna and Paris, 1939, pp. 767–79.

———, *Yehudim be'Itot Mahpekhah* (Jews in Revolutionary Periods), Tel Aviv, 1958.

———, ed., *Geshikhte fun der Yiddisher Arbeter Bavegung in der Faraynigte Shtatn* (History of the Jewish Labour Movement in the United States), 2 vols., New York, 1943.

Thomas, H. Otto, 'The Tee-To-Tum Movement', *The Economic Review*, II, 3 (July, 1892), pp. 351–58.

United Synagogue, *East End Scheme*, London, 1898.

Urinovsky, A. (Ben-Or), *Toledot haSifrut ha'Ibrit haHadashah* (History of Modern Hebrew Literature), 3 vols., Tel Aviv, 1948.

'Wages in Jewish Tailoring Workshops in Leeds and Manchester', *The Labour Gazette*, I, 1 (May, 1893), pp. 8–9.

Walinsky, M., 'The Oldest Jewish Union in England and the Largest in the Provinces', *The Ladies' Garment Worker*, III, 12 (December, 1912), pp. 5–8.

Webb, Beatrice, *My Apprenticeship*, London, 1926. (See Potter, Beatrice.)

Webb, Sidney and Beatrice, *History of Trade Unionism*, rev. ed., London, 1920.

——, *Industrial Democracy*, 2 vols., London, 1897.

——, *Problems of Modern Industry*, new ed., London, 1902. See Potter, Beatrice.

Webb, Sidney, and Arnold Freeman, eds., *Seasonal Trades*. (Studies in Economics and Political Science, No. 23.) London, 1912.

Weizmann, Chaim, *Trial and Error*, New York, 1949.

Whelpley, James D., *The Problem of the Immigrant*, London, 1905.

White, Arnold, *The Modern Jew*, London, 1899.

——, *Problems of a Great City*, London, 1886, new ed., 1895.

——, 'The Invasion of Pauper Foreigners', *The Nineteenth Century*, XXIII, No. 133 (March, 1888), pp. 414–22.

——, 'Alien Immigration—A Rejoinder', *The Fortnightly Review*, N.S. LVII, No. 339 (March 1, 1895), pp. 501–07.

——, 'Europe and the Jews', *Contemporary Review*, LXXII (November, 1897), pp. 733–42.

——, 'A Typical Alien Immigrant', *Contemporary Review*, LXXIII (February, 1898), pp. 241–50.

——, ed., *The Destitute Alien in Great Britain*, London and New York, 1892, 2nd ed., 1905.

Wilde, Oscar, *Die Menshlikhe Zeele unter dem Sotsializmus* (The Soul of Man under Socialism), London, 1905.

Wilkins, W. H., *The Alien Invasion* (Social Questions of To-day, No. 6), London, 1892.

——, *The Bitter Cry of the Voteless Toilers* (*with special reference to the seamstresses of East London*) . . . n.p., n.d. (London, 1893).

Willcox, Walter F., ed., *International Migrations*, 2 vols., New York, 1929, 1931 (I: Statistics, comp. Imre Ferenczi; II: Interpretations, by a Group of Scholars in Different Countries.)

Winchevsky, Morris, *Erinerungen* (*Gezamelte Shriftn, IX, X*) (Memoirs), 2 vols., New York, 1927. (Also Moscow, 1926.)

——, *Yehi Or* (Let There be Light!), London, 1884 (*non vidi*); 2nd ed., Newark, N.J., 1890.

Wischnitzer, Mark, *To Dwell in Safety*, Philadelphia, 1949.

Wolf, Lucien, *Essays in Jewish History*, ed., Cecil Roth, London, 1934.

——, *Manasseh ben Israel's Mission to Oliver Cromwell*, London, 1901.

(World Zionist Organization), *HaProtokol shel haKongress haZioni haRishon beBazel* (Protocol of the First Zionist Congress at Basel), Jerusalem, 1946.

Wortsmann, Ezekiel, *Vos Villen die Tsionisten?* (What do the Zionists Want?), London, 1901.

Wortsmann, Ezekiel, 'Die Iddishe Presse in England', *Der Iddisher Kemfer*, II, 11, 12, 15 (June 14, 21, and July 12, 1907).

Yoffey, Israel Jacob, *Keneset Yisrael* (Sermons and Talmudic Dialectics), Manchester, 1910.

Zimmern, A. E., 'The Aliens Act: A Challenge', *The Economic Review*, XXI, 1 (April, 1911), pp. 187–97.

(Zinkin, Jacob), *Heshbonot shel Mizvah* (Pious Calculations), London, 1920.

Zinkin, Jacob, *Jubal Shai . . . on the Occasion of the Queen's Jubilee . . .* London, 1887.

Zitron, S. L., *Toledot Hibbat Zion* (History of the Love of Zion), I, Odessa, 1914.

Zubrzycki, Jerzy, *Polish Immigrants in Britain*. The Hague, 1956.

INDEX

ADLER, HERMANN (Chief Rabbi), 114–16, 126, 128, 202, 207, 209–10, 212, 215, 217, 225, 237, 245

Adler, Jacob (actor), 260

Adler, Nathan Marcus (Chief Rabbi), 19, 24

Adler, Sarah (actress), 260

Agricultural workers, 58

'*Agunah* (in marriage law), 168–9

Aldgate Pump (London), 146

Alexander, Lionel L., 52, 56, 182

Aliens, census of, in England, 283

Aliens Act, 1905, 28, 49, 250, 278

America: *see* United States of America

Anarchism, 130–7; and Yiddish literature, 256, 268

Angel, Moses (schoolmaster), 222–3, 233

Anglicization of Jews, 221 fol., 239 fol., 268–9, 272 fol.

Anti-Semitism, in England, 28, 61–2, 114, 127, 157, 276, 278; Winchevsky and, 107–8; in Russia, 21–2. *See also* Pogroms

Apostasy, 30, 197

Apprenticeship, 237

Arbeiter Freind, Die (The Worker's Friend; Yiddish journal), 109–13, 115–16, 123, 128, 129, 132, 136, 137, 243

Arbitration boards, 79

Aronsberg, William, 38

Artificial flower-makers, 93

'*Asefat Hakhamin* (Assembly of the Wise), 106

Ashkenazim, 18, 19; Ashkenazi immigrants, 33; synagogue, 144

Atlantic Rate War, 47

Atlantic Shipping Ring, 36, 46

Australia, 'slop' clothing worn in, 84; immigrants to, 270

Austria, 33 ticket agencies, 35

BALFOUR DECLARATION, 263, 281

Banking, 21, 33

Bankruptcies, 81

Basket weaving, 95

Beards, shaving of, 30

'Becker, Simha': *see* Cohen, Simon

Beggars, 20, 39

Benevolent societies, 178–90, 205

Bentwich, Herbert, 51, 262

Bentwich, Matthias, 38

Berlin, Hayyim, 246

Berlin, Meir, 190, 191

Berlin, Nafthali Zvi Judah, 187, 245

Berner Street Club, 111–12, 115–16, 127–8, 131–2

Beth Din (court), 19, 180

Beth HaMidrash HaGadol (Great House of Study), 215

Bethnal Green (London), 146

Bevis Marks Synagogue, 50, 144

Birmingham, tailoring and sweating system, 92–3

trade union membership, 138

residential area, 145–6; schools, 224

Birnbaum, Bernard, 51

Boer War, 47

Boot and shoe makers, 58, 64, 72, 75–81, 279

wages, 98–9

trade unions, 78–80, 122, 130

health hazards, 160–1

Bradford, first immigrants, 33

clothing trade, 85, 88

THE END